The History of British Women's Wri

The History of British Women's Writing
General Editors: **Jennie Batchelor** and **Cora Kaplan**
Advisory Board: Isobel Armstrong, Rachel Bowlby, Carolyn Dinshaw, Margaret Ezell, Margaret Ferguson, Isobel Grundy, and Felicity Nussbaum

The History of British Women's Writing is an innovative and ambitious monograph series that seeks both to synthesize the work of several generations of feminist scholars, and to advance new directions for the study of women's writing. Volume editors and contributors are leading scholars whose work collectively reflects the global excellence in this expanding field of study. It is envisaged that this series will be a key resource for specialist and non-specialist scholars and students alike.

Titles include:
Liz Herbert McAvoy and Diane Watt (*editors*)
THE HISTORY OF BRITISH WOMEN'S WRITING, 700–1500
Volume One

Caroline Bicks and Jennifer Summit (*editors*)
THE HISTORY OF BRITISH WOMEN'S WRITING, 1500–1610
Volume Two

Mihoko Suzuki (*editor*)
THE HISTORY OF BRITISH WOMEN'S WRITING, 1610–1690
Volume Three

Ros Ballaster (*editor*)
THE HISTORY OF BRITISH WOMEN'S WRITING, 1690–1750
Volume Four

Jacqueline M. Labbe (*editor*)
THE HISTORY OF BRITISH WOMEN'S WRITING, 1750–1830
Volume Five

Maroula Joannou (*editor*)
THE HISTORY OF BRITISH WOMEN'S WRITING, 1920–1945
Volume Eight

History of British Women's Writing
Series Standing Order ISBN 978–0–230–20079–1 hardback
(*outside North America only*)

You can receive future titles in this series as they are published by placing a standing order. Please contact your bookseller or, in case of difficulty, write to us at the address below with your name and address, the title of the series and the ISBN quoted above.

Customer Services Department, Macmillan Distribution Ltd, Houndmills, Basingstoke, Hampshire RG21 6XS, England

---

The History of British Women's Writing, 1920–1945

Volume Eight

Edited by
Maroula Joannou

palgrave
macmillan

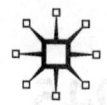

Selection, introduction and editorial matter © Maroula Joannou 2013
Individual chapters © contributors 2013

Softcover reprint of the hardcover 1st edition 2013 978-0-230-28279-7

All rights reserved. No reproduction, copy or transmission of this publication may be made without written permission.

No portion of this publication may be reproduced, copied or transmitted save with written permission or in accordance with the provisions of the Copyright, Designs and Patents Act 1988, or under the terms of any licence permitting limited copying issued by the Copyright Licensing Agency, Saffron House, 6–10 Kirby Street, London EC1N 8TS.

Any person who does any unauthorized act in relation to this publication may be liable to criminal prosecution and civil claims for damages.

The authors have asserted their rights to be identified as the authors of this work in accordance with the Copyright, Designs and Patents Act 1988.

First published 2013 by
PALGRAVE MACMILLAN

Palgrave Macmillan in the UK is an imprint of Macmillan Publishers Limited, registered in England, company number 785998, of Houndmills, Basingstoke, Hampshire RG21 6XS.

Palgrave Macmillan in the US is a division of St Martin's Press LLC,
175 Fifth Avenue, New York, NY 10010.

Palgrave Macmillan is the global academic imprint of the above companies and has companies and representatives throughout the world.

Palgrave® and Macmillan® are registered trademarks in the United States, the United Kingdom, Europe and other countries.

ISBN 978-1-349-32858-1   ISBN 978-1-137-29217-9 (eBook)
DOI 10.1057/9781137292179

A catalogue record for this book is available from the British Library.

A catalog record for this book is available from the Library of Congress.

10 9 8 7 6 5 4 3 2 1
22 21 20 19 18 17 16 15 14 13

Transferred to Digital Printing in 2013

To the Memory of Julia Briggs (1943–2007)

Contents

Series Editors' Preface ix

Acknowledgements x

Notes on the Contributors xi

Chronology 1920–1945 xiv

Introduction: Modernism, Modernity, and the Middlebrow in Context 1
Maroula Joannou

Part I Mapping Modernism

1 Gender in Modernism 23
   Bonnie Kime Scott

2 Exemplary Intermodernists: Stevie Smith, Inez Holden, Betty Miller, and Naomi Mitchison 40
   Kristin Bluemel

3 Virginia Woolf and the Aesthetics of Modernism 57
   Jane Goldman

4 The Art of Bi-Location: Sylvia Townsend Warner 78
   Maud Ellmann

Part II Cultural Hierarchy

5 The Feminine Middlebrow Novel 97
   Nicola Humble

6 Women and Comedy 112
   Sophie Blanch

7 The Woman's Historical Novel 129
   Diana Wallace

8 'Queens of Crime': The 'Golden Age' of Crime Fiction 144
   Cora Kaplan

Part III Gendered Genres

9 Poetry, 1920–1945 161
   Jane Dowson

10 Drama, 1920–1945 182
    Rebecca D'Monté

| 11 | The Woman Journalist, 1920–1945
Catherine Clay | 199 |

Part IV   The Mobile Woman

12	Caught in the Triple Net? Welsh, Scottish, and Irish Women Writers *Katie Gramich*	217
13	Women's Writing in the Second World War *Gill Plain*	233
14	Women Writing Empire *Lisa Regan*	250
15	Women Writing the City *Deborah Longworth*	264
16	Myths of Passage: *Paris* and *Parallax* *Tory Young*	275

Electronic Resources	291
Select Bibliography	292
Index	304

Series Editors' Preface

One of the most significant developments in literary studies in the last quarter of a century has been the remarkable growth of scholarship on women's writing. This was inspired by, and in turn provided inspiration for, a postwar women's movement, which saw women's cultural expression as key to their emancipation. The retrieval, republication and reappraisal of women's writing, beginning in the mid-1960s have radically affected the literary curriculum in schools and universities. A revised canon now includes many more women writers. Literature courses that focus on what women thought and wrote from antiquity onwards have become popular undergraduate and postgraduate options. These new initiatives have meant that gender – in language, authors, texts, audience, and in the history of print culture more generally – are central questions for literary criticism and literary history. A mass of fascinating research and analysis extending over several decades now stands as testimony to a lively and diverse set of debates, in an area of work that is still expanding.

Indeed so rapid has this expansion been, that it has become increasingly difficult for students and academics to have a comprehensive view of the wider field of women's writing outside their own period or specialism. As the research on women has moved from the margins to the confident centre of literary studies it has become rich in essays and monographs dealing with smaller groups of authors, with particular genres and with defined periods of literary production, reflecting the divisions of intellectual labour and development of expertise that are typical of the discipline of literary studies. Collections of essays that provide overviews within particular periods and genres do exist, but no published series has taken on the mapping of the field even within one language group or national culture.

A History of British Women's Writing is intended as just such a cartographic standard work. Its ambition is to provide, in ten volumes edited by leading experts in the field, and comprised of newly commissioned essays by specialist scholars, a clear and integrated picture of women's contribution to the world of letters within Great Britain from medieval times to the present. In taking on such a wide ranging project we were inspired by the founding, in 2003, of Chawton House Library, a UK registered charity with a unique collection of books focusing on women's writing in English from 1600 to 1830, set in the home and working estate of Jane Austen's brother.

JENNIE BATCHELOR
UNIVERSITY OF KENT

CORA KAPLAN
QUEEN MARY, UNIVERSITY OF LONDON

Acknowledgements

I am indebted to the General Editors of the series, Jennie Batchelor and Cora Kaplan, for inviting me to edit this volume and overseeing its progress with great insight, and to Paula Kennedy and Ben Doyle at Palgrave for their understanding, encouragement and patience from beginning to end. I wish to thank Magda Bergman, the departmental administrator for English at Anglia Ruskin and the library staff in the Cambridge University and Anglia Ruskin University libraries (especially John Reynolds and Sue Gilmurray) for their unfailing helpfulness, courtesy, and efficiency. Joan Williams read the final typescript with scrupulous care. Many friends have given me support, encouragement, and incisive critique including Lucie Armitt, Şue Bruley, Chiara Briganti, Cathy Clay, Jane Dowson, Gill Davies, Mary Eagleton, Gill Frith, Faye Hammill, Clare Hanson, Mary Jacobs, Brenda Kirsch, Jan Montefiore, Claire Nicholson, Paulina Palmer, Emma Parker, Helen Phillips, Imelda Whelehan, and Gina Wisker. The book comes at the end of nearly two decades of full-time reading, research, and teaching in the Anglia Ruskin University English Department in Cambridge and benefiting from access to all the cultural riches that our beautiful city has to offer. I owe an incalculable debt to my colleagues at Anglia Ruskin past and present, most recently John Gardner, Colette Paul, Valerie Purton, Julia Swindells, Jeff Wallace, Tory Young, and Rowlie Wymer. Copyright permission for the use of Vanessa Bell's painting 'The Kitchen' on the front cover is by kind permission of Henrietta Garnett. The scholarly expertise, professionalism, and commitment of the contributors have made compiling this volume the pleasure and the privilege that it has been. We wish to dedicate it collectively to the memory of Julia Briggs, whose life and work have been an inspiration.

MARY JOANNOU
ANGLIA RUSKIN UNIVERSITY
CAMBRIDGE

Notes on the Contributors

Sophie Blanch is Lecturer in English Literature at the University of Surrey and formerly a British Academy Postdoctoral Fellow in English at the University of Sussex, where she organised an international conference, *Joking Apart: Gender, Literature & Modernity, 1850–Present*. She is editing a book of collected essays under the same title.

Kristin Bluemel is Professor of English at Monmouth University. She is author of *George Orwell and the Radical Eccentrics: Intermodernism in Literary London* (2004) and editor of *Intermodernism: Literary Culture in Twentieth-Century Britain* (2009).

Catherine Clay is Senior Lecturer in English at Nottingham Trent University. She is author of *British Women Writers 1914–1945: Professional Work and Friendship* (2006), and is currently working on a monograph about the feminist periodical *Time and Tide*.

Rebecca D'Monté is Senior Lecturer at the University of the West of England. She has published essays on Margaret Cavendish, April de Angelis, Judy Upton, Daphne du Maurier, Esther McCracken, and Dodie Smith. She has edited with Nicole Pohl *Female Communities 1600–1800: Literary Visions and Cultural Realities* (1999) and with Grama Saunders *Cool Britannia: British Political Drama in the 1990s* (2008).

Jane Dowson is Reader in Twentieth-Century Literature at De Montfort University. Her publications on women's poetry include *Women's Poetry of the 1930s* (1996), *Women, Modernism and British Poetry 1910–39* (2002), *A History of Twentieth-Century Women's Poetry* (co-authored with Alice Entwistle, 2005), and *The Cambridge Companion to Twentieth-Century British and Irish Women's Poetry* (2011).

Maud Ellmann is the Randy L. and Melvin R. Berlin Professor of the Development of the Novel in English at the University of Chicago. She has written on modernism and literary theory, particularly psychoanalysis and feminism. Her books include *The Hunger Artists: Starving, Writing and Imprisonment* (1993), *Elizabeth Bowen: The Shadow Across the Page* (2003), and *The Nets of Modernism: James, Woolf, Joyce, and Freud* (2010).

Jane Goldman is Reader in English Literature at the University of Glasgow, and a General Editor of the Cambridge University Press Edition of *The Writings of Virginia Woolf*, and volume editor of *To the Lighthouse* and of *A Room of One's Own*. She is author of *The Feminist Aesthetics of Virginia*

Woolf: Modernism, Post-Impressionism and the Politics of the Visual (1998) and co-editor of *Modernism: An Anthology of Sources and Documents* (1998). Her publications include *Modernism, 1910–1945: Image to Apocalypse* (2004) and *The Cambridge Introduction to Virginia Woolf* (2006).

Katie Gramich is Reader in English Literature at Cardiff University. She is the author of *Twentieth Century Women's Writing in Wales: Land, Gender, Belonging* (2007) and a monograph on the Welsh-language novelist and short story writer, *Kate Roberts* (2011).

Nicola Humble is Professor of English at Roehampton University and author of *The Feminine Middlebrow Novel 1920s to 1950s: Class, Domesticity and Bohemianism* (2001), *Cake: A Global History* (2010), and *Culinary Pleasures: Cook Books and the Transformation of British Food* (2005). She has co-edited, with Kimberley Reynolds, *Victorian Heroines: Representations of Femininity in Nineteenth-Century Literature and Art* (1993), and produced editions of Mrs Beeton's *Book of Household Management* (2000) and Jane Austen's *Persuasion* (1997).

Maroula Joannou is Professor of Literary History and Women's Writing at Anglia Ruskin University. Her publications include *'Ladies, Please Don't Smash These Windows': Women's Writing, Feminism and Social Change 1918–1938* (1995), *Contemporary Women's Writing: From the Golden Notebook to The Color Purple* (2000), and *Women's Writing, National and Cultural Identity: The Mobile Woman and the Migrant Voice, 1938–1962* (2012).

Cora Kaplan is an Honorary Professor in the School of English and Drama at Queen Mary, University of London, and is Professor Emerita of English at Southampton University. A General Editor of this series, her publications include *Genders* (with David Glover, 2000, 2009) and *Victoriana – Histories, Fictions, Criticism* (2007).

Deborah Longworth (née Parsons) is a Senior Lecturer at the University of Birmingham. She is the author of *Streetwalking the Metropolis: Women, the City and Modernity* (2000). She edits the journal *Modernist Cultures* with Andrzej Gasiorek and Michael Valdez Moses.

Gill Plain is Professor of English Literature and Popular Culture at St Andrews University. Her publications include *Women's Fiction of the Second World War: Gender, Power and Resistance* (1996), *Twentieth-Century Fiction: Gender, Sexuality and the Body* (2001), *Ian Rankin's Black and Blue: A Reader's Guide* (2002), and *John Mills and British Cinema: Masculinity, Identity and Nation* (2006). She has co-edited *A History of Feminist Literary Criticism* (2007).

Lisa Regan is a Lecturer in English Literature at the University of Liverpool. She is the editor of *Winifred Holtby, 'A Woman in Her Time': Critical Essays* (2010) and has just completed a monograph, *Winifred Holtby's Social Vision: 'Members One of Another'* (2012).

Bonnie Kime Scott is Professor Emerita of Women's Studies at San Diego State University and Professor Emerita of English at the University of Delaware. Her publications include the authored works, *In the Hollow of the Wave: Virginia Woolf and Modernist Uses of Nature* (2012) and *Refiguring Modernism* (1995), and the edited volumes, *Gender in Modernism: New Geographies, Complex Intersections* (2007) and *The Gender of Modernism* (1990).

Diana Wallace is Professor of English Literature at the University of Glamorgan. She is the author of *The Woman's Historical Novel: British Women Writers* (2005) and *Sisters and Rivals in British Women's Fiction 1914–39* (2000) and is currently completing a monograph entitled *Female Gothic Histories: Gender, History and the Gothic*.

Tory Young is a Senior Lecturer at Anglia Ruskin University and the author of *Studying English Literature: A Practical Guide* (2008) and *The Hours by Michael Cunningham* (2003). She co-edits the 20th–21st century section of *Literature Compass* with Laura Winkiel and is writing a monograph provisionally titled *Sex, Narrative and Postfeminism in Contemporary British Fiction*.

Chronology 1920–1945

Year	Events	Works
1918	End of the First World War. Votes for women over thirty. Liberal government under Lloyd George. School leaving age raised to fourteen.	Katherine Mansfield, *Prelude*; Emma Orczy, *The Man in Grey*; Marie Stopes, *Married Love*; Rebecca West, *The Return of the Soldier*.
1919	The Versailles Treaty. Housing Act launches programme of council housing.	Elizabeth von Arnim, *Christopher and Columbus*; Angela Brazil, *A Harum-Scarum Schoolgirl*; Clemence Dane, *Legend*; E.M. Delafield, *Consequences*; Leonora Eyles, *Margaret Protests*; Cicely Hamilton, *William – an Englishman*; E.M. Hull, *The Sheik*; Storm Jameson, *The Pot Boils*; Gertrude Jennings *Waiting for the Bus*; Hope Mirrlees, *Paris* and *Madeleine*; Dorothy Richardson, *The Tunnel* and *Interim*; May Sinclair, *Mary Olivier: A Life*; Mary Augusta Ward, *Cousin Philip*; Edith Wharton, *The Marne*; Virginia Woolf, *Night and Day*.
1920	The League of Nations founded. Prohibition of alcohol in the United States.	Catherine Carswell, *Open the Door!*; Agatha Christie, *The Mysterious Affair at Styles*; O. Douglas, *Penny Plain*; Vernon Lee, *Satan the Waster*; Rose Macaulay, *Potterism*; Katherine Mansfield, *Bliss and Other Stories*; Dorothy Richardson, *Interim*; May Sinclair, *The Romantic*.
1921	Marie Stopes opens first family planning clinic in Holloway, London.	Elizabeth von Arnim, *Vera*; Clemence Dane, *A Bill of Divorcement*; Georgette Heyer, *The Black Moth*; Sheila Kaye Smith, *Joanna Godden*; Dorothy Richardson, *Deadlock*; Virginia Woolf, *Monday or Tuesday*.
1922	The BBC established. Bonar Law Ministry. Mussolini comes to power in Italy. Gandhi imprisoned in India. Insulin discovered.	Elizabeth von Arnim, *The Enchanted April*; Catherine Carswell, *The Camomile*; Richmal Crompton, *Just-William*; Mary Agnes Hamilton, *Follow My Leader*; Rose Macaulay, *Mystery at Geneva*; Katherine Mansfield, *The Garden Party and Other Stories*; May Sinclair, *Life and Death of Harriett Frean*; Edith Sitwell, *Façade*; E.H. Young, *The Bridge Dividing*; Rebecca West, *The Judge*; Virginia Woolf, *Jacob's Room*.
1923	End of Civil War in Ireland. Baldwin's first ministry.	Winifred Holtby, *Anderby Wold*; Vera Brittain, *The Dark Tide*; Sheila Kaye-Smith, *The End of the House of Alard*; Rose Macaulay, *Told by an Idiot*; Katherine Mansfield, *The Dove's Nest and Other Stories*; Naomi Mitchison, *The Conquered*; Mollie Panter-Downes, *The Shoreless Sea*; Dorothy Richardson, *Revolving Lights*.

Chronology 1920–1945   xv

1924	First minority Labour Government. Baldwin's second ministry. Empire Exhibition.	Vera Brittain, *Not Without Honour*; Clemence Dane, *Wandering Stars*; Radclyffe Hall, *The Unlit Lamp*; Cicely Hamilton, *The Old Adam*; Winifred Holtby, *The Crowded Street*; Margaret Kennedy, *The Constant Nymph*; Rose Macaulay, *Orphan Island*; Katherine Mansfield, *Something Childish and Other Stories*; F.M. Mayor, *The Rector's Daughter*; Hope Mirrlees, *The Counterplot*; Eleanor Rathbone, *The Disinherited Family*; Mary Webb, *Precious Bane*.
1925	Hitler, *Mein Kampf*.	Stella Benson, *The Little World*; D.K. Broster, *The Flight of the Heron*; Elinor Brent Dyer, *School at the Chalet*; Ethel Carnie Holdsworth, *This Slavery*; Ethel Mannin, *Sounding Brass*; Naomi Mitchison, *Cloud Cuckoo Land*; Mollie Panter-Downes, *The Chase*; Dorothy Richardson, *The Trap*; Dora Russell, *Hypatia*; E.H. Young, *William*; Virginia Woolf, *Mrs Dalloway* and *The Common Reader*.
1926	The General Strike and Miners' Lock-out.	Stella Benson, *Goodbye, Stranger*; H.D., *Palimpsest*; Charlotte Haldane, *Man's World*; Georgette Heyer, *These Old Shades*; Rose Macaulay, *Crewe Train*; Olive Schreiner, *From Man to Man*; Hope Mirrlees, *Lud-in-the-Mist*; Sylvia Thompson, *The Hounds of Spring*; Sylvia Townsend Warner, *Lolly Willowes*.
1927	Execution of Sacco and Vanzetti.	Elizabeth Bowen, *The Hotel*; D.K. Broster, *The Gleam in the North*; Winifred Holtby, *The Land of Green Ginger*; Storm Jameson, *The Lovely Ship*; Rosamond Lehmann, *Dusty Answer*; Jean Rhys, *The Left Bank*; Dorothy Richardson, *Oberland*; May Sinclair, *The Allinghams*; Sylvia Townsend Warner, *Mr Fortune's Maggot*; Amabel Williams-Ellis, *The Wall of Glass*; Virginia Woolf, *To the Lighthouse*; E.H. Young, *The Vicar's Daughter*.
1928	Votes for women over twenty-one. Discovery of penicillin.	Mary Butts, *Armed with Madness*; Radclyffe Hall, *The Well of Loneliness*; Marie Carmichael, *Love's Creation*; Jean Rhys, *Postures*; E. Arnot Robertson, *Cullum*; Nan Shepherd, *The Quarry Wood*; Ray Strachey, *The Cause*; Rebecca West, *The Strange Necessity*; Virginia Woolf, *Orlando: A Biography*.
1929	Wall Street Crash. Marriage age raised to sixteen for both sexes.	Mary Borden, *The Forbidden Zone*; Elizabeth Bowen, *The Last September*; Ivy Compton-Burnett, *Brothers and Sisters*; Helen Ferguson, *A Charmed Circle*; Inez Holden, *Sweet Charlatan*; Nora James, *Sleeveless Errand*; Fryniwyd Tennyson Jesse, *The Lacquer Lady*; Olive Schreiner, *Undine*; Sylvia Townsend Warner, *The True Heart*; Rebecca West, *Harriet Hume*; Ellen Wilkinson, *Clash*; Virginia Woolf, *A Room of One's Own*.

(continued)

Continued

Year	Events	Works
1930	Gandhi starts civil disobedience campaign in India.	Agatha Christie, *The Murder at the Vicarage*; E.M. Delafield, *Diary of a Provincial Lady*; Rosamond Lehmann, *A Note in Music*; Una Marson, *Tropical Reveries*; Olive Moore, *Spleen*; Jean Rhys, *After Leaving Mr Mackenzie*; Vita Sackville-West, *The Edwardians*; Dorothy Sayers, *Strong Poison*; Nan Shepherd, *The Weatherhouse*; Helen Smith, *Not So Quiet...: Stepdaughters of War*; E.H. Young, *Miss Mole*.
1931	World economic crisis. Nearly 3 million unemployed in Britain. National government under Ramsay Macdonald. Means Test introduced for the unemployed. Japanese invade Manchuria.	Stella Benson, *Tobit Transplanted*; Elizabeth Bowen, *Friends and Relations*; M.J. Farrell, *Mad Puppetstown*; Rachel Ferguson, *The Brontës Went to Woolworths*; Winifred Holtby, *Poor Caroline*; Sheila Kaye-Smith, *The History of Susan Spray, The Female Preacher*; Naomi Mitchison, *The Corn King and the Spring Queen*; Willa Muir, *Imagined Corners*; Kate O' Brien, *Without My Cloak*; Dorothy Richardson, *Dawn's Left Hand*; Vita Sackville-West, *All Passion Spent*; Dodie Smith, *Autumn Crocus*; G.B. Stern, *The Man Who Pays the Piper*; Virginia Woolf, *The Waves*.
1932	First regular TV broadcast, Gandhi interned. Mosley founds British Union of Fascists.	Phyllis Bentley, *Inheritance*; Mary Butts, *Death of Felicity Taverner*; Elizabeth Bowen, *To the North*; Margiad Evans, *Country Dance*; Stella Gibbons, *Cold Comfort Farm*; Rosamond Lehmann, *Invitation to the Waltz*; Olive Moore, *Fugue*; Julia Strachey, *Cheerful Weather for the Wedding*; Dorothy Whipple, *Greenbanks*; Ellen Wilkinson, *The Division Bell Mystery*; Virginia Woolf, *The Common Reader: Second Series*.
1933	New Deal in the United States. Reichstag fire in Germany and Hitler takes power.	Margery Allingham, *Sweet Danger*; Vera Brittain, *Testament of Youth*; Elizabeth Cambridge, *Hostages to Fortune*; Margiad Evans, *The Wooden Doctor*; Inez Holden, *Friend of the Family*; Winifred Holtby, *Mandoa, Mandoa!* and *The Astonishing Island*; Storm Jameson, *Women Against Men*; Ethel Mannin, *Venetian Blinds*; Una Marson, *At What a Price*; Nancy Brysson Morrison, *The Gowk Storm*; Willa Muir, *Mrs Ritchie*; E. Arnot Robertson, *Ordinary Families*; Angela Thirkell, *High Risings*; Antonia White, *Frost in May*; Virginia Woolf, *Flush: A Biography*.
1934	Olympia Exhibition. Left-wing protesters violently ejected by Mosley's blackshirts. Stalin's purges.	Dot Allan, *Hunger March*; Muriel Box, *Peace in Our Time*; Sally Carson, *Crooked Cross*; Nancy Cunard, *Negro*; Winifred Holtby, *Women and a Changing Civilization* and *Truth is Not Sober*; Storm Jameson, *Company Parade*; Fryniwyd Tennyson Jesse, *A Pin to See the Peepshow*; Kate O'Brien, *The Ante Room*; Jean Rhys, *Voyage in the Dark*; Dorothy Whipple, *They Knew Mr Knight*; E.H. Young, *The Curate's Wife*.

Chronology 1920–1945 xvii

1935	Italy invades Abyssinia. Baldwin leads national government. Invention of nylon (first fully synthetic fabric). Baldwin's third ministry. Invention of radar.	Elizabeth Bowen, *The House in Paris*; Muriel Box, *Angels of War*; Mary Butts, *Scenes from the Life of Cleopatra*; Lettice Cooper, *We Have Come to a Country*; Victoria Cross, *Martha Brown, M.P*; Georgette Heyer, *Regency Buck*; Storm Jameson, *Love in Winter*; Ethel Mannin, *Cactus*; Naomi Mitchison, *We Have Been Warned*; Dorothy Richardson, *Clear Horizon*; Dorothy Sayers, *Gaudy Night*; Rebecca West, *The Harsh Voice*.
1936	Death of George V. Accession and abdication of Edward VIII. Berlin Olympics. Spanish Civil War. Germany occupies Rhineland. Jarrow Hunger March. Battle of Cable Street in East End of London.	Valentine Ackland, *Country Conditions*; Phyllis Bentley, *Freedom, Farewell!*; Sarah Campion, *Duet for Female Voices*; Lettice Cooper, *The New House*; Daphne du Maurier, *Jamaica Inn*; Winifred Holtby, *South Riding*; Naomi Jacobs, *Barren Metal*; Storm Jameson, *In The Second Year*; Rosamond Lehmann, *The Weather in the Streets*; Irene Rathbone, *They Call it Peace*; Kate O'Brien, *Mary Lavelle*; Kate Roberts, *Feet in Chains*; Stevie Smith, *Novel on Yellow Paper*; Noel Streatfeild, *Ballet Shoes*; Josephine Tey, *A Shilling for Candles*; Hilda Vaughan, *Harvest Home*; Sylvia Townsend Warner, *Summer Will Show*.
1937	Neville Chamberlain becomes PM. Guernica air raid. Divorce legalized on grounds of desertion and insanity. Second Sino-Japanese war.	Ruth Adam, *War on Saturday Week*; Phyllis Bottome, *The Mortal Storm*; Katharine Burdekin, *Swastika Night*; Carmel Haden-Guest, *Give Us Conflict*; Georgette Heyer, *An Infamous Army*; Winifred Holtby, *Pavements at Anderby*; Olivia Manning, *The Wind Changes*; Freya Stark, *Baghdad Sketches*; Rosalind Wade, *Treasure in Heaven*; Virginia Woolf, *The Years*.
1938	Dr Alex Bourne acquitted of performing an illegal abortion. Germany annexes Austria. Munich crisis. Invention of ballpoint pen.	Margery Allingham, *The Fashion in Shrouds*; Elizabeth Bowen, *The Death of the Heart*; Lettice Cooper, *National Provincial*; Catherine Gavin, *Clyde Valley*; Daphne Du Maurier, *Rebecca*; Kate O'Brien, *Pray for the Wanderer*; Dorothy Richardson, *Pilgrimage* (including *Dimple Hill*); Dodie Smith, *Dear Octopus*; Stevie Smith, *Over The Frontier*; Angela Thirkell, *Pomfret Towers*; Sylvia Townsend Warner, *After the Death of Don Juan*; Winifred Watson, *Miss Pettigrew Lives for a Day*; Virginia Woolf, *Three Guineas*.
1939	Hitler invades Czechoslovakia and Poland. Start of the Second World War.	Mary Borden, *Passport for a Girl*; Clemence Dane, *The Arrogant History of White Ben*; Pamela Frankau, *The Devil We Know*; Rumer Godden, *Black Narcissus*; Elspeth Huxley, *Red Strangers*; Rosamond Lehmann, *No More Music*; Nancy Mitford, *Pigeon Pie*; Jean Rhys, *Good Morning, Midnight*; Mary Renault, *Purposes of Love*; Jan Struther, *Mrs Miniver*; Flora Thompson, *Lark Rise to Candleford*; Dorothy Whipple, *The Priory*.

(continued)

xviii *Chronology 1920–1945*

Continued

1940	Dunkirk. London Blitz. Battle of Britain. Surrender of Belgium and Holland. Germans enter Paris.	Angela Brazil, *The New School at Scawdale*; Enid Blyton, *The Naughtiest Girl in the School*; Vera Brittain, *Testament of Friendship*; Georgette Heyer, *The Corinthian* and *The Spanish Bride*; Mollie Panter-Downes, *Letter from England*; Storm Jameson, *Cousin Honoré* and *Europe to Let*; Pamela Hansford Johnson, *Too Dear for My Possessing*; Anna Kavan, *Asylum Piece*; Freya Stark, *A Winter in Arabia*; Virginia Woolf, *Roger Fry: A Biography*.
1941	Germany invades Russia. Japanese bomb Pearl Harbour. United States enters the war. Conscription of 'mobile women'.	Margery Allingham, *Traitor's Purse*; Phyllis Bottome, *London Pride*; Elizabeth Bowen, *Look at all Those Roses*; Ivy Compton-Burnett, *Parents and Children*; Inez Holden, *Night Shift*; Margaret Irwin, *The Gay Galliard*; Daphne du Maurier, *Frenchman's Creek*; Ethel Mannin, *Red Rose*; Ngaio Marsh, *Surfeit of Lampreys*; Betty Miller, *Farewell Leicester Square*; Kate O'Brien, *The Land of Spices*; Rebecca West, *Black Lamb and Grey Falcon*; Virginia Woolf, *Between the Acts*.
1942	The Beveridge Report. Fall of Singapore. North African campaign and Battle of El Alamein.	Enid Blyton, *Five on a Treasure Island*; Monica Dickens, *One Pair of Feet*; Rumer Godden, *Breakfast with the Nikolides*.
1943	Allied landing in Sicily. Italy surrenders. Men and women at Rolls Royce factory strike for equal pay.	Phyllis Bottome, *Within the Cup*; Monica Dickens, *The Fancy*; Storm Jameson, *Cloudless May*; Mary Lavin, *Tales from Bective Bridge*; Ethel Mannin, *No More Mimosa*; Kate O'Brien, *The Last of Summer*; Mary Renault, *The Friendly Young Ladies*; Dorothy Whipple, *They Were Sisters*.
1944	Butler Education Act. D-Day. Allied Normandy landings. Liberation of Paris.	Daphne du Maurier, *The Years Between*; Georgette Heyer, *Friday's Child*; Inez Holden, *There's No Story There*; Diana Murray Hill, *Ladies May Now Leave their Machines*; Margaret Irwin, *Young Bess*; Magdalen King-Hall, *Life and Death of the Wicked Lady Skelton*; Marghanita Laski, *Love on the Supertax*; Rosamond Lehmann, *The Ballad and the Source*; Esther McCracken, *Living Room* and *No Medals*.
1945	Bombing of Hiroshima and Nagasaki. Labour landslide in General Election. Family Allowances introduced. V-E Day.	Margery Allingham, *Coroner's Pidgin*; Elizabeth Bowen, *The Demon Lover*; Storm Jameson, *The Journal of Mary Hervey Russell*; Ethel Mannin, *Comrade O Comrade*; Katherine Mansfield, *The Collected Stories*; Betty Miller, *On the Side of the Angels*; Nancy Mitford, *The Pursuit of Love*; Noel Streatfeild, *Saplings*; Lesley Storm, *Great Day*; Elizabeth Taylor, *At Mrs Lippincote's*.

Introduction: Modernism, Modernity, and the Middlebrow in Context

Maroula Joannou

Literary Modernism and women's writing, 1920–1945

This book discusses a broad spectrum of writing by women much of which is not widely-known, including forgotten drama, narratives of empire, opinion-shaping journalism, poetry originally published in small magazines, feminine middlebrow fiction, historical novels, and popular crime fiction. The women writers in this book are important to our understanding of which aspects of modernity we privilege in constructing narratives to account for the literary production of the early and middle years of the twentieth century. The majority of women whose work is discussed in volume eight of Palgrave's *History of British Women's Writing* do not fit into a recognized version of the modernist canon. Their complex and often troubled relationship to modernity – as readers, consumers, and travellers at home and abroad – requires new critical frameworks in which to discuss their writing as well as a revision of the territory that has been staked out as the preserve of Modernism by critical theory and practice.

The historical period from 1920 to 1945 is coterminous with the great achievements of literary Modernism dating approximately from the *annus mirabilis* of 1922, which saw T.S. Eliot's *The Waste Land* and James Joyce's *Ulysses*, to the publication of Joyce's *Finnegans Wake* at the apex of 'high Modernism' in 1939. The canonical literary history of Britain in these years has been dominated by the towering figures of James Joyce, T.S. Eliot, Ezra Pound, and Virginia Woolf who, in the spirit of Pound's celebrated injunction to 'Make it New',[1] set their backs to the conventions of Victorian literature.

Such key works as Woolf's *Mrs Dalloway* (1925) or Pound's 'Hugh Selwyn Mauberley' (1920) signalled a radical break with the literary past and an attempt to find new literary techniques to represent consciousness in ways appropriate to the changing understandings of the physical universe and psychic identity. Einstein's theory of relativity altered traditional understandings of space and time and Freud's work on the unconscious focused attention on the complexities of the inner psychic life. The revolutionary new insights afforded by the visual arts, psychology, anthropology, mathematics, and the physical sciences in the early twentieth century dramatically transformed the work of artists, musicians, architects, and writers. As Woolf put it, after visiting the Post-Impressionist Exhibition in London, 'on or about December 1910 human character changed'.[2]

These changes in the perception of consciousness affected women writers profoundly, and in her path-breaking *Women of the Left Bank* (1986)[3] Shari Benstock argued that Gertrude Stein, H.D., Marianne Moore, Djuna Barnes, and others *were* modernists, in the sense that like Joyce and Pound they were avant-garde writers and bohemian expatriates. But they were also significantly different from their male counterparts in that they did not live conventional heterosexual lives, some being lesbian or bisexual, and were sustained by female friendship networks that gave them the freedom to express non-normative textual and sexual identities. Situated in Paris these women invested in new ways of writing to liberate themselves from gendered restrictions upon their freedoms. Hope Mirrlees's *Paris* (1919), discussed here by Tory Young, has been termed 'modernism's lost masterpiece, a work of extraordinary energy and intensity, scope and ambition'[4] by the critic, Julia Briggs. Preceding *The Waste Land*, to which it has some resemblances, by three years, *Paris* enjoyed nothing of the critical recognition that *The Waste Land* received on first publication and subsequently lapsed into obscurity.

The writing of the period 1920–1945 is exceedingly varied and the stylistic innovative features that we associate critically with Modernism represent one set of tendencies that existed alongside and in tension with many others. The term Modernism was still relatively new and unfamiliar and many writers, such as E.H. Young, Rosamond Lehmann, Storm Jameson, and Vera Brittain, considered it irrelevant to themselves. The authors discussed by Sophie Blanch (comedy), Nicola Humble (the feminine middlebrow novel), Rebecca D'Monté (theatre), and Diana Wallace (the historical novel), were distinctly modern in such respects as style, outlook, and social attitudes. They were not, however, modernists in that their writing refused both the avant-garde rupture with the literary past and the male modernists' cultural devaluation of femininity. Moreover, they sought to deal with the contradictions of modern life by writing outside the framework of Modernism.

In *A Very Great Profession: The Woman's Novel 1914–39* (1984)[5] Nicola Beauman identified a significant body of fiction written by women between the wars that she termed the 'woman's novel'; that is, a type of woman-centred narrative written and avidly read, purchased, and enjoyed by, middle-class women like Laura Jesson in *Brief Encounter* (1947). Interest in such woman-centred fiction flourished during the 1970s and 1980s with the establishment of The Women's Press in the United States in 1978, and Virago, a feminist publishing collective in Britain in 1973, making reprints of 'modern classics' available to a new generation of women readers. In 1998 Beauman achieved a remarkable personal triumph with the successful launch of her new company, Persephone Books, which includes Dorothy Whipple, Cicely Hamilton, and other women whom Beauman had discussed in *A Very Great Profession* in its rapidly expanding catalogue.

Alison Light's influential *Forever England* (1991) accounted for the ways in which Ivy Compton-Burnett, Agatha Christie, Jan Struther, and Daphne Du Maurier were able to accommodate the past in the forms of the present and suggested that the feminized 'conservative modernity' that characterized the interwar period represented a qualitatively different kind of conservatism.[6] Taking up Light's invitation to engage critically with the contradictions and tensions of ostensibly conservative literary texts Rebecca D'Monté discusses plays for the mainstream theatre which have received little critical attention because they were considered intellectually lightweight in much the same way as Coward, Rattigan, and Priestley. D'Monté argues that the middlebrow character of much of this drama accounts for the condescension with which it was often greeted but Jane Dowson's essay on poetry in this volume points to a rather different picture. Dowson identifies a range of styles, poetic voices, and allegiances with the avant-garde revolution of the word represented by Edith Sitwell and Lynette Roberts while at the other end of the stylistic spectrum she identifies women like Eleanor Farjeon who favoured traditional lyricism or light verse.

For much of its history the term 'modernist' retained the stylistic and evaluative meanings that it held from its first use in 1927 by Laura Riding and Robert Graves in *A Survey of Modernist Poetry*.[7] However, in a perceptive review of Peter Brooker and Andrew Thacker's edited volume, *The Oxford Critical and Cultural History of Modernist Magazines*, a project that encompasses a number of periodicals that make no claim to be other than traditional in content and form, Stefan Collini has noted the 'marked tendency in recent scholarship to try to expand its range employing [modernist] as a quasi-historical label for a whole period rather than for a cultural style or movement'.[8] Indeed the temporal usage of the term 'modernist', as opposed to its older qualitative and evaluative meanings, has become hegemonic within the academy, latterly coming to refer to virtually all post-Victorian literary production.

The willingness to expand what is now included in the portmanteau of Modernism may also be related to many critics' discomfiture in relation to the negativity that has accrued to 'Eliotic Modernism'. This can appear profoundly at odds with the secular sensibility of the twenty-first century, as well as the recognition that Modernism has been tarnished by its history of association with discredited or exclusionary aesthetics and politics. As Peter Childs puts it, 'Modernism has predominantly been represented in white, male, heterosexist, Euro-American middle class terms, and any of the recent challenges to each of these aspects introduces another one of a plurality of Modernisms'.[9] In *Bad Modernisms* (2006) Douglas Mao and Rebecca Walkowitz summarized critical developments thus:

> Some contemporary scholars have even chosen to apply 'modernist' yet more globally – to say, all writing published in the first half of the twentieth century – thereby transforming the term from an evaluative and stylistic designation to a neutral and temporal one, and thus economically countering the implication that a few experimental works were somehow the only ones authentically representative of their age (in the familiar sequence Romantic-Victorian-Modernist-Postmodernist).[10]

The most inclusive understanding of Modernism contends that this is primarily 'an engagement with the intellectual problems of modernity' and that 'the formal properties of literature are only one means to that end'.[11] Moreover as Peter Brooker, Andrzej Gasiorek, Deborah Longworth, and Andrew Thacker explain, critics no longer assume the aesthetic to be the principle issue of concern in discussions of Modernism and its legacies: 'No less important is the need to grasp where modernism(s) emerged; how they developed; by what means they were produced, disseminated and publicized; in what relationship they stood to other artistic and cultural forms, which might be (or might in the past have been) regarded as non-modernist.'[12] The discussion of Modernism in this volume reflects the well-established critical practice of moving away from the idea of Modernism as a monolith to the consideration of a plurality of Modernisms distinguishing between 'high Modernism' and low. The tiny change of pronoun in the title of Bonnie Kime Scott's two landmark critical anthologies from *The Gender of Modernism* (1990) to *Gender in Modernism: New Geographies, Complex Intersections* (2007)[13] is of major significance in denoting the direction and impetus of feminist scholarship during the years that separate the publication of the two books, which have become standard reference works in Higher Education. Retaining the original recuperative emphasis on the archival recovery of neglected women, and its challenge to the unconscious gendered assumptions that once underpinned modernist scholarship, the second collaborative anthology moves beyond exclusive concern with female authorship to include many more men (from five to just under thirty). *Gender in Modernism* also extends its periodization back to the 'missing' years of 1880–1910, and questions the Eurocentric emphasis on white women by revising its geographies to take account of contemporary concerns with globalization, the transnational, and the ecological, adding these to the more established feminist concern with sexuality, 'race', and class.

In *The Gender of Modernity* (1995) Rita Felski has argued that understanding modernity necessitates looking critically at the roles that women have played in shaping the social and cultural history of the twentieth century.[14]

As Felski puts it in her 'afterword' to Ann L. Ardis and Leslie W. Lewis's *Women's Experience of Modernity* (2003):

> Women have not figured as key players in the theories of modernization or, with some obvious exceptions, in studies of literary modernism. But thinking in terms of popular culture and everyday life cedes them a starring role. Indeed, many of the cultural experiences that we think of as distinctively modern – from shopping to sex, from movies to fashion – are closely tied up with the experience of women in the modern world.[15]

In so far as 'high Modernism' was disdainful of sentiment, sensation, and popular pleasures and was often ironic about the possibilities of social progress it was also disdainful of the ubiquitous feminized cultural modernity of the day and the great gender shifts and transformations that characterized the early twentieth century. These included the impact of the women's suffrage campaigns which, as Jane Goldman and others have argued, were crucial to shaping the feminine aesthetics of Woolf and others.[16]

As a revolution of style Modernism constituted itself by seeking a complete severance from literary tradition as well as refuting domesticity, the matrix of ordinary feeling, and the concerns of everyday life. Early twentieth-century women writers, however, possessed a richly variegated literary inheritance in which passion, reason, and the imagination were diversely represented by such luminaries as the Brontës, Elizabeth Barrett Browning, Jane Austen, George Eliot, and Mary Wollstonecraft, as well as countless writers with lesser reputations; a legacy which had not insisted on the divorce of art and life. While the modernist separation from what had gone before might cut the woman writer off from oppressive patriarchal structures, controls, and responsibilities, it also cut her off from a public community of women and from an important nexus of shared feelings, hopes, experience, and desires. As Suzanne Clark puts it in *Sentimental Modernism* (1991), 'Modernism practiced a politics of style, but it denied that style had a politics.'[17]

In Chapter 4 below, Maud Ellmann ascribes the seemingly incomprehensible absence of a writer of Sylvia Townsend Warner's virtuosity and brilliance, which still befuddles literature syllabuses in colleges and universities, to a 'curious asceticism'. This has:

> descended on our discipline, preventing critics from admiring works that they enjoy, at least in twentieth-century studies; a certain allowance is made for the compelling plots of nineteenth-century fiction, as if its authors were too benighted by the strictures of their age to risk the verbal complexities of Joyce. In this critical context, a modern novelist who strives to captivate rather than to alienate the reader tends to be discounted as a throwback, lacking the gumption to burst the confines of the Victorian novel.

Some useful critical attempts to illuminate the discussion of Modernism and modernity that scrupulously avoid the elision of the two have included Kristin Bluemel's *George Orwell and the Radical Eccentrics* (2004), Alexandra Harris's *Romantic Moderns* (2010), and Chiara Briganti and Kathy Mezei's *Domestic Modernism, the Interwar Novel and E.H. Young* (2006).[18] In *Romantic Moderns* Harris uses the work of John Betjeman, Virginia Woolf, and Evelyn Waugh to show that a love of the countryside or of a particular idea of Englishness need not constitute a betrayal of the modern movement and that the modern need not be at war with the past. Briganti and Mezei examine the exploration of alternative domesticities in novelists such as E.H. Young and the ways in which the representation of domesticity makes possible both feminine pleasure and a feminist critique. Bluemel suggests the use of Intermodernism as a literary-historical category to encompass ex-centric writers before, during and after the Second World War. Initially concerned with George Orwell, Mulk Raj Anand, Stevie Smith, and Inez Holden, labelled as 'radical eccentrics', in this volume Bluemel adds Naomi Mitchison and Betty Miller to Holden and Smith.

'As a woman I have no country'?

The importance of early twentieth-century tourism and travel, cosmopolitanism, African-American Modernism, the Harlem Renaissance, and modernist voices emanating from the Caribbean and Africa all inform the critical understanding of Modernism as a global phenomenon in its geographies, influence, and concerns. Both the cultural export of modernist art, architecture, literature, and music – Matisse, Picasso, Joyce, Stravinsky, Le Corbusier, and so on, globally exemplifying modern European sophistication – and the position of London as a social and cultural Mecca for exiles and émigrés from the English-speaking world raise questions about the extent to which it is possible to discuss British literary Modernism in isolation from the rest of the world. Early twentieth-century globalization deterritorialized, defamiliarized, and delocalized English identification, particularly for those women whose sexual behaviour defied the codes of social acceptability or whose sexual orientation could be more freely expressed far from the strictures of home. Many women writers, such as Katherine Mansfield, Rumer Godden, Una Marson, and Jean Rhys, were either born in the former British Empire and opted to live in England, or like Elspeth Huxley and Stella Benson, spent their formative years or substantial parts of their adult lives living and working abroad. In *Colonial Strangers* Phyllis Lassner has demanded that white women colonial writers are taken with new seriousness and the contradictions of their situation be properly recognized.[19]

As Lisa Regan shows, British feminists were politically active across the world, for example, Winifred Holtby in South Africa, Eleanor Rathbone in Kenya, and Stella Benson in China. Regan draws attention to intrepid female travellers like Freya Stark and suggests that far from being apologists for the British imperial project writers like Godden domesticated colonial space or returned to the foundational moment of colonization to question its meaning and purpose.

The most ambitious work to challenge the dominant attitudes to 'race' in the period is Nancy Cunard's 800-page *Negro: An Anthology* (1934), compiled, financed, and edited as a labour of love by Cunard, whose The Hours Press, based in Paris, published Aldington, Riding, Pound, and Beckett. A ground-breaking compendium in which Cunard sought to represent the entire spectrum of black achievement from music to literature, from art to anthropology, from history to sculpture and ethnology for the first time, *Negro* compelled white readers to question their preconceptions of black people as embodiments of a Eurocentric sense of reality. Cunard, herself a poet, journalist, editor, political activist, and style-setter, is the subject of a critical study by Jane Marcus, her writings on 'race' and empire are edited by Maureen Moynagh.[20] Her poem, *Parallax*, is discussed by Tory Young in this volume.

As Douglas Mao and Rebecca Walkowitz point out, in 'The New Modernist Studies', the transnational is now a major preoccupation within modernist criticism.[21] The significance of translation, collage, linguistic mimicry, and racial masquerade; and of white modernist writers sometimes choosing to adopt black rhythms, voices, and idiolects as an anti-colonial identificatory strategy requires Modernism to be rethought in relation to 'race' and ethnicity in a global and postcolonial context.

However, while the ideal of global feminism envisaged in *Three Guineas* (1938) by Virginia Woolf ('as a woman I have no country, as a woman I want no country')[22] has proved liberating for some women it is problematic for others in so far as it assumes the privileges of cosmopolitan identification and geographical mobility acquired through history, empire, and social class from which many women have been historically excluded. As Katie Gramich points out, ideas of rootedness, loyalty to nation and to local community, are of great importance to women in Scotland, Ireland, and Wales living in the shadow of their powerful English neighbour.

Gramich draws attention to the wealth and diversity of writing by Scottish, Welsh, and Irish women, much of which places emphasis on fixity, geographical place, and the concomitant sense of belonging. Some of the fiction that Gramich discusses in her chapter has been republished by the Honno Press, an independent women's publishing cooperative supported by hundreds of individual subscribers, established in Wales in 1986 and still flourishing a quarter of a century later although little known beyond the Welsh borders. While such writing continues to receive the critical attention it deserves from feminist scholars such as Jane Aaron and Katie Gramich in Wales and Isobel Murray and Dorothy Macmillan in

Scotland, women's writing from Scotland, Ireland, and Wales has regrettably been a structuring absence in literary discussion conducted outside the nations in which it originated. Their inclusion inevitably shifts the terms on which future debate is conducted.

Sexuality

Literary sexuality within this period requires an understanding of the importance of socio-historic changes such as more permissive attitudes to sex, the lifting of many pre-war restrictions on women's freedom – such as the chaperoning of middle-class girls in the aftermath of the war – and the reconfiguration of heterosexuality through the visual signifiers of fashion and dress. The 1920s saw the vogue of the 'boyish' female dressed in trousers or a tailored suit, slim, narrow-hipped, with cropped hair, hands in pockets, and perhaps a monocle, cultivating a look that was severe, masculine, or androgynous. As Laura Doan puts it, fashion 'allowed older women – past the age to be taken as boys – to pass as the masculine "look." Older women who flirted with this "look" would have been more likely to be taken for fashionable than lesbian. The Modern Look and the Lesbian Look would not converge until the trial of *The Well of Loneliness*'[23] in 1928.

The emancipated carefree young woman enjoying sexual affairs to the accompaniment of jazz, fast cars, and alcohol was immortalized in Iris Storm, a character with a 'pagan body and a Chislehurst Mind',[24] loosely based on Nancy Cunard, in Michael Arlen's best-selling novel, *The Green Hat* (1924), but outside raffish, fashionable, and bohemian circles behaviour of this kind 'bore only tangential relation to most women's lives'.[25] Moreover, the increased opportunities for (hetero) sexual experience outside marriage reflected in much of the literature of the period intensified the taboos on the lesbian relationships that had developed between women who had become emotionally reliant on one another during the war.

In *Lesbian Empire: Radical Crosswriting in the Twenties* Gay Wachman shows how Sylvia Townsend Warner uses 'fantasy as a means of escaping, reshaping and critiquing a world fragmented by loss and pain'.[26] Wachman discusses the work of Clemence Dane, Rose Allatini, Evadne Price, and Warner, identifying a tradition of writing from Vernon Lee's *The Ballet of the Nations* (1915) to Warner's *The True Heart* (1929) which she argues 'forms a queer, primitivist predominantly satirical alternative modernist tradition that can be traced back to the aesthetics of excess in the art and literature of the 1890s'.[27] Ancient Greece and Rome were important in enabling writers to transpose the 'otherwise unrepresentable lives of invisible or silenced or simply closeted lesbians into narratives about gay men': Thus historical novelists 'free their imagination from the sex/gender system of their time by writing about men's lives; when they set their novels in a time and place such as ancient Greece that tolerates homosexuality'[28] they are able to celebrate homosexual romance. H.D. based her method of writing poems on classical Greek literature, Sappho in particular.

In *The Pilgrimage of Dorothy Richardson* (2000) Joanne Winning cites the sensual epiphanies in the kiss between Clarissa Dalloway and Sally Seaton in *Mrs Dalloway* (1925) and the rhapsodic moment of recognition between Miriam Henderson and Amabel in Dorothy Richardson's *Dawn's Left Hand* (1931) as representing only two instances of the 'complicated yet insistent traces of lesbian desire and identity in the works of many female modernist writers'.[29] The instantaneous attraction of Bertha Young to Pearl Fulton in Katherine Mansfield's 'Bliss' in *Bliss and other Stories* (1920) is another obvious instance – Mansfield died tragically young in 1923 at the age of thirty-four. Other scholars, including Erin Carlston in *Thinking Fascism: Sapphic Modernism and Fascist Modernity* (1998), Laura Doan and Jane Garrity as the editors of *Sapphic Modernities: Sexuality, Women and National Culture* (2006), and authors of the essay, 'Modernism Queered' (2006), and Robin Hackett in *Sapphic Primitivism* (2004)[30] have attempted to theorize or to explore the lesbian modernist literary subject and the question of what might be meant by a 'lesbian Modernism'. This body of criticism views lesbian sexuality (termed 'Sapphic' in the 1920s and 1930s) as a key radical impetus inspiring modernist literary endeavour and suggests how this might transform our understanding of literary Modernism.

The trial of Radclyffe Hall's *The Well of Loneliness*, the first novel to be written by an unapologetic lesbian, brought lesbianism out of the shadows. Other lesbians were to follow Hall's courageous example of political self-consciousness and public identification. Later fictions often repudiated the particular view of the lesbian as inexorably anguished, suffering, and damned that had informed Hall's novel. However, the historical and political importance of *The Well of Loneliness* lay in its initiating a 'reverse discourse' whereby lesbians were able to articulate their sexuality for the first time and to begin the process of defining themselves rather than accepting the representations imposed upon them by others.

In their pioneering study *Writing for Their Lives: the Modernist Women, 1910–1940* (1987) Gillian Hanscombe and Virginia Smyers located an extensive networks of women writers who 'all seemed to write to each other, or about each other. They introduced one to the other. They sometimes fell in love with each other or with each other's partners. They were all either writing or publishing what the others were writing, because they believed in each other's work.'[31] More recently, Catherine Clay has identified a web of literary and work-based women's friendships based on the metropole, and her 'geographies of work and pleasure' include 'companionate friendships' where women, whether living together or not, provided each other with long-term commitment, understanding, and support; for example, Vera Brittain and Winifred Holtby, Edith Craig and Christopher St John, Elizabeth Robins and Octavia Wilberforce, Virginia Woolf and Vita Sackville-West, and so on. Clay argues that the radical sexual politics of these companionate friendships would have been evident at the time, the 'Smallhyde trio' of Edith Craig, Christopher St John, and 'Tony Atwood', for instance, 'identifying itself in relation to art, with visual codes (notably cross-dressing) indicating a conscious resistance to conventional femininity'.[32]

The 1920s, the 1930s, and the Second World War

The most important political achievement of the 'first-wave feminism' associated in literature with such writers as Olive Schreiner and Virginia Woolf (designated 'first wave' to differentiate it from the second wave of feminism of the late 1960s and 1970s) was the right to vote. Women over the age of thirty acquired the vote in 1918 as the culmination of half a century of struggle that began when John Stuart Mill first put the case for women's suffrage before Parliament in 1866. As Winifred Holtby put it, the suffrage movement 'had disproved those theories about their own nature which were – and sometimes are – among their gravest handicaps'. Moreover, 'An emotional earthquake had shattered the intangible yet suffocating prison of decorum. The standard of values which rated women's persons, positions, interests and pre-occupations as affairs of minor national importance had been challenged.'[33]

While the vote represented an important emancipatory symbol it was still regarded as a privilege to be earned rather than a right, and only after a little-known campaign to demonstrate their fitness for full citizenship in which younger women were prominent was the franchise finally extended to women over twenty-one in 1928. While the First World War cast a long shadow over countless women who had lost their loved ones, women's friendship groups and networks enabled the ideal of feminist community to flourish and provided practical and emotional support for women trying to reform the law relating to marriage, divorce, guardianship, and the welfare of children.

The demographic imbalance of approximately two million more women than men of marriageable age in the population disclosed in the census of 1921 made it imperative that women in this age group should become economically self-supporting and their individual potential and collective importance to the economy be recognized. Organizations such as the London and National Society for Women's Service which sought to further the employment of women were important to those wishing to establish careers for themselves in the professions of medicine, teaching, the law, journalism, and local government; the latter described by the feminist headmistress, Sarah Burton, in Holtby's *South Riding* as the 'first line of defence thrown up by the community against our common enemies – poverty, sickness, ignorance, isolation'.[34] Virginia Woolf's essay, 'Professions for Women', in which she argued that it was the responsibility of the woman writer to put to death the selfless Victorian domestic paragon, the 'Angel in the House', developed out of a talk originally given to the National Society for Women's Service in 1931. Woolf continued to think about entry into the professions throughout the 1930s and retained 'Professions for Women' as a working title for *Three Guineas* (1938).

The 1920s saw a division of ranks between those 'old' feminists such as Winifred Holtby, Vera Brittain, and Margaret, Lady Rhondda, who were primarily concerned with securing equality with men, and the 'new' feminists such as Eleanor Rathbone, who took over from Millicent Fawcett as president when the National Union of Women's Suffrage Societies decided to change its name to the National Union of Societies for Equal Citizenship and to broaden its campaigning base. In *The Disinherited Family* (1924), Rathbone argued persuasively that women's needs were essentially different from men's because of their family responsibilities and that the importance of women's maternal and domestic roles should therefore be properly recognized and remunerated by the state.

In 1920 Margaret, Viscountess Rhondda, established the most important feminist journal of its day, *Time and Tide*, which in its early phase under the editorship of Helen Archdale and Winifred Holtby was closely allied to various radical causes and reflected the politics of the feminist Six Points Group – its political affiliations were to change markedly in its later manifestations. Contributors included well-known political figures such as Margaret Bondfield, Ellen Wilkinson, and Lady Astor, as well as many women who had, or were to acquire, substantial literary reputations, including Elizabeth Bowen, Storm Jameson, Pamela Hansford Johnson, Marghanita Laski, Ethel Mannin, Naomi Mitchison, Kate O'Brien, Jean Rhys, Olive Schreiner, Sylvia Townsend Warner, Rebecca West, Dorothy Whipple, Virginia Woolf, and E.H. Young. Catherine Clay's chapter on *Time and Tide* traces the entry of literary women into journalism and the use of the periodical for the dissemination of feminist ideas. Clay shows that *Time and Tide* played a particularly important role in publishing women poets, who often struggled to place their work, through its policy of publishing new poetry and book reviews.

The 1930s is often called the 'red decade' on account of the hegemony of socialist ideas. What prompted the movement to the left of male and female writers was the soaring unemployment in the Great Depression that followed the crash of the New York Wall Street Stock Exchange in 1929. The resultant misery was brought starkly to the attention of the affluent parts of the country by the hunger marches, most famously the Jarrow March of 1936 from the deserted shipyards of the north-east to London, led by MP Ellen Wilkinson. As Storm Jameson put it in her autobiography, *Journey from the North*, 'on one side Dachau, on the other the "distressed areas" with their ashamed workless men and despairing women. Not many English writers had the hardness of heart to hurry past, handkerchief to nose, intoning, "my concern is with art, what troubles are troubling the world are not my business".'[35] Working-class women regrettably did not find their way into print in any significant numbers during the class-conscious 'red decade'. Despite the strong, albeit short-lived, vogue for fiction written by or about working men we have no female equivalents of Anthony Greenwood's *Love on the Dole* (1933), Lewis Jones's *Cwmardy* (1937), or Walter Brierley's *Means Test Man* (1935).

The growing social division and unrest at home ran in tandem with the growth of Fascism in Europe: the rise to power of Hitler in Germany in 1933, the invasion of Ethiopia by Mussolini in 1934, and the outbreak of the Spanish Civil War in 1936. English Fascists had very little electoral or popular support in comparison with their European counterparts but the violent activities of Mosley's Blackshirts, targeted specifically against the Jewish communities in the East End of London and elsewhere, provoked disquiet and alarm. The consciences of many women on the liberal left, such as Naomi Mitchison, Sylvia Townsend Warner, Lettice Cooper, Nancy Cunard, Vera Brittain, Storm Jameson, Rosamond Lehmann, and Winifred Holtby, were deeply affected by the injustice and suffering that they saw all around them. While the zeitgeist is most clearly discernible in political dystopias like Mitchison's *We Have Been Warned* (1935) or Jameson's *In the Second Year* (1936) the relation of radical politics to literary form that preoccupied each of them is expressed differently in their fiction and often in subtle and complex ways.

Sylvia Townsend Warner's knowledge of Spanish culture and history, acquired on visits to the republic as a medical ancillary and a member of the Association of Writers for Intellectual Liberty during the Spanish Civil War, underpins the finest of her historical novels, *After the Death of Don Juan* (1938). Warner wrote seven novels including *Lolly Willowes* (1926), *Mr Fortune's Maggot* (1927), *The True Heart* (1929), and *Summer Will Show* (1936). A stylist par excellence, whose pellucid prose defies any scholarly attempt to accommodate her within the procrustean bed of modernist critical practice, Warner is the only writer other than Woolf who, for reasons that Maud Ellmann outlines, is sufficiently important to the revised literary history and historiography of this period to merit discussion in a chapter on her own. In *Journey from the North* (1969), Jameson offers the following description of the chastened mood of writers like herself which made inactivity no longer an intellectually credible option:

> The impulse that turned so many of us into pamphleteers and amateur politicians was neither mean nor trivial. The evil we were told off to fight was really evil, the threat to human decency a real threat. I doubt whether any of us believed that books would be burned in England, or eminent English scholars, scientists, writers, forced to beg hospitality in some other country. Or that, like Lorca, we might be murdered.

Or tortured and then killed in concentration camps. But all these things were happening abroad, and intellectuals who refused to protest were in effect blacklegs. In this latest quarrel between Galileo and the Inquisition they were on the side of the Inquisition.[36]

As I have argued elsewhere, feminism suffered significant setbacks in the 1930s in a cultural and economic context where the defeat of Fascism and the defence of democracy took precedent over all else.[37] Women became resistant to feminist ideas not only because there seemed little purpose in further struggle after the vote was won but also because they did not wish to construe men as responsible for women's subordination but as allies in the all-important struggle against totalitarianism. Virginia Woolf's great pacifist polemic, *Three Guineas*, makes a powerful case for gender inequality as the underlying cause of dictatorship and war. Its provocative *auto-da-fé* of feminism is at once an acknowledgement of how redolent of dated politics the word feminism had become for a younger generation of women and a rhetorical strategy to clear the way for men and women to join together to achieve their common dream of peace and freedom.

Winifred Holtby's *Women and a Changing Civilization* (1934), published after the vote in favour of the marriage bar in teaching and the Civil Service in 1932, reflects Holtby's anxieties about women's complicity in the removal of rights achieved through feminist struggle. Like Woolf, she recognized the causal links between masculinity, the upbringing of boys, and Fascist dictatorship. Holtby finished *Women and a Changing Civilization* with a grim warning about the dangers of rigid sexual segregation: '"We want men who are men and women who are women," writes Oswald Mosley. He can find them at their quintessence in the slave markets of Abyssinia, or in the winding alleys of a Chinese city.'[38] Her fascination with Woolf – Holtby was Woolf's first biographer – cautions today's reader against attaching more importance to demarcations between realists and modernists than was attached at the time.

Many women writers had reacted to the devastating losses of their brothers, partners, fathers, sons, and closest friends in the First World War with a strong commitment to pacifist ideals; some, like Vera Brittain and Virginia Woolf, being implacably opposed to war in all circumstances, others, like Storm Jameson and Rose Macaulay, reluctantly prepared to revise their pacifist sympathies in the light of the traumatic events of the late 1930s. The two camps parted company, often with considerable sadness since personal friendships came under intense pressure, when the Second World War was declared in 1939. Reflecting the movement of recent feminist inquiry away from the notion of war as combat to a more inclusive understanding of war as cultural dislocation, Gill Plain explores Elizabeth Bowen's concept of war writing as 'resistance writing' and shows how women writers concerned with questions of everyday survival dissolved the distinction between combatant and non-combatant. However, Plain argues that 'ordinary' citizens were largely powerless in the face of aerial bombardment and the unprecedented regimentation of private life and that gender hierarchy remained despite the ostensibly democratic wartime rhetoric.

Virginia Woolf and the middlebrow

The figure whose importance to virtually all literary-historical accounts of this period remains undisputed is Virginia Woolf. Woolf's name is consistently invoked in both the recognized canon of international modernist authors (Eliot, Pound, Stein, Joyce, Yeats, Mansfield, Conrad, Proust, Kafka, and so on) and in the accounts of feminist critics whose work undermines or questions many of the assumptions on which that canon is founded. Yet while her reputation might today appear impregnable, until relatively recently Woolf was frequently dismissed as an inconsequential exponent of art for art's sake with at best a limited understanding of the social and political realities of her day.

The Virginia Woolf Jane Goldman discusses in this volume is the Woolf whose revised literary reputation – inseparable from her legacy as a feminist and a democrat – owes much to the second wave of feminist criticism from the late 1960s and 1970s onward and to such works of scholarship as Hermione Lee's authoritative biography *Virginia Woolf* (1996), Gillian Beer's *Virginia Woolf: The Common Ground* (1996), Rachel Bowlby's *Virginia Woolf: Feminist Destinations* (1988), and the late Julia Briggs's *Virginia Woolf: An Inner Life* (2005).[39] Woolf's great feminist treatise, *A Room of One's Own* (1928), as Goldman points out, is of particular relevance to readers of this volume of Palgrave's *History of British Women's Writing*. With its insistence on the importance of the material and economic – a woman must have money and a room of her own if she is to write fiction – and its invitation to the reader to 'think back through our mothers', as well as the homage that Woolf makes to a line of writers traced back through history including Fanny Burney, Jane Austen, and Aphra Behn, *A Room of One's Own* remains the twentieth century's most influential attempt to establish a woman's tradition of writing.

Like the term Modernism the term 'middlebrow' is imprecise; referring to a perplexingly unstable combination of popularity, content, style, and readership. It is used both neutrally as a descriptor for a type of enjoyable reading that eludes the category of popular fiction and pejoratively in relation to writing deemed to be unadventurous in content, style, and form. As Nicola Humble puts it in her chapter in this volume, 'It would have been extremely hard in the interwar years to find any writer or publisher who would happily apply the label to their own works, and almost as hard to find a reader who would own the designation.'

Woolf famously dismissed the middlebrow in a letter written in 1927 and published posthumously in *The Death of the Moth* in 1942. Defending the highbrow – such as herself – whose aesthetic taste and intellectual preferences supposedly owed nothing to commercial considerations, Woolf castigated the middlebrow as 'betwixt and between' and 'in pursuit of no single object, neither Art itself nor life itself but both mixed indistinguishably, and rather nastily, with money, fame, power, or prestige'.[40] Woolf initially addressed the controversial letter to the editor of the *New Statesman*, but never posted it. Her failure to do so is perhaps indicative of anxieties about its tone or else of a self-conscious awareness of the contradictions of her own position as an author reliant on her income from writing, her association with publications such as *Good Housekeeping* and *Vogue*, and the importance that she attached publicly to writing as a professional career for women. Thus middlebrow women writers who might well have taken exception to Woolf's opinions were not aware of the letter's contents during her lifetime. Her attitudes had, in any case, mellowed considerably by the end of the 1930s.

While Woolf could be intemperate and even on occasion scathing about what she considered to be bad or meretricious writing her own choice of reading was interestingly eclectic and inclusive, and her responses to middlebrow novelists more generous than is generally recognized. For example, she was impressed by F.M. Mayor's old-fashioned novel, *The Rector's Daughter*, published by The Hogarth Press in 1924, and by E.H. Young's unpretentious *William*: 'I bought a book for 6d in the Penguins called *William* by E.H. Young, and for a wonder, enjoyed it greatly ... I think she must be a very good novelist.'[41] Woolf also disliked being lumped indiscriminately with the male modernists and stressed her difference, to Joyce in particular: 'I dislike *Ulysses* more and more – that is think it more & more unimportant & don't even trouble conscientiously to make out its meanings.'[42]

As Melba Cuddy-Keane argues in *Virginia Woolf, the Intellectual, and the Public Sphere* Woolf was certainly a highbrow in disposition but she was also a democrat intent on making a highbrow intellectual culture available to all.[43] This was consistently demonstrated throughout her life, since her early encounters with 'nice enthusiastic working women who say they love books'[44] as a tutor at Morley College in 1905–1907. Moreover, she was committed to the Co-operative Working Women's Guild which met for many years in her London home and supported the Workers' Educational Association during the bleakest days of the Second World War when the creation of an informed educated public appeared crucial to the defence of a democratic society under threat from invasion by Nazi Germany. As Cuddy-Keane contends in her critique of Jonathan Rose's *The Intellectual Life of the British Working Class*, any monolithic construction of modernist intellectuals such as Woolf in voluntary seclusion from the intellectual pursuits of working people 'produces an unremittingly antagonistic construction of "two rival intelligentsias squared off against each other"' as well as setting up an 'unbridgeable impasse between highbrow and democratic concerns'.[45] Indeed, Woolf's biographer, Hermione Lee, reminds us of Woolf's impassioned principled commitment to the common reader and her belief in the 'democratic function of the library as the university of the non-specialist, uninstructed reader; it is the reading room for the common reader'.[46]

The relationship between 'mass' and 'minority culture' and 'highbrow' and democratic', then, is more complex than it might first appear. Moreover, the critical antipathy to middlebrow fiction and investment in cultural hierarchy that characterizes this historical period must be placed in the context of the massive expansion in the teaching of English literature as a relatively new academic discipline in universities and colleges after the First World War. While the School of English Language and Literature was approved at Oxford University in 1893 the English Tripos at Cambridge University dates back to 1917 and the full independent English Tripos or degree to 1926.

The establishment and consolidation of English as an academic discipline conferred literary critics with unprecedented authority as arbiters of educated taste extending far beyond the universities. Irrespective of their intellectual differences critics such as F.R. Leavis, I.A. Richards, and William Empson were united by their hostility to best-selling fiction, a position forcefully expressed in Leavis's *Mass Civilisation and Minority Culture* (1930), and by their articulate defence of English literature as a respectable subject of academic study that could hold its own in comparison to the older university disciplines such as Divinity and Latin and Greek. Thus the status of English literature in the academy depended on its reputation for intellectual seriousness and concomitantly on the avoidance of any public association between serious literary works and fiction consumed by the undiscriminating reader. As Tory Young puts it, 'English literature as a university subject was constructed against the middlebrow.'[47]

Nicola Humble's pioneering study, *The Feminine Middlebrow Novel 1920s to 1950s*[48] set in motion a train of feminist critical work focused upon the type of woman-centred fiction that came into its own between the wars, aided by the rapid growth of the lending library which supplied the middle-class woman with her weekly library books either free, or in the case of the Boots lending library run by high street pharmacies, at a nominal charge. The Middlebrow Network, a research project funded by the Arts and Humanities Research Council, was launched at Sheffield Hallam University in July 2008 with the purpose of securing a more informed understanding of non-canonical authors and divesting the term 'middlebrow' of the negative associations that it has held for most of its history. As Faye Hammill, a founder of the network, puts it, 'much middlebrow writing has been ignored by the academy because of a misconception that it is so straightforward as to require no analysis'.[49]

One theoretical problem in respect of the term 'middlebrow' is that its very existence is predicated on the terms 'highbrow' and 'lowbrow'. Thus its usage assumes and perpetuates, rather than helping to question or to undermine, the kind of binary oppositions that feminists might wish to erase. Such distinctions have also come to appear increasingly irrelevant in the age of mechanical (and digital) reproduction, when, for example, a grand operatic work to which only a privileged elite would once have had access is transposed to film and can be enjoyed by millions of viewers around the world. Moreover, many postmodern writers after the Second World War deliberately put a critical distance between themselves and what they perceived as the more intractable abstractions, failures, and stylistic extremities of 'high Modernism', self-consciously seeking to establish a different relationship with their readers, for example, by embracing and engaging anew with the ludic and other pleasures of the literary text.

The organization of the book

To reflect recent feminist scholarship this book has been organized into four sections: 'Mapping Modernism', 'Cultural Hierarchy', 'Gendered Genres', and 'The Mobile Woman' although there is inevitably some mutually enriching overlap. The first section 'Mapping Modernism' is dedicated to Modernism with some focus on the vexed questions of its exclusions. Bonnie Kime Scott traces Modernism from its origins in the attempt to revolutionize literature in the early twentieth century to the very different way in which Modernism is perceived retrospectively as a result of the challenges exerted by feminist critique to the thinking of a white male elite. Kristin Bluemel discusses Intermodernism as a kind of writing or aesthetic category associated with the years before and after the war which makes it possible to consider writers and types of writing often occluded in critical discussions of both Modernism and Postmodernism. Jane Goldman and Maud Ellmann provide illuminating case studies of Virginia Woolf and Sylvia Townsend Warner respectively; two authors whose cultural politics were tendentially radical and democratic. Woolf is considered not only as a formally innovative novelist but also as a public intellectual committed to the common reader and to recovering a suppressed lineage of women writers in *A Room of One's Own*. Warner is discussed as an accomplished stylist neglected in the academy because of what Maud Ellmann describes as the 'long-standing over-valuation of experimental Modernism' and the 'curious asceticism' preventing critics from admiring works that they enjoy.

The next two sections, on 'Cultural Hierarchy' and 'Gendered Genres', reflect a common thread that runs through many of the chapters: the way in which women writers have become marginalized in literary history because of their association with low status writing, particularly writing for commercial or mainstream audiences. The crime writers that Cora Kaplan discusses and the writers of historical fiction that are Diana Wallace's subjects were pre-eminent in popular genres that had their heyday or golden age between the wars and rewrite andro-centric narratives, unsettling the distinction between art and politics and 'low' and high art. Journalism has traditionally been viewed with condescension by many writers with aspirations to a literary career but Catherine Clay outlines how women came to regard literary journalism more positively. Much critical discussion about cultural hierarchy, readership, and taste has focused on the feminine middlebrow novel and Nicola Humble's essay on this topic is complemented by Sophie Blanch's discussion of women and comedy. Jane Dowson's chapter on women poets discerns avant-garde disruptions alongside strains of traditional lyricism and unsettles any alignment between 'brow' and 'class' in women publishing poetry in the 1920s and 1930s, and Rebecca D'Monté recuperates a number of women dramatists whose works have been dismissed as 'domestic dramas' and 'trivial comedies'.

The final section, 'The Mobile Woman' begins with Katie Gramich's consideration of Welsh, Scottish, and Irish women writers to allow comparative perspectives on questions of mobility. The chapters by Lisa Regan, Gill Plain, Tory Young, and Deborah Longworth all approach the way in which women's horizons and opportunities were extended by travel, whether in the context of empire or war or shown in the literature associated with women's experiences on the streets of the modern city. All the contributors to this volume have taken a long view of their subjects and have provided a synoptic review of its parts, paying appropriate attention to historical context and locating their chosen authors and texts within the diachronic perspectives of Palgrave's *History of British Women's Writing* in its entirety. All reflect the emphasis of second-wave feminist scholarship on the importance of difference, whether of class, age, religion, 'race', ethnicity, sexuality, or sexual orientation.

Notes

1. Ezra Pound, *Make it New: Essays by Ezra Pound* (London: Faber and Faber, 1934).
2. Virginia Woolf, 'Mr and Mrs Brown', in *The Collected Essays of Virginia Woolf*, ed. Leonard Woolf, 4 vols (London: The Hogarth Press, 1966–1967), II, pp. 319–37.
3. Shari Benstock, *Women of the Left Bank: Paris, 1900–1940* (Austin: University of Texas Press, 1986).
4. See Julia Briggs, 'Hope Mirrlees and Continental Modernism', in *Gender in Modernism: New Geographies, Complex Intersections*, ed. Bonnie Kime Scott (Urbana and Chicago: University of Illinois Press, 2007), pp. 261–9, p. 261.
5. Nicola Beauman, *A Very Great Profession: The Woman's Novel 1914–39* (London: Virago, 1983).
6. Alison Light, *Forever England: Femininity, Literature and Conservatism between the Wars* (London: Routledge, 1991).
7. Laura Graves and Robert Bridges, *A Survey of Modernist Poetry* (London: Heinemann, 1927), p. 270.
8. Stefan Collini, 'Modernism and the little Magazines', *Times Literary Supplement* (7 October 2009), pp. 1–2.
9. Peter Childs, *Modernism* (London: Routledge, 2000), p. 12.
10. Douglas Mao and Rebecca L. Walkowitz, eds, *Bad Modernisms* (Durham: Duke University Press, 2006), pp. 1–2.

11. Stefan Collini, review of Peter Brooker and Andrew Thacker, eds, 'The Oxford Critical and Cultural History of Modernist Magazines', *Times Literary Supplement* (7 October 2009), pp. 3–5, p. 3.
12. Peter Brooker, Andrzej Gasiorek, Deborah Longworth, and Andrew Thacker (eds), *The Oxford Handbook of Modernisms* (Oxford: Oxford University Press, 2010), p. 2.
13. Bonnie Kime Scott, *The Gender of Modernism: a Critical Anthology* (Bloomington: Indiana University Press, 1990); *Gender in Modernism: New Geographies, Complex Intersections* (Urbana and Chicago: University of Illinois Press, 2007).
14. Rita Felski, *The Gender of Modernity* (Cambridge, MA: Harvard University Press, 1995).
15. Rita Felski, 'Afterword', in *Women's Experience of Modernity*, ed. Ann L. Ardis and Leslie W. Lewis (Baltimore: Johns Hopkins University Press, 2003), pp. 290–9, p. 292.
16. Jane Goldman, *The Feminist Aesthetics of Virginia Woolf* (Cambridge: Cambridge University Press, 1998).
17. Suzanne Clark, *Sentimental Modernism: Women Writers and the Revolution of the Word* (Bloomington: Indiana University Press, 1991), p. 5.
18. Kristin Bluemel, *George Orwell and the Radical Eccentrics: Intermodernism in Literary London* (London: Palgrave Macmillan, 2004); Alexandra Harris, *Romantic Moderns: English Writers, Artists and the Imagination from Virginia Woolf to John Piper* (London: Thames and Hudson, 2010); Chiara Briganti and Kathy Mezei, *Domestic Modernism, the Interwar Novel and E.H. Young* (Aldershot: Ashgate, 2006).
19. Phyllis Lassner, *Colonial Strangers: Women Writing the End of the British Empire* (New Brunswick: Rutgers University Press, 2004).
20. Jane Marcus, *Hearts of Darkness: White Women Write Race* (New Brunswick: Rutgers University Press, 2004); Maureen Moynagh, ed., *Essays on Race and Empire: Nancy Cunard* (Peterborough, Ontario: Broadview Press, 2002).
21. Douglas Mao and Rebecca Walkowitz 'The New Modernist Studies', *PMLA*, 123.3 (May 2008), pp. 737–48.
22. Virginia Woolf, *Three Guineas* (London: Hogarth Press, 1938), p. 125.
23. Laura Doan, 'Passing Fashions: Reading Female Masculinities in the 1920s' (1998), reprinted in Bonnie Kime Scott (ed.), *Gender and Modernism: Critical Concepts in Literary and Cultural Studies*, vol. 4, *Diversity of Identities* (London: Routledge, 2008), pp. 297–320, p. 309.
24. Michael Arlen, *The Green Hat* (London: Collins, 1924), p. 58.
25. Lesley A. Hall, *Sex, Gender and Social Change in Britain since 1880* (Basingstoke: Macmillan, 2000), p. 99.
26. Gay Wachman, *Lesbian Empire: Radical Crosswriting in the Twenties* (New Brunswick: Rutgers University Press, 2001), p. 2.
27. Ibid.
28. Ibid., p. 1.
29. Joanne Winning, *The Pilgrimage of Dorothy Richardson* (Madison: University of Wisconsin Press, 2000), p. 4.
30. Erin G. Carlston, *Thinking Fascism: Sapphic Modernism and Fascist Modernity* (Stanford: Stanford University Press, 1998); Laura Doan and Jane Garrity (eds), *Sapphic Modernities: Sexuality, Women and National Culture* (Basingstoke: Palgrave Macmillan, 2006); Laura Doan and Jane Garrity, 'Modernism Queered', in David Bradshaw and Kevin J. Dettmar (eds), *Blackwell Companion to Modernist Literature and Culture* (Oxford: Blackwell, 2006), pp. 542–50; Robin Hackett, *Sapphic Primitivism: Production of Race, Class and Sexuality in Key Works of Modern Fiction* (New Brunswick: Rutgers University Press, 2004).

31. Virginia L. Smyers, 'Preface' to Gillian Hanscombe and Virginia L. Smyers, *Writing for Their Lives: The Modernist Women, 1910–1940* (London: Women's Press, 1987), p. xvii.
32. Catherine Clay, *British Women Writers 1914–1945: Professional Work and Friendship* (Aldershot: Ashgate, 2006), p. 14.
33. Winifred Holtby, *Women and a Changing Civilization* (London: Bodley Head, 1934), pp. 5, 2–3.
34. Winifred Holtby, *South Riding* (London: Collins, 1936), pp. 5–6.
35. Storm Jameson, *Autobiography of Storm Jameson: Journey from the North*, 2 vols (London: Collins and Harvill Press, 1969), I, p. 293.
36. Ibid., pp. 292–3.
37. Maroula Joannou, 'The Woman Writer in the 1930s: On Not Being Mrs Giles of Durham City', in *Women Writers of the 1930s: Gender, Politics and History*, ed. Maroula Joannou (Edinburgh: Edinburgh University Press, 1998), pp. 1–13, pp. 9, 10, 11.
38. Holtby, *Women and a Changing Civilization*, p. 193.
39. Hermione Lee, *Virginia Woolf* ((London: Chatto and Windus, 1996); Gillian Beer, *Virginia Woolf: The Common Ground* (Edinburgh: Edinburgh University Press, 1996); Rachel Bowlby, *Virginia Woolf: Feminist Destinations* (Oxford: Basil Blackwell, 1988); Julia Briggs, *Virginia Woolf: An Inner Life* (London: Allen Lane, 2005).
40. Virginia Woolf, 'Middlebrow', in *The Death of the Moth and Other Essays* (London: Hogarth Press, 1942), pp. 113–19.
41. Virginia Woolf, letter to Lady Ottoline Morrell dated 19 February 1938, in *The Letters of Virginia Woolf*, ed. Nigel Nicolson and Joanne Trautmann, 6 vols (London: Hogarth Press, 1976–1980), VI, pp. 215–16, p. 216.
42. Virginia Woolf, diary entry dated 23 August 1922, in *The Diary of Virginia Woolf*, ed. Anne Olivier Bell and Andrew McNeillie, 5 vols (Harmondsworth: Penguin, 1979–1985), II, pp. 195–6.
43. Melba Cuddy-Keane, *Virginia Woolf, the Intellectual, and the Public Sphere* (Cambridge: Cambridge University Press, 2003), p. 2.
44. Virginia Woolf, *A Passionate Apprentice: The Early Journals, 1897–1909*, ed. Mitchell Leaska (London: Hogarth, 1990), p. 218.
45. Cuddy-Keane, *Virginia Woolf*, p. 4.
46. Hermione Lee, *Virginia Woolf*, p. 414.
47. Tory Young, 'Torrents of Trash', *Cambridge Quarterly*, 33 (2004), pp. 187–9, p. 187.
48. Nicola Humble, *The Feminine Middlebrow Novel 1920s to 1950s: Class, Domesticity, and Bohemianism* (Oxford: Oxford University Press, 2001).
49. Faye Hammill, *Women, Celebrity and Literary Culture between the Wars* (Austin: University of Texas Press, 2007), p. 6.

Part I
Mapping Modernism

1
Gender in Modernism

Bonnie Kime Scott

Coping with gender was an enormous challenge for women writers of the modernist era, on personal, professional, geographical, and theoretical grounds. In her first novel, *The Voyage Out*,[1] Virginia Woolf enlists a young male character, Terence Hewet, to express scepticism about any rapid alteration of gender norms in the early twentieth century. Hewet considers 'the masculine conception of life' to be 'an amazing concoction'.[2] He speaks to Rachel Vinrace, a gifted young pianist belatedly coming into political and self-awareness while visiting an Amazonian location in coastal South America:

> 'It'll take at least six generations before you're sufficiently thick-skinned to go into law courts and business offices. Consider what a bully the ordinary man is,' he continued, 'the ordinary hard-working, rather ambitious solicitor or man of business with a family to bring up and a certain position to maintain. And then, of course the daughters have to give way to the sons; the sons have to be educated; they have to bully and shove for their wives and families, and so it all comes over again. And meanwhile there are the women in the background ... Do you really think that the vote will do you any good?'[3]

Being more concerned with musical goals, Rachel is indifferent to the vote. While the exotic location of the novel might be expected to produce some distance from British gender norms, Rachel and Terence still struggle with custom as they become involved in their own marriage plot. The novel also demonstrates ways in which gender intersects with other social categories, including sexuality and national and imperial attitudes, and it records nightmares and post-impressionist landscapes that usher in Woolf's modernist experimentation. In ultimately denying the marriage plot, Woolf launched herself into a career that would trouble the complex politics of gender in Modernism and modernity. She had a great deal of company, both in Britain and in the wider world of Modernism.

Masculine modernist formulations

Modernism, as an experimental endeavour that aimed at revolutionizing literature in the early decades of the twentieth century, came to be known in decidedly masculine terms, as I first argued in the introduction to *The Gender of Modernism* in 1990.[4] Among the formulators working in London were T.E. Hulme, with his preference for Classicism over Romanticism, Wyndham Lewis, in his influential periodical *BLAST* (published 1914–15) and in his book *Men Without Art*, Ezra Pound, as a definer of 'imagism' and 'vorticism' and as an ambitious editor, and T.S. Eliot, in 'Tradition and the Individual Talent', among his many influential critical pieces. Their views on the forms that writers could employ to engineer literature – to 'make it new' (Pound's phrase, used in 1934 as a title for a collection of his essays) – continued to be privileged well into the 1980s. This privileging began with the New Critics, who helped set academic canons of the 1950s, continued with the influence of Hugh Kenner, and persisted in the early work of Michael Levenson.[5] Kenner coined the phrase 'The Pound Era', using it as the title of one of his most influential books, and spent considerable energy discrediting Woolf and Bloomsbury.[6] Pound and Eliot have remained central figures in the journal *Modernism/modernity* (founded 1994), despite its inclusion of new Modernisms and its insistence upon the broader category of modernity alongside Modernism.

Masculine metaphors of Modernism included 'dry hardness', which Hulme attributed to Classicism, as opposed to attitudes of flight, 'sloppiness', or 'moaning and whining', which he attributes to the Romantics.[7] Pound was fond of genital figurations, even for the brain. In these, active 'making' relied on the male organ. In his postscript to Remy de Gourmont's *The Natural Philosophy of Love*, Pound reports having felt as if 'driving any new idea into the great passive vulva of London, a sensation analogous to the male feeling in copulation'.[8] In both this work and in correspondence with American poet and editor, Marianne Moore, Pound associated women with 'chaos', though he also called attention to H.D. (Hilda Doolittle), another American, then working in England, as an exemplary poet of imagism. When Amy Lowell arrived in London from the United States and began to challenge Pound with her own ideas of imagism, demonstrating that she possessed both the energy and the necessary private resources to produce her own anthologies, Pound turned his attention to the supposedly more dynamic form of vorticism. Wyndham Lewis repeatedly blasted feminine form and sentimentalism, often blending his 'blasts' with homophobic attitudes toward practitioners of decadence and aestheticism. Despite its association with the natural substance of water, Lewis's idea of 'vorticism' is a technical concept, the vortex being geometrically shaped, pointed, and energetic, having 'polished sides' and making swift, repeated, penetrating motions.[9] Practitioners of vorticism such as Nietzsche's superman are 'masters'.[10] To Lewis, Virginia Woolf represented an introverted figure brooding over a subterraneous 'stream of consciousness', which is 'a feminine phenomenon after all'.[11] Eliot offered his own examples of the need for classical and technical control in the creation of art, figured scientifically with his celebrated catalyst, a shred of platinum, which he invokes to represent the mind of the poet.[12]

Since the late 1960s, feminist scholars have done a great deal of work of recovery and revision, not just in identifying the neglected women of Modernism, but also in engaging a wider set of genres and audiences for Modernism as a manifestation of modernity and bringing into the discussion work that was going on outside the urban, cosmopolitan, technological centres of Europe and the United States. Indeed the revision of Modernism has taken place on numerous fronts, including postcolonial and queer Modernisms, and in more elastic groupings, such as the 'intermodern', a classification challenging periodization as well as modernist formal constraints and audiences. Modernism, as codified by the group Lewis defined as the 'men of 1914', was shaped in reaction to numerous cultural forces and further challenged by them as the twentieth century progressed. These included suffragists' endeavours to secure votes for women (only partially satisfied in 1918 in the UK), resistance to forms of popular culture widely dispersed in increasingly globalized cultures of modernity, and the emasculating effects of the First World War. That war brought not only the sacrifice of a generation of promising young men (including Hulme and de Gourmont) but also the gradual acknowledgement of shell-shock as a widespread phenomenon, comparable to forms of hysteria long associated with the female sex. Fought on a world stage, with women assuming new roles in the public sphere, and many of the players originating in the colonies, its later expression in modernist texts brought both greater diversity and awareness of a changing world order and provoked a crisis in masculinity.

Female networks for Modernism

As feminist recovery work has revealed, women were important not just in providing networks and venues for male formulators of Modernism but also for offering critiques that would shape its range and direction. Modernist women assumed active roles as editors or de facto editors of modernist little magazines, and wider circulation in more varied journals, as reviewers and essayists, and in publishing. Many of these relations were sketched out in the introduction to *The Gender of Modernism*, and included here is a figure from that text, representing the complex set of relations that worked intricately across sexes, sexualities, and even race (Figure 1.1). It is based on actual connections made by contributing editors to that text; others certainly existed.

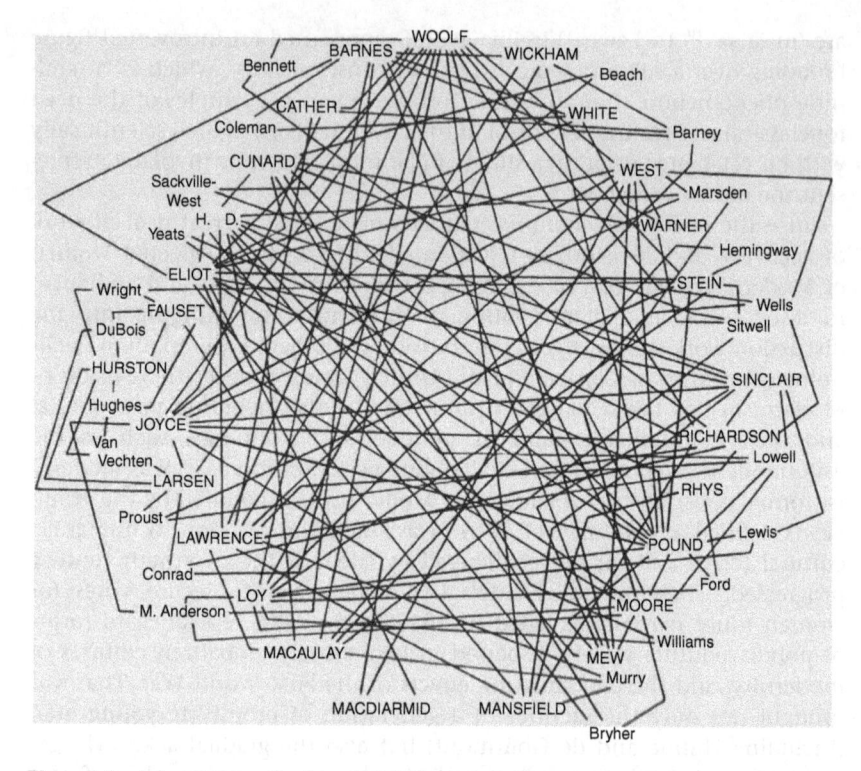

26 *The History of British Women's Writing, 1920–1945*

Figure 1.1 A tangled mesh of modernists
Source: Bonnie Kime Scott, *The Gender of Modernism: A Critical Anthology* (Bloomington: Indiana University Press, 1990), p. 10.

Sitting at the top of this 'mesh of modernists', Woolf has one of the richest arrays of connections, some forged by her published essays and extensive reviewing of contemporary writers, some through the publications of the Hogarth Press, which she and Leonard Woolf established with a small hand press in their home in 1917. Among its early publications were innovative modernist texts, including Woolf's *Kew Gardens*, Katherine Mansfield's *The Prelude*, and Hope Mirrlees's *Paris*, which in many ways anticipated another of its notable publications, T.S. Eliot's *The Waste Land*. Woolf's interest in psychology and in Russian contributions to Modernism later found expression in the Hogarth list, as they did in her important essay, 'Modern Fiction'. Hogarth Press's early covers and illustrations, and its series dedicated to essays and letters further diversified Modernism.[13] British-born Nancy Cunard commands attention for her Hours Press and for editing the anthology *Negro*, published in Paris in 1934. This massive volume had regional sections on America, the West Indies and South America, Europe, and Africa, achieving global range. Samuel Beckett served as a translator, and canonized modernists were scattered among predominant contributions by American blacks, including key writings by Zora Neale Hurston, as well as work by Langston Hughes, Alain Locke, and W.E.B. Du Bois. Similar efforts existed in other global locations such as Argentina where Victoria Ocampo operated Sur Press.

The number of connections generated by the British novelist May Sinclair may seem surprising, but it is indicative of her energetic work both outside and inside modernist circles in the making; many of these connections are with other women who have also remained relatively obscure. Sinclair was one of numerous well-connected women who helped Ezra Pound establish himself among modernists when he arrived in London from the United States in 1908. She provided key introductions to Violet Hunt and her partner at the time, Ford Madox Ford. Another important engineer of connections, Hunt gathered the younger writers at South Lodge – a group that included D.H. Lawrence, H.D., her British husband, Richard Aldington, Wyndham Lewis, G.B. Stern, and Rebecca West. Through Ford, Pound gained access to *The English Review*, where Sinclair made numerous contributions to the conceptualization of Modernism. Indeed Sinclair was an important promoter of modernist women writers, including H.D., who formed her own strong intellectual and personal alliances with British writers, including Aldington, Lawrence, and Bryher (Winifred Ellerman). A reader of Freud and Jung, Sinclair considered psychological realism an important achievement for contemporary writers. She found it in the writing of Hunt and Dorothy Richardson, as well as James Joyce. Sinclair applied the psychologist William James's term, 'stream of consciousness', to Richardson's experimental narrative in her novel sequence *Pilgrimage*. She credited Richardson, not just with moving from the spectator to the mind of the character, but also with a portraying a tragic event so that it 'seizes reality alive', confusing the reader as to what is subjective and what is objective.[14] Virginia Woolf took notes on Sinclair's essay on Richardson, and it may have encouraged her to include 'the dark places of psychology' among the modernist attributes identified in her celebrated essay 'Modern Fiction'.[15] Sinclair's criticism shares some of Pound's attitudes, including distaste for the 'mush' of sentimental writing. She had an interest in imagism, a concept he strongly promoted, particularly as found in the writing of H.D. and Aldington. By Sinclair's definition, 'the Image is not a substitute: it does not stand for anything but itself ... The Image, I take it, is Form. But it is not pure form. It is form *and* substance' and it can be expressive of mood.[16]

The psychological interest she attributes to notable modernists can also be found in Sinclair's own novels – works usually considered late Victorian in nature and consigned to a middlebrow readership, rather than to intellectually elite, modernist readers. In *Mary Olivier: A Life*, for instance, Sinclair enters the thought process of her leading female protagonist, allowing readers to share in the accumulation of impressions that assemble into a dark family history. Her most intense experiences of the feeling of happiness resemble what Woolf would term 'moments of being', and Joyce 'epiphanies'. Even in their most traditionally realistic modes, Sinclair's novels offer a critique of the gender system for its favouring of male over female children, seen even in mothers' priorities. Long considered one of the midwives of Modernism, Sinclair was also a contributor of note.

The Freewoman, a journal founded by Dora Marsden and Mary Gawthorpe, which successively took on the titles *The New Freewoman* and *The Egoist*, represents the confluence of feminism and socialism with literary Modernism, and also the process by which women's contributions were obscured by the ambitions of male modernists on the London scene. Formerly members of the militant suffragette grouping, the WSPU (Women's Social and Political Union), Gawthorpe and Marsden were interested in going far beyond suffrage to secure wider forms of justice for women (an opinion echoed by Woolf's character, Terence Hewet). Gawthorpe favoured movement-based, socialist feminism while Marsden explored philosophy, individualism, and anarchism. As another focus of her activism, Marsden was involved in a protest seeking equal degrees for women graduates of Manchester University, and involved her female university cohort in the journal. Its operations included feminist-style discussion circles as well as journal production, and letters from readers became the material for serious and inclusive intellectual exchange.

When *The Freewoman* succumbed to economic troubles, a host of transitional figures and aspiring modernists came to its rescue, including May Sinclair, H.D., Amy Lowell, Katherine Mansfield, Charlotte Perkins Gilman, Harriet Shaw Weaver (also a key patron of James Joyce), Rebecca West, and H.G. Wells. West started with the *Freewoman* by writing brash reviews that showed sensitivity to the politics of class as well as gender. She advanced to assistant editor, using her own contacts to cultivate a more literary side for the journal. By the time that *The New Freewoman* was renamed *The Egoist* and was publishing Joyce, it had relinquished much of its socialist and feminist purpose, in favour of a more individualist agenda. West no longer felt that she could continue as an editor given that 'there was an *arrivist* American poet who intended to oust me, and his works and those of his friends continually appeared in the paper without having passed me.'[17] Marsden largely ceded editorial power to 'men of letters', including the '*arrivist*', Pound.

West was marginalized for a period by single motherhood, having given birth to a child by H.G. Wells in 1914. But she had established herself as an independent critic and her critical activity persisted into the 1930s, as she evaluated the work of major modernists (Joyce, Woolf, Lawrence, Eliot) as well as middlebrow writers and journalists, among whom she had many friends. Her brashness continued, most notably in challenges to the critical authority of Eliot. In the following example, she challenges him on the controversial topic of 'emotion': 'He registers himself as fastidious by crying out against violence, confusion, and the presentation of unanalyzed emotion. But he appears unable to distinguish between these vices and vigour, the attempts to find new and valid classifications in place of old ones which have proved invalid, and the pressing of the analysis of emotion to a further stage.'[18]

The gender politics of numerous journals reveal the shaping force of additional women editors operating out of Paris and the United States. Among the most notable are Harriet Monroe and Alice Corbin Henderson at *Poetry*, Margaret Anderson and Jane Heap at *The Little Review*, and Marianne Moore at the *Dial* – all little magazines frequently featured in histories of Modernism. Pound attempted with mixed success to influence many of them. Moore had her own musically-based theories of modern poetry, and she and Henderson were broadly inclusive of new forms, including characteristically American work and that of ethnic minorities, as Jayne E. Marek has noted.[19]

Other journals have entered more recently into revisionary histories of Modernism. Beatrice Hastings may well have served as a 'shadow-editor' at the socialist journal *The New Age*, which was under the editorship of her lover at the time, A.R. Orage. Like *The New Freewoman*, this journal had much more than high modernist content. Hastings explored various stances in regard to militant suffragism, critical of the violent tactics to which its supporters occasionally resorted and of its narrow feminist focus, and like West she was willing to challenge the authority of Ezra Pound.[20] The English film journal, *Close Up*, which was published from 1927–33 under the editorship of Kenneth Macpherson, was equally the product of Bryher, H.D., and Dorothy Richardson, who were all major contributors. In the early issues, H.D. offered a multi-part series entitled 'The Cinema and the Classics'. Dorothy Richardson contributed the very significant series 'Continuous Performance', which ran regularly throughout the life of the journal. Poet and novelist Kay Boyle, one of many American expatriates living in Paris between the wars, can be added to the list of influential women reviewing works of Modernism; her reviews were published in *transition* and *New Yorker* magazine (the latter a vehicle for numerous British women writers, including West and Sylvia Townsend Warner). Also on the American scene, Jessie Redmon Fauset had a strong presence as a transnational reporter, author of fiction, and editor for *Crisis*, the journal of the NAACP (National Association for the Advancement of Colored People). *Crisis* editor, the sociologist and feminist sympathizer, W.E.B. Du Bois,[21] made Fauset its literary editor in 1919. Women writers in Japan expressed their own modernity in the journals *Seito* ('Blue Stocking', published 1911–16), which was succeeded by *Nyonin Geijutsu* ('Women's Arts', 1928–32).[22] As these few examples suggest, research redirected at the multiple sites where Modernism was published has complicated and enriched its contexts and its range well beyond London, Paris, and New York.

Traumatic historical contexts

Although the formal qualities of Modernism have long been placed in the foreground, even the most formalist of critics have acknowledged important historical contexts. The First World War, the Irish rising, the Russian Revolution, the Spanish Civil War, and the onset of the Second World War help explain modernist forms of fragmentation, and expressions of trauma and mourning over loss. The second issue of *BLAST* was labelled a war issue. In one of many notable book reviews, Katherine Mansfield chided Virginia Woolf for failing to register the effect of the First World War on modern sensibilities in her postwar novel, *Night and Day* (1919). In *A Room of One's Own*, Woolf may encourage us to reconsider what counts as history when she says, 'towards the end of the eighteenth century a change came about which, if I were rewriting history, I should describe more fully and think of greater importance than the Crusades or the Wars of the Roses. The middle class woman began to write.'[23]

Still, Woolf had a delayed but sustained response to Mansfield's critique, and it came with *Jacob's Room* (1922), *Mrs Dalloway* (1925), and the pacifist arguments of *Three Guineas* (1938). H.D. (who like Mansfield lost a brother in the First World War) suggests in the autobiographical novel, *Bid Me to Live* (1960) that a woman on the home front in London experiences war very differently from her soldier husband, who seems a different person on each return. Her narrative conflates various losses, including that of her protagonist's brother, a stillborn child, and her marriage.[24] Woolf approaches the gendered war intersection differently in *Mrs Dalloway*, offering two characters who are contrasting in sex, age, and class, and yet experience parallel cultural trauma. Septimus Smith, the young clerk who has witnessed the slaughter of a beloved friend at the battle front, ends his life in defiance of a destructive world order that determines 'human nature'; Mrs Dalloway, who has never met him, empathizes and sees triumph in his act. Both seem to share a silenced capacity for same-sex love, adding further complexity to the depiction of war and gender.

Diverse forms of women's writing on the wars of the early twentieth century have emerged from feminist scholarship, with the representation of trauma typically eliciting experimental effects. The heroine of Radclyffe Hall's 1926 short story 'Miss Ogilvy Finds Herself' is distinctly masculine in her physical characteristics and gestures, and is strongly attracted to women. As the story opens, she has flourished in a commanding position in an ambulance corps at the front. This history, and her difficulty returning to the female dependants of her family in England, are all rendered realistically. But Hall ends by transporting her character to a deserted island where the skeletal remains of a slain ancient man have been found. Miss Ogilvy has a vision of herself as this man, in a loving relationship with a young woman, their harmony threatened by internecine war that would presumably kill him. However, Miss Ogilvy is found dead at the opening of a cave. That women can experience war trauma on the front line, and PTSD (post-traumatic stress disorder) thereafter, can be added to the other suggestions of cultural despair in the novel, relating both to frustrated sexuality and seemingly endless cycles of war.

Contrasting attitudes are revealed both in the scholarship and the recovered texts, including women's war reporting, now found in many anthologies.[25] On the one hand, women experienced increased autonomy and the freedom to explore new places in wartime; on the other, they reacted cynically to the machinations of war and its devastating effects on soldiers and civilians alike. Sandra Gilbert and Susan Gubar find many cases of women sensing new opportunities even as men suffered disillusionment at the front.[26] May Sinclair was among these. However, in her novel *The Tree of Heaven* two sons in the Henderson family have given their lives in the First World War and the third goes off to fight at the end of the novel, with parental encouragement, a scenario that questions whether or not nationalist, militant values start at home. The American journalist Martha Gellhorn records grim realities in 'The Third Winter: November 1938', describing the bombed-out city of Barcelona during the Spanish Civil War and basing her account on home-based interviews.[27] Virginia Woolf's *Three Guineas* repeatedly refers to Spanish photographs of ruined buildings and mutilated, dead children in Madrid, available in the media at the time.[28] The assignment of colonial and racialized 'other' men to subordinate, feminine duties in war was also put into question in modernist war reports. This is noted by Sandra Gilbert and Susan Gubar, who cite Alice Dunbar-Nelson's 'Negro Women in War Work', which exposed the lower wages paid to black women in war work.[29] Claire M. Tylee notes the importance of irony as a device for both women and subordinated disaffected groups to write back to the 'dominant viewpoints propagandists of war', which 'reduced working-class "Tommies" and Indian volunteers to the feminine status of object of the gaze' and part of a 'picturesque landscape'.[30] In an article on 'Nationalism and Egypt', the American Jessie Fauset critiqued the effects of British protectionism on women and members of the civil service, as well as racist attitudes carried by British and ANZAC forces into the First World War.[31] National racial violence, particularly in the form of lynching in the United States, also impacts upon modernist expression, particularly as we broaden its formal scope to include journalism and writing formerly dismissed as sentimental.

The struggles of the movement to win women the vote have numerous connections, historical and metaphorical, to the warfare that imploded upon the early twentieth century. The suffrage effort preceded, coincided with, and (in the case of Britain) largely yielded to the First World War, as the WSPU encouraged women to engage in war production. British feminists, particularly those involved with the WSPU, employed militant tactics, smashing the windows of public buildings and slashing a work of art. Suffrage demonstrations were often met with violent crowd control, with police officers wielding batons or mounted on horseback. Evelyn Sharp's short story 'The Women at the Gate' describes one crowd of this sort, with one woman after another courting arrest by coming forward to challenge the ensconced politicians at the gates of Parliament. A comparison of the suffrage struggle to war is threaded through the story in the dialogue of members of the crowd, as if to claim the importance conventionally accorded war for their effort.[32]

As Mary Chapman and Barbara Green have pointed out, suffragism preceded Modernism and shared with it some aspects of popular or mass culture that are usually considered as quite separate phenomena. Suffragism and Modernism made use of banners in the 'arts and crafts style' carried by British suffragettes. They branched out into romance fiction, the New Woman novel, and documentary realism. But in both Britain and the United States, suffragists developed 'new and varied forms of persuasion', including innovations in both visual and print culture and their own networking of a 'counter-public sphere' through organizations of women who had entered the professions of acting and writing.[33] Women collaborated in writing and producing drama that carried the suffrage message in an understandable and amusing way, for example the play *How the Vote Was Won*, by Cicely Hamilton and Christopher St John, directed by Edith Craig, which combined the fantasy of a women's general strike with a narrative of conversion to the cause. They took advantage of urban spaces to stage spectacular marches and in the United States carried banners in 'sleek functional typeface' that anticipated the design of journals such as *BLAST*.[34] There were feminist presses and organizations that fed suffrage stories to the newspapers as well as reporting on prison conditions and forced feedings. Suffragists also made formal innovations. They wrote collectively, created cartoons, and composed 'parody and pastiche in order to disrupt ideology'.[35]

Suffragists appear as characters in fiction by modernists, and in their journalism. One of the daughters in Sinclair's *The Tree of Heaven* has gone into active suffrage work. Virginia Woolf's *Night and Day* follows the struggles of Mary Datchet, working for the cause in a suffrage office, often solitary and late into the night. Miss La Trobe, director and author of the pageant in Woolf's *Between the Acts*, may have been inspired by Edith Craig. Rebecca West's young female protagonist of *The Judge* is employed in suffrage work very similar to that which the author had engaged in as an adolescent growing up in Edinburgh. American novelist Djuna Barnes's essay 'How It Feels to be Forcibly Fed' reports on the actuality of the physical suffering endured by many British suffragists. She feels confined, as in a shroud, and violated by the tube pushed down her throat, stating this in terms akin to rape.

Gender and genre

Virginia Woolf's *A Room of One's Own* encourages an association between women and the genre of the novel. She avers that, having had her way paved by Aphra Behn in the eighteenth century, the middle-class woman writer of the nineteenth century found 'the novel alone was young enough to be soft in her hands'.[36] Woolf's survey history of women novelists suggests that some of the most notable might have been better suited to other genres – Emily Brontë to poetic plays and George Eliot to history or biography.[37] Whether they were the authors of 'old forgotten novels' or such notable writers as Charlotte Brontë, women suffered from 'a mind that was slightly pulled from the straight, and made to alter its clear vision in deference to external authority ... She was admitting that she was "only a woman", or protesting that she was "as good as a man".'[38] Some of this resentment might come from the cultural devaluation of books that deal with basic aspects of women's lives: for example, 'the feelings of a woman in a drawing room', seen as unimportant in comparison to a book that deals with war. As she turns to the twentieth-century novelist, Woolf's formal concerns still mix with her scrutiny of the forces of gender. She is pleased to find an anonymous writer of 1928 experimenting with the sentence, and representing previously unexplored territory, such as the feelings women may have about one another when working together, notably in a scientific laboratory. '"Chloe liked Olivia", I read. And then it struck me how immense a change was there. Chloe liked Olivia perhaps for the first time in literature.'[39] Though aware of the old forgotten novels women have written, Woolf is not interested in their popular success. Indeed the highly successful sentimental novel has only recently been critically considered in relation to Modernism, and this has focused largely on American writers.

The masculinist Wyndham Lewis, T.E. Hulme, and the other formulators of Modernism, eschewed the sentimental as a feminine, maternal, or domestic phenomenon. However, as Suzanne Clark has argued, women's sentimental rhetoric has a powerful history. It contributed, not just to the suffragist movement, but to an array of progressive projects including abolition, temperance, and urban and immigrant welfare – all affecting the lives of women.[40] The same Anglo-American formulators who promoted radical form for Modernism were often politically conservative, wary of communism, blacks, indigenous people, homosexuals and lesbians, and even surrealists.[41] Cultural challenges posed by women writers previously dismissed for sentimentality have their own experimental appeal to feminist critics, and on these grounds, the scope of Modernism has increased. With this has come attention to and respect for a wider range of experience and the literary methods brought to its expression.

The various examples of sentimental Modernism offered by Clark include poetry reflecting lesbian love or racial resistance by Angela Weld

Grimké – intense 'poetic musicality' brought to the expression of same-sex love in 'Your Eyes',[42] which also makes lavish use of natural imagery, as does Amy Lowell in her imagist love poetry. Strategic repetition reinforces resistance to racial violence, including lynching, as in Grimké's 'Beware Lest He Awakes'. Jessie Fauset's fiction, like that of many who shared the stage with high modernists, aims at a middlebrow audience, and is unabashedly sentimental. Like many women modernists in relation to the ideals of the 'men of 1914', Fauset defies Alain Locke's long-accepted characterization of the Harlem Renaissance.[43] Edna St Vincent Millay, typically subject to attack as a woman poet by new critics such as John Crowe Ransom, re-emerges as a writer with a variety of political concerns, including the American suffrage movement (in a poem commemorating Inez Milholland) and sexual revolution. Clark finds in her 'ironic sonnet' 'I, being born a woman and distressed' a response to critics such as Ransom.[44]

Women writing on the left have also emerged as a group to claim the attention of scholars of Modernism/modernity; their revolutionary effort being in part the proposal of new ideas for social reform that challenged the cultural pessimism often equated with the tendency within Modernism represented, for example, by T.S. Eliot.[45] Their work often attends to marginal groups adversely affected by capitalist economics as well as politics. Sylvia Townsend Warner and her lover Valentine Ackland, who were long affiliated with the British Communist Party, visited Spain repeatedly in its Civil War period, recording their observations in journalism and later poetry that supported the Republican cause. The scope of Modernism again widens, finding new content in left-wing American publications such as *The Masses* and collections of writings; reaching back to the democratizing efforts of Lucia Trent and Ralph Cheyney through a series of anthologies, magazines, workshops, and readings in the United States.[46] Their essay, 'What is this Modernism', argues that for all the 'do nots' modernists have shattered, they have invented new prohibitions. It also sets Modernism in a new context: 'it is the feeling aloud of a thinker whose mediations and meditations are burst in upon by a shouting army of workers'.[47] Erupting into such poetry as that selected by Berke are scenes from the ghetto, or race riots by Lola Ridge, wives and mothers facing the stringencies of labour strikes in poetry by Genevieve Taggard, an abortionist's office and a visit to a California labour camp holding the potential of Mexican workers on strike.

Queering and decolonizing gender and Modernism

In the last two decades there have also been new understandings of ways that both gender and Modernism can be queered and decolonized. If modernist studies have gradually worked out of gender binaries, they have also come to recognize a 'homo/hetero binary division', or rather 'a single literary corpus that is torn in various ways by the scission between these (supposedly) incongruent longings' – a queer conjunction, as Colleen Lamos has described it.[48] Sexual fluidity and same-sex communities, while not limited to modernity, were facilitated by the greater freedom afforded to difference in urban settings where Modernism and various ethnic and immigrant cultures also flourished. Through their representations of same sex longing, modernist women's writing helped to create a sense of community, despite the repressions of the legal system, and even the sexology of the day. Radclyffe Hall's 1928 novel, *The Well of Loneliness*, constitutes a watershed in the literary history of sexuality, for its content, its censorship, and for the rallying of other modernists to its defence. Defenders included Virginia Woolf, E.M. Forster, Vera Brittain, and Rebecca West, who critiqued the court proceedings in publications and supported the author and her work in their willingness to testify at the trial. By 1928, Hall felt that she had sufficient reputation as an author, as well as personal, 'medical and psychological' knowledge to take on the task of writing a novel representing the 'invert', as homosexual men and women were then labelled by sexologists such as Havelock Ellis. Hall explains in a recently found letter dating from 1934 that she understood the invert's 'mental and physical reactions, their joys and sorrows, and above all their unceasing battle against a frequently cruel and nearly always thoughtless and ignorant world'.[49]

While the history and tone of Hall's novel are sombre, queer modernists may bring wit and defiance into their creations, particularly by thinking back to their decadent predecessors and especially the literary model of Oscar Wilde, before the tragedy of his trial and incarceration for homosexuality.[50] One leading example is Virginia Woolf's 1928 novel *Orlando*, whose central character is unperturbed by a change of sex in the midst of a life that spans centuries. Even as a female, Orlando enjoys urban encounters with women while costumed as a male. Djuna Barnes's *Ladies' Almanack*, also published in 1928, depicts a Parisian lesbian community resembling that headed by Natalie Barney. Unlike London, Paris was widely recognized as a haven for communities of 'Sapphic modernism', as described in Shari Benstock's *Women of the Left Bank*.[51] Among those in attendance in Barnes's novel are Radclyffe Hall and her lover, Una Troubridge. In Barnes's more sobering *Nightwood*, Dr Matthew O'Connor and Robin Vote pose, costume, and reinvent themselves, readily transgressing the boundaries of sexuality and gender. Less conspicuous transgressions can be found in the 1933 co-published volume of poetry, *Whether a Dove or a Seagull* by Sylvia Townsend Warner and Valentine Ackland. The verses challenge the norms of rural British society as well as any attempt to divide the identities of this long-standing lesbian couple.

Complexity has also been found in the diverse interplay of gender and national identity. Feminine images continued to represent subjected colonial nations such as Ireland, and maternal images were exploited in First World War propaganda urging men to uphold nation and empire, as noted by Tylee. On the other hand, just as evolutionary theory suggested profound connections between species other than the human, cultural geography brought new insistence on relationships between human communities and the land. It attended to patterns of migration, imperial conquest, and racialization found in British colonials returning briefly, or more permanently to London. The Australians Nettie Palmer and Susanna Prichard, Dominican Jean Rhys, and New Zealander, Katherine Mansfield were among them. This brought diverse geographies together, with the identity of one social location dependent upon another. Jessica Berman has found such connection important to Rhys's reclaiming of Dominican identity, inclusive of racialized assumptions inherited from the imperial past, in *Voyage in the Dark*.[52] Writing of her childhood in her unfinished autobiography *Smile Please*, Rhys identifies the confluence of Indian, French, and native Caribbean elements of food and language, and suggests the factors of race and class that make her nurse Meta seem 'always to be alien and angry'.[53] Blended identities, and a mixture of privilege and oppression, are also obvious in Cornelia Sorabji. She was Indian-born, an ethnic Parsee (a group of Persian origin), daughter of a Christian convert, and (unlike Woolf) Oxford-educated, obtaining a law degree. Though she was an advocate for the rights of women in India, her sense of India's move forward is strongly inflected by British legal, educational, and imperial constructs.[54]

The pan-Africanism that arose between the two world wars suggests the power of diasporic African identity in the historical period shared by Modernism. Jessie Fauset followed the Second Pan-African Conference through several European capitals, including London, reporting upon the different level of receptivity provided in each locale. Only recently have efforts been made to map colonial African women's 'engagement with modernity' and to place women in the pan-African dialogue, as Tuzyline Jita Allan has argued.[55] Allan draws attention to Charlotte Manye Maxeke, a native of South Africa who first visited Britain, Canada, and the United States through choir tours organized by the African Methodist Episcopal Church. She later received a college degree from Wilberforce University, in the state of Ohio, where W.E.B. Du Bois was a member of the faculty. Engaged, like Sorabji, in women's advocacy, Maxeke founded the Bantu Women's League. Schooled on the American philosophy of the 'New Negro', Maxeke developed 'a political craft that promoted a relationship with the encroaching modern age but criticized its ruinous effects on black family life'.[56] Adelaide Casely Hayford, a native of Sierra Leone who spent some of her childhood years in England, was both an advocate for girls and a writer of fiction. In an effort to support a girls' school she had established in Freetown, she made extensive travels through the United States, where she met African-American cultural leaders and icons and visited black educational institutions. Her story 'Mista Courifer' satirizes a coffin maker and preacher in the local church for his imposition of Western styles of dress and office employment on his son. The son revolts, opting instead for the native dress of his mother, which he combines with a more egalitarian attitude toward the wife he has selected, not for her cooking, but for their mutual sense of love, adapting selectively the 'English customs' of 'the way white men treat their wives'.[57]

A more global understanding of gender in modernity has again made Modernism new. As suggested above, modernity traverses national boundaries in multiple directions and with diverse energies. It encourages patterns of consumption, and artistic, media, and fashion production that contribute to the global phenomenon of the 'modern girl' and diversify and queer what it means to have 'cosmopolitan style'.[58] The new modernist studies celebrate dynamic critiques that move from the former margins to the centre, as well as the complexity of gender as it intersects with other cultural identifications and positionings. Such understandings have been advanced in the work of feminist analysis and especially in woman of colour feminist analysis. In the nearly two decades that elapsed between the publication of *The Gender of Modernism* and the appearance of *Gender in Modernism: New Geographies, Complex Intersections*, the feminist concept of intersectionality has emerged and indeed has become an essential ingredient in serious analysis.[59] Gender can no longer be seen in terms of feminine vs. masculine traits, or in contests for modernist editorial control between men and women. Indeed, in the modernist focuses provided in this chapter, gender, race, class, sexuality, imperialism, and queer positioning have twined, interacted, and intensified their effects on individuals, on the politics of power and privilege, and on literary form. In this new matrix for Modernism, it becomes evident that one of the major experiments of Modernism was to find new, creative ways to challenge complex systems of inequality.

Notes

1. Published 1915, but begun as early as 1904.
2. Virginia Woolf, *The Voyage Out* (New York: Harcourt Brace & World, 1948), p. 213.
3. Ibid., p. 212.
4. Bonnie Kime Scott, ed., *The Gender of Modernism: A Critical Anthology* (Bloomington: Indiana University Press, 1990), p. 2.
5. Michael H. Levenson, *The Genealogy of Modernism: A Study of English Literary Doctrine, 1908–22* (New York: Cambridge University Press, 1984).
6. Hugh Kenner, *The Pound Era* (Berkeley: University of California Press, 1971).
7. T.E. Hulme, 'Romanticism and Classicism', in *A Modernist Reader: Modernism in England 1910–1930*, ed. Peter Faulkner (London: B.T. Batsford, 1986), pp. 49–50.
8. Quoted in *The Gender of Modernism*, p. 357 n. 1.
9. Wyndham Lewis, 'Our Vortex', *BLAST*, 1 (c. 1914), p. 147.
10. Bonnie Kime Scott, *Re-Figuring Modernism, I: The Women of 1928* (Bloomington: Indiana University Press, 1995), p. 102.
11. Wyndham Lewis, *Men Without Art* (London: Cassell, 1934), p. 138.
12. T.S. Eliot, 'Tradition and the Individual Talent', in *A Modernist Reader*, p. 88.

13. See Helen Southworth, *Leonard and Virginia Woolf, the Hogarth Press, and the Networks of Modernism* (New York: Columbia University Press, 2010).
14. May Sinclair, 'The Novels of Dorothy Richardson', in Scott, *The Gender of Modernism*, p. 446.
15. Virginia Woolf, 'Modern Fiction', in *The Common Reader* (New York: Harcourt, Brace & World, 1953), p. 156.
16. May Sinclair, 'The Poems of H.D.', in Scott, *The Gender of Modernism*, p. 454.
17. Rebecca West, 'The "Freewoman"', in Scott, *The Gender of Modernism*, p. 576.
18. Rebecca West, 'What is Mr T.S. Eliot's Authority as a Critic?', in Scott, *The Gender of Modernism*, p. 589. Originally published in the *Daily Telegraph* (30 September 1932).
19. Jayne E. Marek, 'Women Editors and Modernist Sensibilities', in *Gender in Modernism: New Geographies, Complex Intersections*, ed. Bonnie Kime Scott (Urbana: University of Illinois Press, 2007) p. 226. See *passim*, pp. 225–31.
20. Ann Ardis makes the argument for her 'shadow-editor' identity in 'Debating Feminism, Modernism, and Socialism: Beatrice Hastings's Voices in *The New Age*', in Scott, *Gender in Modernism*, pp. 161–6.
21. See for example Du Bois's 'The Damnation of Women', in W.E.B. Du Bois, *Darkwater: Voices from Within the Veil* (New York: AMS Press, 1969), pp. 163–86; also in *Gender and Modernism: Critical Concepts in Literary and Cultural Studies, 1: Modernists Write Gender*, ed. Bonnie Kime Scott (London: Routledge, 2008), pp. 259–71.
22. See Yasuko Claremont, 'Modernising Japanese Women through Literary Journals', *Hecate* 35.1/2 (2009): 42–56. This special issue was entitled 'Women Writers/Artists and Travelling Modernisms', and is particularly illuminating about the circulation of Australian women writers, who indeed had their own creative networks, centred in Sydney, but circulating in and out of London and Paris.
23. Virginia Woolf, *A Room of One's Own* (Orlando: Harcourt, 2005), p. 64.
24. Suzette Henke, 'Modernism, Trauma, and Narrative Reformulation', in Scott, *Gender in Modernism*, ed. Scott, p. 559.
25. Claire M. Tylee offers an extensive list in 'War, Modernisms, and the Feminized "Other"', in Scott, *Gender in Modernism*, pp. 519–28. She cites in particular the work of Cynthia Enloe and Margaret Higonnet for their attention to the gendering of war.
26. See Sandra M. Gilbert and Susan Gubar, 'Soldier's Heart: Literary Men, Literary Women, and the Great War', chapter 7 of *No Man's Land: The Place of the Woman Writer in the Twentieth Century, II: Sexchanges* (New Haven and London: Yale University Press, 1989), pp. 285–323.
27. Martha Gellhorn, *The Face of War* (London: Granta 1993), pp. 41–6.
28. Virginia Woolf, *Three Guineas*, annotated and with an introduction by Jane Marcus (Orlando: Harcourt, 2006), p. 14.
29. Gilbert and Gubar, p. 273.
30. Tylee, p. 521. Modernist women are well represented in Daniel Gioseffi, ed., *Women on War: An International Anthology of Writings from Antiquity to the Present* (New York: The Feminist Press, 2003).
31. Jessie Fauset. 'Nationalism and Egypt', *Crisis* 19.6: 310–16.
32. Evelyn Sharp, 'The Women at the Gate', in Scott, *Gender in Modernism*, pp. 39, 40, 43.
33. Mary Chapman and Barbara Green, 'Suffrage and Spectacle', in Scott, *Gender in Modernism*, pp. 27–8.
34. Ibid., p. 29.

35. Ibid., p. 31.
36. Woolf, *A Room of One's Own*, p. 76.
37. Ibid., p. 66.
38. Ibid., p. 73.
39. Ibid., p. 81.
40. Suzanne Clark, 'Sentimental Modernism', in Scott, *Gender in Modernism*, p. 126.
41. Ibid., p. 128. She is focusing again on Lewis.
42. Ibid., p. 129.
43. Cheryl A. Wall, 'Jessie Redmon Fauset (1882–1961)', in Scott, *The Gender of Modernism*, pp. 155–6, and *Women of the Harlem Renaissance* (Bloomington: Indiana University Press, 1995).
44. Clark, p. 131.
45. Nancy Berke, 'Radical Moderns: American Women Poets on the Left', in Scott, *Gender in Modernism*, p. 95.
46. Ibid., p. 97.
47. Lucia Trent and Ralph Cheyney, 'What is This Modernism?' in Scott, *Gender in Modernism*, p. 121.
48. Colleen Lamos, 'Queer Conjunctions in Modernism', in Scott, *Gender in Modernism*, p. 336.
49. Radclyffe Hall, 'From "Notes on *The Well of Loneliness*"', in Scott, *Gender in Modernism*, p. 325.
50. Ibid., p. 341.
51. Shari Benstock, *Women of the Left Bank: Paris 1900–1914* (Austin: University of Texas Press, 1986).
52. Jessica Berman, 'Modernism's Possible Geographies', in *Geomodernisms: Race, Modernism, Modernity*, ed. Laura Doyle and Laura Winkiel (Bloomington: Indiana University Press, 2005), pp. 281–96.
53. Sonita Sarker, 'Race, Nation and Modernity: the Anti-Colonial Consciousness of Modernism', in Scott, *Gender in Modernism*, p. 475.
54. Ibid., pp. 475, 477.
55. Tuzyline Jita Allan, 'Modernism, Gender and Africa', in Scott, *Gender in Modernism*, p. 431.
56. Ibid., p. 433.
57. Adelaide Casely Hayford, 'MistaCourifer', in Scott, *Gender in Modernism*, p. 469.
58. See, for example, Rebecca L. Walkowitz, *Cosmopolitan Style: Modernism Beyond the Nation* (New York: Columbia University Press, 2006) and The Modern Girl Around the World Research Group, *The Modern Girl around the World: Consumption, Modernity, and Globalization* (Durham and London: Duke University Press, 2008).
59. Among those who have advanced the long-existing idea of intersectionality are Jacqui Alexander, Gloria Anzaldua, Patricia Hill Collins, Bonnie Thornton Dill, bell hooks, Beverly Guy-Sheftall, Chandra Mohanty, and Barbara Smith.

2
Exemplary Intermodernists: Stevie Smith, Inez Holden, Betty Miller, and Naomi Mitchison
Kristin Bluemel

For most of the twentieth century, Modernism was not kind to British women writers. They have fared much better since the advent of the New Modernist Studies, evidence of which can be found in almost any anthology on Modernism published since 1999.[1] For example, in Stephen Matthews's *Modernism: A Sourcebook* (2008), three of the seven writers included in the chronological list of major literary texts for that astonishing year, 1922, are women.[2] Two of these women writers, Katherine Mansfield and Virginia Woolf, we expect to find on such lists. The other, May Sinclair, who is best known for using the phrase 'stream of consciousness' to describe a narrative style, seems an eccentric choice.[3] Such eccentric choices come as happy discoveries for scholars and students committed to understanding the full history of women's writing from 1920 to 1945, but Modernism as it traditionally has been understood, and even in some cases as it is currently being revised, does not necessarily provide a satisfying framework for understanding Sinclair's writing or the writing of other women whose work has not been perceived as sufficiently formally innovative. For example, when the New Critics of the 1930s and 1940s were busy consolidating the reputations of modernist poets such as T.S. Eliot and Ezra Pound, both of whom knew Sinclair and respected her work, Sinclair herself dropped out of favour.[4] Students who were introduced to Modernism through formal university study did not read her novels or works of philosophy, even as they became accustomed to describing Virginia Woolf's *To the Lighthouse* or James Joyce's *Ulysses* as 'stream of consciousness' novels. Well into the 1980s the term Modernism still functioned as shorthand for the most elite, experimental art of the century, art supposedly untarnished by politics or commerce.[5] While some of Sinclair's novels were experimental and she occasionally published reviews in the elite 'little magazines' associated with Modernism, her work was also characterized by the two qualities most distant from elite Modernism; it was both political and popular.

Like many other women writers active from 1920–1945, Sinclair was rediscovered by feminists in the 1970s and 1980s and then relabelled a 'modernist' in order to accommodate existing academic literary values and institutions. But as the names, places, timelines, genres, styles, and practices of modernist production expanded, so did confusion over historical and ideological relations between the 'old' Modernism and the 'New Modernisms'. 'Intermodernism', a term that names a new critical category in twentieth-century British literary history and culture, is a product of and response to this confusion. It provides an alternative basis for understanding relations between 'Modernisms' as it also provides an alternative way of valuing, analysing, and positioning the work of those women writers who do not fit tidily into traditional literary categories.

While there are many women writers whose novels, short stories, and journalistic prose invite analysis in terms of Intermodernism, for this volume I have designated Stevie Smith (1902–1971), Inez Holden (1903–1974), Betty Miller (1910–1965), and Naomi Mitchison (1897–1999) as exemplary intermodernists based on their historical positioning, favoured genres and styles, and dominant thematic and ideological concerns. These four women writers achieved critical and popular success for their fictions, and in Smith's case, poetry, during the interwar years; they continued to write and publish through the Second World War, and attracted the interest of feminist scholars who began projects of literary recovery at just about the time the writers themselves died.[6] Yet none of these writers is especially well known despite second-wave feminist attention, in part because none has been well served by the vocabularies and genealogies of Modernism. They remain eccentric figures in British literary history when measured against the time lines of Modernism (none had published an article or book by 1922); when measured against the guest lists of the most influential modernists' parties (none could be found at the soirées of Virginia Woolf or Edith Sitwell); or against the backlists of the most widely-recognized modernist publishers (none published with Hogarth Press or Faber and Faber). Instead, all gained recognition for realist fictions published from the late 1920s or mid-1930s; Mitchison threw her own parties in Hammersmith while Smith, Holden, and Miller circulated among members of what Jack Barbera and William McBrien describe as the 'Hampstead set' affiliated with Betty Miller;[7] and all chose to work with publishing houses such as Jonathan Cape, Victor Gollancz, and John Lane, whose editorial policies were targeted towards more popular or political titles and readerships. And very much to the point of this volume, all struggled with their publishers' resistance or refusal to publish their writing, even after having established themselves as influential contributors to the contemporary literary scene. In what follows, I discuss the significance of these historical and biographical details in terms of Intermodernism, suggesting ways in which the term can increase the value and visibility of Smith, Holden, Miller, Mitchison, and other women writers similarly positioned in twentieth-century literary history and criticism.

What is Intermodernism?

Defining and theorizing Intermodernism is no easier than defining Modernism. As the feminist scholar Elizabeth Maslen reminds us, there is 'no consensus about what we mean by the main labels which have been adopted for the novel in the twentieth century'; she mentions as examples of this confusion three approaches to literary Modernism. It can be defined as a period, as a mode of writing, or in relation to modernity.[8] On the one hand, Intermodernism designates the interwar, wartime, and immediately postwar years, and thus offers itself as a 'new' historical period: one that separates certain years from the accepted, and diversely described periods of Modernism and Postmodernism. Of course, Intermodernism is only a 'new' period to the extent that within the discourse of modernist studies it inscribes lines around new dates and thus suggests a reorganization of values. Such a reorganization of values means that Intermodernism, like any other movement category such as Romanticism or Modernism, is clearly, self-consciously, ideological.

It is important *not* to define Intermodernism primarily or only as a period, since all efforts of periodization are open to critique for being arbitrary. On the contrary, Intermodernism, like Modernism, is a category that alludes to period, style, and historical conditions of modernity. Intermodernism should therefore be thought of as a *kind of writing* (by which I mean it is an aesthetic category), a *social formation* (an institutional, materialist category), and an expression of *shared values* (an ideological category). Above all, Intermodernism should be functional, providing scholars with a literary-critical compass, analytical tool, or useful guidepost for finding and valuing vital figures and cultural forms that disappear in discussions of Modernism or Postmodernism. Smith, Holden, Miller, and Mitchison are among Modernism's 'disappeared'; while these four writers might emerge in discussions framed by categories of the 1930s and the 1940s, interwar and war literature, or women's writing, the addition of Intermodernism to these pre-existing discussions promises to foreground exciting new materials and approaches to literature of the period.

I do not claim that all critical projects on the four women writers I describe as exemplary intermodernists, let alone all women writers of the period 1920–1945, should be read within the framework of Intermodernism. However, describing Smith, Holden, Miller, and Mitchison as intermodernists points us toward potentially innovative approaches to their work and the work of other women writers. In contrast to modernist writers, for example, intermodern writers tend to have their origins in or maintain contacts with working- or lower-middle-class cultures. As young people, they generally do not fit into the Oxbridge networks or values that shaped the dominant English literary culture of their time because they are the 'wrong' sex, class, or colonial status. As adults they remain on the margins of celebrated literary groups. Intermodern writers tend to hold down regular jobs (secretary, journalist, war worker, home worker, factory worker, teacher) to supplement their income from writing. Perhaps as a result, they often write about work. When intermodernists experiment with style or form (as Smith does in *Over the Frontier*), their narratives are still within a recognizably realist tradition. They do not often demonstrate that archetypal modernist impulse toward mystic epiphany (Lawrence) or mythic allusion (Joyce or Eliot). The intermodernists' social marginalization, lack of financial independence, and debts to realism, often resulted in writing that attends to politics, especially politics that may improve working conditions. Intermodern texts tend to favour narratives that are intellectually and culturally available to ordinary, non-elite, English working men and women. Intermodernism contributes to what F.R. Leavis famously called England's minority culture, but it also cheerfully partakes of and contributes to the mass culture Leavis distrusted.

Elsewhere I have argued that much of the literature of the 1930s and 1940s, whether by men or women, can be advantageously studied as part of an intermodernist movement.[9] Criticism of Modernism, no matter how revised, expanded, and renovated, still has trouble accounting for the literature of writers associated with the 1930s and 1940s, even male 'highbrow' writers such as W.H. Auden, Henry Green, or Samuel Beckett. On the other hand, widely acclaimed modernist women writers such as Woolf and Sitwell do not seem to be identified as 1930s or 1940s writers, although a significant portion of their literary work dates from those decades. Women born slightly later than Woolf and Sitwell, including Smith, Holden, Miller, and Mitchison, have been recuperated by some feminist scholars as modernists or late modernists; but, curiously, women are never classified as members of the Auden generation, despite their exactly congruent dates with Auden and his contemporaries. Put simply, most writing by British women of the 1930s, irrespective of the educational background, social class, marital status, sexual orientation, religious or political status of the author, remained almost entirely excluded from critical analysis until the last fifteen years. And if we turn to British women's writing of the 1940s, we note that even sophisticated and widely-cited studies on late or Second World War Modernism by Tyrus Miller, Jed Esty, and Marina MacKay have not persuaded many scholars to understand Modernism in terms linked to either the aesthetics, politics, or publishing practices of the previous decades.[10] Left without a critical vocabulary that can account for the continuities between writers of the interwar and war years, scholars have either made do with a too elastic category of Modernism or the too inelastic categories of 1930s and 1940s literature. As a result, the careers of writers like Smith and Miller, which began in the 1930s and flowered in the early 1940s, fit no recognized literary-critical trajectory and appear inconsequential. Intermodernism provides one way out of such apparent incoherence.

Stevie Smith: working it out for herself

We need look no further than Stevie Smith's career as a novelist to understand the value of reading her work as part of an intermodernist movement bridging the 1930s and 1940s, peacetime and wartime, poetry and fiction. Smith first tried to get into print as a poet, but her editor, Ian Parsons at Chatto and Windus, responded with the recommendation that she '"Go away and write a novel."'[11] This she promptly set out to do in the frequently empty moments of her job as a secretary in the offices of the publisher Pearson Newnes. Prior to the merging of the two companies in 1921, Pearson was famous for publishing the *Daily Express*, Newnes for publishing magazines such as *Tit-Bits*. The mass market publishing empire that resulted from their union had a purpose and success measured in completely different terms from those of the elite small presses run or patronized by Woolf and Eliot or the more mainstream presses that I associate with the intermodernists. Yet the stable working environment Pearson Newnes provided for Smith, including a near endless supply of yellow office paper, enabled the writing of the novel subsequently published by Jonathan Cape as *Novel on Yellow Paper* (1936), which had been rejected by both Ian Parsons's manuscript readers and, reluctantly, by Parsons himself.[12]

Novel on Yellow Paper, or, Work it out for Yourself was an almost instant success and made the reclusive Smith a *cause célèbre* among publishing insiders and the public alike.[13] It featured an ebullient first-person narrator named Pompey Casmilus, a thinly disguised version of the then unknown author. Nothing much happens to Pompey – *Novel* has no plot to speak of but rather a compelling female voice that gallops along. Among other things, it describes contemporary life for a spinster secretary who by day works in a publishing office, by night attends parties, and when she is not visiting friends in the country on weekends, remains with her beloved Lion Aunt in her decidedly unfashionable, lower-middle-class north London suburb of Bottle Green. Smith's alter ego talks about everything from Jews in London to Germans in Berlin; Hitler, sexism, sex education; poetry, her boyfriend, Freddy, her boss, Sir Phoebus Ullwater (a disguised Sir Neville Pearson, her employer and son of the founder of Pearsons), and her 'darling friends, [her] less darling friends, [her] acquaintances'.[14] To Smith's delight and profit, the public and Cape wanted more. She promised and produced a second novel, *Over the Frontier* (1938), but closer to her heart, perhaps, was acceptance of her first volume of poems, *A Good Time Was Had by All* (1937), which Cape also published.[15] This volume of poems, like all volumes to follow, was illustrated with Smith's doodles, which more than her plotless first novel marked her out as an eccentric among contemporary British writers.

Writing to Naomi Mitchison in an undated letter, probably composed in early spring 1937, Smith remarked:

> *A Good Time* represents the scourings of about ten years of elicit office scribbling generally as you will see in a rather unsatisfactory and futile

round, or is it square, peggishness. I should like to see you and hear more of what you think of them if it wouldn't bore you ... I had the most awful fight with Cape over the nauseating sum of £2.14.1 – I repeat and a penny, won my point (I'd already fought and won it last September but that is Ganz Gleich the pets Nicht?) Phoebus is getting hot cattish, I mean cat on hot brickish about 'all this yellow paper' and I am beginning to wonder if he will stand for the new novel [*Over the Frontier*] which Cape liked ...[16]

In addition to recording Smith's literary hopes and travails, this letter provides evidence of what I would describe as an intermodern literary network linking Smith to Mitchison, and as I will later demonstrate, to Holden and Miller as well. Review of the women's correspondence, diaries, and book reviews shows that this intermodern network also included Olivia Manning, Storm Jameson, Rosamond Lehmann, and Sally Chilver, together with other less prominent writers and now forgotten editors such as Kay Dick.[17] It was built out of shared personal and professional interests, and what feminist scholars would later recognize as the women writers' special challenges of breaking into and maintaining a profitable presence in a print world largely shaped by male editors, publishers, and directors.

The same year that *Over the Frontier* came out – the year of the Anschluss, of Chamberlain's appeasement of Hitler at Munich, and of *Kristallnacht* – Smith published her second illustrated volume of poems, *Tender Only to One* (1938), again with Cape. In contrast to *Over the Frontier*, her poems were not engaged with contemporary politics, the tragedies of anti-Semitism, or impending war. Instead, they pursued themes, forms, and rhymes that earned Smith comparison to William Blake, Mother Goose, and other children's writers. Smith's fame as a poet did not come until the 1960s; to get there, she had to type, fetch, and write her way through the hard, dry years of wartime scarcity, when even the most well-connected of writers had difficulty winning contracts from publishers or promises of paper. Smith captured this climate of privation, desperation, and heroism beautifully in a third novel titled *The Holiday*.[18] Finished during the war, it was refused by Cape and not published until 1949 by Chapman and Hall. Technically a postwar novel and thus beyond the scope of this volume, the conditions of *The Holiday*'s making demonstrate how Intermodernism can serve critics' needs by supporting the study of women's writing that bridges historical periods and literary-critical divides. Written during war, describing a heroine and landscape of war, *The Holiday* was transformed by Smith into a postwar novel through relatively simple alterations, including inserting 'post-' in front of each iteration of 'war'. The ambiguity over *The Holiday*'s status as a war or postwar novel is neatly captured by her protagonist-narrator, Celia Phoze, who muses about her particular experience of modernity: 'It cannot be said that it is war, it cannot be said that it is peace, it can be said that it is post-war.'[19] These words gesture toward Celia's discomfort with the most common categories of national history and politics and point to a parallel discomfort experienced by literary critics trying to understand Smith's writing: postmodernist? War literature? Postwar? A 1930s novel or maybe 1940s? Reading *The Holiday* as intermodernist eliminates these distracting, anxious questions.

Inez Holden: night shifts

Inez Holden was a good friend of Stevie Smith's. Like Smith, she never married and lived off her modest earnings from novels, book reviews, journalism, BBC contracts, and any other odd jobs she could drum up. An energetic (because impoverished) writer, Holden was ready to try almost anything. Best remembered for her documentary writing of the war years, especially the novel *Night Shift* (1941), she is the only British woman writer to have published fiction translated into C.K. Ogden's experimental language, Basic English.[20] Ogden notes in his preface to the volume, *Death in High Society* (1934), that Holden's stories had appeared originally in *The Sketch*, *Harper's Bazaar*, *Nash's*, and the *Evening Standard*, and he describes them as 'representative of an important part of the reading material on which the value of Basic for general purposes has to be tested'.[21] Ogden's preface ends with a curious reference to his happiness over 'hav[ing] the chance of ornamenting our front page with the picture by Mr. Augustus John'.[22] The picture he alludes to is a black-and-white sketch of Holden done by the modernist artist during the years after the First World War when he was regarded as England's leading portrait painter. John's association with Holden and Ogden's Basic project is of interest to scholars of Intermodernism because the inclusion of John's art intimates the competing aesthetics and markets that shaped the critical reception of Holden's writing. Typical of many other pieces of intermodern writing, *Death in High Society* raises questions about literary values and hierarchies. Is it sensible or absurd to see analogies between Ogden's attempts to promote a literature for 'general purposes' in his pared-down Basic English and other modernists' attempts to create a minimalist art of purified forms? Does reference to Augustus John belong next to references to *Harper's Bazaar*, *Nash's*, and the *Evening Standard*? Such questions are central to Intermodernism and illustrate why Holden is an exemplary intermodernist: her publishing outlets, political choices, social networks, and literary productions of the 1930s and 1940s typify the qualities I associate with the larger movement of Intermodernism.

In contrast to others' images of Holden as a gleeful presence at all the best London parties,[23] Holden's diaries, which she kept throughout most of her adult life, show her serious and constant concern with work, writing, nation, love, and politics. Like her arch 1930s articles on 'Country House Bridge' or 'Fox Hunting – Is It Human?', published in *Harper's Bazaar*, Holden's private diaries and Second World War documentary fictions focus on women's experience.[24] However, in contrast to her writing of the mid-1930s, Holden's private and public writings of the early 1940s dwell on the fate of assembly workers who struggled to maintain their dignity and wages amid institutionalized discrimination evident at every level of working and social life. For example, Holden, who described herself as a socialist, makes the unfair conditions of and compensation for women's industrial work a theme in the piece 'Fellow Travellers in Factory' (1941), which appeared in Cyril Connolly's prestigious *Horizon*.[25] In this sketch, a worker named May narrates the details of a humiliating job interview to her fellow women workers, turning the experience into a joke that works at the expense of a powerful employer of war workers. Holden uses this episode to advocate cooperation and community among factory women, attacking exploitative war employers through winning over potentially politically influential *Horizon* readers to the side of the workers. Readers' political action is more directly invited by Holden's reworking of the material from 'Fellow Travellers in Factory' in her fictionalized war diary, *It Was Different at the Time* (1943).[26] The factual realism of the published diary permits Holden to foreground basic journalistic information that is repressed for the sake of artistry in 'Fellow Travellers'.

By 1944, when Holden's *There's No Story There* came out from John Lane, the signs of Holden's struggle with the representation of relations between a middle-class author and working-class subjects, overt political content, and hollow documentary fact, have disappeared.[27] In this narrative, Holden provides a rich, detailed portrait of working-class life amid the routine and danger of Statedale, a huge munitions factory, in a language of impressionistic, documentary realism that combines the comic sensibility of her 1930s satires like *Born Old, Died Young* with the serious content of war work, violence, social dislocation, and psychological stress.[28] The granddaughter of a Master of Foxhounds, Holden's careful concentration on diverse working-class lives and accomplishments, dialects and characters, represents the last distinctive step in her movement toward writing working-class fiction. Her deployment of the techniques of documentary realism contradicts the traditional notion that the war brought an end to the type of political fiction associated with the 1930s. The overall effect of *There's No Story There* is to persuade readers that precisely the opposite of its title statement is true: that there *is* a story there, if we only learn how to look for it. This is also true of Intermodernism.

Betty Miller: *On the Side of the Angels*

Betty Miller is best known to critics for *On the Side of the Angels* (1945), a home-front novel about the psychological and domestic trauma of militarism as it corrodes the values of civilians.[29] Her protagonist is a gentle young mother named Honor Carmichael, who is married to a small-town doctor.

As Honor finds herself increasingly culturally marginalized at a local and national level, she witnesses her husband and other men in the community succumb to the proto-fascist seductions of uniforms, military hierarchies, and charismatic leaders.[30] Miller was known to Smith and Holden as a friend and successful author who brought literary women together at her home near Regents Park. According to one of Smith's biographers, Miller's husband, the psychiatrist Emanuel Miller, disliked his wife's witty, sarcastic friends. Out of respect for Emanuel Miller's feelings, Betty Miller would remove all evidence of her literary activity – typewriter, paper, books – from the dining room when she heard her husband's key in the door.[31] The disguising of her literary ventures at home did not prevent Miller from pursuing publication throughout the 1940s and beyond; the height of her public recognition followed her publication of a biography of Robert Browning (1952), which won her a place in the Royal Society of Literature and a commission to edit a volume of unpublished letters from Elizabeth Barrett to Mary Russell Mitford.

Miller's first home was in Cork, to which her Lithuanian Jewish father had moved around 1880, but the Irish 'troubles' of the 1920s led Miller and her mother and siblings to leave for Sweden, before they moved to London. There Miller attended University College, graduating with a degree in journalism in 1930. This university education distinguishes her from the other intermodernists discussed in this chapter, but it could not protect her from the shared experience of conflict with and rejection by a trusted publisher, in her case, Victor Gollancz.[32] Gollancz, Miller's first editor and publisher, is most famous for establishing the Left Book Club in 1936 and for refusing, as did Jonathan Cape, George Orwell's *Animal Farm* (1945). In 1933, the year Gollancz published Orwell's *Down and Out in Paris and London*, he published Miller's *The Mere Living*. She was just twenty-two. Taken with his protégée, Gollancz went on to publish in quick succession Miller's *Sunday* (1934) and *Portrait of the Bride* (1935).[33] However, when presented in 1935 with her fourth novel, tentatively titled 'Next Year in Jerusalem', Gollancz rejected the book and traumatized its still very young author, who stuck the manuscript in a bottom drawer and retreated into journalism for six years.

Before Gollancz's rejection of the manuscript, Miller had confidently told a friend that she was soon to be the author of 'one of the best novels Victor Gollancz Ltd have ever published'.[34] Her understanding of the novel's qualities was keener than Gollancz's, although she was naive to expect that readers would admire her aim of 'tackling the social and psychological conflicts of a Jew in the modern world'.[35] This novel was finally brought out by Robert Hale in 1941 as *Farewell Leicester Square*; Hale went on to publish Miller's last three novels, including *On the Side of the Angels*.[36]

Equally a book of the 1930s and 1940s, peacetime and wartime, *Farewell Leicester Square* examines political concerns over Jewish radical assimilation and English anti-Semitism by adopting as its hero an Anglo-Jewish film director named Alec Berman, whose success in the cinema has grown out of his obsession with English middle-class spaces, best represented by his popular movie, *Farewell Leicester Square*. Berman's film is

> [t]he sort of picture of middle-class London life that Alexander Berman could be trusted to do with his eyes shut, a trivial but well-constructed story, adapted from a recent lending-library success, redeemed, brought alive, by his loving insistence on detail, his genius for putting the commonplace on to the screen and somehow illuminating it with his own passion of observation.[37]

The terms of the description encourage us to identify Miller's novels about the 'commonplace' scenes of domestic life with the more popular or 'trivial' films of her hero. As with the writing of Smith and Holden, Miller's novel blurs traditional boundaries of period and style, while describing a peculiar relation of the woman writer, in this case the Jewish woman writer, to modernity.

Farewell Leicester Square begins in a working-class neighbourhood in Brighton, moves to the studios of Ladywell Films in London where Alec Berman becomes a successful film director and eventually son-in-law to Ladywell's genteel and gentile owner, Richard Nicolls, and returns to Brighton after Alec's grand effort at radical assimilation fails. His marriage has fallen apart and his wife, Catherine, is raising their son, David, as a gentile in the home of her brother, who has always regarded Alec with hostility. This plot of domestic tragedy is redeemed by the last chapter of the book in which, after long exile, Alec is reconciled with his father, reunited with his siblings, and brings his ailing mother back from the brink of death. Alec's emotionally charged re-entry into the physical spaces of his working-class childhood reintegrates his sense of shattered self through familial affirmation, and teaches him the futility of efforts to defeat English anti-Semitism through Jewish assimilation. It is indeed unfortunate that his story was not told until the 1940s rather than in the 1930s when anti-Semitism was rife and *Farewell Leicester Square* would have been perceived as a prescient warning. It is equally unfortunate that Betty Miller wrote and published no fiction for years after Gollancz rejected the novel. The story of Miller and Gollancz is as complex and compelling as the oft-told story of Gollancz and Orwell. The intensely supportive and debilitating relations between a woman writer and her male editor provide the foundations of a tragic-comic plot that shaped Betty Miller's career as well as the careers of the three other writers discussed here.

Naomi Mitchison: she had been warned

In 1933, the year that Gollancz published Orwell's *Down and Out in Paris and London* and Miller's *The Mere Living*, Naomi Mitchison asked him to publish her feminist novel about the Labour Party, *We Have Been Warned* (1935).[38] Gollancz was a friend of Mitchison's: he had already published her controversial edited collection of leftist essays for children, *An Outline for Boys and Girls and Their Parents* (1932), and his press seemed a natural placement for the new novel.[39] Yet Gollancz declined *We Have Been Warned*, beginning his letter with the salutation, 'My dear Naomi', and then moving on to this explanation for his rejection of her work:

> It is I believe the first piece of genuinely social art (using the term as parallel with proletarian art and as opposed to art for art's sake) that has been done in England in our time and I believe it to be immensely valuable as such – the sexual parts no less than the political and economic ... But it is absolutely clear to me as a result of reports and conversations that bits of it (and bits which in my view should not be changed) will horrify an overwhelming proportion even of people who would otherwise be sympathetic, and that publication of the book would cause a real outcry.[40]

This letter poured salt in the wounds left by Mitchison's departure from her publisher of ten years, Jonathan Cape, over his attempts to censor this very same novel. In contrast to Gollancz, Cape was known as a conservative house, although it had published Radclyffe Hall's groundbreaking lesbian novel, *The Well of Loneliness* (1928). However, having taken this risk, Cape had been fined and publicly censured for his trouble. Mitchison was feeling the consequences of the *Well of Loneliness* trial as Cape was already trying to get her to change her *Barbarian Stories* (1929).[41] Mitchison's struggle with Cape over *We Have Been Warned* was more prolonged and bitter; in her memoir, Mitchison notes of the break, 'I was very miserable about it, especially about the hurt to my long friendship with Edward Garnett [her reader at Cape].'[42]

Mitchison took her book to John Lane, who turned it down, and then Constable, who agreed to publish it 'as it was', put it into page proof and 'then started querying'.[43] Reading Mitchison's account of this prolonged pre-publication censorship undertaken by diverse, male-directed publishing houses, readers are likely to agree with her that Constable had resorted to dirty tricks. At the time, Mitchison protested to her publisher:

> I told you that Cape wouldn't take the book because of this question of decencies. If I had been willing to castrate the passage in question he would of course have published it this time last year. But I was not willing – hence the fact that you got the book. And never say you weren't warned ...[44]

A more seasoned writer than Miller, Mitchison could never be described as naive in her relations with publishers. Yet even she was discouraged. Finding herself unable to write fiction, she continued publishing her non-fiction with the very publishing houses that had so angered her over censorship of *We Have Been Warned*. Defeat came in 1935 with the reception of the novel, which was universally despised. Its representations of not only free love but rape and abortion alienated readers on the left and horrified those on the political right.

One of the lessons of this intermodern literary drama is that feminist and socialist politics worked out through novels set in the Roman-ruled Gaul of Mitchison's *The Conquered* (1923) or the fifth-century Athens of her *Cloud Cuckoo Land* (1925) were unpalatable in a novel set in present day England.[45] Another lesson is that the term 'The Red Decade' does not describe the publishing or political climate of the early 1930s. This was a time when a newly emboldened Conservative government was flexing its muscles and clamping down on writers through censorship trials. Describing the circumstances in which Mitchison was trying to publish *We Have Been Warned*, her biographer explains, 'surely this [threat of trials and fines] was meant to encourage publishers through their purses to do the dirty work of regulating what might decently be said'.[46] Women writers pursuing themes of female sexual- and self-actualization in their fictions were likely to realize another limit to the decade's radicalism, whether of the right or left. There was little interest in narratives that insisted women were entitled to the same privileges of sexual and emotional and social experience as men. One odd effect of this exclusion is evident in even the most glowing reviews of Mitchison's novel *The Corn King and the Spring Queen* (1931), her 700-page *magnum opus*, which follows Erif Der from her barbarian homeland of Marob to Sparta and Egypt and back.[47] The reviewers failed to notice its penetrating feminist critique of diverse kinds of patriarchal societies; in fact, they failed to notice that it was more concerned with its queen than its king.[48] This may explain why no one objected to the following scene of female sexual pleasure, which appears mid-way through *The Corn King and the Spring Queen* and describes the barbarian heroine's joy in breast-feeding her son:

> Erif's breast answered to the noise with a pleasant hardening, a faint ache waiting to be assuaged. Their tips turned upward and outward, and the centre of the nipple itself grew velvet soft and tender and prepared for the softness of the baby ...
>
> Now by turns he sucked and laughed, and she laughed too; his hands patted her, his whole lovely body was moving with the warmth and sweetness. He lay across her belly and thighs, heavy and utterly alive. She picked him up and held him on her shoulder and buried her nose in his neck, in the sharp dizzying smell of his bodily warmth. He sucked a little at her cheek and lips, the careless beginning of kisses. She laid him down again on the other side; the mutual pleasure of give and take began again.[49]

This passage marks a highly unusual, but not unique, moment in early twentieth-century British literature, in which female bodily processes and maternal sexual pleasures are represented by a woman writer.[50] One of the few other such representations appears not in any celebrated modernist narrative, but in Betty Miller's novel *On the Side of the Angels*. Though no queen or witch of epic feminist ambition, Miller's heroine, like Mitchison's, celebrates the sexual pleasures of breast-feeding. Finding herself abandoned by her husband at a RAMC hospital dance, Honor battles feelings of misery and alienation with thoughts of her son:

> And with that, a sudden yearning filled her. She thought of the quiet nursery; the gentle pulsing of the night-light in its saucer: of the physical presence of the child, so sweet, so infinitely consoling; the penetrating warmth of his being, the tender radiance of his breath upon her face. At once, her armpits, her breast, tingled; she felt the dawning irradiation, the sudden ripeness in each breast. It was time to go; she could stay no longer.[51]

Honor is prevented from leaving the dance by the imperious and magnetic Colonel Mayne, the CO to whom her husband and all the other men in uniform are fawningly, sickeningly subject. Opposed, repelled, and deflated, Honor gives her excuses: 'I've got to – I'm sorry – I have to feed the baby.'[52] When the Colonel finally realizes 'too late' what Honor's words mean, he is horrified: 'his eyes could not rest on her at all; agonized they flitted here, there and everywhere, to escape somehow the indecency her words suggested'.[53] 'Indecency' here carries meanings akin to those adopted by a zealous Home Office in the obscenity trials against publishers during the late 1920s and early 1930s and in publishers' and reviewers' reactions to *We Have Been Warned*. Finding shades of Mitchison's questing heroines in the seemingly passive home-front wife, Honor Carmichael, points to alliances between diverse kinds of intermodern writers and narratives that await analysis in the aesthetic, ideological, cultural, or political terms associated with Intermodernism.

Conclusion

There are many differences in the writings and lives of the four women writers discussed here. Mitchison, in particular, stands out as a Scottish landowner with overt involvement in British political life, a woman who enjoyed the wealth and the freedom to explore countries, cultures, and communities closed to the lower-middle-class Smith, the bohemian Holden, and the socially-privileged Miller. Yet Mitchison as much as the others is an exemplary intermodernist, someone who was committed to advocating the rights of working people. She poured her energies into writing as an art that she understood to serve the people, and her insights into the parallels between ancient patriarchal tribal societies of a tyrannical nature and the capitalist democracies or fascist dictatorships of her own age led to trenchant critiques of the status quo on behalf of outsiders, especially women and workers. Biographers and feminist literary critics have begun the work needed to understand the accomplishments and failures of these British women writers in terms of their interactions with each other, with other writers, with the institutions of interwar and wartime publishing, and with the crises of their historical moment. The category of Intermodernism has grown out of this earlier critical work. As Intermodernism continues to be theorized and applied, it is hoped that it will provide a more accommodating space within literary history and criticism for investigation of the work and lives of Smith, Holden, Miller, and Mitchison. Ideally, it will serve other women equally well: those whose writing shares many of the aesthetic, material, and ideological qualities of these four exemplary intermodernists.

Notes

1. See for example Jon Stallworthy and David Daiches, eds, 'The Twentieth Century', in *The Norton Anthology of English Literature*, 8th edn, ed. S. Greenblatt and M.H. Abrams, 2 vols (New York: W.W. Norton, 2006), II; Joseph Black et al., eds, *The Broadview Anthology of British Literature, VI: The Twentieth Century and Beyond* (Calgary: Broadview Press, 2006); and David Damrosch and Kevin J.H. Dettmar, eds, *The Longman Anthology of British Literature: The Twentieth Century and Beyond* (New York: Pearson Education, 2010). For an Anglo-American anthology see Lawrence Rainey, ed., *Modernism: An Anthology* (Malden, MA: Blackwell Publishing, 2005), and for a good British and Irish poetry anthology, see Keith Tuma, ed., *Anthology of Twentieth-Century British and Irish Poetry* (New York: Oxford University Press, 2001). Of these, the Broadview, Oxford, and Blackwell anthologies contain the most substantial selections by twentieth-century women writers.
2. Steven Matthews, *Modernism: A Sourcebook* (New York: Palgrave, 2008).
3. In 1922 Sinclair published *The Life and Death of Harriett Frean* (London: Virago, 1980), still widely regarded as her best work. In a 1918 review in the elite little magazine, *The Egoist*, Sinclair described Dorothy Richardson's *Pilgrimage* as a 'stream of consciousness' novel. See May Sinclair, 'The Novels of Dorothy Richardson', in *The Gender of Modernism: A Critical Anthology*, ed. Bonnie Kime Scott (Bloomington: University of Indiana Press, 1990), pp. 442–8, as well as Diane F. Gillespie's Introduction to 'May Sinclair (1863–1946)', also in *The Gender of Modernism*, pp. 436–42.
4. Jean Radford, 'Introduction' to May Sinclair's *The Life and Death of Harriett Frean* (London: Virago, 1980), n.p.
5. The myth of modernist disinterest has long ceased to enthrall. See for example Lawrence Rainey's *Institutions of Modernism: Literary Elites and Public Culture* (New Haven: Yale University Press, 1998) for one of the most influential accounts of the commercial savvy – the attention to markets, submarkets, influence, mass media – that fuelled the art and careers of Pound, Eliot, Joyce, and H.D.
6. The early feminist studies that began the work of inserting multiple women into histories of Modernism include those by Nicola Beauman, *A Very Great*

Profession: The Woman's Novel 1914–39 (London: Virago, 1983); Shari Benstock, *Women of the Left Bank: Paris, 1900–1940* (Austin: University of Texas Press, 1986); Jane Dowson, ed., *Women's Poetry of the 1930s: A Critical Anth*ology (London: Routledge, 1996); Sandra Gilbert and Susan Gubar, *No Man's Land: The Place of the Woman's Writer in the Twentieth Century*, 3 vols (New Haven: Yale University Press, 1988, 1989, 1994); Gillian Hanscombe and Virginia L. Smyers, *Writing for Their Lives: The Modernist Women, 1910–1940* (Boston: Northeastern University Press, 1987); and Scott, *The Gender of Modernism*. Mitchison lived until 1999, and thus was able to witness nearly three decades of feminist recovery work, including reprints of her fiction, critical biographies by Jill Benton, *Naomi Mitchison: A Biography* (London: Pandora Press, 1992), and Jenni Calder, *The Nine Lives of Naomi Mitchison* (London: Virago, 1997), and multiple critical treatments of her writing. The Space Between Society, devoted to study of literature and culture, 1914–1945, in 1997 inaugurated a period of intensified publication on works by women writers I would designate intermodernist. See for example Kristin Bluemel, *George Orwell and the Radical Eccentrics: Intermodernism in Literary London* (New York and Basingstoke: Palgrave Macmillan, 2004); Faye Hammill et al., eds, *Encyclopedia of British Women's Writing, 1900–1950* (New York: Palgrave Macmillan, 2006); Nicola Humble, *The Feminine Middlebrow Novel, 1920s–1950s: Class, Domesticity, Bohemianism* (Oxford: Oxford University Press, 2001); Maroula Joannou, ed., *Women Writers of the 1930s: Gender, Politics, and History* (Edinburgh: Edinburgh University Press, 1999); Alison Light, *Forever England: Femininity, Literature and Conservatism between the Wars* (New York: Routledge, 1991); Janet Montefiore, *Men and Women Writers of the 1930s: The Dangerous Flood of History* (New York: Routledge, 1996); Jennifer Poulos Nesbitt, *Narrative Settlements: Geographies of British Women's Fiction between the Wars* (Toronto: University of Toronto Press, 2005); Gill Plain, *Women's Fiction of the Second World War: Gender, Power and Resistance* (New York: St Martin's Press, 1996); and Anthea Trodd, *Women's Writing in English: Britain 1900–1945* (Harlow: Addison, 1998).

7. Jack Barbera and William McBrien, *Stevie: A Biography of Stevie Smith* (London: Heinemann, 1985), p. 156.
8. Elizabeth Maslen, *Political and Social Issues in British Women's Fiction 1928–1968* (London: Palgrave, 2001), p. 9.
9. See my 'Introdction' to *Intermodernism: Literary Culture in Mid-Twentieth-Century Britain*, ed. Kristin Bluemel (Edinburgh: Edinburgh University Press, 2009), pp. 1–18.
10. Tyrus Miller, *Late Modernism: Politics, Fiction, and the Arts Between the Wars* (Berkeley: University of California Press, 1999); Jed Esty, *A Shrinking Island: Modernism and National Culture in England* (Princeton: Princeton University Press, 2004); and Marina MacKay, *Modernism and World War II* (Cambridge: Cambridge University Press, 2007).
11. Frances Spalding, *Stevie Smith: A Biography* (New York: W.W. Norton, 1989), p. 111.
12. Ibid., p. 113.
13. Stevie Smith, *Novel on Yellow Paper, or, Work It out for Yourself* (London: Virago, 1980).
14. Ibid., p. 212.
15. Stevie Smith, *Over the Frontier* (London: Virago, 1980). See *The Collected Poems of Stevie Smith*, ed. James MacGibbon (New York: New Directions, 1983) for contents of all volumes of Smith's poetry.

16. Naomi Mitchison, *You May Well Ask: A Memoir 1920–1940* (London: Flamingo, 1986), p. 153.
17. See for example Frances Spalding, *Stevie Smith*; Jill Benton, *Naomi Mitchison: A Biography* (London: Pandora, 1990); or Sarah Miller, 'Introduction' to Betty Miller, *On the Side of the Angels* (London: Virago, 1985), pp. vii–xviii.
18. Stevie Smith, *The Holiday* (London: Virago, 1980).
19. Ibid., p. 13.
20. Inez Holden, *Night Shift* (London: John Lane, 1941). Basic stands for 'British American Scientific International Commercial'.
21. C.K. Ogden, 'Preface' to Inez Holden, *Death in High Society* (London: Kegan Paul, 1934), p. 9.
22. Ibid., p. 10.
23. See, for example, Celia Goodman, 'Inez Holden: A Memoir', *London Magazine* (December/January 1994): 29–38 or Anthony Powell, 'Inez Holden: A Memoir', *London Magazine* (October/November 1974): 88–94.
24. Inez Holden, 'Country House Bridge', *Harper's Bazaar* (September 1934): 67, and 'Fox Hunting - Is It Human?', *Harper's Bazaar* (November 1935): 94.
25. Inez Holden, 'Fellow Travellers in Factory', *Horizon* (January–June 1941): 117–22.
26. Inez Holden, *It Was Different at the Time* (London: John Lane, 1943).
27. Inez Holden, *There's No Story There* (London: John Lane, 1944).
28. Inez Holden, *Born Old, Died Young* (London: Duckworth, 1932).
29. Betty Miller, *On the Side of the Angels* (London: Virago, 1985).
30. See Phyllis Lassner, *British Women Writers of World War II: Battlefields of Their Own* (New York: Macmillan, 1998); Jenny Hartley, *Millions Like Us: British Women's Fiction of the Second World War* (London: Virago, 1997); Judy Suh, *Fascism and Anti-Fascism in Twentieth-Century British Fiction* (New York: Palgrave, 2009); and Jane Dowson, ed., *Women's Writing 1945–1960: After the Deluge* (New York: Palgrave Macmillan, 2004) for astute analyses of this novel.
31. Spalding, *Stevie Smith*, p. 186
32. Sarah Miller, 'Introduction' to Betty Miller, *On the Side of the Angels*, pp. vii–ix.
33. Betty Miller, *Sunday* (London: Gollancz, 1934) and *Portrait of the Bride* (London: Gollancz, 1935).
34. Jane Miller, 'Introduction' to Betty Miller, *Farewell Leicester Square* (London: Persephone Books, 2000), p. x.
35. Sarah Miller, 'Introduction' to Betty Miller, *On the Side of the Angels*, p. xi.
36. Betty Miller, *Farewell Leicester Square*.
37. Ibid., p. 63.
38. Naomi Mitchison, *We Have Been Warned* (London: Constable, 1935).
39. Naomi Mitchison, ed., *An Outline for Boys and Girls and Their Parents* (London: Gollancz, 1932).
40. Mitchison, *You May Well Ask*, pp. 176–7.
41. Benton, *Naomi Mitchison*, p. 92.
42. Mitchison, *You May Well Ask*, p. 176.
43. Ibid., p. 177.
44. Ibid., pp. 177–8.
45. Naomi Mitchison, *The Conquered* (London: Jonathan Cape, 1923) and *Cloud Cuckoo Land* (London: Jonathan Cape, 1925).
46. Benton, *Naomi Mitchison*, p. 92.
47. Naomi Mitchison, *The Corn King and the Spring Queen* (New York: Soho Press, 1989).
48. Benton, *Naomi Mitchison*, p. 69.

49. Mitchison, *The Corn King and the Spring Queen*, pp. 304–5.
50. Montefiore highlights this scene in *Men and Women Writers of the 1930s*, pp. 163–4.
51. Miller, *On the Side of the Angels*, p. 144.
52. Ibid., p. 145.
53. Ibid., p. 146.

3
Virginia Woolf and the Aesthetics of Modernism
Jane Goldman

By 1920, Virginia Woolf (1882–1941) was an established novelist already attracting serious critical attention, an accomplished critic, and a fledgling publisher. In the two decades that followed she remained a successful, best-selling author, whose reading public bought and read her work without the benefits, or otherwise, of academic mediation. The Hogarth Press, which she founded with her husband, Leonard Woolf, published most of Woolf's writings, and therefore she had significant control of the production of her own work and considerable artistic freedom. She was also responsible for publishing numerous other key modernist works, including T.S. Eliot's *The Waste Land* and many of the first English translations of Sigmund Freud, as well as works by Gertrude Stein, Nancy Cunard, Katherine Mansfield, and several other important (women) writers of the period.

Shortly after her death in 1941, Woolf's tenth novel, *Between the Acts*, was published to great elegiac acclaim. Her reputation as a serious experimental writer and a central figure in the Bloomsbury Group, notorious for its experiments in avant-garde lifestyles and politics as well as in the arts, did not exclude her from popular esteem. She took pride in her professional reputation as a public intellectual. Not only was her 'light' novel *Flush: A Biography* enormously popular; her 'high modernist' novels also sold very well, including *To the Lighthouse* (1927) and *The Waves* (1931). Her two collections of essays, *The Common Reader* (1925 and 1932), also sold well and widely. Her feminist polemic *A Room of One's Own* (1929), itself the foundation for modern feminist literary, cultural, and political theories, had instant and palpable impact not least for its consideration of most women's exclusion from university education, from the professions, and from mainstream as well as highbrow literary discourse. Her feminism consolidated further with pacifism and anti-Fascism in her other major polemic *Three Guineas* (1938). Much of Woolf's own critical writing, such as her essays 'Modern Fiction' (1925) and 'Mr Bennett and Mrs Brown' (1924), was framed to help readers understand the nuances and 'difficulties' of the new, avant-garde literary practices we have come to call 'modernist'. Her modernist aesthetics, even in these essays, are intricately bound up with her feminist politics.

Since her death, Woolf's substantial body of published works has been augmented by editions of letters, diaries, memoirs, and journals, and comprehensive collections of her essays and short stories. Woolf records and explores, questions and refashions everything in modernity and modern life – cinema, sexuality, shopping, education, motor cars, aeroplanes, feminism, politics, war, and so on. This chapter considers Woolf's contributions to the shaping and reshaping of modernist aesthetics, in her fiction and in her critical, polemical, and autobiographical writings, with particular attention to some of her later fragmentary works in process, left unfinished – but perhaps artfully so – and certainly most carefully worked and reworked: 'Reading at Random' (c. 1939–1940), 'Sketch of the Past' (c. 1939–1940), and 'Thoughts on Peace in an Air Raid' (1940). Along with the recent publication of Woolf's final novel *Between the Acts* in a radical new edition,[1] these later works have become more widely available.[2] These late fragments, deceptively fleeting and ephemeral, constitute a rich resource for readings in Woolf's feminist and modernist aesthetics.

> And I want to write another 4 novels: Waves, I mean; & the Tap on the Door; & to go through English Literature, like a string through cheese, or rather like some industrious insect, eating its way from book to book, from Chaucer to Lawrence. This is a programme, considering my slowness, & how I get slower, thicker, more intolerant of the fling & the rash, to last out my 20 years, if I have them.
>
> (Virginia Woolf, 13 January 1932)[3]

Woolf lived a further nine years after making this prediction, eleven years short of her estimated lot. In 1932, she was at the height of her powers, having published numerous short stories and essays and *A Room of One's Own*, as well as seven novels.[4] But, by the fifth of these, she had begun seriously to worry about the adequacy of the generic label 'novel' to account for her work, vowing to 'invent a new name for my books to supplant "novel". A new – by Virginia Woolf. But what? Elegy?'[5] After the publication of the eighth, she seems to take its very title to stand for her radically new genre ('Waves, I mean'). Indeed, *The Waves*, arguably the zenith of her achievement as an avant-garde writer, had been conceived to break literary genres and breach artistic and disciplinary boundaries as 'a new kind of play ... prose yet poetry; a novel & a play'[6] written 'to a rhythm not to a plot', a rhythm furthermore 'in harmony with the painters'.[7] These are the experimental and interdisciplinary terms of her creative ambition for the next four 'Waves' she predicts in 1932.[8] In fact she went on to produce three more works of fiction – *Flush: A Biography* (1933), *The Years* (1937), and *Between the Acts* (1941), as well as her second essay collection,

Three Guineas, and a biography of her friend, the critic and theorist of modern art, Roger Fry.

But what of Woolf's other stated ambition 'to go through English Literature, like a string through cheese'? By 1932 she was seriously intending to 'write a history of English literature' which she envisaged as 'a vast vista of intense and peaceful work stretch[ing] before me – a whole book on English lit'. The feminist advocate of 'think[ing] back through our mothers if we are women'[9] seems to be thinking back exclusively through the fathers in setting her parameters from Chaucer to Lawrence, but this may be her point – she will explore patriarchy's received historical records and canon. No such book came to fruition before Woolf's death, but perhaps the project was transmuted into Miss LaTrobe's avant-garde village pageant in *Between the Acts*, which certainly does 'go through English Literature, like a string through cheese' while interweaving its series of historical tableaux with the parochial action and dialogue offstage and undergoing constant interruption by numerous incidental events, natural and manmade, the mooing of cows, a sudden downpour of rain, the flitting of birds, the flight of military aircraft. Aside from the typescript of this final novel, however, Woolf also left drafts of the first two chapters of a book provisionally entitled 'Reading at Random' or 'Turning the Page', and these unfinished chapters, 'Anon' and 'The Reader',[10] constitute the beginnings of an innovative theory and form of literary history, which her earlier speculative phrase (also of relevance to *The Years*) seems to encapsulate: 'the Tap on the Door'. This unfinished and disjointed work is one of Woolf's final and most careful formulations of her feminist legacy, her continuously developing philosophy of literature.

In a fragmentary series of vignettes, inspired by the anonymously authored songs of early English, Woolf charts the shifting status of 'Anon', who is 'sometimes a man; sometimes a woman' and who 'is the common voice singing out of doors' and 'has no house' and 'lives a roaming life crossing the fields, mounting the hills, lying under the hawthorn to listen to the nightingale'.[11] This figure, in early times, unites audience and performer: 'The audience was itself the singer; "Terly, terlow" they sang; and "By, by lullay" filling in the pauses, helping out with a chorus. Every body shared in the emotion of Anon's song, and supplied the story.'[12] But with the erection of medieval settlements, and then the enclosures, and the rise of urban developments, Anon becomes a more and more reviled and excluded figure: 'Anon singing at the back door was despised. He had no name; he had no place.'[13] Yet, 'nameless, often ribald, obscene', Anon's 'singing his song at the back door' constitutes a continuity in the history of literature and 'the other less visible connection – the common belief'.[14] In 'Anon', anticipating more recent analyses of authorship by Roland Barthes and Michel Foucault,[15] Woolf charts the changing relations between singer and audience, play and audience, poet and reader, until the 'playwright is replaced by the man who writes a book. The audience is replaced by the reader. Anon is dead.'[16]

Anon is a key figure in *A Room of One's Own* where Woolf speculates on the lost historical women it has very possibly masked:

> When, however, one reads of a witch being ducked, of a woman possessed by devils, of a wise woman selling herbs, or even of a very remarkable man who had a mother, then I think we are on the track of a lost novelist, a suppressed poet, of some mute and inglorious Jane Austen, some Emily Brontë who dashed her brains out on the moor or mopped and mowed about the highways crazed with the torture that her gift had put her to. Indeed, I would venture to guess that Anon, who wrote so many poems without signing them, was often a woman.[17]

Woolf marks out a double impetus in feminist literary history and philosophy, both to recover the lost or suppressed lineage of women writers – a matriarchal writing subjectivity, perhaps, to rival that of patriarchy – and yet also somehow simultaneously to develop the democratic and anti-patriarchal potential available in the legacy of Anon by refusing precisely that model of authorial subjectivity constructed in patriarchy. This is the paradox embodied by 'Shakespeare's sister', the feminist messianic revenant celebrated at the close of *A Room of One's Own*:

> Now my belief is that this poet who never wrote a word and was buried at the cross-roads still lives. She lives in you and in me, and in many other women who are not here to-night, for they are washing up the dishes and putting the children to bed. But she lives; for great poets do not die; they are continuing presences; they need only the opportunity to walk among us in the flesh. This opportunity is now coming within your power to give her.[18]

Yet, if this account of Woolf's fictional Judith Shakespeare suggests the return of a suppressed individual feminine subject to match the transcendent national and literary authorial subjectivity of the historical (or mythical) William Shakespeare, then the poly-clausal conditional propositions that follow offer a contradictory model of multiple and collective authorial subjectivity that defers if not belies individual, singular or absolute subjectivity:

> For my belief is that if we live another century or so – I am talking of the common life which is the real life and not of the little separate lives which we live as individuals – and have five hundred a year each of us and rooms of our own; if we have the habit of freedom and the courage to write exactly what we think; if we escape a little from the common sitting-room and see human beings not always in relation to each other but in relation to reality; and the sky, too, and the trees or whatever it may be in themselves; if we look past Milton's bogey, for no human being

should shut out the view; if we face the fact, for it is a fact, that there is no arm to cling to, but that we go alone and that our relation is to the world of reality and not only to the world of men and women, then the opportunity will come and the dead poet who was Shakespeare's sister will put on the body she has so often laid down. Drawing her life from the lives of the unknown who were her forerunners, as her brother did before her, she will be born. As for her coming without that preparation, without that effort on our part, without that determination that when she is born again she shall find it possible to live and write her poetry, that we cannot expect, for that would be impossible. But I maintain that she would come if we worked for her, and that so to work, even in poverty and obscurity, is worth while.[19]

A Room of One's Own urges women collectively to work for the material conditions that will allow women's creativity to flourish: 'Intellectual freedom depends upon material things.'[20] The goal is not to produce an absolute feminine subjectivity ('she') but to find the freedom from gendered hierarchy previously enjoyed by Anon ('we'). In this Möbius logic, 'we' enables 'she' who enables 'we'. And we might compare here Woolf's early conception of *Between the Acts* as 'a centre' in which 'all lit. [is] discussed' and where she plans to have '"I" rejected; "we" substituted'. This 'we', she explains, is 'composed of many different things ... we all life, all art, all waifs & strays – a rambling capricious but somehow unified whole – the present state of my mind?'[21]

This intended intervention in the politics of pronominal gender and number is manifest in the final typescript of *Between the Acts*, which Woolf left at her death and in which the only words (aside from book and newspaper titles) she has rendered for italics are as follows: *'he'* (referring to a man); *'he'* (referring to a dog); *'not'*; *'she's'*; *'he'*; *'our'*; *'we?'* and again *'we?'*; *'that'*; *'has Mr Sibthorpe a wife?'*; *'all'*; *'they'*; *'That'* (referring to the 'music' made by an ominous passing flight of aeroplanes).[22] This spine of italicized words delineating the turns of Woolf's original pronominal gender politics has been obscured for decades by Leonard Woolf's decision, for the posthumous first publication of the novel, to render into italics all the text of the pageant in order to distinguish it from the rest of the text of *Between the Acts*. Mark Hussey's recent edition of the novel, however, has stripped out the posthumously imposed italics to make visible this spine, itself a line through the cheese of the text.[23] Hussey's editing restores a levelling textual politics to the novel, which puts into dissolution divisions between art and life; further muddies carnivalesque boundaries between political classes; and also (in keeping with Woolf's above use of the term 'waifs [people] & strays [dogs]'), does away with the arbitrary and shifting caesura between animal and human, historically imposed, as Giorgio Agamben has identified, by the 'anthropological machine'.[24]

In the unfinished 'Anon', Woolf recounts the advantages of the lost anonymity in collective terms ('we') whilst choosing to refer to the historical figure of the unknown poet as masculine ('he'), perhaps reflecting the historical record of a gendered hierarchy in which 'he' has stood for the universal:

> Anonymity was a great possession. It gave the early writing an impersonality, a generality. It gave us the ballads; it gave us the songs. It allowed us to know nothing of the writer; and so to concentrate upon his song. Anon had great privileges. He was not responsible. He was not self conscious. He is not self conscious. He can borrow. He can repeat. He can say what everyone feels. No one tries to stamp his own name, to discover his own experience, in his work. He keeps at a distance from the present moment. Anon the lyric poet repeats over and over again the flowers fade; that death is the end. He is never tired of celebrating red roses and white breasts. The anonymous playwright has like the singer this nameless vitality, something drawn from the crowd in the penny seats and not yet dead in ourselves. We can still become anonymous and forget something that we have learnt when we read the plays to which no one has troubled to set a name.[25]

This account of impersonality attempts to disentangle a model of collective universal subjectivity, 'drawn from the crowd', from a singular and gendered model of universal absolute subjectivity: 'he is not self conscious'. In doing so it counters T.S. Eliot's influential 'modernist' theory of 'impersonality' as set out in 'Tradition and the Individual Talent' (1919). Woolf was certainly familiar with Eliot's essay which, among other things, attacks the subjectivity of Romanticism.[26] But whereas his argument for a radical new impersonality focuses on the cyclical relationship of the self-sacrificing and self-resurrecting artist to art and to the literary canon of the dead (and it goes without saying his canon and his model of subjectivity are exclusively gendered masculine),[27] she, on the contrary, draws impersonality in terms of collective participation in the making and remaking of art (canonical and otherwise) by the living artist and audience alike, in effect dissolving the distinction between them. Woolf's and Eliot's differing accounts of impersonality therefore mark a fundamentally gendered fault-line in the theorizing of modernist aesthetics.

Woolf's account of impersonality, in 'Anon' and her earlier account of Shakespeare's sister, may inform and underpin her encapsulation of a model of collective subjectivity in the posthumously published late memoir, 'A Sketch of the Past' (1939–1940). This meditation was carefully drafted during the perilous period of German air raids on the English coast and sets out her 'philosophy'

> that behind the cotton wool is hidden a pattern; that we – I mean all human beings – are connected with this; that the whole world is a work

of art; that we are parts of the work of art. Hamlet or a Beethoven quartet is the truth about this vast mass that we call the world. But there is no Shakespeare, there is no Beethoven; certainly and emphatically there is no God; we are the words; we are the music; we are the thing itself.[28]

Woolf's 'philosophy' here again clearly anticipates later literary critical and theoretical declarations of the death of the author by Barthes and Foucault, but its feminist import is perhaps less obvious. Her understanding of the world as a text in which we all – 'all human beings' – participate is only implicitly feminist in its rejection of the authority of Shakespeare, Beethoven, and God. Yet, as her figures 'Anon' and 'Shakespeare's sister' also demonstrate, Woolf urges an alternative, collective, model of authorship, a questioning of canonicity, and a revision of our metaphors of gender. As well as encouraging us to read the works of male authors with a different attention to authority and gender, Woolf also prompts us to consider the nature of a literary canon that includes women authors, and the nature and form of literary texts written by and about women. In doing so, she also simultaneously revises and opens up the very nature and form of literary criticism and theory, forging a new feminist literary critical language, a new feminist agenda.[29] The feminist agenda, however, anticipates the moving through and beyond feminism to a state of commonality, encompassing (if not transcending) both genders, as outlined in the draft chapter, 'The Reader', which follows on from 'Anon', and in which Woolf considers the impact of changing technologies on the politics of reading, in print culture and beyond:

> As the habit of reading becomes universal, readers split off into different classes. There is the specialized reader, who attaches himself to certain aspects of the printed words. Again there is the very large class of perfectly literate people who strip many miles of print yearly from paper to paper yet never read a word. Finally there is the reader who, like Lady Anne Clifford read excellent Chaucer's book when they are in trouble 'and a little part of his beauteous spirit infuses itself in me'. And the curious faculty – the power to make places and houses, men and women and their thoughts and emotions visible on the printed page is always changing. The cinema is now developing his eyes; the Broadcast is developing his ear.[30]

Woolf credits print culture with the capacity both to encourage and deter the democratic collective politics of reading in which men and women of all classes participate and thereby dissolve class differences. She develops this class analysis of literature in her late lecture, 'The Leaning Tower', which she read to the Workers' Educational Association in April 1940. She envisages here a 'common ground' for literature, a postwar 'world without classes or towers',[31] made possible by the prospect, proffered by the politicians, of 'equal opportunities, equal chances of developing whatever gifts we may possess', and by the material underpinning of that prospect by 'income tax'.[32] Woolf's feminist concerns are subsumed and bound up here into class ones; and her concept of the 'common ground' of literature marks out a future egalitarian, republican, democracy of letters that appears to be beyond gender concerns.

Developing her thoughts on the democratic potential inherent in the processes of reading in 'Anon', Woolf finds book-reader to have an advantage over theatregoer: 'he can pause; he can ponder; he can compare ... He can gratify many different moods. He can read directly what is on the page, or, drawing aside, can read what is not written.'[33] The sheer longevity and continuity of print culture, its material and historical accretion, contribute to these intellectual freedoms for Woolf's common reader: 'There is a long drawn continuity in the book that the play has not. It gives a different pace to the mind. We are in a world where nothing is concluded.' Yet Woolf extends print culture, as we have seen, back to include the earliest songs of 'Anon' and to embrace the genesis of theatre, and forward to include works in film and radio. What emerges from her analysis of literary history is the repetition of a set of political choices regarding how we communicate individually, hierarchically, and collectively. She sounds an ominous note, however, in pointing out how the 'importance' of the reader 'can be gauged by the fact that when his attention is distracted in times of public crisis, the writer exclaims: I can write no more'.[34]

The prospect of acute silence, authorial and readerly, was all too real at the turn of the fourth decade of the twentieth century. Woolf's memoir, while reflecting on her enduring 'philosophy' as well as her primal childhood moments, also records glimpses of darker historical moments unfolding as she writes: 'Yesterday (18 August 1940) five German raiders passed so close over Monks House that they brushed the tree at the gate. But being alive today, and having a waste hour on my hands – for I am writing fiction; and cannot write after twelve – I will go on with this loose story.'[35] Writing her final memoir in alternation with her final novel under a sky darkened by warfare constitutes for Woolf and her readers a life-affirming act. But she also makes us realize that *'That'* music, the music of the warplanes overhead,[36] *is* music and it is also *our* music. The responsibility for it is not only *his* but *ours*. The gender politics of modern warfare, of the mass bombardment of unarmed civilians, which was a new phenomenon in Woolf's era (a commonplace in ours), becomes of urgent interest in one of Woolf's last essays written for publication.

'Thoughts on Peace in an Air Raid' (1940) was commissioned by Phyllis Moir for a symposium on 'women & peace' aimed at an American audience. A 'potted version'[37] was read by Woolf at a local Labour Party meeting in September 1940 shortly before publication in the *New Republic*, New York. In October 1938 Woolf responded positively to Moir's invitation, agreeing with her 'that culture was in danger'.[38] By January 1940 Woolf was pondering her task in a letter to the reforming politician, Shena, Lady Simon, speculating on a postwar gender settlement, and wondering:

> about sharing life after the war: about pooling men's and women's work: about the possibility, if disarmament comes, of removing men's disabilities. Can one change sex characteristics? How far is the women's movement a remarkable experiment in that transformation? Mustn't our next task be the emancipation of man? How can we alter the crest and the spur of the fighting cock? Thats the one hope in this war; his soberer hues, and the unreality, (so I feel and I think he feels) of glory. No talk of white feathers anyhow; and the dullness comes through the gilt much more than last time. So it looks as if the sexes can adapt themselves; and here (thats our work) we can, or the young women can, bring immense influence to bear. So many of the young men, could they get prestige and admiration, would give up glory and develop whats now stunted – I mean the life of natural happiness.[39]

Woolf's speculations on the capacity of culture to change entrenched gendered warrior behaviour echoes concerns voiced by two other leading intellectuals of her era. In 1932, under the auspices of the League of Nations, Albert Einstein and Sigmund Freud contemplated similar questions in their correspondence initiated by Einstein's letter to Freud asking 'Is there any way of delivering mankind from the menace of war?' *Why War?*, first published internationally as a League of Nations pamphlet in 1933, was reprinted in 1939 by Woolf's Hogarth Press in *Civilisation, War and Death: Selections from Three Works by Sigmund Freud*, edited by John Rickman.

Woolf's guarded optimism that 'the sexes can adapt themselves' seems to follow on from Einstein's and Freud's lead in *Why War?* 'Is it possible', Einstein asks Freud, 'to control man's mental evolution so as to make him proof against the psychoses of hate and destructiveness? Here I am thinking by no means only of the so-called uncultured masses. Experience proves that it is rather the so-called "Intelligentzia" that is most apt to yield to these disastrous collective suggestions, since the intellectual has no direct contact with life in the raw, but encounters it in its easiest, synthetic form – upon the printed page.'[40] Change, he suggests, is to be wrought culturally and intellectually, and he urges his correspondent 'to present the problem of world peace in the light of your most recent discoveries, for such a presentation well might blaze the trail for new and fruitful modes of action'.[41] If for Woolf, in *A Room of One's Own*, 'intellectual freedom depends upon material things', for Einstein here material freedom – peace – depends upon intellectual change. Freud concurs with this endorsement of cultural and intellectual opposition to war:

> On the psychological side two of the most important phenomena of culture are, firstly, a strengthening of the intellect, which tends to

master our instinctive life, and, secondly, an introversion of the aggressive impulse, with all its consequent benefits and perils. Now war runs most emphatically counter to the psychic disposition imposed on us by the growth of culture; we are therefore bound to resent war, to find it utterly intolerable. With pacifists like us it is not merely an intellectual and affective repulsion, but a constitutional intolerance, an idiosyncrasy in its most drastic form. And it would seem that the aesthetic ignominies of warfare play almost as large a part in this repugnance as war's atrocities.[42]

Freud closes by worrying, 'How long have we to wait before the rest of men turn pacifist?' He finds hope in 'man's cultural disposition and a well-founded dread of the form that future wars will take', which together 'may serve to put an end to war in the near future'; and he concludes with 'the assurance that whatever makes for cultural development is working also against war'.[43] Woolf's development of this concept of cultural pacifism makes more explicit Freud's passing reference to the stumbling block of gender inequality, where he alerts us to the complicating 'fact that, from the outset, the group includes elements of unequal power, men and women, elders and children, and, very soon, as a result of war and conquest, victors and the vanquished – i.e. masters and slaves – as well'.[44] Indeed Freud here comes close to the terms of Woolf's own earlier identification of hard evidence for the cultural engineering of a change in the gender balance of subjectivity, in her influential pamphlet 'Mr Bennett and Mrs Brown' (1924), where she famously asserts 'on or about December, 1910, human character changed',[45] a slogan that remains for modernist aesthetics and modern politics one of her most important, most disputed interventions. Woolf's evidence is in literature – 'the books of Samuel Butler ... the plays of Bernard Shaw',[46] but also in 'life' – 'in the character of one's cook';[47] and she continues to alternate her examples between art and life in such a way that both are bound up in a cultural nexus of change:

> Do you ask for more solemn instances of the power of the human race to change? Read the *Agamemnon*, and see whether, in process of time, your sympathies are not almost entirely with Clytemnestra. Or consider the married life of the Carlyles and bewail the waste, the futility, for him and for her, of the horrible domestic tradition which made it seemly for a woman of genius to spend her time chasing beetles, scouring saucepans, instead of writing books. All human relations have shifted – those between masters and servants, husbands and wives, parents and children. And when human relations change there is at the same time a change in religion, conduct, politics, and literature. Let us agree to place one of these changes about the year 1910.[48]

Woolf posits, then, an abrupt historical change in modernity in tandem with a rupture in the aesthetic order, a concatenation that produces both Modernism and new, modernist subjectivities, as I have argued elsewhere.[49] In modernist representations of 'character' a new discursive and performative model of subjectivity emerges with the recognition that there is no unified identity prior to representation or performance, a condition for the production of art that Woolf celebrates too in figures such as 'Anon' and 'Shakespeare's sister'.

Where Freud identifies 'unequal power' between 'men and women, elders and children, and, very soon, as a result of war and conquest, victors and the vanquished – i.e. masters and slaves', Woolf, anticipating the philosopher Hélène Cixous, understands all of these *hierarchized* binary oppositions to be always and already participating in the dominant cultural and discursive metaphor of gender:[50] 'All human relations have shifted – those between masters and servants, husbands and wives, parents and children.' But whereas, in 'Mr Bennett and Mrs Brown', Woolf seems to be offering up cultural instances as evidence of material character change, in 'Thoughts on Peace in an Air Raid' she more emphatically and more urgently brings out the corollary already implicit in the earlier essay that cultural change not only evidences but may also *produce* character change.

'Thoughts on Peace in an Air Raid' opens in alarm and urgency: 'The Germans are over this house last night and the night before that. Here they are again.'[51] The deictic marker 'Here' unites reader and writer in the textual locus of a shared vulnerability that extends beyond the originating historical experience of the author's enduring of German bombardment of England in the Second World War to the future horizons of successive contemporary readers. Woolf's essay meditates – in the first instance, then, while German bombs drop on British civilian targets, but it also continues to meditate now, while NATO bombs, for example, drop on Libyan civilians – on the 'queer experience, lying in the dark and listening to the zoom of a hornet which may at any moment sting you to death'.[52] Woolf warns of the gender politics inherent in this horrific aspect of modern warfare which has young men bombing unarmed women and children: 'Unless we can think peace into existence we – not this one body in its one bed but millions of bodies yet to be born – will lie in the same darkness and hear the same death rattle overhead. Let us think what we can do to create the only efficient air-raid shelter while the guns now on the hill go pop pop pop and the searchlights finger the clouds and now and then, sometimes close at hand, sometimes far away, a bomb drops.'[53] The 'pop pop pop' here marks a clear gender division whereby men are at war with each other in the sky – 'the defenders are men, the attackers are men' – while women 'must lie weaponless to-night' listening for the bombs.[54]

The onomatopoeic (and fatherly) 'pop pop pop' of these guns, however, has previously sounded in Woolf's writing, in the 1891 chapter of *The*

Years (1937), in rural Devonshire where the pregnant Milly Gibbs handles 'swollen' yellow pears hanging in an orchard: 'Pop pop pop sounded in the distant woods. Someone was shooting.'[55] The bucolic idyll is interrupted, then, by gunfire, which echoes across the years of setting to composition. It echoes all the more ominously in another phrase from Woolf in a letter of 1936 to her nephew Julian Bell who was later to die in the Spanish Civil War: 'As you know, the guns are popping in Spain now; coming nearer and nearer, but since we have left London and turned bucolic, the stress seems lessened.'[56] It eerily reproduces the sound recorded in Woolf's diary entry of 19 August 1940, which in turn corresponds to the inscription made on the same day in her memoir (cited above):

> Yesterday, 18th, Sunday, there was a roar. Right on top of us they came. I looked at the plane, like a minnow at a roaring shark. Over they flashed – 3, I think. Olive green. Then pop pop pop – German? Again pop pop pop, over Kingston. Said to be 5 Bombers hedge hopping on their way to London. The closest shave so far. 144 brought down – no that was last time. And no raid (so far) today. Rehearsal. I cannot read Remorse. Why not say so?[57]

That any prospect of successful cultural antagonism to war is waning is poignantly communicated in Woolf's recorded reluctance to prepare for her local Women's Institute's rehearsal of Samuel Taylor Coleridge's tragic blank verse play, *Remorse*. The same sound recurs in Woolf's letter to Hugh Walpole, 29 September 1940, describing *as they happen* another set of explosions witnessed by Woolf in her Sussex orchard while attempting to write to him about the bombing that destroyed her London flat:

> We drove up to [Mecklenburgh Square] on Tuesday morning and found – well, what you saw. The bomb had fallen that night. I'm glad we weren't there. Then there were three more time bombs in the square. So for ten days we weren't allowed into the Square. Then the bombs went off – most of our ceilings fell, and the Press has had to be evacuated to X
> I make this mark to show the point at which a bomb shook the window so violently that the pen jumped out of my hand. Theres an air raid going on – I've just been out into the garden to have a look. There's a pop-pop pop up in the sky – then a crash somewhere over towards Newhaven. Now its quieted down though theres one hornet up in the clouds – and I continue. Press has been moved to Letchworth.[58]

Not only does this letter written during an air-raid to fellow writer, Walpole, record the present dangerous context of her writing in which her very pen is moved by bomb blast, it also records the recent peril in which the London raids have put Woolf's own means of cultural reproduction, her printing press. She goes on to mention how 'more of [the] Bloomsbury [Group's]' sites of artistic production have been 'destroyed' too: 'Monday Nessa's and Duncan's studios were burnt out – in [No. 8] Fitzroy Street. A frigidaire and a statue the only survivors.'[59] The letter ends with an affirmation of their common acts of reading and writing which smoothly follows on from an intriguing pair of sexual innuendos. She buttonholes Walpole about a 'memorable tea' they took together under similar bombardment ('D'you remember the picture falling, and the lurid light on the Park, and Rupert Hart Davis coming in? I saw they'd been very close at hand – the bombs I mean'), and counters his subsequent apparent 'fears for [his] chastity in the shelter, but wish you were here at the moment; and put out a feeler for another letter, should you be inclined – should this letter reach you. Are you reading, writing? Yes, I hope so.'[60] For to be 'reading, writing' is to be alive, both surviving and fighting the bombings. This is an instance of Woolf's own 'queer experience' of 'thinking peace into existence' by co-creating with a fellow writer and reader the urgently required cultural 'air-raid shelter'.

Returning to the gendered lines of battle delineated in 'Thoughts on Peace in an Air Raid', Woolf cites William Blake's rousing lyric, 'Jerusalem', in urging women to 'fight with the mind', to free the men 'from the machine', and, in openly Freudian terms, to 'compensate the man for the loss of his gun'.[61] One target is the 'subconscious Hitlerism'[62] in men that turns them against women, and this returns us to Woolf's exegesis of domestic dictatorship in her earlier tract, *Three Guineas*, itself written as a fictional response to the approach of a barrister who asks of the narrator, as Einstein asks of Freud: 'How in your opinion are we to prevent war?'[63] The narrator makes the didactic point: 'Should we not help her to crush him in our own country before we ask her to help us crush him abroad?'[64] The narrator therefore gives the second of her three guineas to 'help the daughters of uneducated women to enter the professions', with the proviso that the beneficiaries help 'to prevent war'.[65] Likewise the first guinea goes to the funding of a women's university college, whereas the third is eventually yielded to her interlocutor's pacifist cause but with the observation that the first two guineas donated to women's causes are in themselves donations to this common cause: 'the rights of all – all men and women – to respect their persons of the great principles of Justice and Equality and Liberty'.[66]

Woolf's poignant, late essay, 'Thoughts on Peace in an Air Raid', then, espouses feminist, anti-fascist culture and writing, and defines the 'mental fight' we should muster in times of war as a fierce, intellectual independence. She rallies us to think 'against the current, not with it'.[67] But the essay has much more to yield to its readers than these urgent slogans, these open calls to intellectual arms that press the reader at the surface of its 'conversational' argument, as Judith Allen has it, 'awakening and enabl[ing] critical thinking'.[68] The citation of Blake's popular hymn to 'Jerusalem' is perhaps somewhat over-didactic: '"I will not cease from mental fight", Blake wrote.

Mental fight means thinking against the current, not with it.'[69] Given that these lines are from a highly popular poem internationally co-opted as a socialist and feminist anthem, Woolf's attribution to Blake seems somewhat redundant. Surely most readers, at the time of publication and even now, would know this very well, even if its origin in Blake's Preface to his longer work, *Milton* (1808), might escape them? Not only would Woolf's first live audience for her essay, her comrades in Rodmell's Labour Party, very probably be able to recite the anthem in its entirety, but so too would many of her readers, including in America, including even today.

The interior pastoral urged by Blake's 'Jerusalem / In England's green and pleasant land',[70] quite obviously corresponds to Woolf's mind-forged air-raid shelter in the midst of war. Most readers would have little difficulty too with Woolf's overt citation, if slight misquotation, of Shakespeare's *Othello*: 'Othello's occupation will be gone; but he will remain Othello.'[71] Woolf adjusts Shakespeare's 'Othello's occupation's gone' to enforce her point that physical disarmament per se is not enough to ensure peace since the 'young airman up in the sky is driven not only by the voices of loudspeakers; he is driven by voices in himself – ancient instincts, instincts fostered and cherished by education and tradition'. Perhaps too there are readers of Woolf's essay still educated enough in the English literary canon to catch her quite blatant allusion to Shakespeare's *Two Gentlemen of Verona* when her narrator asks 'Who is Hitler? What is he?', echoing as it does the bard's well-known and frequently anthologized lyric, 'Who is Sylvia? What is she?'[72] And what are we to make of this absurd turning of lyric tables against Hitler?

It is easy enough, furthermore, even (or perhaps *especially*, given the rise of online digital resources) for today's reader, to track down the particular newspaper article that Woolf mentions that carries the 'sawing' 'sound' of 'Lady Astor speaking in *The Times* this morning' on the topic of '"Women of ability"'.[73] But, given these instances of obvious literary and cultural allusion, we might also wonder why, then, it is that Woolf's narrator makes such a studied and veiled reference in the closing paragraph of the essay to 'some half-forgotten words of an old English writer [which] come to mind: "The huntsmen are up in America ..."' without giving source or author's name.[74]

On the heels of this broken elliptical allusion comes the essay's implicitly temporary nocturnal closure:

> Let us send these fragmentary notes to the huntsmen who are up in America, to the men and women whose sleep has not yet been broken by machine-gun fire, in the belief that they will rethink them generously and charitably, perhaps shape them into something serviceable. And now, in the shadowed half of the world, to sleep.[75]

This self-reflexive invitation to American readers to 'shape' the 'fragmentary notes' that constitute the very essay they are currently reading, seems a pretty obvious appeal to American foreign policy regarding the war against Nazism and Fascism currently being conducted on European soil. Has Woolf disavowed her pacifism? Is this a pointed call to join the fray, rousing American huntsmen to arms? She did not live to see this happen since American involvement did not come until the Japanese attacked Pearl Harbor in December 1941, when American sleep was indeed 'broken by gunfire'. But is this, in effect, to read Woolf's writing like that 'very large class of perfectly literate people who strip many miles of print yearly ... yet never read a word'? Perhaps the passage is, after all, asking to be read as an alternative call to 'mental fight' and not to physical combat at all. As such, it puts into practice the democratic processes of reading that Woolf outlines in her draft chapter, 'Anon'. Perhaps American huntsmen, who are ominously 'already up' (and now outside the cited sentence in one of Woolf's), may be roused instead to literary not martial pursuits.

Surely, in this intriguing coda to a most carefully wrought essay, Woolf is playfully inviting the reader to 'pause' and to 'ponder' and 'compare' so that he or she 'can gratify many different moods ... can read directly what is on the page, or, drawing aside, can read what is not written'.[76] If we read the closing passage of 'Thoughts on Peace in an Air Raid' as a call to military rather than mental fight, then presumably the reader will feel obliged to stop reading and enter the theatre of war, taking literally Blake's line, which Woolf elides, 'Nor shall my sword sleep in my hand'. But if we read this same passage as a call to 'not cease from mental fight' and therefore to understand Blake's unsleeping sword in hand as an erotic or writerly metaphor for such continuing and sustained intellectual engagement, then we contract ourselves to explore the intellectual freedoms available to Woolf's common reader in roaming the 'long drawn continuity' of book culture, submitting to 'a different pace to the mind' which discloses to us 'a world where nothing is concluded'.[77]

To conclude in non-conclusion we might return to that heavy-handed allusion in the closing passage of Woolf's essay to 'some half-forgotten words of an old English writer [which] come to mind: "The huntsmen are up in America ..."'[78] The editor Stuart N. Clarke's helpful explanatory note reminds us that the 'old English writer' is Sir Thomas Browne (1605–1682) and the 'half-forgotten words' are from Chapter Five of *The Garden of Cyrus* (1658) 'which continues: "and they are already past their first sleep in Persia"'.[79] Having restored from ellipsis the other half of Browne's semi-occluded sentence, as if to complete quantitatively those 'half-forgotten words' – rather than understanding the words actually cited to be themselves 'half-forgotten' (whatever that might mean) – Clarke helpfully glosses that while Woolf 'is likely to have read this in Browne, it was reprinted in Logan Pearsall Smith's *A Treasury of English Prose* (Constable, 1919), p. 71, which she reviewed'.[80] Even if Woolf herself was au fait with the arcane source text itself, her reviewing of the anthology, then, points to an awareness of Browne's probable common cultural currency, which again makes us wonder why she insists on its semi-forgotten status and on simultaneously eliding Browne's name.

The editor's work may well be done, but the reader's is surely not. Let us 'pause' and 'ponder' and 'compare' and attempt to 'read directly what is on the page, or, drawing aside ... read what is not written'.[81] What is not written by Woolf is the old English author's name, nor does she write the title of his work from which the 'half-forgotten words' return to us. Clarke restores to us the author's name and the work's short title, *The Garden of Cyrus*. What is not written by Clarke is its full title: *The Garden of Cyrus or The Quincuniall, or Lozenge, or Network Plantations of the Ancients, naturally, artificially, mystically considered*. This hermetic work was written and published as companion piece to Browne's *Urn Burial* (1658), itself a learned and witty meditation on death and immortality.[82] A similarly consolatory work, *The Garden of Cyrus*, 'after expounding ancient patterns of planting, including much modern botanical information, and gathering together examples of quintuplicity in human artefacts, the natural world, and pagan and Christian numerology, likewise concludes in religious mood, invoking "the mystical Mathematicks of the City of Heaven" which will ordain "that time, when ... all shall awake again"'.[83]

The Garden of Cyrus appears previously in Woolf's fiction, where she has Ralph Denham, in *Night and Day* (1919), stretch for 'a small and very lovely edition of Sir Thomas Browne, containing the "Urn Burial", the "Hydriotaphia", the "Quincunx Confuted" and the "Garden of Cyrus"' which he opens, reading from 'a passage which he knew very nearly by heart'.[84] Could it be the same half-remembered passage?

Woolf herself was clearly a voracious reader of Browne, and owned a number of editions in which she might read *The Garden of Cyrus* and its companion piece, including Geoffrey Keynes's handsome six-volume edition (1928–1931).[85] She does not directly mention this work in the handful of essays where she considers Browne's legacy, but in 'Reading' (1919) Woolf considers his contribution to theories of authorship, recognizing that his amazing prose 'brings in the whole question, which is afterwards of such importance, of knowing one's author',[86] since the 'poet gives us his essence, but prose takes the mould of the body and mind entire', and as an unpaid 'amateur', Browne 'has no call to conciliate his reader'.[87] In 'Sir Thomas Browne' (1923), her review of the 'beautiful Golden Cockerel edition' (1923),[88] Woolf expands on the reader/writer relations his prose inculcates, claiming 'the desire that makes us turn instinctively to Sir Thomas Browne ... is the desire to be steeped in imagination';[89] but it is also the desire to lose individuated and gendered selfhood and escape pronominal politics: 'Here it is all a question not of you and me, or him and her, but of human fate and death, of the immensity of the past, of the strangeness which surrounds us.'[90] Woolf uses Browne to question the model of readerly and writerly subjectivity produced by the modern(ist) prose of her contemporary Marcel

Proust, whose 'nine volumes' of fiction make 'us more aware of ourselves as individuals' whereas the *Urn Burial* 'is a temple which we can only enter by leaving our muddy boots on the threshold'.[91] She finds in the work of the earlier author a distinctly secular, inconclusive, and non-dogmatic Bible: 'Here, as in no other English prose except the Bible the reader is not left to read alone in his armchair but is made one of the congregation. But here, too, there is a difference; for while the Bible has a gospel to impart, who can be quite sure what Sir Thomas Browne himself believed?'[92] Anonymizing Browne in 'Thoughts on Peace in an Air Raid' may be Woolf's sly homage to his politics of anonymity and textual occlusion. (Perhaps her elusive 'Mrs Brown' is homage too?)

The freely roaming common reader of Woolf's cryptic allusion to Browne might also ponder a shared 'quintuplicity'. Woolf's neatly shaped argument may indeed be a playful nod to Browne's *Quincuniall*, since the essay is organized in five pairs of paragraphs capped by an eleventh, itself the coda that refers us to Browne. The literary amnesia, furthermore, may too be pointed.[93] Omitted 'from many Victorian editions', the *Quincuniall* was not transmitted as widely as its companion piece to modern readers in Woolf's era and beyond.[94] Perhaps Woolf's term 'half-forgotten' refers to this nineteenth-century forgetting of one half of Browne's diptych publication. Also blamed for its semi-obscurity is 'the sheer difficulty of text itself which has baffled all but the most determined reader' as it 'veers abruptly from passages of sublime purple prose to crabbed note-book jotting' cryptically alluding to hermetic and esoteric learning.[95] Woolf herself was just such a determined reader of Browne, and determined readers of Woolf have only just begun to unbury her deep Brownean treasures.[96]

Declaring her essay as 'these fragmentary notes', Woolf heralds feminist and pacifist material salvation in the specific adaptation of Browne's fragmentary form for the construction of a mind-forged air-raid shelter powerful enough to counter war. Woolf invites her reader to participate in endless supplementary construction, to become in effect an avant-garde bricoleur. The participating arranger of 'these fragmentary notes' is charged 'perhaps' with 'shap[ing] them into something serviceable'. Her modernist aesthetics attempt to forge a material, secular, and textual 'world where nothing is concluded'. This domain of 'Anon', 'the whole world', spinning between occlusions, 'is a work of art' where everything is in supplementary process, unified yet not closed, where there is no transcendent (Hitlerian) author, 'certainly and emphatically ... no God; we are the words; we are the music'.

Notes

1. Virginia Woolf, *Between the Acts*, ed. Mark Hussey (Cambridge: Cambridge University Press, 2011).
2. Wider availability has come with the recent publication of the long awaited sixth volume of Woolf's collected essays: Woolf, *The Essays of Virginia Woolf*, ed.

Andrew McNeillie and Stuart N. Clarke, 6 vols (London: Hogarth, 1986–2011). See also Brenda R. Silver, ed., '"Anon" and "The Reader": Virginia Woolf's Last Essays', *Twentieth Century Literature: A Scholarly and Critical Journal*, 25.3–4 (Fall–Winter 1979): 356–441; Nora Eisenberg, 'Virginia Woolf's Last Words on Words: Between the Acts and "Anon"', in *New Feminist Essays on Virginia Woolf*, ed. Jane Marcus (Lincoln: University of Nebraska Press, 1981), pp. 253–66; Maria DiBattista, *Virginia Woolf's Major Novels: The Fables of Anon* (New Haven: Yale University Press, 1980); Shelley Saguaro, 'Telling Trees: Eucalyptus, "Anon", and the Growth of Co-Evolutionary Histories', *Mosaic: A Journal for the Interdisciplinary Study of Literature*, 42.3 (Sept. 2009): 39–56; Sharon O'Dair, 'Laboring in Anonymity', *Symplokē: A Journal for the Intermingling of Literary, Cultural and Theoretical Scholarship*, 16.1–2 (2008): 7–19.
3. Woolf, *The Diary of Virginia Woolf*, ed. Anne Olivier Bell and Andrew MacNeillie, 5 vols (London: Hogarth, 1979–1985), IV, p. 63.
4. *The Voyage Out* (1915), *Night and Day* (1919), *Jacob's Room* (1922), *Mrs Dalloway* (1925), *To the Lighthouse* (1927), *Orlando: A Biography* (1928), and *The Waves* (1931).
5. Woolf, *The Diary of Virginia Woolf*, III, p. 34.
6. Ibid., p. 128.
7. Ibid.
8. Woolf scholarship has long been investigating and debating her engagement with a panoply of avant-garde art and media, in her immediate Bloomsbury circle and beyond, in visual arts, dance, theatre, music, radio, and cinema. See Diane F. Gillespie and Leslie K. Hankins, eds, *Virginia Woolf and the Arts: Selected Papers from the Sixth Annual Conference on Virginia Woolf* (New York: Pace University Press, 1997); Diane F. Gillespie, ed., *The Multiple Muses of Virginia Woolf* (Missouri: University of Missouri Press, 1993); Maggie Humm, ed., *The Edinburgh Companion to Virginia Woolf and the Arts* (Edinburgh: Edinburgh University Press, 2010).
9. Woolf, *A Room of One's Own* (London: Hogarth, 1929), p. 74.
10. Woolf, 'Anon [and] The Reader', *The Essays of Virginia Woolf*, VI, pp. 580–607.
11. Ibid., p. 582.
12. Ibid., p. 581.
13. Ibid., p. 582.
14. Ibid., pp. 582, 583.
15. Roland Barthes, 'The Death of the Author', in *Image–Music–Text*, ed. Stephen Heath (London: Hill & Wang, 1977); Michel Foucault, 'What is an Author?', in *Twentieth-Century Literary Theory*, ed. Vassilis Lambropoulos and David Neal Miller (Albany: State University Press of New York, 1987).
16. Woolf, 'Anon [and] The Reader', p. 599.
17. Woolf, *A Room of One's Own*, p. 74.
18. Ibid., p. 171.
19. Ibid., pp. 171–2.
20. Ibid., pp. 162–3.
21. Woolf, *The Diary of Virginia Woolf*, V, p. 135.
22. Woolf, *Between the Acts*, ed. Hussey, pp. 4, 13, 31, 44, 45, 78, 81, 81, 98, 121, 125, 132, 138.
23. See Hussey, 'Introduction', *Between the Acts*, pp. lxiv–lxviii.
24. Giorgio Agamben, *The Open: Man and Animal*, trans. Kevin Athill (Stanford: Stanford University Press, 2004), p. 92; see also Jane Goldman, '"When Dogs Will Become Men": Melancholia, Canine Allegories and Theriocephalous Figures

in Woolf's Urban Contact Zones', in *Woolf and the City: Selected Papers of the Nineteenth Annual Conference on Virginia Woolf*, ed. Elizabeth F. Evans and Sarah E. Cornish (Clemson: Clemson University Digital Press, 2010), pp. 180–8.
25. Woolf, 'Anon [and] The Reader', p. 598.
26. T.S. Eliot, 'Tradition and the Individual Talent', in *The Selected Essays of T.S. Eliot*, 3rd edn (London: Faber & Faber, 1951), p. 21. Eliot's essay culminates in the identification of '*significant* emotion', which is an aesthetic emotion paradoxically arising from poetic 'impersonality': 'What happens is a continual surrender of himself as he is at the moment to something which is more valuable. The progress of an artist is a continual self-sacrifice, a continual extinction of personality.' For discussion of Woolf's 'Mr Bennett and Mrs Brown' in relation to Eliot's essay, see Jane Goldman, *Modernism, 1910–1945: Image to Apocalypse* (London: Palgrave, 2003), pp. 143–60.
27. Homer, Donne, Dante, and Shakespeare dominate his 'Tradition'.
28. Woolf, 'A Sketch of the Past', in *Moments of Being*, ed. Jeanne Schulkind (London: Hogarth, 1985), p. 72.
29. Goldman, 'The Feminist Criticism of Virginia Woolf', in *A History of Feminist Literary Criticism*, ed. Gill Plain and Susan Sellers (Cambridge: Cambridge University Press, 2007), p. 68.
30. Woolf, 'Anon [and] The Reader', pp. 600–1.
31. Woolf, 'The Leaning Tower', in *The Essays of Virginia Woolf*, VI, p. 274.
32. Ibid., p. 275.
33. Woolf, 'Anon [and] The Reader', p. 601.
34. Ibid.
35. Woolf, 'A Sketch of the Past', *Moments of Being*, p. 137.
36. Woolf, *Between the Acts*, p. 138.
37. Woolf, *The Diary of Virginia Woolf*, V, p. 324.
38. Woolf, *The Letters of Virginia Woolf*, ed. Nigel Nicolson and Joanne Trautmann, 6 vols (London: Hogarth, 1976–1980), VI, p. 277.
39. Ibid., pp. 379–80.
40. Albert Einstein and Sigmund Freud, *Why War? A Correspondence Between Albert Einstein and Sigmund Freud*, trans. Stuart Gilbert (London: Peace Pledge Union, 1939), p. 5. Rickman's edition for Hogarth does not reproduce Einstein's contribution to the dialogue.
41. Ibid, p. 7.
42. Sigmund Freud, 'Why War?', in *Civilisation, War and Death: Selections from Three Works by Sigmund Freud*, ed. John Rickman (London: Hogarth, 1939), p. 95.
43. Ibid., p. 97.
44. Ibid.
45. The essay was also published as 'Character in Fiction', *The Essays of Virginia Woolf*, III, p. 421. 'Mr Bennett and Mrs Brown' was published as a pamphlet by the Hogarth Press in 1924, and in the same year, with minor variants, in the *Criterion*, under the title 'Character in Fiction'. The version cited here is the latter.
46. Woolf, 'Character in Fiction', p. 422.
47. Ibid.
48. Ibid.
49. Goldman, 'Virginia Woolf and Modernist Aesthetics', in *The Edinburgh Companion to Virginia Woolf and the Arts*, p. 36.
50. Hélène Cixous, 'Sorties', in *New French Feminisms*, ed. Elaine Marks and Isabelle de Courvitron (Brighton: Harvester, 1981), p. 90.

51. Woolf, 'Thoughts on Peace in an Air Raid', *The Essays of Virginia Woolf*, VI, p. 242. See also Judith Allen's extensive and fine engagement with this essay in *Virginia Woolf and the Politics of Language* (Edinburgh: Edinburgh University Press, 2011); Judith Allen, 'Conversation as Instigation: Virginia Woolf's "Thoughts on Peace in an Air Raid"', in *Virginia Woolf: Art, Education, and Internationalism*, ed. Diana Royer and Madelyn Detloff (Clemson: Clemson University Digital Press, 2008); Jennifer Cook, 'Radical Impersonality: From Aesthetics to Politics in the Work of Virginia Woolf', in *Impersonality and Emotion in Twentieth-Century British Literature*, ed. Christine Reynier and Jean-Michel Ganteau (Montpellier: Université Montpellier III, 2005).
52. Woolf, 'Thoughts on Peace in an Air Raid', p. 242. For a more sustained account of the contemporary relevance of this essay, see Allen's concluding chapter, 'Thinking Against the Current', in *Virginia Woolf and the Politics of Language*, pp. 113–18.
53. Woolf, 'Thoughts on Peace in an Air Raid', p. 242.
54. Ibid., p. 242.
55. Woolf, *The Years* (London: Hogarth, 1937), p. 90.
56. Woolf, Letter to Julian Bell, 'Nineteen Letters to Eleven Recipients, by Virginia Woolf ', ed. Joanne Trautmann, *Modern Fiction Studies*, 30.2 (1984): 191.
57. Woolf, *The Diary of Virginia Woolf*, V, p. 312.
58. Woolf, *The Letters of Virginia Woolf*, VI, p. 435.
59. Ibid. Woolf is referring to the studios of Bloomsbury artists, her sister Vanessa Bell and her companion, Duncan Grant.
60. Woolf, *The Letters of Virginia Woolf*, VI, p. 435.
61. Woolf, 'Thoughts on Peace in an Air Raid', p. 244.
62. Ibid., p. 243.
63. Woolf, *Three Guineas* (London: Hogarth, 1937), p. 1.
64. Ibid., p. 98.
65. Ibid., p. 152.
66. Ibid., pp. 260–1.
67. Woolf, 'Thoughts on Peace in an Air Raid', p. 243.
68. Allen, *Virginia Woolf and the Politics of Language*, p. 94.
69. Woolf, 'Thoughts on Peace in an Air Raid', p. 243.
70. William Blake's 'Jerusalem', the Preface to *Milton* (1808) was available to Woolf in numerous editions in her library, including *The Lyrical Poems of William Blake*, ed. John Sampson (Oxford: Clarendon Press, 1905).
71. Woolf, 'Thoughts on Peace in an Air Raid', p. 244. Clarke's explanatory note directs us to *Othello* 3.3.361: 'Othello's occupation's gone'. See note 8, *The Essays of Virginia Woolf*, VI, p. 248.
72. Woolf, 'Thoughts on Peace in an Air Raid', p. 243. Clarke's explanatory note directs us to *The Two Gentlemen of Verona* 4.2.38–9: 'Who is Sylvia? What is she, / That all our swains commend her?' See note 5, *The Essays of Virginia Woolf*, VI, p. 248.
73. Woolf, 'Thoughts on Peace in an Air Raid', p. 243. Clarke's explanatory note directs us to 'Waste of Woman Power: Demands for Clearer Direction', *The Times* (22 August 1940): 2. See also *The Essays of Virginia Woolf*, VI, p. 248; Allen, *Virginia Woolf and the Politics of Language*, p. 89.
74. Woolf, 'Thoughts on Peace in an Air Raid', p. 245.
75. Ibid.
76. Woolf, 'Anon [and] The Reader', p. 601.
77. Ibid.

78. Woolf, 'Thoughts on Peace in an Air Raid', p. 245.
79. *The Essays of Virginia Woolf*, VI, p. 248.
80. Ibid.
81. Woolf, 'Anon [and] The Reader', p. 601.
82. The full title is *Hydriotaphia, Urn-Burial, or, A Discourse of the Sepulchral Urns Lately Found in Norfolk for Thomas Le Gros of Crostwick or Crostwight*.
83. R.H. Robbins, 'Browne, Sir Thomas (1605–1682)', *Oxford Dictionary of National Biography* (Oxford: Oxford University Press, 2004); online edn (May 2008) http://www.oxforddnb.com/view/article/3702, accessed 6 July 2011.
84. Woolf, *Night and Day* (London: Duckworth, 1919), p. 72. Browne 'takes [the] fancy' of Orlando as both man and woman, and Woolf describes Orlando reading Browne a number of times, again without specifying which passages. See Woolf, *Orlando: A Biography* (London: Hogarth, 1928), pp. 68, 160. See David Galef, 'Mrs Woolf and Mr Browne', *Notes and Queries*, 36.2 (June 1989): 202–3; Pamela L. Caughie, 'Sir Thomas Browne and *Orlando*', *Virginia Woolf Miscellany*, 25 (Fall 1985): 4.
85. Thomas Browne, *The Works of Sir Thomas Browne*, ed. Geoffrey Keynes, 6 vols (London: Faber & Gwyer, 1928–1931).
86. Woolf, 'Reading' (1919), *The Essays of Virginia Woolf*, III, p. 156.
87. Ibid., p. 157. See also Allen, *Virginia Woolf and the Politics of Language*, p. 32.
88. Woolf, 'Sir Thomas Browne' (1923), *The Essays of Virginia Woolf*, III, p. 368.
89. Ibid., p. 369.
90. Ibid., p. 369. On the other hand, Elena Gualtieri, *Virginia Woolf's Essays: Sketching the Past* (Basingstoke: Macmillan, 2000), p. 53, understands Woolf to find in Browne 'a purely subjective form of writing'.
91. Woolf, 'Sir Thomas Browne', p. 369.
92. Ibid.
93. One (appropriately anonymous) online commentator observes: '*The Garden of Cyrus* is not as familiar to readers of English literature as much as its diptych companion *Urn-Burial*'. Anon., 'The Garden of Cyrus', online article: http://neohumanism.org/t/th/the_garden_of_cyrus.html, accessed 6 July 2011.
94. Anon., 'The Garden of Cyrus', online article.
95. Ibid.
96. See Jane De Gay, *Virginia Woolf's Novels and the Literary Past* (Edinburgh: Edinburgh University Press), pp. 8–9 for passing discussion of Woolf's interest in the dialogism of Browne's prose; Browne is considered in passing in Juliet Dusinberre, *Virginia Woolf's Renaissance: Woman Reader or Common Reader?* (Basingstoke: Macmillan, 1997). See also Sally Greene, 'Brownean Motion in "Solid Objects"', *Virginia Woolf Miscellany*, 50 (Fall 1997): 2–3.

4
The Art of Bi-Location: Sylvia Townsend Warner

Maud Ellmann

In Sylvia Townsend Warner's story 'But at the Stroke of Midnight' (1971), Aston Ridpath returns from his office expecting to find Lucy, his 'middle-aged, plain, badly kept, untravelled' wife, probably pottering in the kitchen.[1] But Lucy is not there. Did she tell him she was going out to tea? It might have slipped his mind. Or perhaps she told him and he didn't attend; he always finds it hard to pay attention to Lucy. The thought crosses Aston's mind that Lucy might be dead, but he blames the presentiment on Wordsworth; if her name had been Angelina he would have been less compelled to suppose that she was dead.

At least she couldn't be visiting her cousin Aurelia, who used to exercise an unaccountably disturbing influence on Lucy.

> It was absurd that visits to a country cousin – a withered virgin and impecunious at that – should be so intoxicating that Lucy returned from them as from an assignation, and acknowledged them as such by leaving him such quantities of soup.

Now that Aurelia is dead and buried, Lucy will no longer come back 'talking in Aurelia's voice, asserting Aurelia's opinions, and aping Aurelia's flightiness, flushed, overexcited, and giggling like a schoolgirl' (*SS* p. 144). Two days having passed with no sign of Lucy, Aston finally telephones his sister Vere, 'a successful widow', who arrives on his doorstep with a suitcase, clearly intending to move in (*SS* p. 145). Taking her brother firmly in hand, Vere insists on reporting Lucy's disappearance to the police, lest they should suspect Aston of murder. To Aston, such a suspicion would be absurd: 'Twenty years and more had passed since they were on murdering terms' (*SS* p. 148).

Meanwhile Aurelia has embarked on a reckless posthumous adventure. She visits the Turners in the Tate, jumps into a taxi with a stranger, and later presumably jumps into his bed, since he is dazzled by 'her ease in nakedness' (*SS* p. 147). The following day she meets a clergyman, who is equally dazzled by her spirituality. This is because Aurelia, 'the replacement of Lucy, [is] a nova – a new appearance in the firmament, the explosion of an ageing star. A nova is seen where no star was and is seen as a portent, a promise of what is variously desired ...' To the stranger at the Tate, she is an artwork that he can't account for, to the clergyman she is the most spiritual woman he has ever met, and to the denizens of St Hilda's hostel, where she now takes up residence, she is something new to talk about – perhaps the most miraculous of her effects. Her housemates are dismayed, however, when Aurelia adopts an injured, mangy tomcat, naming him Lucy, as if 'to call attention to his already too obvious sex' (*SS* p. 155).

Having no money, Aurelia experiments with blackmail: she drafts one letter to Aston demanding fifty pounds to come back home, and another demanding the same sum to stay away. The envelope has been posted before she realizes that both drafts are enclosed. In response Aston sends a niggardly ten pounds, but Vere sends a hundred on condition that Lucy never return. With her new-found wealth, Aurelia moves into a bungalow, accompanied by her feline familiar.

One stormy night, Aurelia is waiting for Lucy the tomcat, much as Aston had waited for Lucy the drudge at the beginning of the story. At last the sodden creature drags himself across the doorstep, his head smashed in, his front leg broken, and one eye sagging on his cheek, like a revenant from Poe. When the cat dies shortly afterwards, a cry breaks from Aurelia: '"Lucy!"' shortly followed by another cry, '"Aurelia!"' (*SS* p. 166). For she has changed back into Lucy Ridpath, looking at a dead cat that has never known her. Clutching its mangled body, she ventures out into the dawning light to discover that the familiar vista has disappeared under a roaring tide of floodwater. She walks into the torrent, which sweeps her onwards, cracks her skull against a concrete post, and spins the cat out of her grasp. Thus both Lucys, like their Wordsworthian namesake, are 'Rolled round in earth's diurnal course / With rocks and stones and trees'.[2]

This tragicomic fantasy exemplifies the wit and inventiveness of Warner's work, its affinity to magic realism, as well as its characteristic fascination with escape. Many of her novels, poems, and short stories, especially in the early part of her career, focus on repressed, middle-aged protagonists who burst out of their dreary lives and embark on sensational adventures. Lolly Willowes, in the novel of that name, abandons her brother's household in London, where she has withered in the role of serviceable maiden aunt, to set herself up as a witch in the village of Great Mop. Elderly, green-fingered Rebecca Random, in Warner's narrative poem *Opus 7* (1931), sells the luxuriant flowers in her cottage garden to finance her thirst for gin. As Jan Montefiore has observed, Rebecca 'finds in gin what Lolly found in magic: freedom, intensity of experience, and the courage to defy God'.[3] In *Mr Fortune's Maggot* (1927), the missionary Mr Fortune, a former bank clerk, sets out to the island of Fanua to convert the savages, only to find himself converted by their carefree ways. His love for Lueli, a faun-like Fanuan boy, releases Mr Fortune from the iron grip of Christianity; when an earthquake strikes and Lueli loses the idol that he worships, Mr Fortune also loses his censorious God. In *Summer Will Show* (1936), the Victorian landowner Sophia Willoughby, having lost two children to smallpox, goes to Paris to ensnare her worthless husband into giving her a third. Instead she falls in love with his mistress Minna Lemuel, a Bohemian Jewess, and ends up fighting with her on the barricades of the Revolution of 1848.

In the course of this novel Sophia effectively turns into Minna, having moved into her lodgings and adopted her beliefs, much as Lucy turns into Aurelia, or Lolly the doormat into Laura the witch. '"Women have such vivid imaginations, and lead such dull lives"', Laura explains to Satan. '"That's why we become witches: to show our scorn of pretending life's a safe business ..."'

> One doesn't become a witch to run around being harmful, or to run around being helpful either, a district visitor on a broomstick. It's to escape all that – to have a life of one's own, not an existence doled out to you by others, charitable refuse of their thoughts, so many ounces of stale bread of life a day, the workhouse dietary ... scientifically calculated to support life.[4]

The phrase 'a life of one's own' looks forward to the title of Woolf's feminist manifesto, *A Room of One's Own* (1929), which was published three years after *Lolly Willowes*. To attain a life of her own, Laura Willowes has to cast off Aunt Lolly, her dutiful false self, just as Aurelia has to cast off Lucy. But the fact that Lucy Ridpath comes back in feline form suggests that social conventions cannot be discarded with impunity. Warner, who joined the Communist Party during the Spanish Civil War, was thoroughly aware of the economic and ideological impediments to a life of one's own. Even so, our mind-forged manacles are often self-imposed; we cling to them for fear of freedom, not of punishment. When Warner embarked on her lesbian affair with Valentine Ackland, which was to continue until Ackland's death in 1969, she noted in her diary that 'Feeling safe and respectable is much more of a strain' than coming out. Despite the limitations on a life of one's own – social, economic, ideological – self-protection can be harder to sustain than liberation: 'life rising up in me again cajoles with unscrupulous power, and I will yield to it gladly, if it leads me away from this death I have sat so snugly in for so long, sheltering myself against joy ...'[5] Just as Warner found release by defying heterosexual norms, so many of her characters – Mr Fortune, Lucy Ridpath, Sophia Willoughby, Thomas Kettle in *The Flint Anchor* (1954) – break out of their snug death through same-sex love.

Yet their liberation rarely brings them lasting happiness. Laura Willowes is exceptional among Warner's escapees for succeeding in her getaway, though only through Satanic intervention. When her nephew Titus threatens to install himself in Great Mop, forcing her back into the death in which she sat so snugly for so long, she calls on the Lord of the Flies to drive away the interloper. A wasp attack, combined with the enticements of a pretty girl, ominously named Pandora, persuades Titus to clear off. For Laura, selling her soul is a small price to pay for this deliverance.

Warner's other fugitives, however, cannot call upon the devil for assistance, or rely on a *diabolus ex machina*. In Sophia's case, as in Lucy Ridpath's, escape concludes in disaster; Minna falls to a soldier's bayonet, Lucy perishes in a flood. Mr Fortune's Polynesian idyll also ends in pain and loss, when he realizes he cannot love Lueli without trying to change him, and therefore sacrifices paradise. The novel concludes with an anguished envoy from the author: '"My poor Timothy, good-bye! I do not know what will become of you".'[6] Warner later explained that she dashed off this envoy impulsively, 'with a feeling of compunction, almost guilt, toward this guiltless man I had created and left in such a fix'.[7]

Yet even though escape is often thwarted or satirized in Warner's fiction, the utopian impulse is not discredited. Lucy Ridpath has her moment of glory as a nova before the flood extinguishes her brilliance. Sophia never gives up hoping that Minna has survived the bayonet-wound, or that the Parisian workers will vanquish their oppressors; *Summer Will Show* ends in 1848 with Sophia engrossed in reading *The Communist Manifesto*, published the same year. This incongruous scene has been attacked as 'doctrinaire', but this is to overlook its irony: Sophia's metamorphosis is too improbable for propaganda.[8] As Gillian Beer has pointed out, the utopian reach of Warner's fictions of the 1930s is 'over and over again, sardonically undermined from within'.[9] Indeed Warner satirizes both the conformist and the escapist sides of Sophia's character; both her previous existence as English landowner, hemmed in by outworn conventions of class and gender, and her transformation into Sapphic revolutionary. What is crucial is her doubleness, her division into straitlaced self and reckless alter ego – a doubleness she shares with Warner's other escape artists, both human and feline.

For cats take a leading or supporting role in much of Warner's poetry and fiction, where they often serve as catalysts for transformation. As we have seen, Lucy the frump morphs into Aurelia the nova through the mysterious intervention of a feline familiar; similarly Lolly turns into Laura by means of a ferocious kitten, who draws her blood to seal her contract with the devil. If cats provoke doubling, this is because they are double in themselves, both tame and wild, *heimlich* and *unheimlich*. Warner's book *Boxwood* (1960), in which her poems 'illustrate' engravings by Reynolds Stone, features a cat who rejoices in his cosy cushion but also in his wild nights.[10]

The fire, the cushion, and the toy,
The curtained room
And my sweet milk to come –
All mine by right feline –
Is this not joy?

The wind, the dangerous dark, the sway
Of bough to ride,
The midnight world so wide –
All mine by right feline –
Is that not joy?

* * *

Sylvia Townsend Warner published four volumes of poetry in the course of her eventful life, as well as a co-authored volume with her lover Valentine Ackland, *Whether a Dove or Seagull* (1933). She also published seven novels and twelve collections of short stories, a translation of Proust's *Contre Saint-Beuve* in 1958, a biography of T.H. White in 1967, and innumerable articles, short stories, and poems in periodicals, pamphlets, and anthologies, including over 140 stories in the *New Yorker* over a forty-year period. Her diary, a tour de force of life-writing, has also been published, as well as many of her letters, including her correspondences with Valentine Ackland, David Garnett, and William Maxwell, which contain some of Warner's finest writing.[11] Her letters reveal her brilliant wit, her 'will to whimsy', and her power of observation, as well as her enormous capacity for love.[12]

Well known as a writer in the 1920s and the early 1930s, with the excitement produced by *Lolly Willowes* in 1926, and the critical esteem accorded to her poetry, Warner later receded from public view. Her reputation revived in the 1960s, when her biography of T.H. White was greeted with acclaim, and her novels and short stories began to be reprinted. Another boost to this revival was Wendy Mulford's innovative critical biography of Warner and Ackland, *This Narrow Place* (1988), which focuses on the lovers' writing and politics during the years 1930–1951, closely followed by Claire Harman's 1989 biography of Warner.[13] Yet despite this renewal of interest, Warner's writings rarely feature in school or college courses. For readers enthralled by her compelling plots, her mordant wit, and her penetrating insight into character – both human and feline – this critical neglect is baffling.

Warner suspected that her leftism caused her to be sidelined by the critical establishment; others have blamed sexism for the oblivion which has engulfed so many women writers of her century. These prejudices aside, the versatility that makes Warner's works so unpredictable has also made them difficult to brand and package for the marketplace. As David Simon has commented, 'Each of her seven novels is an unprecedented new world, and each of them looks, at first glance, as if it were written by a different author.'[14] Each of her novels sets out in a new direction, often by reimagining a previous age: seventeenth-century Spain in *After the Death of Don Juan*, nineteenth-century Norfolk in *The Flint Anchor*, the fourteenth-century convent of *The Corner that Held Them*, or the Essex marshes of 1873 in *The True Heart*, where the romance of Psyche and Eros from *The Golden Ass* of Apuleius is re-enacted by Sukey the skivvy and Eric the fool. These works eschew the extraneous 'period' detail or scene-painting typical of historical novels, thus transcending what Warner calls the 'arthritis of antiquarianism'.[15] The author resists the impulse to educate the reader, or to smuggle superfluous facts into her fiction. Instead of distracting us with historical information, she immerses us in the flow of narrative, imagining what it was like to live, rather than to know the past – or pasts. She crosses into pasts much as she crosses into dreamscapes – the island paradise in *Mr Fortune's Maggot*, the kingdoms of Elfin in her last collection of short stories, or the world of 'catkind' of *The Cat's Cradle-Book* – giving each imagined universe its own validity.

A further reason for Warner's neglect in the academy is the long-standing over-valuation of experimental Modernism. A curious asceticism has descended on our discipline, preventing critics from admiring works that they enjoy, at least in twentieth-century studies; a certain allowance is made for the compelling plots of nineteenth-century fiction, as if its authors were too benighted by the strictures of their age to risk the verbal complexities of Joyce. In this critical context, a modern novelist who strives to captivate rather than to alienate the reader tends to be discounted as a throwback, lacking the gumption to burst the confines of the Victorian novel. Because Warner's writing is not 'difficult', Gay Wachman contends, 'she has not been admitted to the mainstream modernist canon and has rarely been read with the care required by her subtle irony, her shifts in narrative genres and tone, her intricate, musical poems, and her layered and nuanced literary and political intertextuality'.[16] Although Warner constantly experiments with form and content – her later novels subvert the convention of the hero, as well as the expectation of a climax and an ending, while her poetry shows a prosodic versatility akin to Auden – her grammar and sentence structure remain too orthodox to count as 'modernist'. Meanwhile her popular appeal has merely bolstered professorial disdain.

In recent years the stranglehold of Modernism has begun to loosen, enabling a wider range of writing and writers to re-emerge, especially women and minorities. Warner's reputation has benefited from this expansion, her works attracting new attention from gender studies and queer theory. Yet her writing is too cunning, her irony too slippery to be dragooned into position-taking. Although her political views rigidified in later life – to the extent that Warner grieved for the death of 'Uncle Joe' [Stalin] in 1953, and dismissed as capitalist propaganda the mounting evidence of

Stalinist atrocities – her art never ceases to distrust beliefs and their believers, especially those of Christianity.[17] If her politics tended towards absolutism, her fiction moves in the opposite direction, undercutting political and moral certainties. Despite recent efforts to recast her as a lesbian crusader, Warner is too suspicious of identity per se – witness her self-divided heroines – to be co-opted into identity politics. As Jane Garrity has shrewdly observed, 'Warner resists collusion with existing models of "deviant" sexuality and elects, instead, to employ an individualized discourse of inversion that relies on elements of fantasy, evasion, dissimulation, and displacement.'[18]

Warner's own term for these wily stratagems is 'bi-location', the ability to straddle two places at once. In a lecture of 1959, Warner suggests that 'women as writers are obstinate and sly'.

> There is, for instance, bi-location. It is well known that a woman can be two places at once; at her desk and at her washing machine. She can practice a mental bi-location also ... Her mind is so extensive that it can simultaneously follow an intricate train of thought, remember what it was she had to tell the electrician, answer the telephone, keep an eye on the time, and not forget about the potatoes.[19]

It is this capacity for bi-location that launches Warner's heroines into their adventures in alterity, transforming her downtrodden Lollies into mischievous Lauras. As a novelist Warner practises both temporal and spatial bi-location, standing in two times as well as two places at once. Her historical settings provide an ironic distance from the present, yet also bring the past *'near* to a present-day reader', an achievement that the Marxist critic Georg Lukács attributed to the great historical novels of the long nineteenth century. Warner's novels also avoid the pitfalls endemic to this genre, identified by Lukács as the tendency either to modernize the past, or to turn it into a parable of the present, 'to wrest directly from history a "fabula docet"', or instructive fable.[20]

* * *

Warner inherited her interest in history from her much-loved father, George Townsend Warner, a distinguished history master at Harrow, the elite public school. But it was her mother Nora, a beautiful, volatile drama queen, whose stories of her early life in Anglo-India nurtured her daughter's love of fantasy. 'My mother's recollections of her childhood in India were so vivid to her that they became inseparably part of my own childhood, like the arabesques of a wallpaper showing through a coating of distemper.' To her child, Nora unpacked the 'astonishing storehouse' of her memory, 'full of scents and terror, flowers, tempests, monkeys'; a storehouse that Warner later raided to create such exotic settings as the island of Fanua (*SS* 340, 341).

An only child born in 1893, the young Sylvia Townsend Warner was expelled from kindergarten for her unruly behaviour – she mimicked the teachers and distracted the pupils – and thereafter received no formal education. Jealous of her father's attention to the privileged boys at Harrow, most of them her intellectual inferiors, Sylvia nonetheless enjoyed the full run of his library, as well as his intellectual companionship. George Townsend Warner was a staunch atheist, and although Nora taught Sylvia her letters from the Bible, she regarded most of its characters as cheats and charlatans. As a result of this early training, Warner's writing abounds with biblical allusion, yet without the faintest trace of piety. If Marx regards religion as the opiate of the people, Warner condemns it as brute coercion, unrelieved by any narcotic benefits. As opiates go, God is a poor alternative to gin.

George Townsend Warner delighted in his daughter's intelligence and wit, but her mother was dismayed by her looks. As an adolescent she grew lanky and thin; her face was angular, long-jawed, and bespectacled, and she showed no interest in attracting suitors. The young men she met failed to match up to her father, and like Laura Willowes, 'she had no mind to quit her father's company for theirs ...' (*LW* p. 26). At the time of her 'coming out', which she dreaded as a gruesome preparation for 'going in', Warner was devoting much of her energy to music, having benefited from the inspiring instruction of Percy Buck (*STW* p. 23). A handsome musician and musicologist who had joined the staff at Harrow in 1901, Buck was married, had five children, and was twenty-two years older than Warner. Nonetheless they embarked on a clandestine love affair, which began when Warner was nineteen and continued until she fell in love with Ackland in 1930.

In 1914 Sylvia was planning to leave home to study composition with Arnold Schoenberg, but the opportunity was lost when war broke out. Instead she joined a scheme for women of independent means to help out in munitions factories, which were now operating round the clock. Staying in dismal lodgings in Erith, south of the Thames, Warner would make her way to Vickers' factory for night shifts as a shell machinist. Here the regular workers, 'bone-weary, working long hours of necessity, living in the vitiated air of the shop, where the noise eats them like a secret poison', referred to the well-heeled female volunteers as the 'Miaows'. Although she was later to regret having worked as a scab, Warner was grateful for her experience of factory labour, which resulted in her first publication: 'Behind the Firing Line. Some Experience in a Munitions Factory. By a Lady Worker'. Published anonymously in *Blackwood's Magazine* in 1916, this article earned Warner the handsome fee of sixteen guineas (*STW* pp. 30–2).

In the same year George Townsend Warner died suddenly, probably of a heart attack, although his daughter thought he died of grief, having lost so many of his brightest pupils to the bloodbath of the First World War I (see *D* p. 231). 'My father died when I was twenty-two', she later wrote, 'and I was mutilated' (*L* p. 251). To make things worse, her mother took out her despair on her daughter, while also insisting that she share the parental bed. When her mother moved to Dorset the following year, Warner escaped to London, where she lived in a draughty flat over a furrier's in Bayswater Road. She had been hired by the Carnegie United Kingdom Trust to work on its Tudor Church Music Research Project as a member of its editorial committee. The job was probably arranged by Percy Buck, who was also a member of the editorial committee, and it required a good deal of travelling to examine music manuscripts in cathedral archives. These trips came in handy for rendezvous with Buck in the various cathedral towns of England, where the couple called themselves the Arbuthnots (*NP* p. 14).

Meanwhile Warner's interest in composing music had begun to wane, while her interest in writing was intensifying. Her first book of poems, *The Espalier*, received favourable notices when it was published in 1925, but it was her novel, *Lolly Willowes*, published the following year, which made her famous. It was the first book chosen by the newly-launched American Book-of-the-Month Club, and was also nominated for the Prix Femina, which was awarded that year to Radclyffe Hall. On the crest of her success with *Lolly Willowes*, Warner was invited to contribute articles and book reviews to a number of magazines, such as *The Nation*, *Time and Tide*, *Eve*, and *The Forum*. Early in 1927 Warner finished her second novel, *Mr Fortune's Maggot*, 'in a state of semi-hallucination'. The idea had come to her in a dream of 1925: 'A man stood alone on an ocean beach, wringing his hands in an intensity of despair ... He was a missionary ... on an island where he had made only one convert: and at the moment I saw him he had just realized that the convert was no convert at all. I jumped out of bed and began to write it down.'[21]

Since 1922, Warner had been paying regular visits to the Dorset village of East Chaldon, also known as Chaldon Herring, where she made friends with the writer Theodore Powys. It was at the Powys' home in 1927 that she first met Valentine Ackland, who had come to Chaldon as 'Molly Turpin' to recover from a brief, disastrous marriage. Born Mary Kathleen McCrory Ackland in 1906, Ackland reclaimed her maiden name after her marriage was dissolved, and also changed her given name to Valentine. Willowy and slender, dressed in trousers, her hair cut short in an Eton crop, Ackland was frequently mistaken for a handsome young man.

Her first meeting with Warner was not a success. Warner, by her own account, became 'aggressively witty and overbearing', conscious that Ackland was 'young, poised and beautiful, and I was none of these things'.[22] Over the next few years, however, Warner and Ackland had plenty of opportunities to overcome their initial awkwardness. In 1930 Warner, who had purchased a worker's cottage in East Chaldon, known as 'Miss Green' after its previous inhabitant, invited Ackland to move into the spare bedroom. It was in October at Miss Green that the love affair began that was to bind the women together for the rest of their lives.

Warner later said that she was too imaginative to write an autobiography; the closest she came to writing her own life are the stories posthumously collected in *Scenes of Childhood* (1981). By contrast, as Ali Smith has pointed out, Valentine Ackland was too unimaginative not to write an autobiography.[23] The result was *For Sylvia: An Honest Account*, written during a crisis in 1949 when Ackland was torn between Warner and an American lover, Elizabeth Wade White. Published posthumously, *For Sylvia* portrays Ackland as a woman born 'with one layer of skin too few', in Wendy Mulford's words, who lives at the highest pitch of intensity, yet also shows a curious passivity, as though she were the victim rather than the instigator of events (*NP* p. 22). While Warner's passionate devotion to her lover never wavered, Ackland was chronically unfaithful, perhaps as a manic defence against depression. Unbeknown to Warner, Ackland was a secret, guilty drinker, whose alarming headaches, swoons, and 'heart-attacks' resulted from her furtive binges (*STW* p. 99). 'Love ... makes one sensitive, but it also makes one obtuse', Warner writes in *The Cat's Cradle-Book* (p. 19). The novelist may be mocking her own obtuseness to her lover's alcoholism in *The Flint Anchor*, her last novel, where the Victorian patriarch John Barnard fails to notice that his wife Julia, swollen by multiple pregnancies and copious rum, has become 'an incurable drunkard'.[24]

In 1933, when the Nazis came to power in Germany, Ackland grew increasingly alarmed about the threat of Fascism. As her politics moved further to the left, Warner initially maintained a sceptical distance. But the horrifying news of Nazi barbarities soon began to change her mind, and in the spring of 1935 both Ackland and Warner joined the Communist Party of Great Britain. In *Summer Will Show*, which was begun in 1932 and completed in 1935, Sophia's conversion by Minna to the revolutionary cause fictionalizes Warner's own conversion by Ackland.

Summer Will Show was published in 1936, the same year that civil war broke out in Spain, precipitated by a military coup against the legally elected republican government. The British government refused to intervene, but the British Left rose to the defence of Spanish democracy, and Warner and Ackland, like their comrades in the Party, ardently supported the republican side. The couple took two trips to Spain during the civil war, and Warner was enchanted with the country and its people: 'I never again saw a country I loved as much as I loved Spain' (*NP* p. 124). The Spanish Civil War inspired some of Warner's finest writing, such as her poem 'Benicasim', named after a coastal town in Spain. This poem describes a makeshift field hospital, set up on the beach, where the wounded wander in 'bleached cotton pyjamas' in 'a bright painted landscape of Acheron', which is the name of the river of pain in the Homeric underworld. Suspended between battles, the patients 'bathe in the tideless sea', but they cannot resist the tide of history: 'narrow is this space / of garlanded sun and leisure and colour'. Inland loom the mountains, 'rigid as death and unforgiving', mountains that evoke the vastness of the obstacles to be surmounted, as well as the paralysis of death.[25]

This enigmatic ending contrasts with the jingoistic conclusion of 'Journey to Barcelona', another poem of the Spanish Civil War, where a powerful evocation of the sun-baked Spanish landscape – 'Pale is that country like a country of bone' – is spoilt by the final rallying-cry: 'Rain from the red cloud, come to Spain!' (*NCP* p. 258). Here the echo of the nursery rhyme – Rain rain go to Spain! – reduces to bathos the heavy-handed political symbolism of the line. In this poem as in 'Red Front' (1935), another jingoistic poem, Warner's political zeal overwhelms her aesthetic judgement.[26] This is not the case, however, in 'The Red Carnation', one of Warner's greatest short stories about the Spanish conflict, in which the author suspends her own political position to assume the viewpoint of the other side. The central character, a young German soldier, has been sent to Spain to fight for Fascism and quash the communists. Steeped in propaganda, the youth is convinced that 'wherever those red flames sprang up there the German soldier must go, to trample them out under his strong boots'. Nonetheless he thrills with the romance of Spain: 'He would see Seville, the orange trees, the bullfights, those girls who made cigarettes. He would walk about holding a red carnation between his teeth' (*SS* p. 113). What he experiences instead, as he meanders through an ancient town, is the smell of something worse than death, the smell 'not of a corpse but of a ghost' (*SS* p. 125). Spurned by the townspeople, spat at by a child, he is 'left alone with the smell, knowing himself hated' (*SS* p. 126). At this point he realizes that he has come to Spain, not to save its people from the Red threat, but to die. By adopting the perspective of the 'enemy', in this case a deluded innocent, Warner reveals the human tragedy behind the rhetoric of war.

Warner's experience in Spain also inspired what is arguably her greatest novel, *After the Death of Don Juan* (1938). The novel takes up the story of Don Juan where Molière and Mozart left it. The heiress Doña Ana, a betrothed virgin, who resisted Don Juan's attempted rape, is now obsessed with her seducer. Convinced by the rumour that the notorious libertine was dragged by demons into hell, Doña Ana insists on conveying this news in person to his father, Don Saturno. Accompanied by her wimpish husband Ottavio and a large retinue of flunkies, Doña Ana embarks on an arduous seven-day journey to the remote village of Tenorio Viejo, stopping at every church for hand-wringing displays of piety. When the caravan finally reaches its destination and Doña Ana delivers her message, Don Saturno refuses to believe the story of the supernatural comeuppance inflicted on his son. Much as he would like to be relieved of Don Juan's debts, which have crippled the estate and thwarted Don Saturno's philanthropic projects to improve the peasants' lot, he has heard this story too often before. It is a long-standing family legend, appropriated by Leporello, Don Juan's 'rapscallionly valet', the only witness to his master's supposed abduction into hell.[27]

'Slow-witted' though she is, Doña Ana eventually reaches the conclusion that her heart-throb is still alive (*DJ* p. 48). Sure enough, Don Juan reappears, recovering from an attack of nettle-rash that forced his departure from Seville – 'I could not face them with a face covered with blotches' – where he had commissioned Leporello to spread the thrilling story of his death (*DJ* p. 207). Far from pleased to learn that Doña Ana has been stalking him, 'mewing and spitting and caterwauling', the resurrected roué spurns her lust (*DJ* p. 219). Doña Ana's fanatical pursuit of Don Juan, dead or alive, provides the comic framework of the novel, but it is the plight of the peasants, starved by feudalism as they were later to be bled by Fascism, which precipitates its tragic denouement. When these peasants finally revolt, Don Juan calls in troops of henchmen to slaughter them. During the massacre Don Saturno, who had dreamed of irrigating his parched lands with the money that his son has squandered in the gambling dens and bedrooms of Seville, sits helplessly gagged and bound to his chair.

In a letter to Nancy Cunard of 1945, Warner described *After the Death of Don Juan* as 'a parable, if you like the word, or an allegory or what you will, of the political chemistry of the Spanish War, with the Don Juan – more of Molière than of Mozart – developing as the Fascist of the piece' (*L* p. 51, n. 1). In this novel, the mesmerizing evocation of the Spanish landscape, combined with Warner's affectionate portrayal of the common people, which never lapses into schmaltz or condescension, provides a beguiling counterpoint to her acid satire of the grandees, wallowing in self-indulgence, religiosity, and sheer silliness. The pilgrimage to Tenorio Viejo – narrated largely from the point of view of Ottavio, the pusillanimous fop, blind to his wife's erotic obsession and baffled by her excesses of piety – is a comic masterpiece, comparable to Chaucer's *Canterbury Tales*, with its colourful cortege of hypocrites and scoundrels.

Franco declared victory in Spain on 1 April 1939; on 3 September Britain declared war on Germany. When war broke out, Warner and Ackland were visiting the United States, but they returned to Britain to join the home front, accompanied by their wealthy American friend, Elizabeth Wade White, who was already wreaking havoc in their ménage. It was in 1942 that Warner began to write *The Corner that Held Them* (1948), her chronicle of a fourteenth-century convent at Oby in the fenlands between the years 1345 and 1382, which became her favourite novel. Like *After the Death of Don Juan*, only more so, *The Corner that Held Them* does away with the convention of the hero; as Warner later explained, 'the characters are innumerable and insignificant'.[28] The action begins when a drunken beggar, seeking alms at the convent, is mistaken for a priest and therefore enlisted to perform the sacrament. Once installed in this sinecure, 'Father Ralph' never corrects the error except when he is talking in his sleep, but his nocturnal indiscretions are discounted as deliria. Apart from this impostor, five prioresses and four bishops come and go; novices arrive, grow up, and die, while the novel focuses on the collective life of the community. Warner later said that she began the book 'on the purest Marxian principles ... if you were going to give an accurate picture of the monastic life, you'd have to put in all their finances ...' (*STW* p. 216). Marxism may also have persuaded her to eschew the hero of the bourgeois novel and to focus on social relations rather than individuals.

For readers who enjoy identifying with the hero and reading for the plot, it is hard to explain what makes this novel so compelling. But its effect could be compared to the addictive power of a soap opera, where we become absorbed in the low-key events of daily life, rather than panting for the climax. *The Corner that Held Them* brings the novel back to its origins in gossip, a form of collective storytelling in which local heroes wax and wane, constantly overtaken by new intrigues and embarrassments. Warner's novel also bears comparison to Mass Observation, the organization founded in 1937 by Tom Harrisson and others to study the everyday lives of ordinary people in Britain. The Mass Observation archives now provide an invaluable record of the home front experience in the Second World War. From all the corners that held them, contributors were asked to report on bomb shelters, food shortages, black-out regulations, and even to record their dreams which – as Elizabeth Bowen remembers – gained a strange new intensity in wartime.[29] In *The Corner that Held Them*, Warner transposes to the fourteenth century the new attention focused by Mass Observation on the local experience of total war.

As Warner forged on with her writing, Ackland continued to oscillate between her lovers, unable to choose between her long-standing attachment to Warner and her newer infatuation with Elizabeth Wade White. In 1949, when Warner and Ackland were living at Frome Vauchurch, near the site of Miss Green which was destroyed by a bomb in the Second World War, it was decided that White should move into the couple's house with Ackland while Warner spent a 'trial month' in a hotel. In preparation for White's arrival, Warner burst into an orgy of housecleaning, removing all traces of her own presence, even to unpicking her monograms from the pillows and towels. In her story 'Winter in the Air' (1955), based on this harrowing experience, the husband Willie, who is moving his mistress into the marital home, protests against his wife's 'revengeful housekeeping'. 'It's only fair to Annalies', Barbara explains, 'to get my smell out of the house.' Yet privately she knows that Willie's accusation is closer to the mark: by now 'she had no more magnanimity than a criminal on the run. There must be nothing left behind by which she could be tracked' (*SS* p. 24). Ackland's affair with White came to an end a few months after this ordeal, followed by the death of Thomas the cat, Warner's confidant in her loneliness. 'It will always seem to me', she later wrote, 'that [Thomas] did, in his faithfulness, stay by me till she came back' (*STW* p. 240).

But Warner's tribulations were not over. Now that White was out of the picture, Ackland found a new way to test Warner's devotion and abuse her love by pursuing a secret flirtation with the Catholic Church, which she rejoined in 1956. Warner reacted to this news with 'severe shock', blaming herself for Ackland's rosary-clutching mania: 'this Roman Catholic business is like a third person in the house' (*STW* pp. 261, 266). After the Vatican reforms of the early 1960s, Ackland grew disillusioned with the Church and in 1969 she joined the Quakers, which Warner found easier to stomach. By this time Ackland's health was failing, and she died of cancer on 9 November 1969. 'Total grief is like a minefield', Warner wrote in her diary. 'No knowing when one will touch the tripwire' (*STW* p. 301).

Warner survived her lover by nine lonely years, during which she kept two diaries, one enlivened with her customary brilliance, the other abject and distraught, as if she had incorporated Ackland's life-long sadness into her own divided consciousness. Meanwhile Warner gave up writing realist stories, turning to fantasy in her last book *Kingdoms of Elfin* (1977), an interlinked series of 'exceeding grown-up fairy stories about the political, sexual and aesthetic lives of a group of articulate elves', as Terry Castle has described them.[30] In an interview Warner said, 'I suddenly looked round on my career and thought, "Good God, I've been understanding the human heart for all these decades. Bother the human heart, I'm tired of the human heart. I want to write about something entirely different"' (*STW* p. 312). Warner's fairies have no souls; they cannot weep or hate, and their love affairs tend to be brief. From time to time they snatch a human child, attaching a fasting weasel to its neck to drink its blood, which also siphons off its human propensity to melodrama. This procedure increases its longevity, adding a hundred years or so to human life.[31]

In *The Cat's Cradle-Book*, the narrator of the frame story claims that all our fairy-tales derive from cats, which is why the mood of these stories is not heated and sentimental, but 'cool and dispassionate ... objective – and cat-like'.[32] Accordingly Warner strives to 'inhumanize' her prose in *The Kingdoms of Elfin*, cultivating a catlike insouciance in her diminutive protagonists (*KE* p. 2). Like the historical settings of her earlier novels, elfindom enables her to practice 'bi-location', standing in two places at once and casting an ironic glance at both the human and the fairy worlds. While fairies are immune to the appalling suffering that Warner experienced with Ackland's death, they live in constant dread of boredom. The implication, Alison Lurie suggests, is that 'there is something to be said for a short human life of work and struggle and strong emotions'.[33]

To do justice to the rich variety of Warner's work would require far more than my allotted space. I can only hope that this foretaste will tempt new readers to explore this cornucopia. Sylvia Townsend Warner stands alongside Virginia Woolf and Elizabeth Bowen as one of the finest British fiction writers of her century, and she also achieved distinction as a poet. In view of the originality of both her life and her work, it is crass to disparage her as insufficiently 'modernist'. In a review of Warner's *New Collected Poems*, John Wilkinson suggests that 'these poems can act as a reminder that poetic change does not involve supersession'.[34] The same could be said of the novels and short stories that Warner wrote over the five decades of her long career, as well as the fascinating record of her life and times conserved in her diary and letters. To put it bluntly, Sylvia Townsend Warner is much too good to miss.

Notes

1. Sylvia Townsend Warner, 'But at the Stroke of Midnight', in *Selected Stories* (London: Virago, 1990), p. 147; henceforth cited as *SS*.
2. William Wordsworth, 'A Slumber Did My Spirit Seal', in *The Major Works: Including 'The Prelude'*, ed. Stephen Gill (Oxford: Oxford University Press, 2008), p. 147.
3. Jan Montefiore, *Men and Women Writers of the 1930s: The Dangerous Flood of History* (London: Routledge, 1996), p. 138.
4. Sylvia Townsend Warner, *Lolly Willowes, or The Loving Huntsman* (London: Virago, 2000), pp. 234, 238–9; henceforth cited as *LW*.
5. *The Diaries of Sylvia Townsend Warner*, ed. Claire Harman (London: Virago, 1995), pp. 70, 71; henceforth cited as *D*.
6. Sylvia Townsend Warner, *Mr. Fortune's Maggot* (London: Virago, 1978), p. 250; henceforth cited as *MFM*.
7. A note on *MFM*, in Sylvia Townsend Warner, *Letters*, ed. William Maxwell (London: Chatto and Windus, 1982), p. 11; henceforth cited as *L*.
8. See Brooke Allen, 'Sylvia Townsend Warner's "Very Cultured Voice"', *New Criterion*, 19.7 (2001): 20–7, p. 24.
9. See Gillian Beer, 'Sylvia Townsend Warner: The Centrifugal Kick', in *Women Writers of the 1930s: Gender, Power, Resistance*, ed. Maroula Joannou (Edinburgh: Edinburgh University Press, 1999), pp. 76–7.
10. Sylvia Townsend Warner, *Boxwood* (London: Chatto and Windus, 1960), p. 24.
11. In addition to *L*, see *I'll Stand by You: The Letters of Sylvia Townsend Warner and Valentine Ackland*, ed. Susanna Pinney (London: Pimlico, 1998); *Sylvia and David: The Townsend Warner–Garnett Letters*, ed. Richard Garnett (London: Sinclair-Stevenson, 1994); *The Element of Lavishness: Letters of Sylvia Townsend Warner and William Maxwell, 1938–1978*, ed. Michael Steinman (Washington, DC: Counterpoint, 2001).
12. See Terry Castle, 'The Will to Whimsy', review of Claire Harman, *The Diaries of Sylvia Townsend Warner*, TLS (3 June 1994): 8–9.
13. Claire Harman, *Sylvia Townsend Warner: A Biography* (1989; London: Minerva, 1991); henceforth cited as *STW*; Wendy Mulford, *This Narrow Place: Sylvia Townsend Warner and Valentine Ackland: Life, Letters and Politics 1930–1951* (London: Pandora, 1998); henceforth cited as *NP*.
14. David Carroll Simon, 'History Unforeseen: On Sylvia Townsend Warner', *Nation* 25 January 2010: http://www.thenation.com/article/history-unforeseen-sylvia-townsend-warner.
15. Sylvia Townsend Warner, 'Edmund Fellowes as Editor', *Musical Times*, 93.1308 (February, 1952): 59–60, p. 60.
16. Gay Wachman, *Lesbian Empire: Radical Crosswriting in the Twenties* (New Brunswick: Rutgers University Press, 2001), p. 3.
17. See Harman, *Sylvia Townsend Warner*, pp. 252–3.

18. Jane Garrity, *Step-Daughters of England: British Women Modernists and the National Imaginary* (Manchester: Manchester University Press, 2003), p. 142.
19. Sylvia Townsend Warner, 'Women as Writers', *Royal Society of Arts Journal*, 107.5034 (1959): 379–86, p. 380; quoted in Garrity, *Step-Daughters*, p. 147.
20. Quoted by Chris Hopkins, 'Sylvia Townsend Warner and the Marxist Historical Novel', *Literature and History*, Ser. 3, 4.1 (1995): 50–64, pp. 58, 61.
21. Preface to *MFM*.
22. Warner, *I'll Stand by You*, p. 6.
23. Ali Smith, 'Sylvia Townsend Warner, Ghost Writer', *TLS* (2 January 2009): 3–5, p. 3.
24. Sylvia Townsend Warner, *The Flint Anchor* (London: Virago, 1997), p. 125.
25. Sylvia Townsend Warner, *New Collected Poems*, ed. Claire Harman (Manchester: Carcanet, 2008), p. 256; henceforth cited as *NCP*.
26. *Left Review*, 1:7 (1935): 255–7; omitted by Claire Harman from *NCP*. See Montefiore, *Men and Women Writers*, p. 234, n. 12.
27. Sylvia Townsend Warner, *After the Death of Don Juan* (London: Virago, 1989), p. 13; henceforth cited as *DJ*.
28. Quoted by Claire Harman, introduction to Sylvia Townsend Warner, *The Corner that Held Them* (London: Virago, 1988), p. v.
29. See Elizabeth Bowen, Postscript to *The Demon Lover* (1945), in *The Mulberry Tree: Writings of Elizabeth Bowen*, ed. Hermione Lee (London: Virago, 1986), p. 96.
30. Castle, 'The Will to Whimsy', p. 8.
31. Sylvia Townsend Warner, *Kingdoms of Elfin* (Harmondsworth: Penguin, 1979), pp. 1–2; henceforth cited as *KE*.
32. Sylvia Townsend Warner, *The Cat's Cradle-Book* (New York: Viking, 1940), p. 28; henceforth cited as *CCB*.
33. Alison Lurie, 'Sylvia Townsend Warner', in *The Oxford Companion to Fairy-Tales*, ed. Jack Zipes (Oxford: Oxford University Press, 2000), p. 545.
34. John Wilkinson, Review of *NCP*, *Modernism/Modernity*, 16:2 (2009): 457–9, p. 459.

Part II
Cultural Hierarchy

5
The Feminine Middlebrow Novel
Nicola Humble

In a very real sense, there is no such thing as the middlebrow. It would have been extremely hard in the interwar years to find any writer or publisher who would happily apply the label to their own works, and almost as hard to find a reader who would own the designation. Much like 'lower-middle class' it is a label almost exclusively applied to others: a form of dismissal, sounding a powerful note of contempt. It remains a highly contentious term, one that even today produces anxiety and a curious sort of shame within academic circles. And yet I and other critics continue to argue that there is some value in the revivification of this ossified literary snobbery, some work of understanding that can only be achieved by the active examination and deployment of the concept of the middlebrow.[1]

It is easier to say what the middlebrow is not than what it is. It is not straightforwardly a generic category, nor does it have a fixed canon. Books slip in and out of its defining field over the period from the 1920s to the mid-1950s when the concept held most sway. Nonetheless, I would argue that the books so defined had more in common than highbrow dismissal: that in these decades middlebrow fiction, and in particular the middlebrow fiction largely read and written by women, acquired something like a generic identity – a characteristic voice, a set of ideological assumptions, a particular attitude to itself and its readers. The middlebrow novel, I suggest, is identifiable as such not simply because of external factors such as its adoption by a book club or its popularity in the lending libraries but because of particular formal qualities and ideological concerns and, most notably, by a particular engagement with its readers.

The term middlebrow is first recorded in 1924, fracturing the simple binary opposition between highbrow and lowbrow, terms which had been in operation since shortly before the First World War, and on the existence of which the middlebrow depends for its meaning. The new term quickly acquired currency. The fact that the period of the 1920s was apparently in need of the concepts of 'the person of average or moderate cultural attainments' and the cultural phenomenon 'claiming to be or regarded as only moderately intellectual' (*OED*) tells us a great deal about the cultural politics of the day. This was a period in which cultural battle-lines were being drawn. On the one hand, we have the increasing might of publishing and entertainment industries serving a mass public; on the other, we have the proponents of various avant garde movements, including Modernism, who saw the rise of commodified literature as threatening the high seriousness of art, and central to whose aesthetic was a notion of literature as *difficult*, resistant to easy understanding. The contempt that the highbrow felt for the lowbrow was complicated by politics. For many of these writers and artists, a literary elitism went hand in hand with an at least notional commitment to mass politics, an ideological fellowship with the interests of the working classes. What was needed was a way of more sharply directing their contempt: of distinguishing different forms of commercial literature, of dividing the reading of the shop-girl from that of the complacent bourgeois housewife. It is this need that the concept of the middlebrow fulfilled. The class dimension that inflected all contemporary understanding of the 'battle of the brows' is most clearly revealed in Virginia Woolf's famous essay 'Middlebrow', written in 1932 in the form of an unsent letter to the *New Statesman* and finally published in 1942 in the posthumous collection *The Death of the Moth and Other Essays*. Here, using a curious rural metaphor that evokes a lost world of secure social hierarchies and cap-doffing, Woolf defines the highbrow as 'the man or woman of thoroughbred intelligence who rides his mind at a gallop across country in pursuit of an idea' and the lowbrow (whom she professes, along with all true highbrows, to much admire) as 'a man or a woman of thoroughbred vitality who rides his body in pursuit of a living at a gallop across life'.

The middlebrow, on the other hand, is 'betwixt and between': 'the middlebrow is the man, or woman, of middlebred intelligence who ambles and saunters now on this side of the hedge, now on that, in pursuit of no single object, neither art itself nor life itself, but both mixed indistinguishably, and rather nastily, with money, fame, power, or prestige'.[2] It is here that Woolf's tongue-in-cheek self-mocking tone breaks down. There is real contempt and antipathy contained in her portrait of the middlebrow, which may account for the fact that she never sent the letter. We find this contempt underlying virtually all contemporary accounts of the middlebrow. It is notable, for instance, in George Orwell's account of Ethel M. Dell, whose books are read, he remarks 'solely by women, but by women of all kinds and ages and not, as one might expect, merely by wistful spinsters and the fat wives of tobacconists'.[3] Such contempt is compounded partly, I would suggest, of class snobbery, with the middlebrow seen predominantly as the readership of the lower-middle class, and partly of a sense – probably correct – that highbrow culture was under threat from the middlebrow. Because the middlebrow is not essentially separate from the highbrow (or, indeed, the lowbrow). It is a literature of imitation, of incorporation. To quote my own earlier definition:

> The middlebrow novel is one that straddles the divide between the trashy romance or thriller on the one hand, and the philosophically or formally challenging novel on the other: offering narrative excitement without guilt and intellectual stimulation without undue effort. It is an essentially parasitical form, dependent on the existence of both a high and a low brow for its identity, reworking their structures and aping their insights, while at the same time fastidiously holding its skirts away from lowbrow contamination and gleefully mocking highbrow intellectual pretensions.[4]

Alternatively, we might suggest that the middlebrow is the place where highbrow and lowbrow distinctions break down: that it is dangerous precisely because it threatens the security of those literary definitions. Defined largely by the fear and contempt of its detractors, the concept of the middlebrow does, nonetheless, designate a significant body of the commercial literature of the interwar years. And while it might be more comfortable to consider this literature under some more anodyne, less snobbish rubric, the notion is worth retaining, I would argue, for the significant insights it affords us into the ideological and cultural status of these works and the relationship they establish with their readers.

The middlebrow as a concept is one that is entirely dependent on readers, and on the development of a particular sort of reading culture in the interwar years. A number of institutions emerged in those years which created both a new sort of readership for fiction and a culture of snobbery directed at those readers. One of the most important was the private lending library, which underwent a massive programme of expansion during and after the First World War. The Boots Booklovers' libraries, in particular, with their comfortable country-house-style furnishings and innovative lending system, soon acquired an iconic status as suppliers of books to the middle classes. Boots' librarians were trained to treat books as commodities and to offer their subscribers more of what they liked. The library appears repeatedly in the fiction of the period as a site of intense social judgements: E.M. Delafield's Provincial Lady, meeting the overbearing Lady Kingsley-Browne in the local circulating library, finds herself pressured to take *Georgian Poems* in place of one of the many new novels that she wanted to read. George Orwell's *Keep the Aspidistra Flying* (1936) opens with a lengthy scene in a lending library in which Gordon Comstock, the librarian-cum-bookshop-assistant, ably negotiates the complex intersections of class and literary taste among his customers, playing up to their snobberies while roundly despising them all.[5] The librarian is repeatedly characterized as a dragon guarding the cave of readerly pleasure, withholding as much as supplying the books that are her stock in trade. In Elizabeth Bowen's *The Death of the Heart* (1938) the glamorous Daphne works as a library assistant at Smoot's, where she is understood to bring a certain refinement to the establishment, in part because of her refusal to read: 'It was clear that Daphne added, and knew she added, cachet to Smoot's by her air of barely condoning the traffic that went on there. Her palpable wish never to read placed at a disadvantage those who had become dependent on this habit.'[6] Daphne and her fellow librarians enjoy their power, bullying hapless subscribers into taking books that they feel they ought to read instead of the bright new novels they long for. 'Library books' becomes a recognizable category in this period, a synonym for pleasurable, absorbing books, invariably written by women: books that you consume rather than buy to display; books that you might want to hide from those you wish to impress, a literature of self-indulgence rather than improvement.

The other key institution in establishing a middlebrow reading culture was the book club, large commercial institutions which offered their own editions of newly published books at hugely reduced rates. The most influential was the American Book-of-the-Month Club, which was founded in 1926 and boasted in its literature of the many literary reputations it had been responsible for establishing.[7] In Britain it was imitated by the Book Society (started 1927), the Book Guild (1930), and many others which followed the same model. A selection committee of reviewers, journalists, and novelists would make a monthly choice of books to be offered to readers. The first selection would be dispatched to all members, who then had the option of retaining it or exchanging it for another on the list. The draw for the many who joined book clubs was primarily the price: the Book Club, run by Foyle's bookshop, announced that books previously sold for up to 12/6 would be available through their club at 2/6. But there was also a distinct element of upward mobility being sold along with the books: eager to promote a culture of book-buying in a section of the population who had not previously been able to afford it, the book clubs sought to transform ephemeral best-sellers into 'modern classics', decking them out in 'dignified' uniform bindings and employing in their advertising copy language carefully designed to evoke a life of cultured and leisured gentility.

The processes of commodification and the expectations of its readers worked to create a very particular sort of literature. While there is a case to be made that the middlebrow label, at its broadest and most perniciously hostile, simply encompassed virtually all non-formulaic realist fiction, and particularly all such fiction written by women, I would argue that there are a number of more specific features that led to the adoption of a book by the commercial institutions that established middlebrow taste. Moreover, a combination of commercial and readerly expectations led to the creation of a body of writing that demonstrates a considerable number of shared preoccupations and ideological concerns. While there was, of course, a masculine middlebrow (P.G. Wodehouse, John Buchan, Arnold Bennett, for example), the contemporary consensus saw the middlebrow as a particularly feminine sphere. Q.D. Leavis argued in her influential *Fiction and the Reading Public* (1932) that women were responsible for determining what she saw as the low standard of public literary taste because they 'rather than men change the [library] books (that is, determine the family reading)' and George Orwell observed that 'roughly speaking, what one might call the average novel – the ordinary good-bad, Galsworthy-and-water stuff which is the norm of the English novel – seems to exist only for women. Men read the stuff it is possible to respect, or detective stories.'[8]

My preferred formulation of the concept of a feminine middlebrow would include not just novels written by women, but those largely read by them: the works of E.F. Benson, Warwick Deeping, and Gilbert Frankau among others, but for the purposes of this discussion I shall focus on works written by and for women which were generally considered to be middlebrow: the authors considered include Stella Gibbons, Rachel Ferguson, E.M. Delafield, Margery Allingham, Nancy Mitford, Rosamond Lehmann, and E. Arnot Robertson. I suggest that the feminine middlebrow novel had a significant role in the negotiation of new class and gender identities in the interwar period, and also that its oscillations between the challenges of the highbrow and the pleasures of the lowbrow led it to develop both a distinctive voice and a very particular relationship to its readers.

Women's middlebrow fiction demonstrates an intense preoccupation with readers and reading. Repeatedly within its pages we find discussions of book collections and favourite books, of lending libraries and book shops, of old favourites and new best-sellers, of the differences in practices, status, and incomes between male and female writers, of reading for pleasure and reading for instruction, all alongside determined re-castings of the terms of the battle of the brows. Most typically, middlebrow fiction combines a gentle mocking of the effortful intellectual attitudes of the highbrow. E.M. Delafield's Provincial Lady series derived much of its humour from its protagonist's exposure of both social and intellectual snobs. Among the latter is her neighbour Miss Pankerton who 'wears pince-nez and is said to have been at Oxford' and introduces herself as 'the most unconventional person in the whole world' (pp. 98–9). Along with her effete intellectual friend Jahsper she pursues the Provincial Lady with learned conversation through social gatherings and chance encounters, and is met with finally at the fancy dress party with which the first novel ends:

> I am greeted by an unpleasant looking Hamlet, who suddenly turns out to be Miss Pankerton. Why, she asks accusingly, am I not in fancy dress? It would do me all the good in the world to give myself over to the Carnival spirit. It is what I *need*. I make enquiry for Jahsper – should never be surprised to hear that he had come as Ophelia – but Miss

P. replies that Jahsper is in Bloomsbury again. Bloomsbury can do nothing without Jahsper. I say, No, I suppose not, in order to avoid hearing any more about either Jahsper or Bloomsbury.

(p. 120)

Bloomsbury and its arch exemplar Virginia Woolf function as key talismans of the highbrow in the middlebrow novel. In Rose Macaulay's 1926 *Crewe Train*, a novel which contains a number of thinly disguised parodies of the actual Bloomsbury set, the 'artistic, literary, political, musical and cultured' Gresham family are described as 'all right in Chelsea, though, except Humphrey, they were not quite fit for Bloomsbury'.[9] The note the Provincial Lady strikes – one of grudging tolerance, as of a mother to a misbehaving adolescent – is typical of the way in which the feminine middlebrow treats its highbrow characters. Their self-importance and eccentricities are indulged, fully-comprehended, and forgiven. There is never a whiff of the abjection or anxiety that guardians of the highbrow then and since would expect: rather, the middlebrow incorporates the highbrow by patronizing it and by demonstrating an easy familiarity with its key texts and debates.

In the 1933 sequel, *The Provincial Lady Goes Further*, the protagonist has become a successful writer (clearly of the middlebrow variety), and frequents smart literary gatherings at which she is amused by the games of intellectual one-upmanship and the many lively discussions about books none of the participants have read. Again, she is continually sought out and bored by intellectuals: 'London regained, though not before I have endured further spate of conversation from several lights of literature.'[10] The anxiety of the highbrows to shock is particularly noted: participants at a literary conference in Brussels exclaim over *Lady Chatterley's Lover*, advising the Provincial Lady to take a detour via Paris to secure a copy (p. 141), and a Bloomsbury literary party buzzes with the news that one of the guests has written a book that will 'undoubtedly be seized before publication and burnt' (p. 179). Stella Gibbons's *Cold Comfort Farm* makes similar mileage out of the pretensions of intellectuals in the form of 'Mr Mybug', the repellent self-proclaimed genius who pursues Flora through the Sussex countryside declaiming about the phallic beauty of the chestnut blooms. Like Delafield's Jahsper, he is a member of the Bloomsbury set, whom Flora caricatures by interpreting their determinedly outlandish way of life as actually highly conventional:

> And was it quite fair to fling Elfine, all unprepared, to those Bloomsbury-cum-Charlotte-Street lions which exchanged husbands and wives every weekend in the most broad-minded fashion? They always made Flora think of the description of the wild boars painted on the vases in Dickens's story – 'each wild boar having his leg elevated in the air at a painful angle to show his perfect freedom and gaiety'. And it must be so discouraging for them to find each new love exactly resembling the old

one: just like trying balloon after balloon at a bad party and finding that they all had holes in and would not blow up properly.[11]

As the epitome of middlebrow sensibilities, Flora's disdain is carefully balanced: she expresses no shock at the antics of the free-living highbrows, rather a weary contempt, produced partly by over-familiarity. This is a world that holds no mysteries or glamour for her: she moves in social circles in which these 'types' are encountered only too frequently. The eternal literary standards of Dickens and (elsewhere) Jane Austen are her counters against the ephemeral intellectual fripperies and fashions of the highbrow.

Characters in women's middlebrow fiction are frequently judged by their attitudes to reading, with the ideal middlebrow readers distinguished from those who read wrongly or fail to understand their reading. The undiscriminating readers reviled by Orwell for their treatment of books as a commodity available by the yard is treated ironically in a number of novels.[12] In E. Arnot Robertson's *Cullum* (1928) the youthful female narrator is trapped by a boring woman at a dinner party:

> Mrs Cole settled herself by me on the sofa and, unaware of my hatred of being touched, pawed my arm while she chatted with her restful vigour, which allowed no time for replies; I had been thankful to it before. She had latterly finished a book which she insisted that I must read; it was marvellously well written, quite too fascinating, she said, and though at the moment she could not remember the title she knew it was by the man who wrote *The Crock* – (or it might have been *The Arrow*) – *of Gold*. Anyway, it was by whichever of these authors had also written *Fortitude*.[13]

In a novel in which the passionate (if misguided) central relationship between the narrator and the young novelist, Cullum, is founded on a mutual love of and respect for books, Mrs Cole's vague and uninformed attitude to reading marks her out as worthy of contempt. It is by delineating such empty attitudes to reading that the feminine middlebrow novel gestures towards the sort of discriminating yet emotionally responsive reader it desires. The ideal reader as imagined by these novels is one for whom literature is an intelligent passion: she is a re-reader, devoted to the literature of the past (the Brontës, Charlotte M. Yonge, Jane Austen) and of her childhood (with childhood reading denoting an abandoned immersion in textual pleasure that is more difficult to recreate in adulthood). She understands the intimate connection between bodily and readerly pleasures: like *Cold Comfort Farm*'s Flora, who 'liked Victorian novels. They were the only kind of novel you could read while eating an apple' (p. 53).

The readers within middlebrow fiction read in bed (by guttering candlelight in the case of the bohemianly-impoverished sisters in Dodie Smith's

I Capture the Castle), by the fireside (where two virginally-clean library books await Mrs Miniver at the start of Jan Struther's eponymous classic of bourgeois complacency), and while eating.[14] They read compulsively, surrendering to the emotional power of the text with abandonment, weeping over old favourites. At their most self-indulgent they allow books to replace real life, like Deirdre Carne in Rachel Ferguson's curious 1931 novel *The Brontës Went to Woolworths*, who has been unable to marry because she was in love with Sherlock Holmes for whose 'personality and brain [she] had a force of feeling which, for the time, converted living men to shadows'.[15] Above all else, the ideal middlebrow reader (both as depicted in the texts and as demanded by them) is capable of a dual approach to reading: she must be able to read both actively and passively. Time and again middlebrow novels require of their reader a sort of double vision: they demand to be taken seriously at precisely the same time as they wryly mock themselves and the world they depict. E.F. Benson's Mapp and Lucia novels are one example, with their exuberantly surrealistic take on the minutiae of domestic experience (where exclusion from dinner parties leads to revenge schemes as elaborate as those of Jacobean drama, and the theft of a recipe leads to the protagonists being washed out to sea on an upturned kitchen table): they work by treating with profound affection the thing they are so clearly revealing as ridiculous. Or we might think of the many middlebrow romances that flip from emotional wallowing to cynical anti-romance. Far from being formulaic, the middlebrow novel typically displays fairly sophisticated narrative structures, and demands of its readers the ability to slip easily from knowing to surrendered reading practices – from serious focus to relaxed pleasure and back again. It is as a result of this complex positioning of its readers that the feminine middlebrow novel is able to pick its way through a number of ideological minefields, the most potentially explosive of which is class.

The interwar years, the 1930s in particular, were a time of heightened class tensions and of a class-consciousness so intense that it tipped over into neurosis. As well as the tensions between workers and the governing class that reached their apotheosis with the General Strike of 1926, the period was marked by powerful antagonisms within the middle class. The decline of the wealth and political power of the aristocracy, the reduction of incomes of the gentry and professional middle class and the rise in numbers and influence of a new technocratic lower-middle to middle-middle class all contributed to an atmosphere of toxic resentment, hostility, and snobbery. As the influence and standard of living of the upper-middle class declined, they defended their class values and status with ever more intensity, and with ever sparser cultural capital. Where in an earlier age class was determined by factors such as job, income, education, and family, in the new postwar world it seemed dependent on murkier, harder-to-define categories of taste, leisure, and social and domestic habits (by the time another war had been fought it would depend, as Nancy Mitford's *Noblesse Oblige* (1956) concedes, on nothing more than tricks of speech).[16]

The feminine middlebrow novel responds to these intra-middle-class tensions in a very distinctive way. Often intensely snobbish, it also cracks the codes of its own snobberies. It functions, in other words, as a curious form of 'conduct literature', offering its readers access to the jealously guarded rituals and values that mark the borders of upper-middle-class identity, allowing them to 'pass' if they read correctly and apply the results of their reading. Rachel Ferguson's *The Brontës Went to Woolworths* is a good example. The three Carne sisters at its centre spend much of their time involved in elaborate shared fantasies. As the eldest sister Deirdre, a journalist, explains, 'meals in our family are usually eaten amid a cloud of witnesses, unless there are visitors' (p. 28). It takes the reader a while to establish that most of the characters who people their conversation are imaginary, though some are based on real-life public figures. The brow-beaten governesses employed to teach the youngest sister never do fully grasp the intricacies of the game, and much of the operation of the text seems to be to engage the reader on the side of the sophisticated, self-consciously bohemian upper-middle-class Carnes in their favourite game of wrong-footing these anxiously respectable figures. The intricacies of class play a key part in both their fantasies and their attacks on the governesses. They imagine Mildred Toddington, the wife of a high court judge once glimpsed and then incorporated into their fantasy world, as 'not as top-shelfish as she thinks she is' (pp. 40–1) and enjoy conjuring up situations in which her solecisms grate on her husband's sensibilities. They also spend a lot of time mocking the speech patterns of Freddie Pipson, a music hall comedian of their acquaintance:

> The latest Carne joke, it appeared, was to say 'Pleased to meet you', when they passed each other on the stair, and to do what they described as 'pipsoning' at meal-times. Deirdre would say, 'If you'll pardon me, Mrs Carne, you're commencing to cut the beef wrongly, if you know what I mean,' and Katrine would reply, 'If I'm not robbing *you*, may I ask you to pass the cruet?' then both together would enquire, 'Is your tea as you like it?' And even Shiel would call out, 'Don't spill it, Miss Carne; if I may pass the remark, whatever are you doing?'
>
> (p. 112)

Miss Martin, the governess, objects to the unkindness of the pastiche but is sternly countered by Deirdre who insists that the game is a mark of their affection for the comedian. It is also, however, a warning to any reader not in the know of precisely the phrases and overly-careful conversational tone to avoid if they wish to avoid dismissal as 'not our sort'. Deirdre's pretended class tolerance comes back to bite her when Katrine, the second sister, working in a revue chorus alongside Freddie, falls in love with him. Deirdre dismisses with a virtually eugenic passion the possibility of her marrying Freddie, despite conceding his many virtues and attractions: 'Oh, what a husband and father and lover were there' (p. 221). Notably, the main objection to Freddie is not his own upper-working-class status, but his lower-middle-class relatives: 'I've seen some of his relations, you know, in the dressing-room. One of them is called Sidney, and looks it, and he says "Naow" and "Haow" and lives at Herne Hill' (p. 219). Just as the highbrow tolerates the lowbrow and dismisses the middlebrow, so the upper-middle-class Carnes are far more uncomfortable with the aspirant gentility of Sidney than with the cheerful 'lowness' (he is a 'low' comedian as well as 'lower class') of Freddie.

E. Arnot Robertson is another of the many middlebrow novelists who demonstrate a painfully acute response to class. In her 1928 *Cullum*, the protagonist, Esther, wanting to train as a journalist, gets a job at the Cameron Press, a periodical publisher producing lowbrow romance magazines. As well as being surprised to find herself incapable of writing the romance stories she finds so facile and meretricious, she is forced to reconsider the simple binary model of class (in or out, our sort or not our sort) she has been offered by her upper-middle-class upbringing:

> Before going there I had always thought, when the subject entered my mind at all, that there were only two sets of people; those who conformed to a certain standard, and those who did not. Whether they barely missed it or had no pretensions of attaining it made no difference, but I found in the Cameron Press innumerable nice distinctions, especially among the women, who discussed endlessly whether So-and-so was a lady, a real lady, quite a lady, not quite a lady or – final and incomprehensible damnation – 'No-class'.
>
> (p. 163)

From her *haute bourgeois* perspective, her initial response is to find this jockeying for what she sees as entirely illusory status 'only pitiable and amusing', but she is forced to reconsider, when 'by degrees it was borne upon me that they did their work far more efficiently than I did mine; their brains were more alert, and they succeeded where I failed' (p. 163). It is a point that the novel insists must be understood in socio-political terms rather than simply in the light of a complication of snobberies: when Esther fails to write a story for the third time it is handed over to another girl who completes it well and effortlessly: 'ill-educated and a year younger than I was, she was the first person to make me realise the mental superiority of the rising lower middle class over the falling upper middle class' (p. 164). Such acknowledgements occur frequently in women's middlebrow novels, but the shift in power is rarely treated with equanimity. However broadly sympathetic the text is to its lower-middle-class characters, their depiction is never free of an almost visceral level of snobbery.

Elizabeth Bowen's *The Death of the Heart* (1938) contains one of the most lyrical accounts of the pleasures of the newly leisured new middle class in its description of the Heccomb house in Seale-on-Sea where the teenage protagonist Portia is sent to stay when her brother and his stuffy *haute bourgeois* wife go abroad. The first account of the house overflows with class signifiers: there is a locked 'show' bookcase, a modern brown-glazed tile fireplace, and bought cakes for tea. Most damningly of all, 'she learned later that Daphne called this the lounge' (p. 134). The text nudges the sophisticated reader with its hints about the lower-middle-class status of the household, but the room seen through Portia's class-innocent eyes is above all else comfortable, with 'a scarlet portable gramophone, a tray with a painting outfit, a half-painted lampshade, a mountain of magazines'. With its crumpled arm chairs and settee, its blazing fire, its carpet ready to be rolled up for impromptu dances, this is a room designed for enjoyment, a stark contrast to the chilly grandeur of her brother's house on the edge of Regent's Park. Daphne is an active apologist for her class, and the text treats her with some sympathy until the moment that she turns on Portia, at which point she becomes a sort of monster of bad taste:

> Daphne's reaction time was not quick: it took her about two seconds to go rigid all over on the chaise longue. Then her eyes ran together, her features thickened ... 'Now look here', she said ... 'there's no reason for you to be vulgar ... I had no idea you were so *common*, and nor had Mumsie the least idea, I'm sure, or she wouldn't have ever obliged your sister-in-law by having you to stop here, convenient or not.'
> (pp. 203–4)

It is a veritable explosion of the sort of language the upper-middle class considered irredeemably coarse, words such as 'vulgar' and 'common' being paradoxically the acme of vulgarity. By actively caricaturing Daphne's speech the novel removes all sympathy from her. The reader of this and similar novels is asked to recognize and even approve the diminution of the power of the upper-middle class while at the same time being taught to adhere to its cultural and linguistic norms. The feminine middlebrow novel thereby performs a curious transposition: simultaneously breaking the codes that protect a rarefied *haute bourgeois* identity and ensuring the hegemonic authority of the cultural values of the upper-middle class, if not of its original members.

If the feminine middlebrow engages with and renegotiates the elaborate class distinctions of the interwar years, it also responds with striking immediacy to the altered gender roles and changing sexual mores of the period. As has frequently been noted, the disillusionment following the Great War effected a fundamental shift in the coding of gender in the ensuing years, with men increasingly being represented as brittle and effete and women as practical and competent. These new social stereotypes people most forms of contemporary fiction: Wodehouse's effete and dapper Bertie Wooster and the hearty golf-playing girls from whom he flees; the self-deprecating detective heroes of Margery Allingham and Dorothy Sayers; the cynical bright young things satirized by Evelyn Waugh and Aldous Huxley: these are just the most obvious manifestations of a redefining of gender roles that transformed the novel of the period. For Virginia Woolf, the shifts in gender identity had a fundamental impact on the notion of romance: 'When the guns fired in August 1914', she asked, 'did the faces of men and women show so plain in each others eyes that romance was killed?'[17] It is a sensibility shared by the feminine middlebrow. A new convention is evolved in which romance is figured primarily by reticence: evasion rather than declaration becomes the new textual currency of love. An example is Margery Allingham's 1933 *Sweet Danger*, in which series detective Albert Campion is provided with a long-term love interest. As in Allingham's other novels an exuberant and convoluted plot covers a highly acute analysis of contemporary mores. Campion's frivolous pose and evasive manner is threatened for the first time in *Sweet Danger* by his meeting with the adolescent Amanda Fitton; red-haired, bravely independent, and passionately interested in radios and engines (she becomes an aeronautical engineer in the 1938 *The Fashion in Shrouds*, so borrowing a touch of the glamour of female flyers Amy Johnson and Amelia Erhardt). Amanda and Campion's relationship is figured in almost entirely comradely terms throughout the novel, yet the reader is expected to pick up the strong emotional subtext. This is conveyed by what remains unspoken: reticence becomes the key guarantor of emotional and especially romantic authenticity. So the pair communicate for much of the novel in a bantering short-hand, and when Amanda parts from Campion at a moment of high drama and strong danger the lack of romance signifies the opposite:

> She rose cautiously to her feet, slipped the gun in her jacket pocket, and turned towards the house. Then, looking back suddenly, she stopped and kissed him unromantically on the nose.
> 'That's by way of *pourboire*, in case we don't meet again', she said lightly.
>
> (p. 207)

Amanda here adopts the casual heroism of the cinematic hero, striding off to do battle while revealing his deep emotional attachment in the very gestures he employs to make light of it.

Declarative romantic passion is treated with deep suspicion by many middlebrow texts: it is sometimes sought after by youthful protagonists, but it is invariably found to be illusory. It is this fantastical chimera that *Dusty Answer*'s lonely only-child Judith pursues in the glamorous next-door family in Rosamond Lehmann's 1927 novel, particularly in the elusive Roddy, for whom she constructs an elaborate (and false) personality, reading his evasiveness as mystery and his self-centredness as vulnerability. The novel functions on one level as a *Bildungsroman* in which the idealistic Judith must learn the inadequacies of her romantic illusions. Her one long-awaited night of passion with Roddy she assumes to be the start of a relationship that will naturally lead to marriage, but he sees it as a trivial dalliance. In a reversal of conventional sexual morality he is so shocked when she sends him a love letter the next day that he cannot bring himself to speak to her for years. Judith's mistake is not, as with the fallen literary heroines of previous generations, to give herself to a man, but to try to talk about it afterwards. Emotional outpourings, rather than sexual experience, are the new taboo. After a succession of failed romances with both men and women, Judith ultimately, painfully, learns that romantic love is an illusion and that she is finally alone. In the novel's bleakly satisfying conclusion she accepts that 'the futile obsession of dependence on other people' leads only to pain, and that 'this was to be happy – this emptiness, this light uncoloured state, this no-thought and no-feeling'.[18] With the conventional language of romance now firmly belonging to the lowbrow love stories of magazines, the middlebrow reinvents the form, assumptions, and language of the genre, giving with one hand what it takes away with the other. For every moment of transcendent emotion there is an inevitable fall, as with the ending of Nancy Mitford's *The Pursuit of Love* (1945), which offers us high, tragic romance (the death of Linda in childbirth; the death of her true love in war), only to simultaneously snatch it away by giving the last word to the cynical, much-married Bolter:

> 'But I think she would have been happy with Fabrice,' I said. 'He was the great love of her life, you know.'
> 'Oh, dulling,' said my mother, sadly. 'One always thinks that. Every, every time.'[19]

Condemned by its detractors as undemanding and complacent, the feminine middlebrow in fact rewrites the conventions of the various seemingly formulaic genres in which it deals. The domestic novel is inflected with doubts, with marriage seen as the antithesis rather than the apotheosis of romantic love, and the domestic sphere as a cage rather than a haven. The family saga (great staple of the lending libraries) is remade with a deep sense of the family as an eccentric, profoundly anti-social organization, a source of intense neuroses for its female members.[20] Determinedly modern, though anxious about censorship and prosecution, these novels carefully pick their way through the minefield of sexual description, discussing childbirth, homosexuality, abortion, and intercourse, evolving a respectable discourse for the representation of the previously unmentionable. Above all else, in both its tone and content the feminine middlebrow aims for *sophistication*. In its flirtations with bohemianism (the imagined lives of the artistic outsider remade in the selection of daring colours for the home or the serving of unconventional, garlic-laden dishes), in its simultaneous annexing of and assumed contempt for the highbrow, in the knowing codedness of its sexual references, in its eschewal of conventional romance, its adoption of the language of Freudianism, and its playfully self-defeating snobberies, the feminine middlebrow demonstrates a sophisticated slipperiness, a refusal to be pinned down. Dealing mostly in conventionally 'feminine' subjects such as the home, romance, marriage, motherhood, the family, it remakes the everyday into something strange, slightly off-centre. Closely attuned to the shifting demands of its readers, it is subtle and flexible, renegotiating changing social structures and ideologies, balancing the conservative and the radical. Demanding always a dual reading lens, both serious and light-hearted, it gets to have it both – or rather all – ways.

Notes

1. Nicola Beauman's *A Very Great Profession: The Woman's Novel 1914–39* (London: Virago, 1983) and Alison Light's *Forever England: Femininity, Literature and Conservatism between the Wars* (London: Routledge, 1991) were pioneering studies that approach the concept of the middlebrow with some hesitation. My own *The Feminine Middlebrow Novel 1920s to 1950s: Class, Domesticity and Bohemianism* (Oxford: Oxford University Press, 2001) was the first critical work to foreground the middlebrow in the British context. Recent books include Faye Hammill, *Women, Celebrity, and Literary Culture between the Wars* (Austin: University of Texas Press, 2008); Mary Grover, *The Ordeal of Warwick Deeping: Middlebrow Authorship and Cultural Embarrassment* (Madison, NJ: Fairleigh Dickinson University Press, 2009); and Ina Habermann, *Myth, Memory and the Middlebrow: Priestley, du Maurier and the Symbolic Form of Englishness* (Basingstoke: Palgrave Macmillan, 2010).
2. Virginia Woolf, 'Middlebrow', in *The Death of the Moth and Other Essays* (London: Hogarth Press, 1942), p. 115.
3. George Orwell, 'Bookshop Memories', in *The Collected Essays, Journalism and Letters*, ed. Sonia Orwell and Ian Angus, 4 vols (London: Secker and Warburg, 1968), I, p. 244.
4. Humble, *The Feminine Middlebrow Novel*, pp. 11–12.
5. E.M. Delafield, *Diary of a Provincial Lady* (1930), collected with other novels in the series as *The Diary of a Provincial Lady* (London: Virago, 1991), p. 64.
6. Elizabeth Bowen, *The Death of the Heart* (Harmondsworth: Penguin, 1962), p. 157.
7. See Janice Radway's account of the Book-of-the-Month Club in interwar America: *A Feeling for Books: The Book-of-the-Month Club, Literary Taste and Middle-Class Desire* (Chapel Hill: University of North Carolina Press, 1997).
8. Q.D. Leavis, *Fiction and the Reading Public* (London: Chatto and Windus, 1978), p. 7; Orwell, 'Bookshop Memories', p. 244. For further discussion of the masculine middlebrow, see Kate Macdonald, ed., *The Masculine Middlebrow, 1880–1950: What Mr Miniver Read* (Basingstoke: Palgrave Macmillan, 2011).
9. Rose Macaulay, *Crewe Train* (London: E. Collins Sons and Co. Ltd, 1926), p. 20.

10. E.M. Delafield, *The Provincial Lady Goes Further*, reprinted in *The Diary of a Provincial Lady*, p. 143.
11. Stella Gibbons, *Cold Comfort Farm* (Harmondsworth: Penguin, 1983), p. 112.
12. Orwell, 'Bookshop Memories', p. 245.
13. E. Arnot Robertson, *Cullum* (London: Virago, 1990), p. 22.
14. Dodie Smith, *I Capture the Castle* (London: The Reprint Society, 1950), p. 24; Jan Struther, *Mrs Miniver* (London: Virago, 1989), pp. 2–3.
15. Rachel Ferguson, *The Brontës Went to Woolworths* (London: Virago, 1988), p. 12.
16. Nancy Mitford, 'The English Aristocracy', in *Noblesse Oblige*, ed. Nancy Mitford (Harmondsworth: Penguin, 1968).
17. Virginia Woolf, *A Room of One's Own* (Oxford: World's Classics, 1992), pp. 18–19.
18. Rosamond Lehmann, *Dusty Answer* (Harmondsworth: Penguin, 1986), p. 303.
19. Nancy Mitford, *The Pursuit of Love* (Harmondsworth: Penguin, 1970), p. 192. I suggest elsewhere that doubleness of vision in the interwar women's middlebrow novel functions as a kind of camp: Nicola Humble, 'The Queer Pleasures of Reading: Camp and the Middlebrow', in *Middlebrow Matters: Cultural Hierarchy and Literary Value*, ed. Mary Grover and Erica Brown (Basingstoke: Palgrave Macmillan, 2011).
20. Examples of the former include Rose Macaulay's *Crewe Train* (1926), E.M. Delafield's *The Way Things Are* (1927), Margaret Kennedy's *Together and Apart* (1936), and Elizabeth Taylor's *At Mrs Lippincote's* (1945). The family is re-made as eccentric in Margaret Kennedy's *The Constant Nymph* (1924), Stella Gibbons's *Cold Comfort Farm* (1932), E. Arnot Robertson's *Ordinary Families* (1933), Ngaio Marsh's *A Surfeit of Lampreys* (1941), Nancy Mitford's *The Pursuit of Love* (1945), Josephine Tey's *Brat Farrar* (1947), and in Ivy Compton Burnett's entire oeuvre.

6
Women and Comedy
Sophie Blanch

Until very recently, the central preoccupation of feminist critics and researchers working on twentieth-century literary culture has been to ensure that women's contributions to Modernism are taken 'seriously'. This has meant that much of the pleasure and playfulness associated with this writing as well as the significant social, sexual, and psychological insights that emerge from the relationship between women and comedy in this period have been strategically overlooked. There is, however, an alternative history beginning to emerge which reveals the comic potential of a generation of women writers who deploy laughter, jokes, satire, comedy, and humour to significant effect. This chapter addresses the varied and, indeed, contradictory ways in which British women writers have made use of comedy and humour. Beyond the parameters of British Modernism the tradition of American women's literary humour has been mapped with surprising coverage and consistency. First published in 1885, Kate Sanborn's critical anthology, *The Wit of Women* responded to an ongoing debate in *The Critic* relating to the contested existence of a female sense of humour. The anthology roams widely across literary form and comic style, including excerpts from children's stories, magazine articles, poetry, and illustrated satires. Importantly, Sanborn's book reveals the variety of late nineteenth-century women's humour, which included political and social subject matter as well as domestic and family life.

The first significant overview of women's comic writing of the early twentieth century appears in 1934 with the publication of Martha Bensley Bruere and Mary Ritter Beard's *Laughing Their Way: Women's Humor in America*. Bruere and Beard shift the emphasis from the earlier 'corrective for ill-conceived notions of female humorlessness', seeking instead to 'correct America's "partial view" – i.e., masculine view – of its traditions of humor'.[1] Popular writers and journalists such as Anita Loos, Carolyn Wells, Josephine Daskam, Dorothy Parker, and Helen Rowland are featured in order to counter a seemingly all-male 'Golden Age' of American humour. In the decades since these two influential anthologies many more critical assessments of women's literary humour as well as articles, book chapters and special journal issues have been published in the United States.[2]

While several of these influential studies, Barecca and Little in particular, offer re-readings of Virginia Woolf, Muriel Spark, and Elizabeth Bowen, among others, there has been no similar project to assert the significance of a female voice in twentieth-century British literary humour with the exception of Margaret Stetz's recent *British Women's Comic Fiction 1890–1990: Not Drowning, But Laughing* (2001). The historical sweep of Stetz's assessment places most emphasis on the late nineteenth and late twentieth centuries, finding little to laugh at, or about, in the decades in between.[3]

British women's relationship to comedy has been historicized, albeit obliquely, through the prominent role of propagandist humour in the early years of the British suffrage movement. Until the introduction of direct action, campaigners for the vote had courted attention largely through appeals to the comic sensibility of their supporters and, notably, the public's desire to laugh at a staid and inflexible political authority. Through satirical commentary, visual and lyrical lampooning, caricature, punning, gendered word-play, specially commissioned comic plays, and ironic stereotyping of both themselves and their anti-suffrage opponents, large numbers of articulate, well educated women were openly engaged in comic performance and production for political ends. Here again, however, while examples of comic plays, verse, and published articles from *The Vote, Votes for Women*, and other key suffrage periodicals have been catalogued under 'suffrage humour' by the Women's Library in London in recent years, the mapping of humour and comedy as a primary mode of popular campaign rhetoric exists largely in an American context. A useful and under-researched example can be found in the cultural history of Heterodoxy, a feminist collective in Greenwich Village, New York, active from 1912 to the early years of the Second World War.[4]

In the United States a tradition of suffrage humour set the tone for what was to become an alternative Golden Age in American journalism. Writers, columnists, and commentators including Heterodites Alice Duer Miller and Florence Seabury, as well as the now legendary figures of Dorothy Parker, Edna Ferber, and Anita Loos, perfected a brand of social satire, sexual parody, and easy cynicism that came to define these women as world-weary veterans of the 'war between the sexes'; their acerbic, tightly observed musings on marriage and motherhood, suburban domesticity, suffrage, and the sexual double standard became instantly recognizable points of cultural reference and provided the *New Yorker*, the *Washington Post, Harper's*, and the *New Republic* with a high profile female perspective throughout the interwar years.[5] This is important in that it offers a contextual vantage point for tracing the gradual seepage of suffrage humour and comic strategies into the satirical journalism that directly followed it. In a British context the opportunities identified by the suffrage movement for gender-conscious, socially engaged, subversive, and highly literate, if not *literary*, comedy are played out in the work of a series of unlikely women writers throughout the 1920s, 1930s, and 1940s.

Humour, wit, and comic effect are encoded and released in a variety of ways in British women's writing, often regardless of its ostensible status as 'serious', 'highbrow', 'popular', or 'comic'. Despite scholarly insistence on the overarching seriousness of modernist literary production, there is much to suggest that women writers were interested in using comedy, of various sorts, to underscore their own social, sexual, and artistic difference. Some of the most familiar figures and texts to be productively re-read in these terms include Virginia Woolf and her pained mockery of London high society in *Mrs Dalloway* (1925), absurdities of character and class in *To The Lighthouse* (1927), the exuberant deployment of transformational gender-play in *Orlando* (1928), and the theatrical burlesque and historical satire present in *Between the Acts* (1941). In addition, there are Edith Sitwell's experiments in sardonically stylized poetic constructions from *The Wooden Pegasus* (1920) and *Façade* (1922); Rose Macaulay's skilful re-working of the comic double and duplicitous social positioning in her satirical novel, *Potterism* (1920); Rosamond Lehmann's unlaughing protagonist and her sexually and socially coded use of laughter in *Dusty Answer* (1927); E.M. Delafield's mockery of interwar domestic culture and middle-class manners in *Diary of a Provincial Lady* (1930); Stella Gibbons's pitch-perfect pastiche of the rural idyll novel, *Cold Comfort Farm* (1932); and Elizabeth Bowen's subversion of the 'joke' in *The Death of the Heart* (1938).

Even in the context of this indicative selection of writers and texts comedy allows for a kind of literary or cultural judgement about the nature of the writing itself. Where comedy is emphasized as a legitimate subject for critique, there is also a distinction to be made between those texts in which comedy is used transgressively or subversively to question accepted literary and/or gendered norms, and those in which the comedy is socially and politically conservative. The underlying assumption is that the more acutely 'literary' the text (and, therefore, the writer) the more likely it is that the comedy will exist at the level of language, or heightened satirical observation. Similarly, the more 'popular' or immediately accessible the writing appears to be, the more common the reader's expectation that the comedy be attached to character and to the machinations of plot. Elsewhere in this volume Cora Kaplan makes the points that a light comic tone was a signature of Golden Age crime writing and that the banter in Dorothy Sayers's *Strong Poison* (1930) echoes the rhythm of Noel Coward's witty dialogue for the stage. Moreover, the 'jokey repartee and near farcical scenes and plots of much interwar crime makes it patent that mystery writers were chasing the same audience'.[6] This chapter considers the ways in which particular women writers have negotiated their literary identities through their recourse to comedy and humour during a phase of literary history consumed by notions of cultural elitism and accessibility.

Virginia Woolf has been at the centre of important critical attempts to re-think Modernism and a relatively small body of critical work has foregrounded Woolf's humour as a meaningful tone or technique within her writing. Judy Little's *Comedy and the Woman Writer*, and Regina Barreca's *Untamed and Unabashed* and *Last Laughs* explore Woolf's use of comedy as central to her broader sense of a female, if not feminist, aesthetic. As Little explains in her introduction, she is primarily concerned with reading Woolf's brand of comic production as 'subversive, revolutionary, renegade'.[7] It is, she goes on to say, 'comedy which implies, or perhaps even advocates a permanently inverted world, a radical re-ordering of social structures, a real rather than temporary and merely playful redefinition of sexual identity' (p. 2). In less author-specific terms, Regina Barreca has 'de-limited' the pleasure that might be found in humorous or satiric fiction written by women. She argues that while they 'may contain joyous celebration, they do not rely, finally, on the idea of perpetual celebration. [Women] use comedy not as a safety valve but as an inflammatory device, seeking ultimately, not to purge desire and frustration but to transform it into action.'[8] Ultimately for Barreca, 'Comedy is dangerous. Humour is a weapon. Laughter is a refusal and triumph' (p. 30). In 'Slaying the Angel and the Patriarch: the Grinning Woolf' Denise Marshall notes that 'the image of Woolf as smiling and never laughing' is perpetuated throughout the cultural industry that has exploded around her work. She argues that her 'humour, her comic range, her scorn, her sardonic funny satire became invisible because she pinned the patriarchy to the wall'.[9]

This sense of laughing at culturally accepted mythologies and assumptions about gender roles persists throughout Woolf's own fiction as a powerful, and potentially destabilizing, mode of female resistance. Woolf is interested in the fictions men and women construct and ultimately inflict upon each another. She is amused by male fantasies of femininity that seek to return the newly independent 'modern woman' to a less threatening narrative of their own making. In *Mrs Dalloway* (1925), it is the spurned lover, Peter Walsh, who is subjected to Woolf's wry sense of comic timing. Dismissed in the politest terms by Clarissa Dalloway, just as he had been thirty years earlier, Peter imagines himself into a romantic pursuit that works to restore his sense of sexual dominance. Glimpsing an attractive young woman who passes him in the street, Peter follows her, invigorated by the restoration of the role of male hunter to his female prey. It is worth the reader re-tracing the steps of this journey to appreciate the deliberateness of Woolf's mocking set piece:

> Straightening himself and stealthily fingering his pocket-knife he started after her to follow this woman, this excitement, which seemed even with its back turned to shed on him a light which connected

them, which singled him out, as if the uproar of the traffic had whispered through hollowed hands his name, not Peter, but his private name which he called himself in his own thoughts. 'you,' she said, only 'you'.[10]

What is actually in progress, of course, is an increasingly desperate and absurdly amusing attempt to reclaim an idealized sexual scenario in which 'he was a romantic buccaneer, careless of all these damned proprieties', and 'she would answer, perfectly simply, "Oh yes"' (p. 60). It is the female object of Peter's quest who delivers Woolf's perfectly timed punch-line here. Described earlier in the chase as having 'mockery in her eyes' (p. 60), this unknown woman seems to have a sense of the game that is being played, and concludes her part in it with apparent relish:

> Laughing and delightful, she had crossed Oxford Street and Great Portland Street and turned down one of the little streets, and now, and now, she slackened, opened her bag, and with one look in his direction, but not at him, one look that bade farewell, summed up the whole situation and dismissed it triumphantly, for ever, had fitted her key, opened the door, and gone!
>
> (p. 60)

Played out against the backdrop of London's streets, this encounter functions in one way to confound modernist preoccupations with the male *flâneur* and the female streetwalker, or *'passante'*. More dramatic, however, is the way in which the scene overturns masculine control over the 'rules of the game'. As Peter Walsh is forced to admit, even in the context of his own fantasy – his 'exquisite amusement' (p. 61) – the joke was finally on him. He acknowledges that 'it was smashed to atoms – his fun' because it was an invention; he had been 'making oneself up; making her up' (p. 61). And this is why the scene remains 'exquisitely amusing' for Woolf's readers; there is pleasure to be found in Woolf's gleeful manipulation of this most enduring male fantasy.

This is not to suggest, however, that Woolf reserves her attentions solely for representations of masculinity. In *Mrs Dalloway*, Clarissa laughs openly at the spinsterish seriousness of her daughter's tutor Miss Kilman; and Sally Seton is transformed from Clarissa's passionate girlhood love into a ridiculous, preening mother of 'five enormous boys!' (p. 188). In *To the Lighthouse* (1927), Woolf is concerned with questioning the underlying structures that hold gender stereotypes in place, rather than ridiculing individual character traits. Despite functioning for some critics as the magnetic force around which all other characters and narrative elements revolve, the figure of Mrs Ramsay can also be read as Woolf's satire of an obsessive, all-consuming bourgeois motherhood. Reflecting the likely loss of her pivotal role in her children lives, Mrs Ramsay indulges in a gushing maternal reverie:

> Oh, but she never wanted James to grow a day older or Cam either. These two she would have liked to keep for ever, just as they were, demons of wickedness, angels of delight ... Prue, a perfect angel with the others ... Andrew – even her husband admitted that his gift for mathematics was extraordinary ... As for Rose, her mouth was too big, but she had a wonderful gift with her hands ... She did not like it that Jasper should shoot birds; but it was only a stage; they all went through stages.[11]

Mr Ramsay stands as an excessively masculine archetype. Rather than be defined by and through his family, this patrician scholar charts his intellectual successes in absurdly abstract terms:

> It was a splendid mind. For if thought is like the keyboard of a piano, divided into so many notes, or like the alphabet is ranged in twenty-six letters all in order, then his splendid mind had no sort of difficulty in running over those letters one by one, firmly and accurately, until it had reached, say the letter Q. He reached Q. Very few people in the whole of England ever reached Q.
>
> (p. 39)

But if Mr. Ramsay's achievements can be measured in this way, then so can his failures, and while convinced of the accuracy of his system his painful realization of failure informs this laughable and oddly pathetic scene:

> But after Q? What comes next? After Q there are a number of letters the last of which is scarcely visible to mortal eyes, but glimmers red in the distance. Z is only reached by one man in a generation. Still, if he could reach R it would be something. Here at least was Q ... 'Then R ...' He braced himself. He clenched himself.
>
> (p. 39)

Despite her alertness to, and skilful experiments in, literary humour, it is interesting to note that Woolf did not produce her own theory of comedy. However, in its richness and complexity, Virginia Woolf's body of writing has room to accommodate many different comic influences: her political satires (*A Room of One's Own, Three Guineas*) and theatrical burlesques (*Orlando, Between the Acts*) owe much to the tradition of the eighteenth-century 'Wits'. At the other extreme, perhaps, her assessments of family, class, and female subjectivity (*Mrs Dalloway, To the Lighthouse*) find commonalities with the textual parlour games and social comedies of a generation of privileged women writers in this period.

Laughter and mockery, polite or otherwise, ruptures the seemingly placid narrative surface of the 'middlebrow' novel in this period. Among many other examples, there is comic potential to be found in Rose Macaulay's caustic social satires, in the acutely observant genre parody of Stella Gibbons's *Cold Comfort Farm*, throughout the wry character studies in the work of Barbara Pym and Elizabeth Taylor, and in the domestic comedy of manners that structures E.M. Delafield's series of Provincial Lady novels. As such, humour remains a critical, and critically under-examined, mode of discharging gender anxiety and fragile constructions of class superiority in the interwar years. Regardless of its desire to provoke laughter in its reader, the 'middlebrow' (or culturally contested) novel can often be described as 'ludic' in its use of game-playing, or joke-telling, as a central motif or structuring device. This emerges as a particularly disarming narrative technique in texts that are not outwardly 'funny' or comic in tone. In his wide-ranging study *The Alchemy of Laughter*, Glen Cavaliero identifies this kind of writing as 'intellectual comedy'. He goes on to argue that for novels so clearly invested in the ritualized practices of social and domestic reality, a certain kind of humour emerges from an otherwise tight-lipped earnestness as an effect of the way that the writing mimics the 'rules of the game'.[12]

Sub-titled, 'A Tragi-Farcical Tract', Rose Macaulay's 1920 novel *Potterism* reads as an experiment in satiric genre-play, fusing elements of cultural polemic, literary parody, murder mystery, and a barely veiled attack on the conduct of the popular press. As Susan Squier has noted, Macaulay stood in open defiance of the politics of canon creation, and targeted her acerbic wit at deserving literary modes regardless of their perceived cultural prestige.[13] *Potterism* takes a well-aimed swipe at moral and political duplicity as this is voiced in populist literary and cultural production. The text playfully invokes these central themes through the strategic use of the comic double. Johnny and Jane Potter are introduced to the reader as reflections of one another: 'Johnny came up from Rugby and Jane from Roedean. Johnny was at Balliol and Jane at Somerville.'[14] Their striking similarities extend to a shared animosity towards their parents' professional endeavours; the Potter twins come to be founding members of the Anti-Potter League. Potterism, figured by the Anti-Potter League as 'ignorance, vulgarity, mental laziness, sentimentality, and greed' (p. 19), is a widespread moral contagion, but takes its name from the double onslaught of Mr Potter's newspaper industry, and his wife Leila Yorke's novel-writing habit:

> Potterism had certainly not been created by the Potters, and was indeed no better represented by the goods with which they supplied the market than by those of many others; but it was a handy name, and it had taken the public fancy that here you had two Potters linked together, two souls nobly yoked, one supplying Potterism in fictional, the other in

newspaper, form. So the name caught ... The way the twins put it was, 'our family is responsible for more than its share of the beastly thing; the least we can do is to help to do it in.'

(p. 21)

Although an immediate bestseller *Potterism* has been critically overlooked; in what little discussion there is of Macaulay's early serio-comic technique, criticism has focused on her acerbic treatment of the popular press – most notably of the Northcliffe and Beaverbrook newspaper empires with their sensational and sentimental distortions of modern life. While the Potter's paper, *The Daily Haste* is certainly subject to Macaulay's witty derision, ventriloquized by the attacks of the Anti-Potter League, Macaulay arguably reserves her fiercest and funniest satire for the category of women's popular fiction exemplified by Leila Yorke's dubious output. Appropriately enough, as Macaulay voices Mrs Potter's self-assessment as a writer, it is her keen sense of humour that she values above all else:

> I think, in my books, I am almost too frank sometimes; I give offence, and hurt people's egotism and vanity by speaking out; but it is the way I have to write; I cannot soften down facts just to please. Just as I cannot restrain my sense of the ridiculous, even though it may offend those who take themselves solemnly; I am afraid I am naughty about such people, and often give offence; it is one of the penalties attached to the gift of humour. Percy often tells me that I should be more careful; but my dear Percy's wonderful caution, that has helped to make him what he is, is a thing that no mere reckless woman can hope to emulate.

(pp. 14–15)

As the critics Nicola Humble and Faye Hammill have indicated, writers such as E.M. Delafield and Stella Gibbons frequently engage with the 'highbrow' through the lens of gentle humour, often parodying the intellectual and literary pretensions attendant upon elite cultural forms. Especially interesting is the case of *Potterism* where Macaulay, increasingly aligned with a modernist aesthetic, caricatures the aspirations and prejudices of a commercially successful 'lowbrow' mode. The implication here is that the 'middlebrow' acts as a crucial cultural barometer, conscious of its own contradictions, and capable of delivering commentary on the status anxiety at both poles of literary distinction.

Rosamond Lehmann's *Dusty Answer* cannot easily be described as a funny or comic novel. Instead it has variously been read as nostalgic reverie, anti-romantic romance plot, female *Bildungsroman*, and as a largely obedient *gynaeceum* novel with some tendencies towards deviancy. While the text clearly speaks to each of these traditions Lehmann's first novel is also consumed with the politics and poetics of laughter.[15] The novel traces the romantic and sexual education of Judith Earle and the lives of the family who move next door to her childhood home. The beguiling family of cousins, with whom Judith maintains a collective love affair, are introduced in ways that define their roles within the private joke that structures their shared identity: Mariella's lips 'smiled their limited smile' (p. 10); there was 'stupid funny serious Martin' (p. 11); Julian, who 'could not laugh at himself, only at others' (p. 18); and Roddy, who had 'a queer smile that you watched for because it was not like anyone else's' (p. 18). By contrast Judith is repeatedly mocked in their company for being 'so incredibly serious' (p. 77), 'so incredibly solemn' (p. 91). Laughter is encoded as an alternative, private lexicon, able to describe the subtle and shifting power dynamics within each encounter. But despite its power as a mark of non-verbal intimacy within the particular bounds of Lehmann's writing, a preoccupation with the deployment and reception of humour can be understood as a disturbance to the internal politics of the novel, caught between the lingering appeal of the backward glance and an uncertain meeting with modernity.

What is perhaps most interesting in the context of Lehmann's novel, however, is that laughter is never given its full, unqualified expression. *Dusty Answer* is full of compromised or disproportionate expressions of amusement. So, just as Judith is cast as the unlaughing girl, her sobriety is juxtaposed at various moments with other partial, transitory, and marginal responses. Without the natural exuberance of his cousins, Julian's theatrical and 'humourless' jesting appears 'so affected that it crushed the spirit' (p. 64). Similarly, long after his death on the battlefield, Judith is reminded of Charlie 'as a small boy, difficult, petulant, imperious, and yet all the time half laughing at himself in a way that disarmed rebuke' (p. 202). It is Roddy's 'silent laughter' that is most persistent throughout the text, however, and which ensures that for Judith as much as for the reader, the occasion for genuine laughter lies far beneath the surface of the narrative: 'He threw back his head to laugh at his ease, silently, as always, as if his joke were too deep down and individual for audible laughter' (p. 77). Even where laughter is full and unambiguous it retains the quality of an oversized threat; invited into the home of the cousins Judith finds herself disoriented by the aggressive force that greets her:

> 'You're Martin – you're Roddy – you're – ' she hesitated. Julian stood aloof, looking unyouthful and haughty. She finished lamely – 'Mr F–Fyfe.'
> There was a roar of laughter, a chorus of teasing voices to which, plunged once more in a welter of blushes and confusion, she could pay no heed.
> (p. 54)

Rather than mediating the laughter that surrounds her, as someone of her middling status is ideally positioned to do, Judith Earle finds herself always on the edge of these encounters: either cast adrift by uncertain sentiment, or seeking refuge from the violence of full-bodied hilarity.

In her essay exploring 'risibility' in the fiction of Ivy Compton-Burnett, Sara Crangle argues that 'humour underscores the present moment', that, 'if there is something forward-looking in otherwise retro-focused novels, it may well be discernible in representations of laughter'.[16] For Crangle these humorous ruptures are 'fundamental to Modernism's mantra, "make it new"' (p. 100), and therefore challenge the identification of middlebrow humour with the seductive pull of the past. As well as functioning as a form of modernist interruption, Lehmann's strategic use of laughter gestures towards its modernity in a more determined sense, by subtly re-encoding prevailing modernist theories of humour and comic meaning. Published in 1900, and thus a cultural response to the new century, Bergson's essay, 'Laughter: An Essay on the Meaning of the Comic', famously constructs the significance of laughter as a social practice aimed at punishing the unsocial and the inflexible; 'rigidity is the comic, and laughter is its corrective.'[17] The formulation at play here is that of the ultimate comedy of manners in which laughter unites social groups against the unlaughing outsider. Bergson writes:

> You would hardly appreciate the comic if you felt isolated from others. Laughter appears to stand in need of an echo ... It can travel within as wide a circle as you please: the circle remains nonetheless a closed one. Our laughter is always the laughter of a group. However spontaneous it seems, laughter always implies a kind of secret freemasonry, or even complicity with other laughers, real or imaginary.
>
> (p. 64)

For Judith Earle, these 'other laughers' are both real *and* imaginary, at once the occupiers of her present moment and the figments of an idealized past. While the cousins are suspended in a youthful haze above the mundane and the mirthless in Judith's memory, she experiences her own unlaughing nature as further evidence of her insular and unsatisfactory feminine education:

> 'Oh Roddy, how you do laugh at me!'
> 'I can't help it Judy. You are so incredibly solemn. You don't mind do you? Please don't mind. I adore people who make me laugh.'
> It was that his laughter left her out, making her feel heavy and unhumorous. If only he would teach her to play with him, how quick and apt he would find her!
>
> (p. 91)

Unlike Freud's positioning of the woman in his gendered construction of humour, Lehmann is not concerned with identifying her female protagonist as the object of other people's derision. Judith Earle is not the butt of the joke. Neither is her inability to see the point merely symptomatic of a Bergsonian rigidity: particularly as the narrative is largely tasked with tracing her evolving sense of herself from girlhood to graduation. More crucially than that, Judith's displacement from the site of laughter is indicative of her increasingly peripheral status within the social world of the narrative, despite her apparent centrality to the novel's traditional plot structures. Rather than standing as the object of ridicule to be pointed to and openly laughed *at*, Judith stands at a sober distance, allowing the laughter to echo within its closely defined borders.

In the early stage of the narrative it is the orthodoxy of the heterosexual plot that is radically undermined by the marginalization of its female subject. Figured, however uneasily, as the romantic heroine in her brief affair with Roddy, Judith finds that her ability to fulfil her leading role is thwarted by the laughter of others.

> As she opened the door, laughter and talk came suddenly to her from below, – a faint roar of male voices that struck her with strange alarm, and seemed to threaten her. She took a step back into the room again ... The voices came up to her again, like a reiterated warning. 'Keep away. You are not wanted here. We are all friends, men content together. We want no female to trouble us.'
>
> (p. 100)

Laughter in this overtly homosocial context functions as a highly successful intimidation technique. Perhaps taking her cue from the gender-specific solidarity of this encounter, Judith comes finally to abandon her attachment to Roddy in favour of the same-sex bonds she finds in student life at Cambridge. However, her initiation into the familiar scene of *gynaeceum* narrative convention is again frustrated by her self-conscious removal from the exuberant collective spirit: 'Crowds of dresses of all colours, shapes and sizes, all running about briskly, knowing where to go; a sea of faces bobbing and turning, chattering, bright-eyed, nodding and laughing to other faces, sure of themselves ... "I am lost, lost, abandoned, alone, lost," thought Judith wildly' (pp. 107–8).

As Lehmann's deft manipulation of form translates female friendship into proto-lesbian erotics in the central phase of the novel, the panic that strikes Judith at this moment can be seen to effectively foreshadow her later betrayal by the enigmatic Jennifer and the predatory Geraldine Manners: 'Judith returning from her bath, heard voices and laughter behind Jennifer's door. Should she stop? ... She alone had excluded herself, sitting with a pile of books in her room, pretending to have important work. It was her own fault' (p. 158). Eventually summoned to meet Geraldine as the rival for Jennifer's affection, Judith is also forced to confront all that she has been excluded from. In a single moment, the residual laughter that Judith was not invited to share finally demands expression, as though in response to her own intensely private joke: 'Judith broke into a sort of laugh; and then checked herself with a vast effort: for the suppressed hysteria of weeks was climbing upwards within her and if it broke loose, it might never, never cease' (p. 165).

Lehmann's relentlessly unlaughing appeal to laughter as a highly charged form of social and sexual currency captures the solemn frustrations of her protagonist, always on the cusp of experience. The same effect also speaks to the transitional and still marginalized status of the feminine 'middlebrow' itself, held outside the narratives of Victorian realism and the bold departures of modernist innovation. By instructing her reader in the subtle workings of laughter as a potent marker of social power, Lehmann allows her thoughtful, unlaughing heroine to articulate this sense of occupying the space 'in-between'. From that space she is able to imagine what it might mean to be on the other side of that 'excluding circle' from where she could 'look outward and laugh, accepting life as an easy exciting thing; and yet was checked by a voice that said doubtfully that there were dark ideas behind it all, tangling the web' (p. 137). It is this same lingering sense of doubt that brings the novel to a close, as, despite her claims to self-sufficiency, Judith remains hesitant – not yet able to laughingly embrace the future – and, in her reluctance, Lehmann seems to capture the mood of this transitional moment: 'Soon she must begin to think: What next? But not quite yet' (p. 303).

Laughter as a barometer of social, sexual, and familial unease is a familiar trope in much women's writing of the period. Published the year after *Potterism*, in 1921, Macaulay's *Dangerous Ages* explores the less than comedic resentments and regrets of a middle-aged woman as she assesses the impact on her own life of her marital and maternal sacrifices. As she celebrates her forty-third birthday with her family, Neville is struck by the reality that she and her children no longer laugh at the same things; that in fact her persistent sense of humour functions as a further indication of her growing dislocation within her own family:

> They would read and discuss Freud, whom Neville, unfairly prejudiced, found both an obscene maniac and a liar. They might laugh at Freud with her when he expanded on that complex on account of which mothers and daughters hate each other, and fathers and sons – but they both, all the same, took seriously things which seemed to Neville merely loathsome imbecilities. Gerda and Kay didn't, in point of fact, find many things either funny or disgusting as Neville did; throwing her mind back twenty years, Neville tried to remember whether she had found the world as funny and as frightful when she was a medical student as she did now; on the whole she thought not. Boys and girls are for all their high spirits, creatures of infinite solemnities and pomposities. They laugh; but the

twinkling irony, mocking at itself and everything else, they have not yet learnt.[18]

Laughter emerges as a disquieting sound once more in Elizabeth Bowen's short story 'Daffodils', which again is engaged with questions of ageing and feminine redundancy. In this story's brief encounter, however, it is the retired schoolmistress who is left unsmiling when after hearing laughter outside her window, she invites a group of her former pupils to have tea with her in her spinsterish rooms:

> She dreamed, and was awakened by familiar laughter. Nobody's laughter in particular, but surely it was the laughter of the High School? Three girls were passing with arms close linked, along the pavement underneath her window ... Instantly they turned up three pink faces of surprise, which broadened into smiles of recognition.
> 'Hullo, Miss Murcheson!'
> 'Hullo, children! Come in for a minute and talk to me. I'm all alone.'
> Millicent, Rosemary and Doris hesitated, eyeing one another, poised for flight. 'Righto!' they agreed unanimously.
> Miss Murcheson, all of a flutter, went round to open the front door. She looked back at the sitting room as though she had never seen it before. Why had she asked them in, those terrible girls whom she had scarcely spoken to? They would laugh at her, they would tell the others.
> The room was full of them, of their curiosity and embarrassment and furtive laughter.[19]

The unbearable bursts of 'furtive laughter' in this scene signal what Bowen later identifies in her novel *The Heat of the Day*, as 'the joke or agony' without seeing anything odd about the juxtaposition of those elements.[20] This is not the sound of the empowering or revolutionary female laughter described by Little and Barreca; it is instead the sound of women laughing at other women, and as such demands a different kind of analysis.

E.M. Delafield's 1927 novel, *The Way Things Are*, opens with a scene of failed comic exchange which, again, hints at the ways in which comedy and laughter only serve to underscore gender discord in the domestic sphere. In this instance, Laura Temple breaks into the post-dinner silence to share with her husband an amusing incident from her day:

> 'Did I tell you what Johnnie said, after he'd had his reading-lesson today?'
> 'No.'
> Laura embarked upon her anecdote.[21]

Despite her valiant efforts to enliven the familiar marital lull, Laura's delivery of her story is quickly stymied in the face of her less than captive audience: 'She knew well that her husband did not want to hear it.' However, Laura perseveres:

> Nevertheless, she told it. And her secret sense of her own futility and weakness took all conviction from the manner of her telling, so that even a much more amusing story than that of a five-year-old's repartee would have been bereft of sense and all spirit.
> When the recital of his son's witticism had petered out, Alfred Temple said, 'H'm,' compromising between a short, unamused laugh and a curt ejaculation, and then he and Laura were silent again.
> They had been married seven years.
>
> (p. 1)

Delafield's own delivery of this scene is, of course, far more perfectly-pitched than her protagonist's. She captures the all-too familiar absurdity of the gendered status quo of the period: the long-suffering provincial housewife, and her laconic, semi-detached husband. As an expression of anxious domestic comedy, Delafield's timing is expertly judged, revealing an otherwise unspoken tension in the idealized middle-class existence. Delafield's *Diary of a Provincial Lady* (1930), first expresses, by contrast a very different comic tone; the scholarly sobriety of much middlebrow women's writing is replaced with a relentless tone of spirited resilience and ironizing observation. Unlike her precursor, Laura Temple, the unnamed provincial lady translates resignation into what Nicola Beauman describes as 'a continual and irrepressible fight for life and vigour'.[22]

Much of the pleasure of the text is located at the level of the light-hearted lampooning of the codes and institutions that govern this most unremarkable of English, middle-class landscapes; provincial snobbery, domestic routine, marital disharmony, the 'servant problem', and the dilemma posed by the school holidays are all positioned as entirely worthy subjects of polite, and occasionally renegade, laughter. However, while these aspects of the novel capture the external absurdities of the provincial lady's social and domestic sphere, its contemporary resonances are found in the struggles to reconcile expectation with mundane reality, and Delafield's ability to articulate the embarrassing gaps that exist between the two.

The first entry of the *Diary* introduces both the provincial lady's comic interlocutor, Lady Boxe, and a running joke relating to the planting of indoor bulbs. In a series of almost identical encounters, Delafield familiarizes her reader with the wryly observed interplay of voices adopted by her protagonist:

> Do I know that the only really reliable firm for Hyacinths is Somebody of Haarlem? Cannot catch the name of the firm, which is Dutch, but reply, Yes, I do know, but think it is my duty to buy Empire products. Feel at the time and still think, that this is an excellent reply. Unfortunately Vicky

comes into the drawing-room later and says: 'Oh, Mummie, are those the bulbs we got at Woolworth's'.[23]

Lady Boxe's overbearing aristocratic tone is matched by the voice of the provincial lady's reasonableness passing critical judgement over her own achievement in a comic internal monologue that casually undermines the pomposities of polite society. This voice presents comic asides throughout the course of the diary in the form of carefully positioned 'queries' that interrupt the monologue and reflect more pointedly on the accepted status quo. Following her husband Robert's marked disapproval of the provincial lady's 'brand-new and expensive' lipstick, she privately poses the question, 'If Robert could be induced to go to London rather oftener, would he perhaps take broader view of things?' (p. 10). Encoded in this seemingly off-hand enquiry is a larger question about the smallness of provincial respectability and an unresolved tension over the control of the household economy. Ironically, then, these entirely self-directed queries enable the provincial lady to speak directly in the quiet constraints of her environment, and in a tone more overtly satirical than the self-deprecation of her everyday demeanour.

Ultimately, of course, the humour that distinguishes the provincial lady's mode of life-writing is not incisive social commentary. Through her refusal to take herself or her surroundings entirely seriously, her daily recollections provide a kind of critically amused distance from which she responds to her often joyless domestic reality:

> *January 22nd* – Robert startles me at breakfast by asking if my cold – which he has hitherto ignored – is better. I reply that it has gone. Then why, he asks, do I look like that? Refrain from asking like what, as I know only too well. Feel that life is wholly unendurable, and decide madly to get a new hat.
> (p. 29)

There is a spark of joyous audacity here that sustains the daily routine. Delafield's lightly controlled timing and delivery of this female voice as it narrates domestic farce, class, and gendered caricature signals her skill as a female humorist. The comic potential of the diary occupies an entirely separate category, of course, from the arch satire of Rose Macaulay's tragic-farcical *Potterism*, just as Delafield's relentlessly amused diarist has little in common with the unlaughing protagonist of Lehmann's *Dusty Answer*, or the self-aggrandizing petty patriarchs of Woolf's interwar fiction. Yet each of these writers and their texts exploit and examine the alternative vocabulary that comedy provides, whether at the level of tone, character, genre-play or narrative observation. It is this language of polite laughter, 'double-speak', and comic delivery that works to articulate the unspoken tensions of a transitional moment in the social, sexual, and gendered culture of Britain in the first half of the twentieth century.

Notes

1. Martha Bruere and Mary Beard, eds, *Laughing Their Way: Women's Humor in America* (New York: Macmillan, 1934), pp. v–viii. Kate Sanborn's *The Wit of Women* is available from Project Gutenberg: http://www.gutenberg.org/ebooks/28503.
2. Most notable among these are Deanne Stillman and Anne Beatt's misleadingly titled *Titters: The First Collection of Humor by Women* (New York: Collier, 1976); Gloria Kaufman and Mary Kay Blakely, eds, *Pulling Our Own Strings* (Bloomington: Indiana University Press, 1980) and Gloria Kaufman, ed., *In Stitches* (Bloomington: Indiana University Press, 1991); Judy Little, *Comedy and the Woman Writer: Woolf, Spark, and Feminism* (Lincoln: University of Nebraska Press, 1983); Nancy Walker, *A Very Serious Thing: Women's Humor and American Culture* (Minneapolis: University of Minnesota Press, 1988); Regina Barecca, *Last Laughs: Perspectives on Women and Comedy* (New York: Gordon and Breach, 1988) and *Untamed and Unabashed: Essays on Women and Humor in British Literature* (Detroit: Wayne State University Press, 1994); June Sochen, ed., *Women's Comic Visions* (Detroit: Wayne State University Press, 1991); Gail Finney, ed., *Look Who's Laughing: Gender and Comedy* (London: Taylor and Francis, 1994).
3. Margaret D. Stetz, *British Women's Comic Fiction, 1890–1990: Not Drowning, But Laughing* (Aldershot: Ashgate, 2001).
4. Judith Schwartz, *Radical Feminists of Heterodoxy: Greenwich Village 1912–1940* (Lebanon, NH: New Victoria, 1982).
5. Dorothy Parker's journalistic output, along with her short fiction, poetry, plays, and ephemera has been widely collected and re-published: see particularly *The Portable Dorothy Parker*, ed. Marian Meade (New York: Penguin Books, 1973; revised 2006). Alice Duer Miller's suffrage satires are collected in two volumes: *Are Women People? A Book of Rhymes for Suffrage Times* (New York: George H. Doran Company, 1915) and *Women Are People!* (New York: George H. Doran Company, 1917). Selections from Florence Seabury's journalism, short fiction, and suffrage satire can be found in *The Delicatessen Husband and Other Essays* (New York: Harcourt Brace, 1926).
6. Chapter 8 below, p. 153.
7. Little, *Comedy and the Woman Writer*, p. 2.
8. Barreca, *Untamed and Unabashed*, p. 18.
9. Denise Marshall, 'Slaying the Angel and the Patriarch: The Grinning Woolf', in *Last Laughs*, pp. 149–77, p. 175.
10. Virginia Woolf, *Mrs Dalloway* (Harmondsworth: Penguin, 1996), p. 55.
11. Virginia Woolf, *To the Lighthouse* (Harmondsworth: Penguin, 1992), pp. 64–5.
12. Glen Cavaliero, *The Alchemy of Laughter: Comedy in English Fiction* (Basingstoke: Macmillan, 2000), p. 171.
13. Susan M. Squier, 'Rose Macaulay', in *The Gender of Modernism: A Critical Anthology*, ed. Bonnie Kime Scott (Bloomington and Indianapolis: University of Indiana Press, 1990), pp. 252–9.
14. Rose Macaulay, *Potterism: A Tragi-Farcical Tract* (London and New York: Collins, 1920), p. 1.
15. Rosamond Lehmann, *Dusty Answer* (London: Virago Press, 2000).
16. Sara Crangle, 'Ivy Compton-Burnett and Risibility', in *British Fiction after Modernism: The Novel at Mid-Century*, ed. Marina MacKay and Lyndsey Stonebridge (New York: Palgrave, 2007), pp. 99–120, p. 100.
17. Henri Bergson, 'Laughter: An Essay on the Meaning of the Comic', reprinted in *Comedy*, ed. Wylie Sypher (New York: Doubleday Anchor, 1956), p. 74.

18. Rose Macaulay, *Dangerous Ages* (New York: Boni and Liveright, 1921), pp. 6–7.
19. Elizabeth Bowen, 'Daffodils', in *Collected Stories* (London: Vintage Classics, 1999), pp. 23–4.
20. Elizabeth Bowen, *The Heat of the Day* (London: Vintage Classics, 1998), p. 322.
21. E.M. Delafield, *The Way Things Are* (London: Virago Press, 1988), p. 1.
22. Nicola Beauman, *A Very Great Profession: Woman's Novel, 1914–39* (London: Virago, 1983), p. 114.
23. E.M. Delafield, *Diary of a Provincial Lady* (London: Virago Press, 1984), p. 3.

7
The Woman's Historical Novel
Diana Wallace

Drawing attention to the absence of women in mainstream histories, Virginia Woolf suggested to the students of 'Fernham' in *A Room Of One's Own* (1929) that they might 'add a supplement to history', adding with palpable irony that they should 'call ... it, of course, by some inconspicuous name so that women might figure there without impropriety'.[1] In the imagined story of Shakespeare's sister which forms the influential centrepiece of *A Room of One's Own*, however, Woolf demonstrated the power of the imagination not just to supplement but radically to rewrite the 'unreal, lop-sided' history[2] she found in the works of historians like G.M. Trevelyan. A historical novel in miniature, Judith Shakespeare's story of thwarted literary ambition, seduction, and suicide is a narrative of defeat which is echoed in many other novels in this period. In Rose Macaulay's *They Were Defeated* (1932), for instance, the heroine Julian Conybeare, who can only love a poet rather than being one, is accidentally killed during a fight between her Cavalier lover and her Puritan brother. Historical fiction allowed women writers the freedom to re-imagine the unrecorded lives of women but it did more than that. Refuting the oft-made accusation that 'fiction is not history', Woolf argued that 'though it would be easier to write history ... that method of telling the truth seems to me so elementary, and so clumsy, that I prefer, where truth is important, to write fiction'.[3] As Woolf understood, historical fiction has the power to recast our conceptions of history itself, opening up other interpretations and possibilities, for the future as well as the past.

Despite critical proclamations of the death of the historical novel at the end of the nineteenth century, the years between 1920 and 1945 are extraordinarily rich in innovative historical fiction by women and mark a critical turning point in the development of the genre. While women had been writing historical fictions since the eighteenth century (well before Scott claimed in the opening of *Waverley* (1814) to have invented a new genre), it is in the interwar period that women writers most energetically reinvent the historical novel, taking it in a variety of new directions which include the classical novels of Naomi Mitchison, the popular romances of Georgette

Heyer, the Welsh-set historical novels of Margiad Evans and Hilda Vaughan, the modernist historical fictions of Mary Butts and H.D., and the socialist-feminist novels of Sylvia Townsend Warner.

Traditional accounts of the development of historical fiction have been slow to engage with the richly diverse body of novels produced by women in this period. This is partly the result of the stranglehold exerted by Georg Lukács's Marxist *The Historical Novel* (1936/7) which takes Scott's *Waverley* as the exemplary model of a 'classical historical novel'.[4] The historical novel is thus seen as reaching its apogee in the nineteenth century and thereafter declining into costume romance. Following Lukács, Avrom Fleishman in *The English Historical Novel* (1971), for instance, argues that *Orlando* (1928) and *Between the Acts* (1941) bring 'the tradition of the English historical novel to a self-conscious close'.[5] However, the work of women writers rarely fits the Lukácsian paradigm, partly because women are far less likely to depict history as a dialectical 'progress'. In the past few decades there has been important work, notably by Alison Light, Terry Castle, Ruth Hoberman, Helen Hughes, Janet Montefiore, Elizabeth Maslen, Chris Hopkins, and Sue Harper, which has begun to reshape our thinking about women's historical fiction between 1920 and 1945.

The reinvigoration of historical fiction by women writers in the 1920s is closely related to historical changes in the position of women, including women's new status as enfranchised citizens, the aftermath of the First World War, and the opening up of university education to female students. During the 'Great War', the 'mass of people became, for the first time, active citizens'.[6] For women who moved into the public world by taking jobs vacated by men during the war and gained – at least partially – the vote in 1918, this sense of entering into history as active citizens was particularly intense. This new historical sensibility can be compared with that resulting from the French Revolution and the revolutionary wars, to which Lukács attributes the emergence of the 'classical historical novel' as a genre. The European scale of these events, he argued, 'for the first time made history a *mass experience*', allowing 'men [sic] to comprehend their existence as something historically conditioned'.[7] In early twentieth-century Britain this sense of being part of history extended for the first time to the new *woman* citizen exercising her vote. A sense of women's new responsibilities as citizens is evident, for instance, in *They Were Defeated*: 'I live in the State and should know of what passes in it', asserts Julian. 'My father says if I do not I should be shamed and count myself most ignorant, and not fit for a citizen.'[8] Rose Macaulay's point, of course, is that seventeenth-century Julian, excluded from Cambridge University because of her gender, does not have the rights of a citizen and even her only surviving poem is purloined by her Cavalier lover, John Cleveland, who publishes it as his own.

These years also saw the emergence of the first generations of university-educated women, many of whom studied history or English. While some of these women (such as Eileen Power, Margaret Murray, and Jane Harrison) continued their work within the universities, others turned to fiction outside the academy. University-educated writers of historical fiction include Rose Macaulay, Hilda Reid, Margaret Kennedy, Margaret Irwin, D.K. Broster, and Phyllis Bentley. Their scholarly credentials are often visible in the metatextual convention of the 'Author's Note', but frequently in ways that question the hierarchies of 'history' and 'fiction'. 'As it seems to be the habit to furnish such information', Macaulay notes wryly in the 'Note' to *They Were Defeated*, 'I would add that only a very few people in this book are imaginary.'[9]

Feminism, as Anthea Trodd argues, 'created a demand for information about the lives of women in history and a need to understand how they lived'.[10] The Equal Franchise Act of 1928 intensified interest in women's history with the publication of books like Ray Strachey's *The Cause* (1928) taking stock of the gains made by the women's movement. But by the mid-1930s histories like Winifred Holtby's *Women and a Changing Civilisation* (1934), written under the shadow of Fascism and the probability of another war, were keenly aware of a backlash, as Holtby put it, 'not only against feminism, but against democracy, liberty, and reason, against international co-operation and political tolerance'.[11] Alongside such factual accounts, women writers turned to fiction to fill the lacunae in recorded history and re-imagine history from a female point of view. Moreover, far from being merely nostalgic or escapist, historical fiction was frequently used as a cover under which women writers could write about allegedly 'male' subjects, such as war or politics, and explore taboo issues around sexuality and gendered identity.

Classicism and *The Conquered*

The publication of Naomi Mitchison's first novel, *The Conquered*, in 1923 marked a recognizable shift in the genre. 'With *The Conquered* Mrs Mitchison establishes herself as the best, if not the only, English historical novelist now writing', wrote Raymond Mortimer in the *New Statesman*.[12] Mitchison was, as she herself recorded, 'the first to see that one could write historical novels in a modern idiom',[13] and this made the past seem fresh, modern, and real. Ironically, it is precisely this use of an accessible, even 'lowbrow' idiom, as Elizabeth Maslen has pointed out, that makes it easy to underestimate Mitchison.[14]

Nowhere is that more evident than in the iconoclastic 'Note on Books and One's Funny Idea of Ancient History' that Mitchison appended to *When the Bough Breaks* (1924). This emphasizes the partial and subjective nature of historical knowledge, its roots in a fertile muddle of sources from childhood where classical texts, histories, translations, children's and historical fiction, and poetry jostle together: 'One probably starts with a few fixed ideas about the Romans', Mitchison hazards, 'because one always has to learn [Macaulay's] Lays as soon as one goes to school. I think one is rather hazy for a few centuries after that.'[15] She highlights an emotional connection to history, as well as an empathy with the underdog: 'Not unnaturally one always used to take sides with the barbarians against Rome ... But it's the Northerner, one's possible ancestor, who is really thrilling ... And that makes one interested in the Roman idea of slavery.'[16]

Slavery is the subject of *The Conquered*, the story of Meromic, a young Gaul enslaved by the Romans during the conquest of Gaul in the first century BC, who is torn between his loyalty to his defeated people and a close relationship with his Roman master, Titus. The novel is a sensitive meditation on the experience of being conquered and enslaved, history written by the vanquished rather than the victors. After the defeat of the Gauls' leader Vercingetorix, Meromic has his right hand cut off, and the final image is of a wolf's footprints, lame in the right foreleg, heading north, suggesting Meromic has metamorphosed into his totem, the wolf. While Mitchison uses a male protagonist, the epigraph of the novel – 'Victix causa diis placvit sed victa puellis' [The victorious cause is pleasing to the gods, but the conquered cause to girls][17] – signals a potentially gendered reading. In contrast to the Lukácsian 'classical historical novel' with its dialectical progress, women writers from this period far more often focus on defeated and conquered individuals and peoples.

The use of a Latin epigraph has two important functions. On the one hand, it asserts Mitchison's credentials as one of the few women of her generation to have benefited from the kind of classical education usually reserved for boys (until she started to menstruate she attended the Dragon School for Boys in Oxford). As Ruth Hoberman shows in *Gendering Classicism* (1997), a classical education 'set young men apart from their female counterparts' and 'played a particularly vital role in the national image'.[18] In trespassing on this traditionally male ground by using classical settings, historical novelists like Mitchison and Phyllis Bentley were challenging the authority of some of the most influential narratives of their culture. Their novels explore how the existence of women was erased both in antiquity (women were excluded, for instance, from participation in Athenian democracy) and in its modern representations. In *Freedom, Farewell!* (1936), her novel of Caesar's rise to power, Bentley shows how women, like countries, are taken by force and silenced. The novel's most haunting image is of Porcia stifling herself with the fumes of burning charcoal after hearing of the defeat and death of Brutus. The juxtaposition of the Latin epigraph with Mitchison's 'lowbrow' idiom, like her ironic explication of 'one's Funny Idea' of history, is part of a self-conscious undermining of those discourses that keep the powerful in power.

Mitchison's epigraph, however, is also part of her use of what Elizabeth Maslen calls 'Aesopian language'.[19] It is a way of getting politically sensitive material past the censor by signalling a subversive level to an ostensibly conservative text. Many of the epigraphs for *The Conquered*, for instance, are from W.B. Yeats or traditional Irish ballads such as 'The Croppy Boy' which allude to the history of oppression in Ireland. Mitchison was inspired to write by 'the troubles in Ireland in my own year of grace – 1921': 'Yet I didn't want to write directly about Ireland', she wrote, 'So it was that Gaul presented itself to me, plastic material for my parallel with Ireland.'[20] Similarly, Bentley wrote *Freedom Farewell!*, as she put it, 'on account of Hitler',[21] looking back to Rome to provide a parallel with the contemporaneous rise of Fascism.

Popular romances: history as 'escapism'

Georgette Heyer shares with Mitchison the distinction of reinventing the historical novel for women writers in the 1920s, although she turns it in a very different direction. Her first novel, *The Black Moth* (1921), with its gentleman-turned-highwayman hero, was in the tradition of Baroness Orczy's Scarlet Pimpernel novels and the swashbucklers of Jeffrey Farnol and Rafael Sabatini. History here is used, as Helen Hughes argues, 'as an exotic setting to add to the "escape value" of their stories'.[22] It was with her sixth novel, *These Old Shades* (1926), featuring a cross-dressed heroine who falls in love with the saturnine duke who rescues her from the Paris backstreets, that Heyer found her winning formula. A reliable best-seller, she produced a stream of romances, almost all after the mid-1930s set in the Regency period. Her innovation was to make the historical romance a female form, focusing it on the heroine and her desires, and creating a densely textured pseudo-realism through her use of historically accurate surface detail and stylized period language.

Two other forms of popular historical novel developed during this period which were also closely associated with women writers and readers. The 'costume fiction' of Magdalen King-Hall, Norah Lofts, and Eleanor Smith, as Sue Harper has shown, emerged but the war years but differed from the historical romance in using melodrama to explore anxieties about the ways in which marriage confined women.[23] In Magdalen King-Hall's *Life and Death of the Wicked Lady Skelton* (1942), Barbara Skelton, bored with married life in the aptly named 'Maryiot Cells', dresses as a highwayman to find adventure. Similarly, in Daphne du Maurier's *Frenchman's Creek* (1941) Dona St Columb has an affair with a French pirate before returning to her husband and children.

The third form is the biographical historical novel which fictionalizes the life of a real historical figure, usually a queen or princess, epitomized by Margaret Irwin's novels including *The Gay Galliard: The Love Story of Mary Queen of Scots* (1941) and *Young Bess* (1944), which is about Elizabeth I. As the subtitle of *The Gay Galliard* suggests, Irwin's interest is in women as sexually desirous beings, and she uses romance to reshape history into a form which will accommodate women's stories.

While all three types of novel centralize women, they differ in their approach to 'real' history. Although Irwin fictionalized actual historical figures and Heyer used imaginary protagonists, both based their novels on extensive research. In the 'Author's Note' to *An Infamous Army* (1937), her novel about Waterloo, Heyer provides a bibliography of forty-five items and adds that 'wherever possible I have allowed the Duke [of Wellington] to speak for himself, borrowing freely from the twelve volumes of his Despatches'.[24] Even Heyer's more flimsy romances benefit from her knowledge of Regency fashions and language. In contrast, the costume fiction used history as merely a colourful backcloth against which to play out its melodramatic plots.

The success of these writers meant that historical fiction became identified with female writers and readers and the 'popular', and increasingly stigmatized as 'escapist'. The term 'escapism', Alison Light points out, only came into common currency after 1933 and so 'belongs to modernity'.[25] The desire for escapist reading intensified during the war, despite paper rationing. One twenty-four-year-old woman war worker described her favourite reading as 'Books dealing with some costume period' such as Orczy and *Frenchman's Creek*, which 'take me into another world far from the realities of this'.[26] While the wartime setting of many of the historical romances and costume novels may at first seem at odds with this desire for 'escape', what is noticeable is their focus on conflicts that suggest Britain's inevitable victory. In *Young Bess*, Elizabeth Tudor is confident that 'England won't be invaded. She never has been.'[27] Similarly, the appeal of the Regency period was partly the reassuringly iconic status of Waterloo as a British victory.

Alison Light has emphasized the conservatism of much women's writing in this period. Historical novels like *Young Bess* 'fed a conservative vision', she argues, yet they are unusual in giving femininity 'the lead role in the national drama', even 'keeping open the potential for wayward subjectivities outside the norms on offer'.[28] The dominant mood between the wars, nevertheless, she argues in *Forever England*, was 'a conservatism itself in revolt against the past, trying to make room for the present'.[29] She identifies in du Maurier's writing, for instance, a 'romantic Toryism ... which invokes the past as a nobler, loftier place where it was possible to live a more expansive and exciting life'.[30]

Indeed, these popular historical novels obsessively turn to the past to depict wicked ladies and wayward women who transgress the boundaries of the proper feminine. They cross-dress as highwaymen like Skelton's Barbara or cabin boys like du Maurier's Dona, both of whom have adulterous affairs. Heyer's heroines also rebel – like Leonie in *These Old Shades* bemoaning her petticoats or Barbara Childe in *An Infamous Army* painting her toenails – but in her novels marriage is represented as the solution rather than the problem. The endings of both costume fiction (where transgression is frequently punished with death) and historical romance (where the heroine is rewarded with marriage) suggest a conservative ideology. Nevertheless, as Light acknowledges, 'it is the *escape*, rather than the return, which these novels warm to.'[31] Very different from the 'Aesopean' historical novels, these romances can still, through their depiction of transgressive femininity, offer resisting readers a proto-feminist message.

On the 'borders': Welsh and Scottish histories

The dialectical model of historical progress deployed by Lukács and Fleishman is not only andro-centric but also Anglocentric: conflicts – Norman/Saxon, English/Scottish – are seen as moving towards a synthesized 'English' national identity. While the male-authored Scottish novel has retained a place within accounts of historical fiction, partly because of the influence of Scott, fictions of Wales have been remarkably neglected by critics outside Wales. Yet both Scottish and Welsh historical settings have proven fertile ground for women writers and these novels raise important issues around the gendering of nationality as well as history.

D.K. (Dorothy Kathleen) Broster was not Scottish, nor was she, as many of her readers assumed, a man, but her Jacobite trilogy (*The Flight of the Heron*, 1925; *The Gleam in the North*, 1927; *The Dark Mile*, 1929) reworks the tradition of Scott and Robert Louis Stevenson, allowing her, as a woman novelist, to write about male protagonists. One of the first women to graduate from Oxford in 1920, she had actually achieved her second-class honours in history at St Hilda's in 1900, after which she worked for thirteen years as secretary to the Regius Professor of History at Oxford. Her early novels were influenced by Orczy, but the turn to Scottish history with its wild landscapes and supernatural associations, allowed her to develop a mix of well-researched history (she consulted eighty works for *The Flight of the Heron*),[32] adventure story, and psychological realism.

Like Mitchison, Broster used history as an imaginative space within which she could inhabit male characters and explore forbidden or repressed emotions. The emotional core of the trilogy is an exploration of divided loyalties within close male friendships. The two male protagonists of *The Flight of the Heron*, the Scottish Ewen Cameron and the English Keith Windham, recall Scott's Edward Waverley and Fergus Mac-Ivor; but it is the Englishman who dies and Ewen who survives to name his second son 'Keith', suggesting an incorporation of the English into Scotland, rather than vice versa. The friendship they develop is represented in terms we now read as homoerotic. Windham imagines their friendship 'like the roots of two trees growing secretly towards each other in darkness'.[33] Indeed, the potential for such cross-writing and cross-reading seems to be one of the major reasons why women were drawn to the historical novel.

The divided loyalties of border countries are also the subject of Margiad Evans's *Country Dance* (1932), set in the 1850s. The text is presented as the diary of Ann Goodman, discovered by 'Margiad Evans' (pseudonym of the English Peggy Whistler), and offers the kind of re-imagined day-to-day detail of women's lives for which Woolf called. Born of an English father and a Welsh mother, Ann represents 'the entire history of the Border ... that history which belongs to all border lands and tells of incessant warfare'.[34] The title metaphor figures her movements across the border between England and Wales, and between the two men who fight over her, the English Gabriel Ford and the Welsh Evan ap Evans. Initially betrothed to Gabriel, Ann finally chooses Evans, who courts her using the Welsh language spoken by her mother. That Ann's choice of suitors is also a choice of nation illustrates the peculiarly fraught issue of national identity for women given the fact that up until 1948 their nationality depended upon their husband. As Woolf commented in *Three Guineas* (1938): 'that [women] are stepdaughters, not full daughters of England is shown by the fact that they change nationality on marriage'.[35] Ann's murder, and the implied doubt as to which of the two men killed her, exemplifies the ways in which women are repeatedly aligned with the 'defeated' and 'conquered' in these historical novels.

The novels of Evans and Hilda Vaughan can be set within the context of a rising interest in Welsh nationalism during this period, signalled by the establishment of Plaid Cymru in 1925. While Evans and Broster are 'English' novelists who found their writing identities through an identification with the Celtic 'borders', Vaughan, a solicitor's daughter from Builth Wells, was a member of the Anglicized Welsh middle class. Her historical novels are distinctive for the use they make of Welsh folklore and mythology. In *Harvest Home* (1936), set in 1800, Vaughan uses the myth of the creation of Blodeuwedd from blossom in the *Mabinogi* to explore the connections between male ownership of women and of property. Frustrated in his attempts to court his dairymaid, Eiluned, the new Master of the Great House, Daniel Hafod, uses the (misremembered) myth to seduce her fellow maidservant, Lizzie: '"I'll tell you a story o' sorcery," he said, "There was once a monarch, by name Gwyddion ... He made himself a fair woman – the one he wanted out o' the whole world – for his delight. He *made* her, mind you."'[36] Here Vaughan uses historical fiction to critique myths, in the *Mabinogi* as much as the Bible, where the female function of creation is usurped by a male god or wizard, and women are seen as subservient objects to be used by men. Like Woolf, Macaulay, and Mitchison, Evans and Vaughan re-imagine the unrecorded lives of women in the past, but they do so in a specifically Welsh context which allows an interrogation of the fraught and complex nature of nationality for women.

The modernist historical novel

If the term 'historical fiction' is a kind of oxymoron, then 'modernist historical novel' with its yoking of 'modern' and 'historical' seems even more contradictory. The modernist emphasis on the subjective nature of experience, linguistic experimentalism, and the fragmentation of traditional notions of time and space, seems particularly at odds with a genre associated with realist techniques, representative or typical characters, and linear chronology. Yet female modernists, as Hoberman has shown, frequently used myth 'to explore and challenge their culture's assumptions about gender',[37] and Mary Butts and H.D. do this within the historical novel. The modernist fictions of Woolf, Butts, and H.D. offer some of the most radical revisions of historiography as well as the historical novel.

In *Orlando* (1928) Woolf uses fantasy to play subversive games with the historical novel, disrupting traditional notions of time and period by stretching her protagonist's life across several centuries and destabilizing notions of character and identity by transforming 'him' into 'her' half-way through. What Woolf has in common with Walter Scott, however, is her recognition of the determining force of historical period. Orlando may be the same person, regardless of his/her gender, but the way s/he is treated exposes the culturally constructed nature of gender: as an Elizabethan man he is free to adventure, fight, and make love; as a Victorian woman she is 'dragged down by the weight of the crinoline which she had submissively adopted'.[38] Her inability, as a woman, to inherit her ancestral home symbolizes the harsh realities of her position outside history. It is only in the twentieth century that Orlando can emerge into history at 'the twelfth stroke of midnight, Thursday, the eleventh of October, Nineteen Hundred and Twenty Eight'[39] not only as a woman writer but, newly enfranchised that July, as a female citizen.

Turning to classical history, H.D. and Mary Butts also break with realist forms and linear chronology, experimenting with language and image to convey a female subjectivity associated with lost cultures. An American by birth who held a British passport (through her marriage to Richard Aldington), H.D. became the long-term companion of the historical novelist Bryher. She is still mainly associated with her early imagist poetry, but in the 1920s she produced three experimental historical fictions set in the classical world. H.D.'s Hellenism is, Eileen Gregory argues, 'the major trope or fiction within her writing, providing her orientation within historical, aesthetic, and psychological mappings'.[40] The three sections of *Palimpsest* (1926) each portray female writers caught in the cycles of war that dominate history: the translator and compiler Hipparchia, a captive Greek in 'War Rome' (around 75 BC); the poet Raymonde Ransome/Ray Bart, who has lost her husband and a stillborn child in wartime and postwar London (1916–26); and the scholar Helen Fairwood, engaged as a secretary in Egypt during the excavations of King Tut's tomb (1925). The motif of the palimpsest, 'a parchment from which one writing has been erased to make room for another',[41] suggests the violence with which each culture erases and then 'writes' over those it conquers. The three protagonists attempt to counter these losses,

Hipparchia through preserving antique fragments, Ray Bart through writing classically-inflected poetry, and Helen through a mystical encounter with a little Egyptian 'temple or tomb or birth-house'[42] which represents an older culture associated with the lost maternal.

H.D.'s imaging of history as a palimpsest where 'antiquity showed through the semi-transparence of shallow modernity like a blue flame through the texture of some jelly-fish-like deep-sea creature'[43] is one of the most important counters to the Lukácsian emphasis on history as dialectical progress. It centralizes the place of writing within history and, like Woolf, H.D. asserts the historical authority of imaginative art: 'Poetry was to remember', a way of 'diving, deep, deep, deep' through the layers of the past.[44] 'Perversely', Susan Stanford Friedman suggests, 'H.D. used the historical novel to define modernity.'[45] Her palimpsestic layering of past and present, classical and modern, personal and collective, figures their interconnection.

In *Scenes from the Life of Cleopatra* (1935) Butts attacks the misrepresentation of women in history. The traditional depiction of Cleopatra as a harlot has its origins, she argues, in 'scandals circulated before and after her death, by Octavian, anxious and indeed obliged to justify the annexation of Egypt, her death and Antony's'.[46] But she goes further than this to uncover the gender assumptions which skew the interpretation of historical 'fact'. A historian, she writes, 'may be a man with a miraculous gift for discovering lost facts, and an equal inability to interpret them ... men – historians or not – do not like to think, and so refuse to believe, in an active woman, alone, enjoying the use of power'.[47] Butts's novel offers an explicit corrective to such biased views, depicting 'a girl in a desperate situation',[48] who matures into a woman of power. In rejecting the allegedly 'objective' viewpoint of traditional historiography, Butts also rejects linear historical sequence, presenting Cleopatra's life instead through fragmentary 'scenes', each of which is 'slanted through the perspective of someone, its version of reality obviously incomplete and self-serving'.[49] This emphasis on the discontinuities and inconsistencies which make a single version of history impossible, Hoberman notes, is replicated at the level of the sentence: 'Butts's very syntax insists on gaps and elisions, offering frequent fragments, and sentences like ... "She was not seventeen, in whose veins ran not one drop of eastern blood".'[50]

The experimentation of modernist historical novelists at the level of narrative, sentence, and word, demonstrates particularly clearly the understanding of women writers during this period, that they cannot simply provide a 'supplement' to history. Instead, their fictions question the conceptualization and forms of 'history' itself.

The feminist-socialist historical novel

Critical recuperation of the feminist-socialist historical novel of the 1930s is further developed than work on the modernist historical novel. Chris

Hopkins has, for instance, demonstrated the interpretative value of a Lukácsian Marxist context for the work of Sylvia Townsend Warner, while Janet Montefiore has offered an important reading of the 'anti-Fascist historical novels' of Warner and Mitchison as 'parables of the past'.[51] The diversity of these two writers' experimentation within the genre is striking: Warner, for instance, uses classic realism in *Summer Will Show* (1936), and parable or allegory of the present in *After the Death of Don Juan* (1938), while Mitchison deploys myth and anthropology to reinsert women into history in *The Corn King and the Spring Queen* (1931), and also to develop the historical short story. What connects them is their commitment to historical fiction as a vehicle for the socialist-feminist analysis of oppressive structures of gender, class, sexuality, and race.

In *The Corn King and the Spring Queen*, Mitchison depicts three different societies: the imaginary Marob of her 'barbarian' heroine Erif Der ('Red Fire' backwards); Sparta during and after Kleomanes's attempt to effect a protosocialist revolution; and decadent Egyptian Alexandria. In her Foreword, Mitchison emphasizes the unknowability of history: 'it is all a game of hide-and-seek in the dark', she writes, and Marob is 'just as likely, or as unlikely, as the rest of the world'.[52] Like the female characters of Mitchison's earlier novels, the Spartan heroine, Phillyla, is silenced and erased by the violent male-driven conflicts of 'real' history. She represents a passive femininity so extreme that she facilitates her own execution by 'smoothing out her dress and wrapping it tightly about her so that she would be certain to fall with decency, thus giving no trouble to anyone'.[53] In contrast, freed from the constraints of 'real' history in the imaginary Marob, Mitchison creates a vibrant questing heroine in the 'Spring Queen', Erif Der, whose sexual and maternal sensuality is celebrated.

While the political parallels with Mitchison's own times are there for the discerning reader, it is in her treatment of sexual politics through her rewriting of Freud, Marx, and Frazer that this novel really moves forward. As Hoberman shows, Mitchison borrows selectively from Frazer's *Golden Bough*, turning his account of fertility as 'phallic prowess, death and rebirth' into a 'matter of womb and breast'.[54] In the fertility ritual which gives the book its title, Erif Der, as Spring Queen, is supposed to simulate the killing of the Old Corn, her father, but angry because he has killed her son, she puts her father to death. This is, Montefiore argues, 'a feminist-Socialist rewriting of the Aeschylean Myth', whereby Clytemnestra kills her husband in revenge for the murder of their daughter.[55] Like Orestes, Erif Der incurs a curse for her parricide which necessitates her cleansing through her part in the redemptive death of Kleomanes, the 'king-who-dies-for-the-people'.

Warner's superb *Summer Will Show* (1936) is also more formally innovative than it might at first appear. Warner's experimentalism is, as Gillian Beer astutely notes, 'narratological rather than verbal'.[56] When her children die of smallpox, Sophia Willoughby follows her husband to Paris in 1848 and there falls in love with his mistress, Minna Lemuel, a Jewish storyteller, and becomes involved in the June revolutions. Like Woolf's Orlando, Sophia experiences in very material ways her outsider status as a woman when her husband asserts his ownership of her property (jewels, scent bottles, and the house she inherited from her parents): '"It's mine, do you understand?"' he tells her, '"By the law it's mine. When you married me it became mine."'[57] It is, as the communist Ingelbrecht tells her, drawing the parallel between structures of class and gender, '"A lock-out"'.[58] Sophia works for the revolution by collecting old iron for ammunition. But the further parallel she cannot draw is that which acknowledges the oppressions of race, and Minna is shot on the barricades by Casper, the black illegitimate son of Sophia's uncle, whom Sophia has failed to protect. At the end of the novel Sophia, unsure whether Minna is dead, sits down and begins to read the opening of Marx's *Communist Manifesto*: 'A spectre is haunting Europe – the spectre of Communism.'[59]

The spectre which haunts Warner's text, however, is not just communism but lesbianism. In her important essay on the novel Terry Castle shows how it self-consciously reworks the triangular plot of male homosocial bonding which characterizes the Western canon. Castle suggests that Warner's 'counter-plotting' produces a triangle of female desire which looks 'odd, fantastical, implausible, "not there"', but in fact makes *Summer Will Show* an exemplary lesbian text.[60] However, Castle's analysis, as Montefiore argues, risks dehistoricizing the novel.[61] The daughter of a history master at Harrow School and herself a distinguished musicologist, Warner was intensely aware that the historical novelist must be 'historian enough to do a little research'.[62] In a lecture on the genre in 1940, she stressed that, 'There must, it seems, be some recognition, of history in the historical novel.'[63] But this 'obligation' is more than just imitating period speech. 'Human nature does not change, etc.', Warner argues, 'but human thinking alters a great deal, is conditioned by what it has been taught or what it believes, or disbelieves ...'[64] In offering a gendered revision of 1848, *Summer Will Show* explores significant historical shifts in thinking, explicitly connecting the personal and political, and writing in what has been left out. The extraordinary ending, which reprints the opening of the *Manifesto*, tips the reader out of fiction and back into history, but it is a history that they are now differently equipped to (re-)read.

Conclusion

In comparison with the rapidly-growing body of work on the contemporary historical novel, interwar historical fiction, particularly the modernist historical novel, has been neglected. A critical disdain of historical novels has contributed to the neglect (now being partially rectified) of writers such as Warner and Mitchison who wrote mainly within this genre, but the dominance of Lukácsian critical paradigms has meant that novels which do not fit this model, such as H.D.'s *Palimpsest*, have also been excluded from accounts of the development of the genre. Yet the ways in which these texts fail to fit dominant critical paradigms are often signals that they are self-consciously attempting something different, and that we need to reconstruct our accounts of both the genre and the period to acknowledge this. Like Woolf, these novelists understand that it is not enough simply to produce a 'supplement' to history. Instead, they aim to turn history upside down and inside out, recognizing that 'where truth is important' fiction can allow us to reinvent what has been lost.

Notes

1. Virginia Woolf, *A Room of One's Own* (London: Granada, 1977), p. 45.
2. Ibid.
3. Virginia Woolf, *The Pargiters* (London: Hogarth, 1978), p. 9.
4. Georg Lukács, *The Historical Novel* (Lincoln: University of Nebraska Press, 1983).
5. Avrom Fleishman, *The English Historical Novel: From Walter Scott to Virginia Woolf* (Baltimore: Johns Hopkins University Press, 1971), p. 233.
6. A.J.P. Taylor, *English History 1914–1945* (Harmondsworth: Penguin, 1970), p. 26
7. Lukács, *Historical Novel*, pp. 23, 24.
8. Rose Macaulay, *They Were Defeated* (Oxford: Oxford University Press, 1982), p. 345.
9. Ibid., p. 7.
10. Anthea Trodd, *Women's Writing in English: Britain 1900–1945* (London: Longman, 1998), p. 110.
11. Winifred Holtby, *Women and a Changing Civilisation* (London: John Lane The Bodley Head, 1934), p. 151.
12. Raymond Mortimer, 'New Novels', *New Statesman*, 28 April 1923: 82.
13. Naomi Mitchison, *You May Well Ask: A Memoir 1920–1940* (London: Victor Gollancz, 1979), p. 163.
14. Elizabeth Maslen, 'Naomi Mitchison's Historical Fiction', in *Women Writers of the 1930s: Gender Politics and History*, ed. Maroula Joannou (Edinburgh: Edinburgh University Press, 1999), p. 141.
15. Naomi Mitchison, *When the Bough Breaks and other Stories* (London: Jonathan Cape, 1924), p. 315.
16. Ibid., p. 316.
17. Ruth Hoberman, *Gendering Classicism: The Ancient World in Twentieth-Century Women's Historical Fiction* (Albany: State University of New York Press, 1997), pp. 121–2.
18. Ibid., p. 16.
19. Maslen, 'Naomi Mitchison', p. 139.
20. Naomi Mitchison, 'Writing Historical Novels', *Saturday Review of Literature* 11.41 (27 April 1935): 643.
21. Phyllis Bentley, *O Dreams O Destinations: An Autobiography* (London: Victor Gollancz, 1962), p. 202.
22. Helen Hughes, *The Historical Romance* (London and New York: Routledge, 1993), p. 5.

23. Sue Harper, 'History with Frills: "Costume" Fiction in World War II', *Red Letters* 14 (1983): 14–23.
24. Georgette Heyer, *An Infamous Army* (London: Arrow, 2001), p. 5.
25. Alison Light, *Forever England: Femininity, Literature and Conservatism Between the Wars* (London: Routledge, 1991), p. 256.
26. Joseph McAleer, *Popular Reading and Publishing in Britain 1914–1950* (Oxford: Clarendon Press, 1992), p. 96.
27. Margaret Irwin, *Young Bess* (London: Alison and Busby, 1999), p. 1.
28. Alison Light, '"Young Bess": Historical Novels and Growing Up', *Feminist Review*, 33 (Autumn 1989): 58, 60, 63.
29. Light, *Forever*, pp. 10, 11.
30. Ibid., p. 156.
31. Light, '"Young Bess"', p. 63.
32. D.K. Broster, *The Dark Mile* (London: Heinemann, 1968), jacket note.
33. D.K. Broster, *The Flight of the Heron* (London: Heinemann, 1927), p. 319.
34. Margiad Evans, *Country Dance* (London: John Calder, 1978), p. 95.
35. Virginia Woolf, *Three Guineas* (London: Hogarth, 1986), p. 168.
36. Hilda Vaughan, *Harvest Home* (London: Victor Gollancz, 1936), pp. 144, 141.
37. Hoberman, *Gendering*, p. 22.
38. Virginia Woolf, *Orlando: A Biography* (London: Granada, 1977), p. 153.
39. Ibid., p. 205.
40. Eileen Gregory, *H.D. and Hellenism: Classic Lines* (Cambridge: Cambridge University Press, 1997), p. 1.
41. H.D., *Palimpsest* (Carbondale and Edwardsville: Southern Illinois University Press, 1926), epigraph.
42. Ibid., p. 214.
43. Ibid., p. 158.
44. Ibid., pp. 155, 160.
45. Susan Stanford Friedman, *Penelope's Web: Gender, Modernity, H.D.'s Fiction* (Cambridge: Cambridge University Press, 1990), p. 236.
46. Mary Butts, *Scenes from the Life of Cleopatra* (New York: Ecco Press, 1974), p. 280.
47. Ibid., p. 282.
48. Ibid., p. 279.
49. Hoberman, *Gendering*, pp. 145–6.
50. Ibid., p. 147.
51. Chris Hopkins, 'Sylvia Townsend Warner and the Marxist Historical Novel', *Literature and History*, 4.1 (Spring 1995): 50–64; Janet Montefiore, *Men and Women Writers of the 1930s: The Dangerous Flood of History* (London: Routledge, 1996), Chapter 5.
52. Naomi Mitchison, *The Corn King and the Spring Queen* (London: Virago, 1983), p. 17.
53. Ibid., p. 672.
54. Hoberman, *Gendering*, p. 40.
55. Montefiore, *Men and Women Writers*, p. 165.
56. Gillian Beer, 'Sylvia Townsend Warner: "The Centrifugal Kick"', in *Women Writers of the 1930s*, ed. Joannou, p. 77.
57. Sylvia Townsend Warner, *Summer Will Show* (London: Virago, 1987), p. 264.
58. Ibid., p. 266.
59. Ibid., p. 405 (emphasis in the original).

60. Terry Castle, *The Apparitional Lesbian: Female Homosexuality and Modern Culture* (New York: Columbia University Press, 1993), p. 91.
61. Montefiore, *Men and Women Writers*, p. 177.
62. Sylvia Townsend Warner, 'The Historical Novel', *Journal of the Sylvia Townsend Warner Society* (2007): 53–5.
63. Ibid., p. 54.
64. Ibid., p. 55.

8
'Queens of Crime': The 'Golden Age' of Crime Fiction

Cora Kaplan

The book and souvenir shop of the British Library, whose customers are an eclectic mix of international tourists and the odd researcher furtively seeking distraction from her current project in the reading rooms, is one of the best places in London to go for women's interwar crime writing. The small literature section holds a heterogeneous collection of classic and current novels but it always has a few shelves devoted to crime fiction, old and new. In the former category women writers dominate – Agatha Christie (1890–1976), Ngaio Marsh (1895–1982), Margery Allingham (1904–1966), Dorothy L. Sayers (1893–1957), Gladys Mitchell (1901–1983), Elizabeth Mackintosh (Josephine Tey) (1896–1952) – all of whose careers began in the interwar years. The first four are often dubbed the so-called 'queens of crime' of Britain's 'Golden Age' of crime fiction. Allingham and Mitchell experienced some decades of obscurity after their death, but Christie, Marsh, Sayers, and Tey remained defiantly in print, acknowledged collectively and individually as innovators of twentieth- and twenty-first-century British crime writing. Although Christie's uninterrupted presence on the stage and in the cinema has kept her work in the public eye since the inception of her career, all of these writers have had their work adapted for television in high quality, high profile series starring major actors – in the last three decades especially, feeding the seemingly endless appetite of modern film and television audiences for historical drama. Their reincarnation as 'heritage' authors, often – and with justice – interpreted by critics as both pandering to and constructing an airbrushed, insular, class-bound view of Britain and its history should not obscure their originality or their influence as writers. Their unbroken lineage is represented on these same shelves by later, living generations of celebrated women mystery writers – P.D. James, Ruth Rendell, and Sarah Waters – who regularly pay tribute to their formidable talents and originality. Christie's long-standing position as the best-selling global author of all time has only recently been challenged, most significantly by another woman writer, J.K. Rowling.

The continued popularity of this group of women with readers in a competitive, hard-pressed book market, where many female novelists from the period, both avant garde and middlebrow (with the significant exception of Woolf), have not remained in print, is itself an interesting phenomenon. More curious still, given their durable favour with readers is their relative ghettoization within their chosen genre. Even amongst feminist critics an unacknowledged *cordon sanitaire* has been drawn to separate these writers from their more 'literary' sisters. Extended analyses of their work and careers take place largely apart from discussions of middle and highbrow women writers of the period.[1] Neither have they found a secure home in more demotic and inclusive revisions of Modernism in the last quarter century. Both modernist and postmodern criticism has sometimes seen crime and its investigation as the epistemological imperative of the novel form itself, likening it to fiction's insatiable curiosity, its desire to 'know' and expose the secrets of everyday life driving its narrative, but this argument has done more for the reputation of mainstream fiction than for interwar twentieth-century crime writing by women.[2]

In her definitive chapter on Agatha Christie, in *Forever England: Femininity, Literature and Conservatism between the Wars*, Alison Light suggested that women crime fiction writers, creative contributors to the middlebrow novel of the interwar period, should be read in a continuum with their highbrow sisters. Ivy Compton-Burnett and Christie, Light argues, have in common a 'modernist spirit', 'iconoclasts' both, 'monitoring the plots of family life', each dealing in 'domestic inquisitions', sharing a 'compulsive focus on family secrets, reworking the conventional forms of Victorian transgression – the inheritance drama, mistaken identities, hidden madness'.[3] The threatened instability of the seemingly fixed family, community, and nation marks the work of both authors. Christie frequently falls foul of critics who see her fictional worlds as narrowly concerned with the upper classes and the closed worlds of the village or the country house.[4] Light, however, reveals how surprisingly little her novels engage with the aristocracy, how minimally even the grand estates of the lesser gentry figure, and how rarely the hereditary rich are celebrated as detectives, suspects, victims, or criminals (*FE* pp. 70–80). Allingham, Marsh, and Sayers all give centre stage to their well connected or high born gentleman detectives, Albert Campion, Roderick Alleyn, and Lord Peter Wimsey, while Christie's protagonists, if perfectly genteel, are a fat, ageing Belgian bourgeois, Hercule Poirot, and an elderly provincial spinster, Jane Marple. It is outside the crime genre that great houses have the most symbolic resonance as the nostalgic, romanticized repositories of English or imperial history, even if externally challenged by the modern mutations of culture and gender as in Virginia Woolf's *Orlando* (1928) or threatened by the violence of political modernity as in Elizabeth Bowen's *The Last September* (1929).

Christie is, as Light suggests, a supremely 'anti-sentimental' writer (*FE* p. 70): everything in her developing style, from the early high comic register in which the sprightly detective duo, Tommy and Tuppence Beresford operate, to the later, and more psychologically freighted, Jane Marple in the mysteries of the 1950s and 1960s resists both the bathos and the emotional extremities of melodrama. By making her pair of amateur detectives youthfully cheerful and callous and her elderly and more enduring inventions, Hercule Poirot and Miss Marple, essentially cerebral, astute non-participant observers of life, shockingly unshockable if never heartless, Christie carefully turns down the emotional temperature of the novels, aligning the readers' identification not with characters at all but with the problem-solving pleasures of the sleuths. The whodunnits in general were distanced from the affect surrounding the dead bodies that so necessarily litter the genre. The characteristic 'insensibility' to violence, the supposed comfort to the reader of resolution through the identification and elimination of the perpetrator (though only rarely through trial and execution), the very solvable nature of literary 'puzzles' after the social and political chaos and incoherence of wartime were key to their appeal – in the 1920s and 1930s at least. Briefly a nurse in the First World War, Christie was well acquainted with death in the real, as were her first readers.[5]

Julian Symons is among the first of many critics to argue that while crime fiction may highlight the instability of social relations 'for half a century from 1890 onwards' what 'crime literature offered its readers' was a reassuring world in which those who tried to disturb the established order were always discovered and punished.[6] Yet a fictional world – however stylized and parodic – where almost all of the players are suspects, and almost none without some form of transgressive behaviour or desires, hardly suggests a society at peace with itself.[7] Rather than mythologizing settled, traditional communities little changed by time, the settings and plots of crime fiction in the interwar years imagine a restless, mobile population; part of the productive vigour of the period is a society on the move. Plots dictate that every village and hamlet is a host to 'strange' persons out of place – an influx of louche men and women 'of the world'. Ngaio Marsh's *Death at the Bar* (1939), for example, set in a pub in a remote south Devon village, features a leading London barrister, a successful portraitist, a well-known actor and a conman perpetrator, also an outsider, who has become the treasurer of the thriving Coombe Left Society. Many of Christie's best tales are set abroad or in transit. Women's crime fiction represents with a specially charged intensity this disruptive, seductive, threatening sense of movement, possibility, and change which is the *raison d'être* of the genre's creative energy in these years. The denouement and resolution so often claimed to be the whole point of the genre, is perhaps better seen as a secondary effect, almost a necessary evil. Similarly the term 'cosy', so often mechanically applied to Golden Age crime, and so patronizingly gendered feminine whether the authors are male or female,[8] needs more careful parsing, not least when we try to assign it to the books themselves rather than to the more complicated interactions between writer, text, and reader.

However dangerous it may be, women crime writers of the period take the relentless forward movement of modernity as a given, and if for most its freedoms outweigh its terrors, the latter are always under scrutiny and never underestimated. The social fears are habitually expressed through a class-bound, mildly xenophobic, crudely anti-Semitic, and racist consciousness, very 'modern' prejudices that they share with many other men and women writers of the period. A recognition of the fresh air that blows through a democratizing society is often – but not always – juxtaposed with a sentimental affection for the gentry and aristocracy as well as with a lingering nostalgia for the more deferential homogeneous pre-war society. Golden Age women writers are tacitly if not always polemically committed to the political and social advances for women, or at least middle-class women, by which they are also enabled.

In what follows I want to suggest just some of the ways in which these writers use crime writing to investigate the contradictions and uneven development of modernity in the interwar years in Britain. They all do so within the boundaries of what Light has felicitously called 'conservative modernity', an oxymoron only if we make the easy assumption that to be 'modern' is always to be politically and socially progressive. Yet the real tension in the phrase suggests something of the struggles, many of them of a very everyday kind, that are dramatized in their work.

Born between 1890 and 1904, the lives and careers of these writers were shaped by the shift in sensibility at the end of the Edwardian period. For most, the New Zealander Marsh excepted, the immediate trauma of the war years also brought enhanced possibilities. Their central role in the creation of a new type of crime genre allowed all these women to write their way into lucrative publishing and a mass readership, a route into professional life and out of the confining tradition of nineteenth-century domestic fiction. The 'impersonality' of whodunnits and police procedurals was emphatically not of the epic variety that Woolf, in 1929 in 'Women and Fiction', imagined the newly enfranchised woman author might produce – ambitious, serious novels representing 'social evils and remedies' and the ways in which people 'cohere and clash in groups and classes and races' – but in a less exalted vein it achieved its own considerable authorial emancipations.[9] Christie, the oldest and earliest of the group, tried her hand initially at the kind of political thriller that John Buchan and Edgar Wallace had made famous, but this was not easily adaptable to her talents and local knowledge; there was too much of the 'boys' own adventure' in the thriller, and, one suspects, too much idealized imperial masculinity. She quickly shifted to detective fiction. The subject matter of the mid-Victorian sensation novels of Ellen Wood, Mrs Braddon or Wilkie Collins – adultery, theft, insanity, bigamy, forgery, seduction, and murder – the dark side of family and commercial life were retained, but rewritten as social comedy and sometimes even as farce, the histrionics deployed by sensation writers both silenced and sent up. In *The Murder at the Vicarage* (1930) the language of the vicar's disquiet at the appearance of 'such a woman as Mrs LeStrange in St Mary Mead' whose 'clothes were perfect', who had 'all the ease of manner of a well-bred woman' but who appeared 'incongruous', 'baffling', even '*sinister*' has earlier been the subject of his own self-mockery as straight out of the kind of downmarket detective stories, like '*The Stain on the Stairs*', that he and his irreverent young wife have both been reading.[10] The couple's susceptibility to such imaginings are a sly reference perhaps to the fantasies stoked by Catherine Morland's overheated imagination, fuelled by her avid consumption of gothic novels, in Jane Austen's *Northanger Abbey* (1818).

Although reference to imaginary whodunnit competitors may be the easiest way of signalling to the reader that Mrs LeStrange is a literary type (and therefore unlikely to be the guilty party) her pedigree goes back further. The runaway ex-wife of the universally hated murder victim, Colonel Protheroe, she is a caricature of a sensation heroine par excellence. Her presence in *The Murder at the Vicarage*, especially her narrative fate, is typical of the clever way in which Christie both borrows and relegates older popular forms. At the end, in true sensation-novel fashion, we learn that she is fatally ill and has come to claim Lettice, the daughter she has abandoned. Lettice herself is an only too modern girl, not vicious, but, the narrator thinks, in certain respects 'morally colour blind' (*MAV* p. 227), that is, uncaring about the odd lie, or social and sexual conventions, seen by her as relics of the past. Yet that past, like so much else in Christie, is not idealized and, the novel suggests, is always with us – its crimes and its literary styles linger on even as they are transformed. Lettice herself feels a natural affinity with and sympathy for her newly encountered and less than virtuous mother, their rapprochement cleverly turning into narrative the novel's simultaneous break from and kinship with older popular literature.

Literary appropriation and allusion provide the underpinning and the rhetorical surface of interwar crime fiction, their radical rearrangement of older materials to create a different aesthetic, one which, in true modernist fashion, calls attention not to literal but literary realism. What makes its older stock characters credible is in part their historic familiarity as fictional or dramatic creations. If sensation novels serve as both a resource and target for the interwar genre so does Edwardian crime fiction: Holmes and Watson are fair game for all of these women writers, morphing as they do into the infinitely respectable but always mildly ridiculous Poirot and Hastings, the breezy, mysterious Albert Campion and his companion the ex-convict 'Lugg', or the erudite, nervy Wimsey and his loyal valet, Bunter. Wimsey and Bunter are at once a reinvention of the master detective and his man, and a knowingly satirical competitor to P.G. Wodehouse's hugely successful postwar comic duo, Bertie Wooster and his resourceful butler Jeeves, who entered the cultural imagination of readers in 1917. In Sayers's early stories and novels Wimsey's manner is often that of a Woosterish empty-headed aristocrat; but this is, we are told, a mask, a disguise as effective as Holmes's Dickensian make-up and costumes, adopted to disarm the object of his enquiries. Christie and Gladys Mitchell in particular rely on pastiche and parody of the high seriousness of the highly-coloured Victorian and Edwardian novel, undoubtedly one of the pleasures of their work for its early readership, made more complex in Mitchell's case because she is quick to parody her competitor, Christie.

Crime fiction of this period is never nihilistic, consistently defending a mild, vaguely Christian but mostly secular ethics. However the rejection of the moralizing *tone* of nineteenth-century fiction, if not of morality itself, is as much an absolute as it is in avant-garde modernist writing, and the genre's forms of resistance to it are sophisticated and various. All the writers rely on breezy colloquial dialogue: the social not the inner voice prevails. In the interwar years however, we come to know characters psychologically through their actions and what others say about them rather than through their thoughts. Nevertheless 'Alienists' make regular appearances, and common-sense psychological explanations of characters' behaviour are rife. Although frequently disowned by one character or another, the fashionable language of psychology and psychoanalysis is often dotted through their conversation. Indeed Gladys Mitchell even makes her formidable woman detective, the much-married, Dame Beatrice Adela Lestrange Bradley, a Freudian psychoanalyst. In a 1976 interview Mitchell admits that she 'had read some of Freud's work before I thought of Mrs. Bradley, but Freud has no influence, so far as I know, on my characters'.[11] In *The Murder at the Vicarage* it is Raymond West, Jane Marple's pretentious novelist nephew, a writer who snootily sees no literary interest in the 'crude' act of 'murder', who gabbles on about inferiority complexes and 'inhibitions' (*MAV* pp. 149–50).

The creation in the early 1920s of Hercule Poirot and his dim English foil, Major Hastings – Miss Marple was an invention of the latter end of the decade – offers Christie an interesting strategy around gender. An absurd protagonist with a serious point of view allows her to hold masculinity, both European and English, at arm's length, while avoiding too close an association with contemporary femininity. Bald, vain, fussy, foreign, yet with an old-fashioned courtliness to women, an unthreatening Belgian, like the refugees Christie encountered in the war years, Poirot is hardly the 'new man' of women writers' dreams in the 1920s and 1930s. Without his charisma or cruelty but with something of his egocentrism and intellectual authority he could, just possibly, be a revamp of Charlotte Brontë's beloved Belgian schoolmaster, twice fictionalized by her, in *Villette* (1853) and *The Professor* (1857). Christie got bored with Poirot by the late 1930s, greatly preferring Miss Marple, but her public loved her little anti-hero, so he was allowed to live on – and on. His 'last case' and very final appearance in print in *Curtain* (1975) was actually written in the mid-1930s. The 'new men', gentler, less macho but still masculine, are represented by Marsh's gentleman policeman, Roderick Alleyn, and those amateur detectives and men-about-town, Allingham's Campion and Sayers's Wimsey, all three of whom court and marry during their fictional lives, Alleyn a celebrated portraitist, and Wimsey, the detective-fiction writer, Harriet Vane. Women's crime fiction allows their detectives romance, even passion: its model is modern: companionate, egalitarian marriage. Wimsey, in particular, often thought to be a figure of desire and identification for his creator, must engage in a long agonistic negotiation with his love object to persuade her that in spite of his birth and fortune and her tarnished reputation – she was once accused of the murder of a former lover – they can have an equal partnership.

The negotiation of female autonomy is a leading though by no means universal theme in interwar women's crime fiction, but it is certainly a favoured mode through which modernity and its discontents are figured. In 1928 the franchise for women in Britain, which had been limited since 1918 to women over thirty, was brought into line with that for men. It is surely more than coincidental that the late 1920s and early 1930s see the introduction of Christie's Jane Marple, Harriet Vane (who, once acquitted, will help Wimsey with his enquiries in future books), and Gladys Mitchell's fearless psychoanalyst Beatrice Adela Lestrange Bradley, as well as Sayers's creation of an all women's investigatory agency run by the redoubtable Miss Climpson. Of these inventions, Mitchell's frightening, even grotesque, '*saurian*', Mrs Bradley, is by far the boldest and most bizarre figure, and, like her author, one of the longest lived – she starred in sixty-six mysteries. However, the very tentative entry of Jane Marple and Harriet Vane into their respective narratives as well as their relationships to the wider gender politics of the plots suggests just how freighted and anxious these representations of modern life were – especially in relation to gender.

Christie's *The Murder at the Vicarage*, the first novel in which Jane Marple figures, and Sayers's *Strong Poison*, which introduces Harriet Vane, both appeared in 1930. Although one is a village tale and the other set in London they both debate the effects of the loosening of sexual conventions and the negative consequences of 'free love' in the postwar period. In Christie's novel the narrator is the nice, liberal vicar, Len Clement, whose younger, 'distractingly' pretty wife, ironically called Griselda, unapologetically confesses to her entire absence of domestic skills. She is, nevertheless, a perfectly dutiful 'Vicaress', as she calls herself, hosting those 'old cats', the village spinsters, for 'tea and scandal at 4:30' (*MAV* p. 4). The tea-table, where the reader meets Jane Marple, is the setting for female conversation, a social venue and a literary device with its origins in the eighteenth century. The gossipy gathering of unmarried or widowed village women recalls the *mise-en-scène* of Elizabeth Gaskell's *Cranford*. In Christie's fiction stereotypes are 'turned' like a thriftily remodelled dress: same material, different look. But Miss Marple is no naive Miss Mattie. The real innocents in *The Murder at the Vicarage* are the young women in their teens and twenties. The idle, vague, flirtatious Lettice with her excellent command of modern slang reports the 'shemozzle' around the activities of the visiting artist, Lawrence. Griselda, a loyal, loving wife, plays with the modern idiom in another way by teasing her vulnerable husband with the flippant suggestion that she'll 'have an affair' with Lawrence, who is painting her portrait.

Miss Marple, like Len Clement, knows that 'the worst' of human nature is often the truth. Hoping to persuade Len that they should 'work together' on the crime, she represents her intrusive interest in 'Human Nature' to him as a harmless gentlewoman's 'hobby'. Other women, she explains, take up 'woolwork and Guides, and Welfare, and sketching', but she pursues an amateur interest in the natural science of classification – 'genus this' and 'species that' like 'birds or flowers' (*MAV* p. 195). If Miss Marple thinks of herself as an amalgam of Beatrix Potter and Beatrice Webb, Len offers a more readerly rationale for his desire to find the murderer: 'I think each one of us in his secret heart fancies himself as Sherlock Holmes' (*MAV* p. 196), he suggests, as he agrees to join forces, and Jane Marple tacitly endorses his masculine, literary fantasy, giving it an international twist by admitting that she has been 'reading a lot of American detective stories from the library lately' (*MAV* p. 196). Christie's 'vinegary' spinster's innate curiosity and well-honed detective skills are thus given a double source: the first grounded in the natural sciences with its respected, traditional niche for female amateurs but updated in line with the newer human sciences of psychology and sociology, and the second, which highlights not only the rational and affective stimulus of reading, but also its ability to inspire androgynous fantasy and identification. As Miss Marple develops over time, the police and other male authority figures with whom she works, regularly find her 'terrifying' precisely because her appearance and manner are so at odds with her coolly objective talents. Like Peter Wimsey's disarming impersonation of an 'upper-class twit', Miss Marple's 'woolly', 'scatty' old lady is a strategic performance of femininity.

In the penultimate novel in which she appears (published in 1971), physically quite frail but mentally still sharp, she is, simply, *Nemesis*, a divine figure of retributive justice in a humble, seemingly harmless human incarnation. The early, interwar Miss Marple is a more tentative invention; Christie can be seen to be negotiating, somewhat hesitantly, the level of social transgression her creation would be allowed. A similar kind of 'trying-out' is evident in relation to the crime genre and its complicated genealogy in *The Murder at the Vicarage*, where Christie works hard to distinguish her trademark kind of narrative from both its sensational predecessors and contemporaries, while highlighting the influence (for good and ill) of all such popular fictions on the making of modern subjectivity and the social imaginary.

While the knowing internal reference to other crime fiction, past and present, is a hallmark of Golden Age texts, only Dorothy Sayers, through the creation of the mystery writer Harriet Vane in *Strong Poison* and her reappearance as a central figure in *Gaudy Night* (1935), inaugurates an explicit, extended discussion within the novels themselves of the relationship between women's status, sexual mores, and literary hierarchies. Sayers was, in fact, a leading critic, definer, and defender of crime fiction; her position elaborated in a series of introductions to three anthologies and a key essay between 1929 and 1936. Her history of the genre is almost exclusively masculine: Wilkie Collins, Charles Dickens, and Conan Doyle represent the high point of literary excellence in Victorian and Edwardian crime writing. Sayers is much less complimentary about sensation fiction by women in the same period, and about her female contemporaries. She greatly admired the work of E.C. Bentley and G.K. Chesterton (fellow members of the newly formed Detection Club[12]), arguing in 1930 that men of 'literary distinction' had been increasingly turning their talents to writing 'good mystery fiction'.[13] Their books moreover were not being read in 'back kitchens' but in 'Downing Street, and in Bloomsbury studios, in bishops' palaces, and in the libraries of eminent scientists' (PSMS p. 47).

Yet there was, she thought, a problem. The mystery story was 'indeed becoming more and more high-brow in its appeal, more subtle, literary and dessicated' (PSMS p. 47). The present vogue for the 'pure puzzle' among educated mystery readers was, she suggests, largely conjunctural, 'the product of a period of emotional exhaustion', one in which 'religion, morals and sentiment' are 'in difficulties' (PSMS p. 49). The aftermath of war together with the accelerated pace of technological change ('the triumphant march of science and the machine') made the 'detective problem' an attractive mental recreation (PSMS, p. 49). This moment, Sayers believed, could easily be supplanted by a humanist resurgence, marked by the return of philosophy, rationalism, and 'the glorification of the Natural Man' (PSMS p. 49). For twentieth-century crime fiction to endure in the way that Collins and Conan Doyle have done, and become 'classics of their kind', it must, she argues, be able to create living characters, and to possess in literary and in emotional and philosophical terms, 'a certain power and force' (PSMS p. 51).[14]

For the educated, devout, but staunchly feminist Sayers, the translator of Dante, and the author of a series of religious plays in the 1940s, interwar modernity had an inexorable trajectory, but its effects could be damaging as well as liberating. The lack of affect, morality, and realist characterization in the purely cerebral detective stories of her competitors was, she thought, itself a troubling sign of the social and ethical crisis of the times. *Strong Poison* maintains the light comic tone that was a signature of Golden Age crime, and which the earlier Wimsey novels shared with Christie and others, but 1930 is the year of Noel Coward's *Private Lives*, and the banter between the imprisoned Harriet and her would-be rescuer successfully echoes the rhythm of Coward's witty dialogue, which had become, by the end of a decade in which his work was rarely off the West End stage, an almost unconscious part of the metropolitan, if not national, idiom.

Sayers was very conscious of her debt to P.G. Wodehouse, and in *Strong Poison* Wimsey admonishes Bunter not to 'talk like Jeeves'.[15] The jokey repartee and near farcical scenes and plots of much interwar crime makes it patent that mystery writers were chasing the same audience. Yet beneath the comic skin of *Strong Poison* we can see Sayers beginning, cautiously, to put into practice her call for a more fleshed-out approach to the genre and to social issues. Its plot hinges, in part, on Harriet Vane's seemingly perverse refusal of her live-in lover's marriage proposal, a rejection that becomes, in the eyes of the law, a clue to her complicity in his murder. Vane's indignant rejection of Philip Noyes's offer stemmed from the fact that the louche writer had persuaded her to live with him on the grounds that he had a philosophical objection to marriage, when in fact he was simply trying out the relationship to see if he cared enough about her. 'Free love', Harriet argues plausibly, always seems to benefit men rather than woman. Even Peter Wimsey's gallant and successful campaign to find the true culprit and free Harriet, to whom he proposes, represents for her a burden of gratitude and dependency that she, and the novel, resists. Although never mentioned, the exemplary figures of Mary Wollstonecraft and William Godwin, lovers and then married partners from that 'age of reason' and its split-off corollary 'sentiment', which Sayers predicts may be due for a twentieth-century renaissance, seem to hover over Harriet's twentieth-century predicament. Her position is made worse, in the eyes of the law, because she is a highly successful writer of crime fiction, who was, at the time of her ex-lover's death, researching a book involving poisons. Independent, university-educated, professional women with a 'tarnished' sexual history are presented in *Strong Poison* as seen by the authorities and the public as dangerous both to men and to the social order.

Sexual desire, even heterosexual love, is the 'wild card', the Achilles heel, of the emancipated woman, threatening her civic, mental, and emotional independence. It takes Sayers several novels to resolve the question for Harriet Vane, but *Strong Poison*, like *The Murder at the Vicarage*, finds a simpler and more satisfactory fictional solution for single or widowed women – 'mostly elderly, but a few still young and attractive' all 'women ... of the class unkindly known as "superfluous"'.

> There were spinsters with small fixed incomes, or no incomes at all; widows without family; women deserted by peripatetic husbands and living on a restricted alimony ... retired and disappointed school-teachers; out-of-work actresses; courageous people who had failed with hat shops and tea parlours; and even a few Bright Young Things, for whom the cocktail party and the nightclub had grown boring.
>
> (*SP* pp. 54–5)

These women worked for an ageing spinster, Miss Katharine Climpson, in a secret investigative agency set up and financed by Peter Wimsey, a business whose 'front' was a 'typing bureau' but which had 'a private telephone to Scotland Yard'. His 'Cattery', as Lord Peter calls it, provides an essential, if informal service as well as giving a livelihood and occupation to the impoverished gentry. Miss Climpson, whose previous employment had been as a ladies' companion, is a member of that slowly-disappearing class. With her heavily italicized epistolary style, 'spare, lace-covered wrists', and her firm Christian beliefs, she is also a recognizable literary type, which reaches back as far as Charlotte Brontë's *Shirley* (1849) and Elizabeth Gaskell's *Cranford* (1851). As in Christie, the stereotype is 'turned'. Kitty Climpson may look like an Edwardian throwback, but she embraces modernity. She loves Charlie Chaplin films and emphatically rejects the 'old conditions' of female respectability in 'Queen Victoria's time' as *'difficult* and humiliating' (*SP* p. 190).

Kitty Climpson's staff represent a much wider spectrum of indigent females, some reminiscent of George Gissing's *The Odd Women* (1893), others more like the brisk, liberated characters in Sarah Grand and allied New Women fiction. Wimsey's benevolent patronage of the 'superfluous' women offers them a new life and useful, interesting work, bringing to justice men guilty of 'fraud, blackmail and attempted procuration' who preyed on women by advertising in the small ads. This is surely Sayers's mischievous, feminist send-up of those nineteenth-century peers, politicians, and authors, Dickens and Gladstone for example, who became so suspiciously involved in the 'rescue' of prostitutes. Miss Climpson and her undercover 'cats' conducting their 'espionage' in the gendered domain of provincial tea rooms and the haberdashery sections of department stores are also a witty domestication of the female spy, a figure made famous in the First World War by the notorious Mata Hari. Like Jane Marple, Miss Climpson's cover is the persona of a dotty old lady. *Strong Poison* devotes some sixty very funny pages to 'Kitty' Climpson's daring infiltration of the all-female household of the murdered man's dying aunt, where, through a hilarious *faux* séance that she orchestrates, a lost will is discovered. Another shorter section follows the antics of her younger colleague, Miss Murchison's undercover operations in the law office of the real murderer. These comic set pieces, which include Bunter's interrogation of the broadly drawn cockney servants in the murder scene's household, and Wimsey's researches at a ghastly bohemian party, make up much of the novel. Yet in spite of the fact that we are never inside Harriet's consciousness, in narrative terms she has a great deal of agency. Her ordeal, which includes her bitter self-recrimination about the mistaken passion that led her there is the sober, social, and emotional note at the heart of the story.

Gaudy Night (1935), set in an Oxford's women's college, Sayers's own Somerville, thinly disguised, extends the discussion of modernity and women to the vocation of female academics.[16] It represents Sayers's most ambitious attempt to marry crime writing to mainstream fiction, combining a novel of ideas, a mystery and a love story in the resolution of the Peter/Harriet anti-romance. Here Harriet's inner life is given a full and compelling exposition. *Gaudy Night*'s elite but eloquent feminism makes a powerful, detailed case for the life of the mind, and for professional women in general, but its anti-fascist subtext is marred by the attribution of the most reactionary sexual politics to working-class characters, no longer simply present as an excuse for low comedy. The perpetrator turns out to be a college servant, the widow of a failed academic and suicide. Annie Wilson hates not only the female dons who robbed her husband of his profession and his life but also all women who aren't married and mothers. In a novel that, in passing, prophetically describes Europe as under the shadow of impending war, the enraged maternalistic Annie becomes, outrageously, an explicit stand-in for proto-fascist philosophy.

Critics who dislike Sayers's attempt in *Gaudy Night* to make crime fiction more philosophical and more mainstream, more like the middlebrow and highbrow fiction by women writers of the period, see the introduction of Harriet Vane as a literary disaster. However, Sayers's model of crime writing, in which social issues and rounded realistic characters keep company with ingenious plots, has proved hugely influential in the development of the genre, especially as practised by women. Josephine Tey's immediate postwar mysteries are darker, more psychological studies, if still lightened by traces of the social comedy that dominated the work of the 1920s and 1930s.[17]

In later life both Christie and Marsh were given formal recognition by the establishment, both made 'Dames' for their contribution to literature, a tradition upgraded when P.D. James and Ruth Rendell were awarded the higher rank of Baroness by Conservative and Labour governments respectively. From the 1970s onwards feminist crime writing became a highly successful sub-genre reinventing the female sleuth in relation to the mood and demands of second-wave feminism, liberating them from the oversight of male collaborators. But there was room too for figures more reminiscent of the conservative modernity and class-bound feminism espoused by Sayers or Christie. Carolyn Heilbrun, an American academic, who wrote as Amanda Cross from the mid-1960s, invents an alter ego, the amateur detective, feminist English professor Kate Fansler, as a direct twentieth-century tribute to Sayers's intellectual Harriet Vane. And in *An Unsuitable Job for a Woman* (1972), one of her earliest and best mysteries, P.D. James, now a Conservative peer, uses a Cambridge University setting (less idealistically rendered than Sayers's beloved Oxford) for the first investigation by Cordelia Grey, her young woman private eye. The gentlemen policeman and upper-class amateurs of the Golden Age come to life again in the provincial and metropolitan chief inspectors of James and Ruth Rendell – not so new, new men for late twentieth- and twenty-first century readers.

Marsh's and Allingham's well tailored fictions stick closer to the schematic model that Christie made so famous, while still developing their own distinctive voices. Marsh weaves her theatrical experience into her crime writing, and Mitchell's comically offbeat, slightly surreal mysteries make fun of the puzzle form it nevertheless replicates, drawing from other elements of modernist style. There is no space here to consider their intimate and creative intersection with contemporary theatre, radio, and cinema: Marsh was an internationally acclaimed theatre director; Christie, and Tey as Gordon Daviot, wrote for the stage and Sayers for the radio.

As I have suggested, the literary and social interest and innovation of Golden Age women's crime writing does not, and ought not, depend on either a negative comparison to realist fictional traditions on the one hand or to 'high Modernism' on the other. Eclectic, inventive, and like other modernist writing making the open appropriation of other genres and art-forms a virtue, the work of these writers deserves much more serious, collective cultural and critical attention. Their achievements, well written about within the criticism on crime fiction, should be considered and situated more firmly in the wider field of contemporary literature and its genealogy.

Notes

1. See for example Jessica Mann, *Deadlier than the Male* (Newton Abbot: David & Charles, 1981), one of the earliest feminist studies which treats Christie, Sayers, Allingham, Tey, and Marsh; Katherine Gregory Klein, *The Woman Detective: Gender and Genre* (Chicago: University of Illinois Press, 1988); Maureen T. Reddy, *Sisters in Crime: Feminism and the Crime Novel* (New York: Continuum, 1988); and Sally R. Munt, *Murder by the Book? Feminism and the Crime Novel* (London: Routledge, 1994), all of which are very interesting, informative but genre-specific studies.
2. See Laura Marcus, 'Detection and Literary Fiction', in *The Cambridge Companion to Crime Fiction*, ed. Martin Priestman (Cambridge: Cambridge University Press, 2003), pp. 245–68.
3. 'Agatha Christie and Conservative Modernity', in Alison Light, *Forever England: Femininity, Literature and Conservatism between the Wars* (London and New York: Routledge, 1991) p. 61 (hereafter *FE*).
4. See summary discussion in Stephen Knight, 'The Golden Age', in *The Cambridge Companion to Crime Fiction*, p. 82.
5. See Agatha Christie, *An Autobiography* (London: Collins, 1977).
6. Julian Symons, *Bloody Murder* (London: Pan, 1994), p. 24.
7. Robert Barnard makes this point in relation to Christie in *A Talent to Deceive: An Appreciation of Agatha Christie* (London: Collins, 1980), Chapter 6, *passim*. Light also emphasizes the 'instability' of the society described. Yet the idea of conservative closure as the ideological effect of the genre is hard to dislodge: more recently Stephen Knight argues that the identification of criminals in the 'mandarin' upper-middle-class world that Christie creates 'is a process of exorcising the threats that this society nervously anticipates within its own membership: the

multiple-suspect structure has a special meaning in a competitive individualistic world'. Stephen Knight, 'The Golden Age', p. 82.
8. See Raymond Chandler's famous 1944 critical essay on the genre which contains an egregiously misogynist and homophobic attack on Golden Age British crime writing: Raymond Chandler, 'The Simple Art of Murder', in *Later Novels and Other Writings* (New York: Library of America, 1995).
9. Virginia Woolf, 'Women and Fiction', in *Virginia Woolf on Women and Writing*, ed. Michele Barrett (London: Women's Press, 1979), pp. 43–52, p. 51.
10. Agatha Christie, *The Murder at the Vicarage* (New York: Berkley Books, 1986), pp. 17, 5 (hereafter *MAV*).
11. Interview with Gladys Mitchell in B.A. Pike, 'In Praise of Gladys Mitchell', *Armchair Detective*, 9.4 (October 1976).
12. Formed in 1930 by a group of British mystery writers, the club, still in existence, counted Christie and Sayers among its founder members. Its 'oath' and 'rules' were tongue-in-cheek rather than prescriptive. The club held annual dinners, but also initiated some collaborative projects. Mitchell and Allingham were elected members in 1933 and 1934, and Marsh in 1974.
13. Dorothy L. Sayers, 'The Present Status of the Mystery Story', *London Mercury*, 23.133 (November 1930): 47–52, p. 47 (hereafter PSMS). Sayers points out that the mystery story in Britain 'has never been completely divorced from a certain fine artistic seriousness', p. 49.
14. In *Gaudy Night*, Harriet and Peter discuss, without fully resolving, the problem of too little and too much realistic characterization in the novel that Harriet is currently writing.
15. Dorothy L. Sayers, *Strong Poison* (London: Hodder & Stoughton, 2003), p. 257 (hereafter *SP*).
16. See Janet Hitchman, *Such a Strange Lady: An Introduction to Dorothy L. Sayers* (London: New English Library, 1975).
17. On Tey's 'conservative modernity' see Alison Light, 'Writing Fictions: Femininity and the 1950s', in *The Progress of Romance: The Politics of Popular Fiction*, ed. Jean Radford (London: Routledge & Kegan Paul, 1986), pp. 139–56.

Part III
Gendered Genres

9
Poetry, 1920–1945
Jane Dowson

Revisionary anthologies were integral to the debates in conferences, books, and articles that considered women's participation in the experimental avant-garde poetry associated with the 1920s, the left-wing public poetry that characterizes orthodox versions of the 1930s, and the still-evolving documentary literature about the Second World War. In the 1970s, editors retrieved forgotten poets through anthologies with a broad historical and national sweep.[1] Into the 1980s, editors began to evaluate poets' contribution to literary periods and movements and feminist critics looked for the female-specific features that run within and across these periodizing categories. Fleur Adcock's seminal *The Faber Book of Twentieth-Century Women's Poetry* (1987) brought to prominence poets who showed intellectual 'wit', such as Charlotte Mew (1869–1928), Anna Wickham (1884–1947), Frances Cornford (1886–1960), Elizabeth Daryush (1887–1975), Stevie Smith (1902–1971), E.J. Scovell (1886–1961), and the American-born H.D. (1886–1961). In 1984, Catherine Reilly uncovered a number of poets in *Chaos of the Night: Women's Poetry and Verse of the Second World War*, a sequel to her equivalent collection of First World War poetry,[2] and Jane Dowson's *Women's Poetry of the 1930s* filled in the gap for that decade.[3]

Looking back on the years 1920–1945, we can claim that women poets held their own in established literary categories and also require a critical response that attends to their anti-feminine strategies. The best poets moved from a gender-denying abstract lyricism to more adventurous verse styles and dynamic dramatic monologues whereby the poet could speak through a constructed female, and sometimes male, voice. Throughout the period, Edith Sitwell, Mew, Wickham, Smith, and Sylvia Townsend Warner stand out for their varied proddings at literary and social conventions. These include poetry of radical anti-poetic disruptions, coded lesbian desire, bold feminist protest and left-wing social commentary. Their avoidance of the sentimental subject matter and clichéd language associated with the denigrated 'poetess' links them to the further thirty poets who published volumes of poetry in this period.[4]

Context: '(You seldom get the impression of femininity from a woman's book.)'[5]

The above parenthetical statement by the imagist poet Richard Aldington in 1915 registers the heightened consciousness of gender as a cultural construct during the first two decades of the twentieth century. Wickham, whose book Aldington is reviewing, laments how social ideals of femininity prohibited female self-expression:

> It's so, good Sirs, a Woman-poet sings
> Sick self, and not exterior things,
> She'd joy enough in flowers, and lakes and light,
> Before she won soul's freedom in a fight.[6]

In her Introduction to the first woman-edited anthology of the century, *A Book of Verse by Living Women* (1910), Lady Margaret Sackville also associated women's creative development with social emancipation: 'When women have fully proved their capacity for freedom, we can begin to estimate better their capacity for poetry.'[7] A decade of suffragism later, the *Times Literary Supplement* (*TLS*) reviewer of 'The Poetry of Women' (1920), used three new books of sentimental verse from which to homogenize all women's poems. He channelled social anxiety about women's new freedoms in support of barring their entry to the most elite genre: 'But though we allow the novel to be abused in the interests of sex propaganda, lyrical poetry, by the very strict limits of its constitution, will permit no such transgression.'[8] In 1921, J.C. Squire, the notoriously traditionalist Georgian, published *A Book of Women's Verse* in which he observed the phenomenon of women's literary activity:

> Today we scarcely bother about the distinction between male and female writers. With thousands of women writing, with women's verses in every magazine and women represented in every newspaper office, when literary women congregate in clubs, and robust women novelists haggle with editors and discuss royalties with their male rivals, we take composition for granted as a feminine occupation.[9]

Significantly, however, most of Squire's poets were dead and his collection perpetuated them as constituting a segregated and inferior backwater. In *The Bookman*, Rebecca West observed that it was 'a remarkably thin volume and a remarkably poor one', advising that 'feminist societies should buy up all copies of this book and suppress them'.[10] Squire's anthology provoked a long article in the *Times Literary Supplement* headed 'Poetesses' which embellished mythologies of sentimental femininity: 'sincere women's poetry will have the warmth, the wholeness, the grace, the allurement, the tenderness, or the mockery of the feminine mind'.[11] In *Time and Tide*, E. Macbeam's review of Squire's anthology pointed to the need to distinguish the best from the weakest: 'Women *do* write verse, far more of it than men do; a great deal of it gets into print in the *Poetry Review*, the prize page of *The Bookman*, and in minor publications. Women do not, however, always excepting the "star" names, produce great or lasting poetry.'[12]

The desire of intellectual poets to integrate in a male-dominated industry can be seen in their initiatives. They promoted modern poetry by running publishing houses, bookshops, and journals and through editing, reviewing, and journalism. Nancy Cunard's The Hours Press, in Réanville and then Paris, printed twenty-four books between 1928 and 1931, including the poetry of Richard Aldington, Louis Aragon, Robert Graves, Laura Riding, Ezra Pound, William Carlos Williams, Kay Boyle, and Gertrude Stein. Riding and Graves ran the Seizin Press (1927–1939) to encourage new, mostly male, poets and later edited a critical review, *Epilogue* (1935–1937). In Paris, Sylvia Beach's Shakespeare and Company was an international meeting place[13] and the Poetry Bookshop in London provided a platform for new poets, including Cornford, Mew, May Sinclair, and Wickham. Alida Monro took over the shop after her husband was called for war service; he was subsequently too unwell to run it and died in 1932.[14] The less well-known Bermondsey Bookshop was started by Ethel Gutman in 1921 to provide free access to literature and foster the local community's ardour for self-improvement. She also initiated *The Bermondsey Book*, a quarterly literary review where working-class writers were positioned alongside famous authors and thinkers.[15] Dorothy Wellesley edited the Hogarth Living Poets series and Anne Ridler worked with T.S. Eliot at Faber and Faber.

Their unconventional lives additionally demonstrate that the 'cult of femininity' propagated during and after the First World War was alien to these poets. Lilian Bowes Lyon, Cunard, and Edith Sitwell were distanced from the social elitism of their upper-class families, particularly because, as women, they could not hold power or inherit property. Vita Sackville-West, Wellesley, Warner, Valentine Ackland, and H.D. rejected heterosexual for same-sex relationships. Mina Loy and Riding divorced and remarried. Cornford and Wickham were married with children but Cornford suffered from severe depressions and Wickham separated from her husband for a while and eventually committed suicide. Elizabeth Daryush, who spent time in Persia with her husband, chose not to have children. Sitwell, Winifred Holtby, Mew, May Sinclair, Smith, Bowes Lyon, and Pitter were single.

Suzanne Clark identifies women as both losers and drivers in a literary climate that valued objectivity, impersonality, and 'intellection':[16]

> The modernist revolution turned away from ordinary language and everyday life. This disconnection from social consequence, from history,

has everything to do with the gendering of intellectuality ... Modernism developed its anti-sentimentality into a contemptuous treatment of women, who had to struggle both internally and externally with that contempt ... [and] these women seized the moment to escape from categories of gender.[17]

As Clark observes, Sitwell's famous renunciation of her literary foremothers expresses the urgency of distancing 'woman poet' from 'sentimentality':

> Women's poetry, with the exception of Sappho (I have no Greek and speak with great humility on that subject), and with the exception of 'Goblin Market' and a few deep and concentrated, but fearfully incompetent poems of Emily Dickinson, is *simply awful* – incompetent, floppy, whining, arch, trivial, self-pitying, – and any woman learning to write, if she is going to be any good at all, would, until she had made a technique for herself (and one has to forge it for oneself, there is no help to be got) write in as hard and glittering a manner as possible, and with as strange images as possible – strange, but believed in. Anything to avoid that ghastly wallowing.[18]

In an earlier article 'Some Observations on Women's Poetry' (1925), Sitwell had asserted that women should not write like men either:

> Women poets will do best if they realise that male technique is not suitable to them. No woman writing in the English language has ever written a great sonnet, no woman has ever written great blank verse. Then again, speaking generally, as we cannot dispense with our rules, so we find free verse difficult.[19]

In *New Verse* in 1934, Riding echoes that women were ineffectual when they 'assume the manner of men'.[20] Thus, poets who wished to be considered on equal terms with men had to negate the stereotypes of archetypal femininity and also negotiate with the forms, styles, and symbols of the male literary tradition they inherited.

The British avant-garde

A group of independent upper-class writers broke into and away from male-dominated traditions, fuelled by opposition to both cultural elitism and social prescriptions of femininity. Sitwell, along with Nancy Cunard and Iris Tree, also daughters of aristocrats, and Helen Rootham, her former governess and lifelong companion, produced the controversial *Wheels* anthologies (1916–1921) in which they published their work. Intended as an antidote to Edward Marsh's anodyne *Georgian Poetry* books, *Wheels* launched a generation of innovative poets, men and women, on equal terms. Tree's poems were printed in anthologies, magazines like *Vanity Fair*, and four collections. Cunard's poetry also appeared in *The English Review* and *New Age*; she published four collections between 1921 and 1930, worked in French and Spanish, and was a meticulous translator. Tree and Cunard feature in the literary reviews, memoirs, and correspondence of their contemporaries.[21] Sitwell's publishing history spans eight decades: she was a prolific literary reviewer and critic, wrote a novel, historical and satirical biographies, edited several poetry anthologies, and gave poetry readings and lectures on poetry in Europe and the United States. Her most successful period was from 1922 to 1929, during which she visited Paris where she was influenced by European art; her meeting with Gertrude Stein in 1924 began an important alliance between the two champions of avant-garde poetics, although it became tinged with rivalry. Sitwell was awarded the Royal Society of Literature's medal for poetry in 1934.

During the 1920s, there was frequent correspondence in the papers about 'the Sitwells' in connection with the new poetry.[22] They resuscitated a revolutionary zeal that had inspired the imagist and other poets before the war. Edith particularly maintained the momentum for stylistic innovation when the literary press was wary of radical forms because they were conceptually associated with violence. She held weekly soirées and according to Geoffrey Gorer, the leader of the Cambridge University Poetry Society:

> These tea parties of hers really *were* one of the most extraordinary literary affairs of the twenties when you think of them. For there she was, all but penniless, in a dingy little flat in an unfashionable part of London. All she could offer was strong tea and buns. Yet because of who she was she attracted to that flat almost every major literary figure of the twenties.[23]

Sitwell's outlandish clothing and caustic manner can be seen as part of her anti-feminine self-masking.[24] In a letter to Stephen Spender, she confessed to lacking an adequate female model 'to point the way ... I had to learn everything – learn, among other things, not to be timid, and that was one of the most difficult things of all.'[25] Sitwell's reviews of women's books and her frequent references to the nature of women's poetry illustrate her preoccupation with the gendering of poetic techniques that confronted her in the rhetoric of male criticism.

The impersonality of modernist principles provided a legitimate way out of identifying as a woman. Sitwell explains her defamiliarizing strategies in her lengthy article, 'Modern Poetry' (1928) and the Introduction to her *Collected Poems* (1957).[26] *Façade* (1922) marks the stage, between the greater realism of Sitwell's earlier and later work, where she experimented with the equivalent to abstract art and the rhythms of music. In the last section, 'Sir Beelzebub', exaggerated iambic pentameter parodies rigid Victorian values:

> Alfred Lord Tennyson crossing the bar laid
> With cold vegetation from pale deputations
> Of temperance workers (all signed In Memoriam)
> Hoping with glory to trip up the laureate's feet,
> (Moving in classical metres) ... [27]

In 'Fox Trot' and 'Hornpipe', the aristocratic customs of foxhunting and dancing are mocked through similar play with nineteenth-century nonsense and Tennysonian narrative verse. The evocation of an outworn culture in *Façade* connects with *The Waste Land* (1922), which Sitwell admired. She first met T.S. Eliot in 1917 and their acquaintance continued, if somewhat intermittently, for many years. The twenty-one part *Bucolic Comedies* (1923) operates on the level of verbal experiment, particularly rhythm and rhyme, but also explores the psychological effects of Sitwell's unhappy childhood at Renishaw Hall: 'She was made to walk with her three tall aunts / Drooping beneath the snow's cold plants.'[28] In *The Sleeping Beauty* (1924),[29] set in her maternal grandmother's home at Londsborough,[30] Sitwell similarly negotiates between psychological realism and a substitute world of dreams and enchantments. The poem experiments with discordant rhymes and juxtaposes allusions from popular and high artistic forms and traditions – classical and Christian, literary and nursery rhyme.

As we have seen, Sitwell's disruptions of literary traditionalism were contingent with disturbing traditional power structures. Inspired by the hunger marches, *Gold Coast Customs* (1929) was also an attack on fashionable society, personified in Lady Bamburgher who hosts champagne parties while men starve. It got a good, lengthy review in the *Times Literary Supplement* although the social realities were denied.[31] The poem's longer lines and the despair at human barbarity anticipate Sitwell's later poems, which respond to extreme national upheavals in a return to realism that was taking precedence over avant-garde aesthetics during the 1930s and the Second World War.

Transatlantic exchanges

The classification 'Transatlantic' accommodates the ex-patriation of H.D. and Laura Riding from the United States to England, and Mina Loy from England to New York. North American poets are subject to competing interpretations: were they impelled by Ezra Pound's dictum to 'make it new' and 'broke form *for* the boys'[32] or do their anti-traditional structures, myth-making, and elliptical typography, features associated with feminine writing, support the claim that modernist experimentation was driven *by* women? As Celeste Schenck puts it: 'For Woolf and H.D. the notion of breaking sentence and sequence was a way of rupturing political assumptions of great pertinacity and of making a radical criticism of power and status.'[33] Like Sitwell, but more so, the poets' gender-conscious stylistic experiments unsettle a clear line between expressive and self-reflexive poetry.

H.D. became known in Britain and America through imagist and other anthologies and through the progressive journals. She famously won the respect of Pound, Aldington, and D.H. Lawrence and throughout her career was one of the most active practitioners and promoters of free verse. She championed her American contemporaries Marianne Moore and Amy Lowell, and in Britain she enjoyed the mutual regard of May Sinclair, Dorothy Richardson, and Sitwell. *Sea Garden* (1916) was published in London and her two subsequent collections (1921, 1924) in both London and the United States. In the 1920s she more explicitly explored and expressed female desires and perspectives, often through revising Greek mythologies, as in the dramatic monologue 'Cassandra' where the beautiful prophetess addresses the Roman god Hymen: 'when will you break my wings / or leave them utterly free?'[34]

Laura Riding left the United States in 1926 and spent her time in Mallorca and London. She did not align herself with literary groups, although she associated with members of the Paris–Bloomsbury avant-garde including Virginia Woolf, T.S. Eliot, Ezra Pound, Sitwell, and Stein. She published ten books of poems during the 1920s and 1930s, influencing some younger poets whom she published through her Seizin Press. The term 'Modernist' was first used by Riding and Graves in *A Survey of Modernist Poetry* (1927)[35] and Michael Roberts consulted her extensively during the formation of *The Faber Book of Modern Verse* (1936) in which nine of her poems were included. As Jeanne Heuving observes, 'Within existing periodizing concepts, (Riding) Jackson's poetry can only be seen as a strange kind of amalgam of modernist, New Critical, and postmodernist poetics.'[36] Riding's poetry is illuminated by her Preface to *Collected Poems* (1938) where she explains that her experiments with shedding 'literary conventionalities of poetic idiom' – rhyme, image, symbol or form – were aimed at achieving the diction of uncontaminated thought.[37] Riding's ideal of cultural sanctification through linguistic purity is also illustrated in *A Pamphlet against Anthologies* (1928). Heuving believes that 'crucial to (Riding) Jackson's utopian vision of a new human universality is her gender critique'.[38] Riding refused to be in women-only anthologies to avoid the general 'declassing' of woman poets.[39] In 'The Word "Woman"' she looks at the alienation of women in language[40] that is dramatized in 'Postponement of Self': 'Is this Me I think / In all the different ways till twenty. / At twenty I say She.'[41] 'Helen's Faces', a monologue by Helen of Troy, states, 'the original woman is mythical' and 'The Lady of the Apple', envisages a condition of pre-lapsarian sex equality.[42]

London-born Mina Loy can justly be claimed as 'a pioneer of international modernism'[43] and the number of memoirs in which she features can gauge her influence. In addition to critical essays, stories, and plays, she published two books of poems in her lifetime, but individual poems were printed in *The Dial, The Little Review,* and other experimental American journals. These were available in Sylvia Beach's Paris bookshop visited by Wickham and Sitwell. Loy's verse portrait 'Nancy Cunard' registers her admiration[44] while her veneration of Stein is evident in her reviews, essays, and verse portrait.[45] As she sets out in her article 'Modern Poetry' (1925),[46] Loy's commitment to revolutionizing English verse was fuelled by her antipathy towards her background. Her long poem 'Anglo-Mongrels and the Rose' needs to be understood in the context of her mixed parentage: her father was a Jewish immigrant and her mother a bourgeois Englishwoman. Like Eliot and Sitwell, Loy was influenced by Baudelaire in her belief that artists had a prophetic role: 'Ostracised as we are with God / The watchers of the civilised wastes.'[47] Loy made the case that by involving readers in interpretation and by destabilizing high cultural norms, Modernism worked on democratic principles: 'through cubism the newspaper has assumed an aesthetic quality, through Cézanne a plate has become more than something to put an apple upon'.[48] She experimented with the textual correspondences to modern art and jazz to overcome 'the cold barrier of print', as in 'The Widow's Jazz' ('White man quit his actin' wise / colored folk hab de moon in dere eyes').[49]

As Alicia Ostriker observes, 'In an age when it was widely believed that "women are the cause of modernism, whatever that is" – as one journalist put it – these writers were at the provocative edge of the avant-garde. ... they strove to escape the ghetto of feminine poetry by the leaps and bounds of undisguised intelligence.'[50]

Female-centred modernists

Whereas Ostriker emphasizes rupturing literary norms, another band of critics, headed by Bonnie Kime Scott, Celeste Schenck, and Suzanne Clark, challenge language-centred interpretations of modernism, 'favoured in the canonisation process from Ezra Pound to Julia Kristeva', which ignore other breaks with tradition.[51] The modernists in this section appropriated literary tradition to their female-centric and feminist agendas; they experimented with metrical variation, free verse, irregular line lengths, half rhyme, new symbolism, and colloquial idioms. Drawing on the newly available vocabulary of psychoanalysis they investigated female subjectivity and sexual relations. They did not disguise themselves as men nor dissociate themselves from each other. In *Writing for Their Lives 1910–1940*, Hanscombe and Smyers prove how female friendships were vital to female creativity. Although not included in the survey, the relationship between poets Mew and Sinclair, albeit complicated, was arguably integral to their writing.[52] Both Mew and Sinclair were steeped in the Brontës and connect to their Victorian predecessors in exploring women's warring impulses for self-renunciation and self-realization but go further in their evocations of repressed desire.[53]

Records of the reception to Mew endorse how she crosses orthodox literary groups. She won the good opinion of Victorian novelist and poet Thomas Hardy – 'far and away the best living woman poet who will be read when they [the others] are forgotten'[54] – and appealed to avant-garde writers like Woolf, who famously called her 'the greatest living poetess',[55] and Sitwell, who in *Time and Tide*, proclaimed that only the few 'who care anything for poets are reading her work'.[56] Mew's literary centre was the Poetry Bookshop where she helped Alida Monro; her poems were printed in Harold Monro's *New Shilling Magazines*, various periodicals, including *The Egoist*, and anthologies of modern poetry. Mew's reputation was largely established by *The Farmer's Bride* in 1916 and in 1921 it was reprinted with new poems and simultaneously published with an American edition called *Saturday Market*. In America it caught the eye of Louis Untermeyer and at home it received favourable reviews. Both 1924 and 1925 were successful years during which her reputation spread and her supporters stretched from Robert Bridges to Siegfried Sassoon.

The thematic arrangement of *Collected Poems* (1951) makes a largely unclassifiable range seem manageable, but it does not allow for consideration of Mew's stylistic evolution. Val Warner's collection (1997) is more usefully chronological and includes prose selections. As Warner observes:

> Her innovative modernist technique of rhyming free verse, probably derived from Matthew Arnold and others, was closer to the iambic beat than her later work. Recent feminist or lesbian criticism, sometimes citing her use of repeated rhyme that chimed with her American champion Marianne Moore's concerns, often places Mew outside 'male-dominated' modernism, yet within this movement Mew innovated.[57]

The combination of rhyme with irregular metre structurally supports the unfathomable tension between social restraints and personal liberty that Mew explores. Her striking experiments with line lengths and their attendant enjambments allow the representation of identity as a process, as in the opening lines of 'On the Road to the Sea':

> We passed each other, turned and stopped for half an hour,
>   then went our way,
>   I who make other women smile did not make you –

Here, the ungendered pronouns, and elsewhere monologues in a male voice, enabled Mew to express her repressed love for women. With reference to her suicide in 1928, Mew's biographers agree that the conflicts produced by her love for women remained unresolved and were projected onto her representations of mental conflict.

The publication of *The Writings of Anna Wickham* in 1984 brought out her poetry from obscurity. British born, she grew up in Australia, returned to Britain in 1904, and married in 1906. Wickham held soirées at home in London, mingling entertainment with publicity for women's suffrage. Her literary acquaintances included Nancy Cunard, the Poetry Bookshop circle, and the bohemian writers associated with D.H. Lawrence. She spent five months in Paris in 1922, during which she met Ezra Pound as well as Natalie Barney, Sylvia Beach, Robert MacAlmon, Edna St Vincent Millay, and Djuna Barnes. Wickham had a stormy marriage and when her husband died following a climbing accident in 1929, she was freed from its bonds. Freedom of expression is Wickham's central preoccupation in *Fragment of an Autobiography*:

> The relief of writing will give me nervous and physical energy to continue with my task. I write also because I am a woman artist and the story of my failure should be known. I have a European reputation: my poetry is mentioned with honour in the *Encyclopaedia Britannica*: that should give me the right to live. I have very little newspaper reputation.[58]

Surprisingly, some poems were included in *Edwardian Poetry* (1937) and *Neo-Georgian Poetry* (1937) but they have nothing of the formal restraint or agreeableness associated with either. The *Times Literary Supplement* reviewer of *The Little Old House* (1921) commented on her 'lively rhythm and vigorous expression' but undermined the poems as 'flung-off stanzas' and 'sudden unrevised inspirations, sometimes even despising punctuation in her haste'.[59]

In 'Return of Pleasure', Wickham asserts that psychological and creative freedom are interdependent:

> I thought there was no pleasure in the world
> Because of my fears.
> Then I remembered life and all the words in my language.
> And I had courage even to despise form.
> I thought, 'I have skill to make words dance,
> To clap hands and to shake feet,
> But I will put myself and everything I see, upon the page.'[60]

Nevertheless, Wickham suffered the familiar dilemma about aligning the poet and woman in herself. 'Suppression' asserts women's right to write – 'If you deny her right to think, / If you deny her pride of ink / She will smile like a slave' – while 'Woman and Artist' states: 'There's no excuse for expression from a woman / Unless she be representative human.'[61] In 'The Angry Woman', a lengthy discourse on sex differences and equality, the concept of the androgynous imagination parallels other writers' search to avoid gender imperatives: 'There is the sexless part of me that is my mind.'[62]

Wickham's dramatic monologues boldly delve into and present complex psychology, often in domestic conflict. In 'Marriage', a couple's competing instincts for love and liberty are depicted as inextricable and inevitable and 'The Revolt of Wives' contradicts the ideal that childbearing is woman's greatest gift, goal, and pleasure.[63] In 'The Wife' we find Wickham's characteristic combination of rhyme and a colloquial voice that mediates competing forces:

> 'Twere better for my man and me,
> If I were free,
> Not to be done by, but to be.
> But I am tied.[64]

The mix of form and formlessness links Wickham to Mew and also to Stevie Smith. It pushes the reader to ask, 'is this poetry?' and search for a new critical vocabulary.[65]

Martin Pumphrey believes that although Smith 'is not a writer who can easily be recruited as a feminist', she connects to 'other women writers whose poetic strategies have been directed not towards the construction of an authoritative and consistent poetic persona or self but towards disruption, discontinuity and indirection' which are 'strategies of (covert) resistance to the silencing or muting experienced by women within mainstream culture'.[66] Among her gallery of characters, there are assertive women of the moneyed classes, like the mother-in-law in 'Octopus', but most sympathy is directed towards ordinary women like Sally Soo, 'Poor Maria',[67] or the 'patient Griselda of a wife with a heart of gold' who are the casualties of men's freedom to speak and choose: 'Such men as these, such selfish cruel men / Hurting what most they love what most loves them.'[68] Rarely as direct in the language of feminist awareness, Smith's treatment of organized feminism was characteristically liberal. In 'Dear Female Heart' the narrator expresses sympathy for the female species but urges women not to play the victim with a miserable face.[69]

Warner's poetry best unhinges the association between conventional verse forms and ideological conservatism. Jane Marcus endorses Schenck's case for 'elasticizing' stylistic considerations in order to include writers such as her.

> Revising modernism to include this poem [*Opus 7* (1931)] unsettles definitions ... If we privilege lyric fragmented voices from this period, what to do with this other tradition, the daughters of Aurora Leigh? Townsend Warner wrote the verse novel as well as Tudor metrical conceits, the dark and dramatic Hardyesque as well as the committed communist ballad. Her multivoicedness and creation of character in dramatic soliloquy call out for a critical extension of Bakhtin's work on the novel to poetry. In the age of metropolitan modernism, Warner politicizes the pastoral ... she set all the forms at her disposal dancing to the tune of politics.[70]

Warner wrote in her diary in November 1927, 'I want to read and write nothing but poetry'[71] and in October 1929, recorded writing a poem a day. Her poems were printed in literary journals and anthologies and she contributed articles on contemporary literature to *Time and Tide*. Her collection *The Espalier* (1925) was followed by *Time Importuned* (1928), which was given a long complimentary review in the *TLS*. In *The Criterion*, it received a favourable verdict, albeit with the deadly 'poetess' word: 'Now that Miss Charlotte Mew is dead, I think Miss Warner should be proclaimed the best poetess in England', and a *Time and Tide* reviewer noted, 'there are epitaphs and ironic tragedies on the roads of Wessex and psychoanalysis'.[72]

As in her highly imaginative, feminist novel *Lolly Willowes* (1926) and narrative poem *Opus 7*, Warner, a socialist, 'politicizes the pastoral', often in the democratic forms of ballad or narrative quatrains. In 'Wish in Spring', which is concerned with the right to write,[73] Warner uses homely images – 'cups and saucers on a shelf' – to register the competition between the woman's domestic role and her identity as a poet. An uncollected poem, 'Ornaments of Gold', is a dialogue between a mother and daughter about conventional femininity.[74] 'The Rival', ostensibly a light-hearted monologue by a farmer's wife about her husband's absorption in his work, depicts her sense of confinement and neglect, 'Twelve times I've put my neck into the halter: / You'd think / So much might knit my husband's love to me', while 'The Absence' goes further in depicting carefree independence, 'How happy I can be with my love away!'[75] Akin to the spirit of Wickham, Warner is contrastingly 'formally tight in thought and expression'.[76]

Apart from Ridler's 'The Letter', a verse epistle to her husband, love poetry is scarce, except for the lesbian lyrics by Sackville-West and between Warner and Ackland, published in their combined volume *Whether a Dove or a Seagull* in 1934.[77] These lyrics indicate covert lesbian identity in the safety of traditional form and gender indeterminate pronouns. In Ackland's quasi-sonnet, 'What must we do if we cannot do this', the 'this' is the love which dare not speak its name –'our tightened cord, our secret tether' – and in 'Drawing You Heavy with Sleep', Warner's metaphors of liquidity are paradigmatic representations of female sexuality:[78] 'Your arm fell / Across me as a river throws / An arm of flood across meadows.'[79] The representation of female desire was brave in a cultural climate that expected women, particularly poets, to conform to conservative precepts of sexless femininity.

War and social class, 1930–1945

The fierce egalitarianism of Smith and the political engagement of Warner, Ackland, Mitchison, Holtby, and Cunard challenged any lingering assumptions that women belonged to domestic, not public, spheres. These and other poets were active in communist, socialist, and feminist movements and attempted to write poetry of commitment that avoided propaganda.

Kathleen Raine's 'Fata Morgana', published in *New Verse* and several anthologies, registers the political/aesthetic interface with which many writers wrestled: 'Books, idle books, and hours, unfruitful hours, / Weigh on my genius and lay waste my will.'[80] Holtby suffered a lifelong quarrel between the artist and social reformer in her[81] whereas Warner reconciled the tension in her 'discovery that the pen could be used as a sword'.[82] She was active in socialist and communist movements and joining the Communist Party in 1933 concluded her journey to Marxism during the 1920s.[83] Warner's best poems on the Spanish Civil War, notably 'El Heroe', 'Port Bou', 'Journey to Barcelona', 'Waiting at Cerbere', and 'Benicasim' combine her skills as a narrator and observer.[84] As Barbara Brothers states, they 'do not romanticise or sentimentalise the soldier. Her poems are written in the context of suffering and unheroic battlefield conditions that the poets of World War One such as Wilfred Owen, pictured for those who remained at home.'[85] Warner's two most militant poems, 'Red Front' and 'In This Midwinter', are not included in her *Collected Poems* or *Selected Poems*. 'Red Front' was printed in *Left Review*, 1935,[86] and draws upon the associations of the French Revolution to cultivate the sense of horror in those looking on at the war. Its anachronistic vocabulary, 'mire' and 'blight', sits oddly with the rousing refrain:

> Comrade, are you mired enough,
> Sad enough, tired enough –
> Hush! – to march with us tonight
> Through the mist and through the blight?

While the Spanish War poems demonstrate the 'immediacy' that Warner commended in her lecture 'Women as Writers',[87] they carry no hint of gender distinction, partly because they echo Hardy and the First World War poets and partly perhaps because the Marxist emphasis on collective not individual identity transcends sex differences. Warner assumes the persona of a rebellious male civilian in 'Some Make This Answer', published in *Left Review* in February 1936. The speakers in Ackland's 'Communist Poem 1935' are ungendered republican supporters and 'Instructions for England' is gender-neutral polemic. Like Warner and Ackland, Cunard also channelled much of her political anger into journalism, but her poem 'To Eat Today' is a strikingly successful dramatization of a Spanish peasant family ravaged by the civil war. Cunard's unusual 'Sonnet in Five Languages' is printed with her explanatory notes in Valentine Cunningham's anthology, *The Penguin Book of Spanish Civil War Verse* (1980). The anthology also reproduces some of her translations, such as Pablo Neruda's 'Almeria', which provided another outlet for her hostility to upper-class complacency.

Naomi Mitchison was outspoken about her democratic politics and 'To Some Young Communists from an Older Socialist' was printed in *New Verse* in January 1933. Smith distanced herself from Mitchison's politics in a letter to

Denis Johnson, 1937: 'more talkie from Naomi Mitchison, and she's got world problems on the brain too ... but if she thinks she is going to rope me in to the Haldane-communismus gang she is mistaken'.[88] Smith was more opposed to what she called the 'groupismus' of party politics than to Mitchison's socialist principles. Her deceptively playful aesthetics are symptoms of her hostility to the pretensions of the upper classes towards high culture. Again and again, Smith mimics the voices of power in order to expose and scrutinize them. Her association between voice and status is reflected in her reference to 'A lot of highclass people with irritating voices' in a letter to John Hayward in 1942.[89] Her essay 'Private Views', printed in the *New Statesman and Nation*, 7 May 1938, almost imperceptibly mocks the viewers at the Royal Academy exhibition of classic art,[90] and her pastiche poem 'Salon D'Automne' reduces the exclusivity of modern artists to male voyeurism: 'This is the Slap school of art, / It would be nice / To smack them.'[91] Smith was a prolific poet during the 1930s but not published until David Garnett risked printing some of her poems in the *New Statesman* in 1936. There was sufficient response to these to convince Jonathan Cape to produce *A Good Time Was Had by All* in 1937 and *Tender Only to One* in 1938. 'Souvenir de Monsieur Poop' – with the words, 'I am the self-appointed guardian of English Literature' – is one of several swipes at the literary establishment which made it so difficult for her to get her poems published and properly reviewed.

For Smith, feminism and socialism, never articulated as such, were parallel impulses rooted in a liberal temperament which sided with the downtrodden. In 'Lord Barrenstock', the baron is a 'seducer of a hundred little boys' who has cheated people of their status and property and fiddled his gains at the stock exchange with intolerable indifference. Controversially, the poem explores the *response* to such a man as much as his wrongdoings: '"Tis not for these unsocial acts not these / I wet my pen.'[92] In 'The Bishops of the Church of England',[93] 'Major Macroo', and 'Lord Mope', Smith maintains the comitragic register but is more vitriolic. Like other 1930s poets, Smith wrote about the new developments on the edge of towns and cities, but unlike them she is more critical of snobbery than suburban uniformity: 'There is far too much of the suburban classes / Spiritually not geographically speaking. They're asses.'[94] Her treatment of the working class similarly did not patronize but praised unsung heroes like 'Alfred the Great': 'Honour and magnify this man of men / Who keeps a wife and seven children on £2.10.'[95]

In 'The Lads of the Village', Smith undermines the poetry of war (and implicitly those who market and consume it) for aestheticizing pain rather than war per se, but this was daring during a period where patriotic war sensitivities were still acute:

> Oh sing no more: Away with folly of commanders.
> This will not make a better song upon the field of Flanders,
> Or upon any field of experience where pain makes patterns the
>   poet slanders.[96]

Here, Smith's potency derives from her persistent transgression of conventional frontiers which she mediates by transgressing literary norms: 'Oh talking voice that is so sweet, how hold you alive in captivity, how point you with commas, semi-colons, dashes, and pauses and paragraphs?'[97]

Many women poets of the Second World War look stylistically more conventional but frequently blend lyric with narrative devices to present the interaction of individual with collective experience. Since all men and women were involved, there was less scope for the rhetorical and imaginative juxtapositions between 'home' and 'front' that characterized First World War poetry. Warner's 'Road 1940' combines her skills as a short story writer and poet in the lament of a woman left with someone else's sick child.[98] Mitchison's dramatic monologue 'The Farm Woman 1942' also draws in the reader as audience, and shifts between the local and the global.[99] Set in the same year, Wellesley's resonating 'Milk Boy', is a filmic clip of the war's devastation enhanced by a starkly elegiac voice-over.[100] Scovell's 'A Wartime Story' tells how a woman burns her dead baby, conceived with an airman while her husband was overseas.[101] Other memorable snapshots of the war's atrocities, notably Hiroshima and the concentration camps, include Karen Gershon's 'A Jew's Calendar'.[102] Her colloquial understatement and disconcerting detachment are characteristic of this war's literary anti-heroism. Ada Jackson's collection *World in Labour* (1942) is one of the most original: 'Maimed Baby' is a shocking cameo of the effects of 'the *Fuehrer*' which she also confronts in the monologue 'Hitler Youth' where a duped young Nazi disciple has been run over.[103]

In this climate of social upheaval, in which traditional gender roles were decisively unsettled, Hugh Lyon clings to ideals of feminine gentility in his Foreword to *Poems by Contemporary Women* (1944):

> But here is a fresh claimant to favour, a chorus of voices, speaking to him not only of war, but of home, of the dreams of his heart and the ardours of his soul; songs to drown for a moment the urgent tumult into which he is thrust. For the quieter the voice of the poet, the more powerful its spell; and the reader will find quiet voices here – 'soft, gentle and low, an excellent thing in a woman'.[104]

Like other editors before him, Lyon selects poems that fit his own model of women. Such mythologies of domestic poetry can be further refuted by the number and quality of neglected proclamatory poems by women. These can only be surveyed in this chapter but warrant further attention. Sitwell's 'Still Falls the Rain: The Raids, 1940. Night and Dawn' registers many writers' blend of modernist fragmentation with expressive realism. Lynette Roberts's *Gods with Stainless Ears*, dedicated to Sitwell, was explicitly written for filming. Subtitled 'a heroic poem', it maintains classical blank verse throughout its fifty pages. Each of the five parts is prefaced with an 'Argument' to set the scene. Roberts uniquely directs an apocalyptic vision of monstrous war which includes close-ups of personal anguish and culminates in the gunner entering a 'Mental Home for Poets'. Sheila Wingfield's *Beat Drum Beat Heart* (1946, composed by 1944) is a neglected oratorio on war. Pushing home the prejudices against women as public commentators, G.S. Fraser announced: 'Sheila Wingfield is something rather unusual in women poets, an objectivist ... The emotions get expressed indirectly through her grasp on the outer world.'[105] Jackson's candid opposition to Hitler's regime is fulsomely realized in the nineteen-page prizewinning pamphlet poem *Behold The Jew* (1943). She celebrates Jewish identity and major talents along with compassion for the race's history of suffering that is repeated in each person's quotidian experiences. Although based on rhyming iambic quatrameter, which is varied for changes of mood, the poem has epic stature. H.D.'s *Trilogy* (1944–1946) is considered a masterpiece of war writing; it offers a visionary version of contemporary history while evoking the unconscious personal and collective drives that war involves.

Conclusion

Collectively, women poets demonstrate the cultural cross-currents of the period. Their public activities challenged lingering myths of feminine domesticity, naivety, conservatism, and piety. Their poetry was published in progressive publications, including left-wing journals and seminal anthologies such as *Twentieth-Century Poetry* (1929), *Recent Poetry* (1933), *The Faber Book of Modern Verse* (1936), *The Oxford Book of English Verse* (1936), and *Poems of Today* (1938). Retrospectively, they can be positioned in such established categories as avant-garde, Anglo-American, the 1930s, and war poetry. Their work also unsettles and stretches the boundaries of these literary groups with their female-centred perspectives and blend of formal and experimental verse styles. Some reflected the new female autonomy in their stylistic independence, self-asserting colloquial voice, and bold dramatizations of gender. Where stylistically avant-garde poems might appear ungendered, the woman-consciousness can be perceived through its denial or disruption.

Celeste Schenck argues for expanding Modernism to include 'anything written between 1910 and 1940', judging that the loss of 'a certain stylistic designation' is less than the gain of 'all other modernisms against which a single strain of white male, international modernism has achieved such relief'.[106] Accordingly, we might recognize poets who are hard to classify but published in this period, notably Eleanor Farjeon (1881–1965) and 'Susan Miles' (Ursula Roberts, née Wyllie, 1887–1975). In the guise of 'Tomfool' during the 1920s, Farjeon made subversive comments on the news which appeared serially in the socialist *Daily Herald* and were published in books by the Labour Publishing Company (1920, 1921). Roberts produced three socially aware collections in the 1920s and edited two poetry anthologies.

Other poets who have been overlooked or sidelined include Sackville-West, Muriel Stuart, Cornford, Pitter, E.J. Scovell, Elizabeth Daryush, Ridler, Bowes Lyons, and Wellesley, all of whom were particularly successful in terms of publishing and critical reception. Instead of counting as achievements, their popularity and awards like the Hawthornden Prize (Sackville-West and Pitter) and the Queen's Medal for Poetry (Cornford) have tended to align them with the conservative literary establishment and reading public. Nevertheless, in their rejection of high poetic diction, they also participated in the literary revolt against Victorianism that had been precipitated and complicated by the First World War.

Notes

1. Cora Kaplan, *Salt and Bitter and Good: Three Centuries of English and American Women Poets* (New York and London: Paddington Press, 1975); Louise Bernikow, *The World Split Open: Four Centuries of Women Poets in England and America 1552–1950* (London: Woman's Press, 1979); *The Penguin Book of Women Poets*, ed. Carol Cosman, Joan Keefe, and Kathleen Weaver (Harmondsworth: Penguin: 1978).
2. Catherine Reilly, *Scars upon My Heart: Women's Poetry and Verse of the First World War* (London: Virago, 1981).
3. Jane Dowson, ed., *Women's Poetry of the 1930s* (London: Routledge, 1996).
4. The material is dealt with in more detail in Jane Dowson, *Women, Poetry and British Modernism 1910–39* (Aldershot: Ashgate, 2002) and Jane Dowson and Alice Entwistle, *A History of Twentieth Century Women's Poetry* (Cambridge: Cambridge University Press, 2006).
5. Richard Aldington, 'New Poetry', review of *The Contemplative Quarry*, by Anna Wickham (London: Poetry Bookshop, 1915), *Egoist*, 2 (1 June 1915): 89–90.
6. Anna Wickham, 'Explanation', in *The Writings of Anna Wickham: Free Woman and Poet*, ed. R.D. Smith (London: Virago, 1984), p. 296.
7. Margaret Sackville, *A Book of Verse by Living Women* (London: Herbert and Daniel, 1910).
8. 'The Poetry of Women', review of Gladys Mary Hazel, *The House*, Dorothea Still, *Poems of Motherhood* and Fay Inchfawn, *The Verse Book of a Homely Woman*, *Times Literary Supplement* (9 December 1920): 810.
9. J.C. Squire, ed., *An Anthology of Women's Verse* (Oxford: Clarendon, 1921). See John Pearson, *Facades: Edith, Osbert and Sacheverell Sitwell* (Basingstoke: Macmillan, 1978), pp. 146–50.
10. Rebecca West, 'Women Poets', *Bookman* (May 1921): 92–3.
11. 'Poetesses', *Times Literary Supplement* (24 November 1921): 267.
12. E. Macbeam, 'Poetry and the Woman: The Creative Power', *Time and Tide* (9 June 1922): 545.
13. Sylvia Beach, *Shakespeare and Company* (London: Faber and Faber, 1960).
14. See 'Letters from Edith Sitwell and Alida Monro', *Time and Tide* (2 and 9 April 1932), pp. 371, 395; Joy Grant, *Harold Monro and the Poetry Bookshop* (London: Routledge and Kegan Paul, 1967).
15. Editorial Notes, *The Bermondsey Book*, 1.2 (March 1924): 3–4. See Jane Dowson, '*Time and Tide* (1920–76) and *The Bermondsey Book* (1923–30): Interventions

in the Public Sphere', in *The Oxford Critical and Cultural History of Modernist Magazines, vol 1: Britain and Ireland 1880–1945*, ed. Peter Brooker and Andrew Thacker (Oxford: Oxford University Press, 2009), pp. 530–51.
16. 'Intellection' was a favourite term of approval in T.S. Eliot's literary magazine, *The Criterion*.
17. Suzanne Clark, *Sentimental Modernism: Women Writers and the Revolution of the Word* (Bloomington and Indianapolis: Indiana University Press, 1991), pp. 13, 3, 4–5, 8.
18. Edith Sitwell, Letter to Maurice Bowra (24 January 1944), in *Edith Sitwell: Selected Letters*, ed. John Lehmann and Derek Parker (Basingstoke: Macmillan, 1970), p. 116.
19. Edith Sitwell, 'Some Observations on Women's Poetry', *Vogue* [London], 65.5 (March 1925): 117–18; Elizabeth Salter and Allanah Harper, eds, *Edith Sitwell: Fire of the Mind* (London: Michael Joseph, 1976), pp. 187–92.
20. Laura Riding, 'An Enquiry', *New Verse*, 11 (October 1934): 5.
21. William Carlos Williams and Samuel Putnam, in *Nancy Cunard: Brave Poet, Indomitable Rebel 1896–1965*, ed. Hugh D. Ford (Philadelphia: Chilton Book Company, 1968), pp. 56–7.
22. See, for example, review of *England Reclaimed: A Book of Eclogues*, by Osbert Sitwell, *Times Literary Supplement* (27 October 1927): 760; Letter from Lawrence Housman, *Time and Tide* (22 June 1928): 612.
23. Geoffrey Gorer, in Pearson, *Facades*, p. 155.
24. Current criticism perpetuates the personal mythologies. See headlines to reviews of *Selected Letters of Edith Sitwell*, ed. Richard Greene (London: Virago, 1997): 'Epistles of a Great English Eccentric' by Philip Zeiger, *Daily Telegraph* (1 March 1997) and 'Withering Heights' by Miranda Seymour, *Sunday Times* (9 March 1997).
25. Edith Sitwell, Letter to Stephen Spender (16 March 1946), in *Edith Sitwell: Selected Letters*, ed. Lehmann and Parker, pp. 136–7.
26. Edith Sitwell, 'Modern Poetry', *Time and Tide* (30 March 1928): 308–9; Edith Sitwell, *The Collected Poems* (1957; London: Macmillan, 1961). [All subsequent page numbers to *CP* are from this edition.]
27. Sitwell, 'Sir Beelzebub', *CP*, p. 158.
28. Sitwell, 'Winter', *CP*, pp. 33–5.
29. Sitwell, 'The Sleeping Beauty', *CP*, pp. 64–5.
30. Edith Sitwell, *Taken Care of: An Autobiography* (London: Hutchinson, 1965), p. 61.
31. Review of *Gold Coast Customs*, *Times Literary Supplement* (21 February 1929): 137.
32. Celeste M. Schenck,'Exiled by Genre: Modernism, Canonicity, and the Politics of Exclusion', in *Women's Writing in Exile*, ed. Mary Lynn Broe and Angela Ingram (Chapel Hill: University of Carolina Press, 1989), p. 246, note 6.
33. Ibid.
34. H.D., 'Cassandra', in *Collected Poems of H.D.* (New York: Boni and Liveright, 1925), pp. 250–2, 250.
35. Laura Riding and Robert Graves, *A Survey of Modernist Poetry* (London: Heinemann, 1927), pp. 155–6.
36. Jeanne Heuving, 'Laura Riding Jackson's "Really New" Poem', in *Gendered Modernisms: American Women Poets and Their Readers*, ed. Margaret Dickie and Thomas Travisano (Philadelphia: University of Pennsylvania Press, 1996), pp. 192–213.
37. Laura Riding, *The Poems of Laura Riding* (Manchester: Carcanet, 1980), p. 1.
38. Heuving, 'Laura Riding Jackson's "Really New" Poem', p. 192.

39. Riding, Preface to *Collected Poems* 1938, reprinted in *The Poems*, p. 418.
40. Laura Riding and Schuyler B. Jackson, *The Word 'Woman' and Other Related Writings*, ed. Elizabeth Friedman and Alan J. Clark (New York: Persea, 1993), p. 13.
41. Riding, 'Postponement of Self', *The Poems*, p. 59.
42. Riding, 'Helen's Faces', in *The Close Chaplet* (London: Hogarth Press, 1926); 'The Lady of the Apple', Preface to Riding and Jackson, *The Word 'Woman'*, pp. v–vii.
43. Fleur Adcock, ed., *The Faber Book of Twentieth Century Women's Poetry* (London: Faber, 1987) p. 7.
44. Mina Loy, 'Nancy Cunard', in *Nancy Cunard: Brave Poet, Indomitable Rebel*, p. 103.
45. Mina Loy, 'Gertrude Stein', in *Mina Loy: The Lost Lunar Baedeker*, ed. Roger Condover (Manchester: Carcanet, 1997), p. 94.
46. Loy, 'Modern Poetry', *Charm*, 3.3 (April 1925): 16–17, reprinted in *Mina Loy: The Lost Lunar Baedeker*, pp. 157–61.
47. Loy, 'Apology of Genius', *Mina Loy: The Lost Lunar Baedeker*, pp. 77–8.
48. Mina Loy, 'Gertrude Stein', *Transatlantic Review*, 2.2 (1924): 305–9, 427–30, reprinted in *The Gender of Modernism*, ed. Bonnie Kime Scott (Bloomington and Indianapolis: Indiana University Press, 1990), pp. 238–45.
49. Mina Loy, 'The Widow's Jazz', in *Mina Loy: The Lost Lunar Baedeker*, pp. 95–7. It is an elegy to the memory of her second husband, the American, Arthur Cravan.
50. Alicia Ostriker, *Stealing the Language: The Emergence of Women's Poetry in America* (London: The Women's Press, 1987), pp. 48, 53.
51. *The Gender of Modernism*, ed. Scott, p. 5.
52. See Suzanne Raitt, 'Charlotte Mew and May Sinclair: A Love Song', *Critical Quarterly*, 37.3 (Autumn 1995): 3–17.
53. Charlotte Mew wrote an introductory essay to preface a new edition of Emily Brontë's poems, but she was beaten to it. See 'The Poems of Emily Brontë', in *Charlotte Mew: Collected Poems & Selected Prose*, ed. Val Warner (Manchester: Carcanet, 1997), pp. 363–5 (hereafter referred to as *CP* 1997).
54. Penelope Fitzgerald, *Charlotte Mew and Her Friends* (London: Collins, 1985), pp. 170–4.
55. Virginia Woolf, Letter to Vita Sackville-West (9 November 1924), in *The Letters of Virginia Woolf, vol. 3, 1924–1928: A Change of Perspective*, ed. Nigel Nicolson and Joanne Trautman (London: Hogarth Press, 1977), pp. 140–1. An editor's note suggests that this was Hardy's opinion, not Woolf's. Earlier, however, Woolf had written, '[I] have got Charlotte Mew's book [*The Farmer's Bride*], and think her very good and interesting and unlike anyone else.' (Letter to Robert Trevelyan (25 January 1925), in *The Letters of Virginia Woolf, vol. 2, 1912–1922: The Question of Things Happening*, ed. Nigel Nicolson and Joanne Trautman (London: Hogarth Press, 1976), p. 419.)
56. Edith Sitwell, review of Charlotte Mew, *The Farmer's Bride* and *The Rambling Sailor*, *Time and Tide* (21 June 1929): 755. See also Sitwell's reviews in *The Criterion*, 9 (34 October 1929): 130, and *Daily Herald* (4 April 1922), reprinted in Fitzgerald, *Charlotte Mew and Her Friends*, p. 179.
57. Val Warner, Introduction, *CP* 1997, p. 45.
58. Anna Wickham, 'Fragment of an Autobiography', in *The Writings of Anna Wickham: Free Woman and Poet*, ed. R.D. Smith (London: Virago, 1984), p. 52.
59. Review of Anna Wickham, *The Little Old House*, *Times Literary Supplement* (18 August 1921): 535.
60. Wickham, 'Return of Pleasure', in *Writings*, p. 194.

61. Wickham, 'Suppression', 'Woman and Artist', in *Writings*, pp. 327, 331. (Both are undated.)
62. Wickham, 'The Angry Woman', in *Writings*, pp. 202–4.
63. Wickham, 'The Revolt of Wives', in *Writings*, pp. 180–1.
64. Wickham, 'The Wife', in *Writings*, p. 199.
65. See Martin Pumphrey, 'Play, Fantasy and Strange Laughter: Stevie Smith's Uncomfortable Poetry', *Critical Quarterly*, 28.3 (Autumn 1986): 85–96.
66. Ibid., p. 87.
67. Stevie Smith, 'Octopus', 'The Word', 'Marriage I Think', in *Me Again: The Uncollected Writings of Stevie Smith* (London, Virago, 1981), p. 216; *Women's Poetry of the 1930s: A Critical Anthology*, ed. Jane Dowson (London: Routledge, 1996), pp. 147–8.
68. Smith, 'Major Macroo', in *Collected Poems* (London: Allen Lane, 1975), p. 72.
69. Smith, 'Dear Female Heart', in *Collected Poems*, p. 130.
70. Jane Marcus, 'Sylvia Townsend Warner', in *Gender of Modernism*, ed. Scott, pp. 531–8.
71. Sylvia Townsend Warner, *The Diaries of Sylvia Townsend Warner*, ed. Clare Harman (London: Chatto and Windus, 1994), p. 78.
72. Reviews of Warner, *Time Importuned* (London: Chatto & Windus, 1928), in *Times Literary Supplement* (20 September 1928):665; J.G. Fletcher, *Criterion*, 8 (30 September 1928): 128; Naomi Boyd Smith, *Time and Tide* (3 August 1928): 29.
73. Warner, 'Wish in Spring', in *Collected Poems* (Manchester: Carcanet, 1982), pp. 83–4.
74. Warner, 'Ornaments of Gold', *Collected Poems*, p. 5.
75. Warner, 'The Rival', 'The Absence', *Collected Poems*, pp. 162, 12.
76. Claire Harman, *Sylvia Townsend Warner: A Biography* (London: Minerva, 1985), p. 79.
77. Sylvia Townsend Warner and Valentine Ackland, *Whether a Dove or a Seagull* (New York: Viking, 1933). Some poems are reproduced in Warner's *Collected Poems* and in *Women's Poetry of the 1930s*, ed. Dowson.
78. Jan Montefiore, *Feminism and Poetry* (London: Pandora, 1987), p. 158.
79. *Women's Poetry of the 1930s*, ed. Dowson, p. 157.
80. Kathleen Raine, 'Fata Morgana', *New Verse*, 25 (May 1937): 7–9. Raine's poems were printed as much as any poet's in literary journals during the 1930s.
81. Vera Brittain, *Testament of Friendship: The Story of Winifred Holtby* (London: Virago, 1980), p. 87.
82. Sylvia Townsend Warner, 'The Way by Which I Have Come', *Countryman*, 19.2 (1939): 475.
83. John Lucas, *The Radical Twenties* (Nottingham: Five Leaves, 1997).
84. Warner, 'El Heroe', in *Women's Poetry of the 1930s*, ed. Dowson, pp. 153–4 ; 'Port Bou', ibid., p. 154; 'Journey to Barcelona', *Left Review*, 2 (Dec. 1936): 812; 'Waiting at Cerbere', *Collected Poems*, p. 36; 'Benicasim', *Left Review*, 3 (March 1938): 841.
85. Barbara Brothers, 'Writing Against the Grain: Sylvia Townsend Warner and the Spanish Civil War', in *Women Writers in Exile*, ed. Mary Lynn Broe and Angela Ingram (University of Carolina Press, 1989), p. 358.
86. Warner, 'Red Front', *Left Review*, 1 (April 1935): 255–6.
87. Warner, 'Women as Writers', *Collected Poems*, pp. 265–70.
88. Stevie Smith, Letter to Denis Johnson (10 June 1937), in *Me Again: The Uncollected Writings of Stevie Smith*, p. 259.
89. Smith, Letter to John Hayward (24 April 1942), ibid., p. 283.

90. Smith, 'Private Views', ibid., pp. 130–3.
91. Smith, 'Salon D'Automne', ibid., pp. 130–3; *Women's Poetry of the 1930s*, ed. Dowson, pp. 144–5.
92. Smith, 'Lord Barrenstock', *Collected Poems*, p. 69.
93. Smith, 'The Bishops of the Church of England', ibid., p. 96.
94. Smith, 'The Suburban Classes', ibid., p. 26.
95. Smith, 'Alfred the Great', ibid., p. 19.
96. Smith, 'The Lads of the Village', ibid., p. 142.
97. Smith, *Novel on Yellow Paper* (London: Virago, 1986), p. 39.
98. Warner, 'Road 1940', in *Collected Poems*, p. 45.
99. Naomi Mitchison, 'The Farm Woman 1942', in *Women's War Poetry and Verse*, ed. Catherine Reilly (London: Virago, 1997), p. 219.
100. Dorothy Wellesley, 'Milk Boy', ibid., p. 254.
101. E.J. Scovell, 'A Wartime Story', ibid., p. 242.
102. Karen Gershon, 'A Jew's Calendar', ibid., pp. 177–8.
103. Ada Jackson, 'Hitler Youth', in *World in Labour* (Birmingham: Cornish, 1942), p. 3.
104. Hugh Lyon, Foreword, *Poems by Contemporary Women*, ed. Theodora Roscoe and Mary Winter Were (London: Hutcheons, 1944).
105. G.S. Fraser, Preface, Sheila Wingfield, *Collected Poems 1938–1983* (London: Enitharmon, 1983), p. xv.
106. Celeste M. Schenck in *The Gender of Modernism*, ed. Scott, p. 317.

10
Drama, 1920–1945
Rebecca D'Monté

Women dramatists enjoyed considerable success between 1920 and 1945, a period that has traditionally but inaccurately been perceived as theatrically moribund.[1] Yet censure was also directed towards women's production and reception of drama, as when W.A. Darlington, one of the leading theatre critics of the time, described the popular dramatist, Esther McCracken, as a 'curious mixture of professional and amateur' because she wrote surrounded by the noisiness and mess of domestic life.[2] Sir John Ervine felt the theatre was becoming 'womanised', and Ernest Short believed the influx of women to the theatre would 'determine the sort of play the public wants', whilst the poet Louis MacNeice criticized 'interwar female theatre audiences, "who use theatre as an uncritical escape from their daily lives"'.[3] Such anxieties stemmed from the greater presence of women in society after the First World War, with increasing numbers of women attending and working in the theatre.

Behind these fears about the influence of women in the theatre lies a wider debate about class, gender, and historiography. Many plays of the interwar and war years written for the commercial, mainstream theatre, have been dismissed pejoratively as 'middlebrow' and 'middle class'. Theatre at this time was still affected by changes made during the Victorian period, when managers such as Madame de Vestris and Lady Bancroft deliberately pursued the middle-class female audience by making playhouse interiors more 'feminine' and staging 'respectable' drama.[4] The large seating capacity of the majority of London theatres also meant that later managements and producers such as H.M. Tennent, Hugh 'Binkie' Beaumont, and Basil Dean, were resistant to taking risks in the type of drama put on, which had a concomitant effect on touring and regional theatre.

It was not until the end of the nineteenth century that a noticeable split occurred between a self-consciously difficult and elitist high culture and the mass culture it defined itself against.[5] By the 1930s, 'the common terms "highbrow", "lowbrow" and "middlebrow" created a convenient aesthetic and psychological equivalent to the British class system, labelling authors and readers in one epigrammatic blow'.[6] In general, it was thought that readers or audiences of the lowbrow enjoyed genre works such as romances or sensational thrillers and melodrama, while the highbrow was drawn towards the experimental or avant-garde. The middlebrow, Anthea Trodd states, is 'the most contested of the three terms'.[7] It is also the one that is most often applied to the reading of women and to the middle classes, and describes works that are well written but not obscure or intellectually challenging. In drama, the plot often revolves around a middle-class family, the setting is the living room, and the genre domestic realism. Realism has been criticized for being more concerned with tradition, continuity, and outward appearances than with modernity, experimentation, and interiority, and for remaining doggedly middlebrow.[8]

If Trodd sees a correlation between class mobility during the wars and the creation of a new literary market, Tania Modleski remarks on the gendering of mass culture, where female and popular genres, romance and the Gothic, for example – to which I would add comedy and domestic drama – are 'somehow associated with women while "real", authentic culture remains the prerogative of men'.[9] We can certainly see these views echoed by drama critics and theatre historians of the time, who consistently made a connection between gender and genre, as when Lynton Hudson complained of the 1920s and 1930s that

> the play-going public suddenly ... picked on a new type of comedy ... predominately female. It is completely undramatic ... ran interminably ... About? The ditherings of ordinary people seen through the magnifying glass of an observant sentimental humour. It is the vindication of the woman playwright, for it is usually written by a woman ... the delight of mainly female audiences.[10]

This has had a twofold effect: women's drama is neatly, if not necessarily accurately, labelled as domestic, and other material misread or ignored if it does not fit into this category. Concomitant upon this was the domination of the theatrical world by a small group of men whose tastes shaped and determined the success of plays in the commercial theatre, and helped create its historical legacy.[11]

Susan Bennett rightly claims that if one type of drama is privileged over another 'Historiography, then, "legitimises" a place, that of its production, by "including" others in a relation of filiation or of exteriority. It is authorised by this place which allows it to explain whatever is different as "foreign", and whatever is inside as "unique".'[12] Thus, even feminist theatre historians have hindered the process of recuperating interwar women dramatists, because, as Elaine Aston makes clear, this was 'de-valued as less interesting, politically (viewed as conservative rather than radical), and formally (as playwriting in the dominant realistic, rather than alternative, experimental tradition)'; ironically, this cultural and class prejudice has also helped to mask more innovative work by women dramatists of the time.[13]

However, during the last couple of decades, the parameters of historiographic discourse have shifted as a result of the work of scholars including Fidelis Morgan (1994), Aston (2000), Bennett (2000), and pre-eminently Maggie B. Gale (1996, 2000, and so on), who have done much to recuperate a period of theatre history that has been 'traditionally seen as trite, middle class and conventional ... and one which did not produce overtly feminist women playwrights easily slotted into ready-made contemporary categories for analysis'.[14] Attention has also been alerted to the synergies between 'political' and 'commercial', 'avant-garde' and 'mainstream'. So, for example, while critical attention had been drawn to the earlier suffrage plays of the Actresses' Franchise League (AFL), there were, as Gale tells us, 'many cross-over points between the legitimate theatre, the commercial theatre, and the AFL', and their work continued 'during the interwar years in a far less "political" and often more commercial context'. Furthermore, 'the threads of political activism – larger female casts, plots centred around female heroines, women as subject rather than object within the domestic sphere and so on – prevail'.[15]

Thus, if we accept Alison Light's premise that 'feminist work must deal with the conservative as well as the radical imagination', then two patterns begin to emerge in women's drama of this time: the plays of the 1920s and 1930s show the impact of the First World War and the suffrage movement; the 1930s and 1940s show the slide towards, and into, the Second World War.[16] Within this appear smaller thematic circles to do with the empowerment and disempowerment of women, particularly in relation to economics, work, sexuality, public and private space, and nationhood.

Both male and female playwrights had been involved in producing patriotic plays during and immediately after the First World War: Mrs Horace Porter and George Bidder's *Patriotic Pence* (1917) falls into this category, as do the one-act plays of Rudolf Besier and Sybil Spottiswoode (the xenophobic *Kultur at Home*, 1916), Mrs Arthur Hankey (*A House-Warming in War-Time*, 1917), and Gertrude Jennings (*Waiting for the Bus*, 1919). However, Claire Tylee reminds us that two of the main literary narratives about the First World War were '"The Somme Myth" as Paul Fussell calls it, the other is what [Robert] Wohl identified as "The Lost Generation Myth" ... Both myths deal with the loss of English manhood.'[17] The first of these ideas is taken up in plays by male dramatists, including Harry Wall's *Havoc* (1923), Hubert Griffiths's *Tunnel Trench* (1925), R.C. Sherriff's *Journey's End* (1928), and Lawrence du Gard Peach's *Shells* (1937). The physical and psychological effects of the war are covered in plays like Miles Malleson's *Black 'Ell* (1916), Sean O'Casey's *The Silver Tassie* (1928), Robert Graves's *But It Still Goes On* (1930), and Somerset Maugham's *The Sacred Flame* (1928) and *For Services Rendered* (1932).[18]

Women certainly did tackle front-line drama, and explore political themes, even if they did not go as far as their male counterparts, whose work was sometimes banned for its forthrightness in depicting the savagery of war. Yet this has been 'hidden' for a number of reasons. The most obvious is the assumption by theatre management and scholars alike that war was not a suitable topic for women, or that they would only be interested in the home front. We can also point to the fact that several of these plays were staged in unconventional spaces, remained unpublished (or quickly fell out of print), or were not produced professionally. A surprisingly large number also took the form of the usually less well regarded one-act drama, as with M.E. Atkinson's *The Chimney Corner* (1934), which like Bosworth Crocker's [Mary Arnold Lewisohn] *Pawns of War* (1918) was set in Belgium. The suffragette writer and actress, Cicely Hamilton, who had worked on the front line in a military hospital, and took theatre to the trenches with Lena Ashwell's company, collaborated with members of the Women's Auxiliary Army Corps (WAACs) at Abbeville. With *The Child in Flanders* (1917) she cleverly subverts the idea of masculine trench drama through her domestication of the nativity scene: in this three soldiers from England, Australia, and India, are transformed by their encounter with a French husband and wife, and their new-born baby, as they seek refuge with them on their way to Arras. The end of the play, which eschews sentimentality, brings together a chorus of 'Alleluia' and the wartime song, 'The Trail That Leads to Home', with Liz Whitelaw suggesting that 'It must have been very affecting for those who had spent much of the previous year amid the mud and shell-holes of the Flanders plain.'[19] Like Sherriff's *Journey's End*, Muriel Box's *Angels at War* was originally written for amateurs in 1935, but does not seem to have achieved a British professional production until 1981. Given that Box was only nine at the start of the war, it is surprising that her play focuses on life on the front line in 1918 of eight members of Queen Mary's Army Auxiliary Corps, who work mainly as ambulance drivers. Like many of her male counterparts, Box raises the idea of the combatant's patriotic duty, only to subvert it by commenting dryly on the discrepancy between the real and the romanticized experience of war; a visiting VIP refers to the women as 'Britain's brave and beautiful daughters', but in private, the women talk of the permanent fear, harsh conditions, sickening mess, and prosaic nature of war work, all done to keep 'the old flag, flying'.[20]

Female dramatists used their work to comment on the moral ambiguities of war and the dangers of mechanized violence. *Peace in Our Time* (1934), written by Box, this time with her husband, Sydney, is set at a meeting of the League of Nations, where women from four different nations are visited by a Lady in Black: notice comes of the outbreak of war between Britain and Russia, and America and Japan. As each attacks her enemy, the allegorical figure reveals herself to be Death, the moral being that warfare is a natural state for humans unless they can manage to move beyond this through negotiation. Hamilton's *The Old Adam* (1924) gives a similar message. She uses a dramatic distancing effect to comment on the absurdity of war by creating the state of Paphlagonia as a stand-in for Britain. Farcical scenes ensue as both warring sides invent the same weapon, which will immobilize all machinery. Nations are reduced to fighting with old swords taken from museums: the implication again is that 'Old Adam' will always find a way to fight. Three one-act plays also take up a similar idea.[21] In Clemence Dane's *Shivering Shocks* (1935) a new explosive is discovered to 'crumple the armies of the earth like a gardener spraying green fly'.[22] The plot of Cicely Louise Evans's *Antic Disposition* (1935), in which a scientist is contacted by the War Office about the possibilities of transporting bacteria seems horribly prescient today, and at the time recognized that 'the war to end all wars' may not yet have taken place. This is also taken up in Ida Gandy's allegorical *In the House of Despair* (1937). Despair, with her servants Fear and Stupidity, attempts to spoil all attempts at peace by allowing battleships and fighter planes to be built. Despair welcomes victims of the war into her house and, although the play ends on an optimistic note, the tone is bleak.

Allegory represented a frequent, if often overlooked attempt to find a dramatic language in which to speak of the complex experiences of warfare. Such allegorical plays were not usually well received by audiences more used to realist drama, as is exemplified by C.K. Munro's *The Rumour* (1922), O'Casey's *The Silver Tassie* (1928), Hans Chlumberg's *Miracle at Verdun* (1932), and Priestley's fantastical *Johnson over Jordan* (1939). Women used allegory for the same reason as men, as had Hamilton with *The Old Adam* and Box with *Peace in Our Time*. Interestingly, two of the most experimental works of the period were by women. Velona Pilcher co-founded the Gate Theatre Studio in London with Peter Godfrey in 1927; influenced by German Expressionism, she was inspired to make a place for new writing in Britain, an ambition encouraged by the fact that the studio was run as a club and therefore was outside the jurisdiction of the Lord Chamberlain. Ironically, her play *The Searcher* (1929) was considered too uncompromisingly expressionistic, and was rejected, so that it only found a home at the Grafton Theatre, another of London's 'little' theatres, in 1930. Utilizing the *mise-en-scène* Pilcher creates an overall tunnel effect which causes her audience to become experientially involved in the drama. The female 'Searcher' of the title is both looking for lost men and for Truth. Vernon Lee's [Violet Paget] extraordinary pacifist play, *Satan the Waster* (1920) is another fascinating attempt to dramatize the experiences of 1914–1918. Inspired by her anti-war book, *The Ballet of the Nations* (1915), Lee rewrites her story as drama, incorporating a masque directed by Death and staged by Satan for Clio, the Muse of History. Within this, events of the war are allegorically represented, and framed by a prologue and epilogue. Heinz Kosok states that this is 'not so much a play-within-a-play as a metadramatic exploration of the staging of a metaphysical pageant', with the ballet seen by Death described in the play as 'the vastest and most new-fashioned spectacle of Slaughter and Ruin I have so far had the honour of putting on to the World's Stage'.[23] Published with a lengthy introduction and 190 pages of notes, it was immediately attacked by critics who were baffled by its unusual staging and format, but it also garnered praise from Edith Wharton and George Bernard Shaw, the latter of whom admired Lee's intellect and commitment to aesthetics.[24]

Like women novelists such as Vera Brittain, Virginia Woolf, Winifred Holtby, and Storm Jameson, then, many of the female dramatists mentioned present a pacifist message within their plays. Sometimes this not only referred to the horrors of war, but also to the need for change, with women represented as being instrumental in bringing this about. Olive Popplewell's *The Pacifist* (1934) frames this in terms of domestic realism. Plans for a pacifist meeting about a forthcoming war are disrupted by members of the Meresdale Women's Institute, but the heroine, Mavis, who ends her engagement when she finds her fiancé is leading the opposition, refuses to be beaten. Spurred on by knowledge of her father's war experiences, she goes ahead with the meeting, and sways the crowd with her rousing speech about the necessity for peace. Some dramatists also drew a connection between the feminist movement and pacifism, as in Popplewell's *This Bondage* (1935), which shows, in a series of sharp scenes, the development of women's political action from 1891 to the present day. One scene, set in 1914, shows suffragettes having become fervent nationalists, pushing their menfolk to enlist through taunts of cowardice.[25] Popplewell's final act rather weakly posits pacifism as the most reasoned response to the threat of war. Elizabeth Rye takes this further in her chronicle play, *The Three-Fold Path* (1935). Using an all-female cast, Rye provides snapshots of important moments in women's history, ending with the First World War. Power, peace, and love are seen as the most important forces, and the feminist and pacifist stance is made clear at the end, when a character remarks, 'Perhaps if women had more power there wouldn't be so many wars.'[26]

If women found ways to feminize the 'Somme Myth', they also turned to the myth of the 'Lost Generation' as a way of exploring tensions between, on the one hand, the damaging effects of the First World War, and on the other, its potential for empowerment. Most obviously, this can be seen through the representation of female sexuality, and the nexus of ideas surrounding economics, work, and creativity. The start of female enfranchisement inopportunely coincided with the loss of over 700,000 men, along with the rise in unemployment for returning soldiers, and a steady demographic shift towards female births and longevity that had been under way since the nineteenth century. This led to spinsters ('surplus women') often being viewed in the media as a 'menace to the country's economy and its social and political order ... particularly when it was touted that the franchise should be extended to women under 30': this would have put female voters in the majority.[27]

With the shift in the visibility of women, politically, socially, and physically, the figure of the unmarried older woman acted as a repository during the interwar period for society's trauma over the lost generation of men and the growing public presence of women. In the 1920s spinsters were broadly viewed as a disruptive and sexually disturbing influence on every part of society. Equally, because many had entered the workplace, willingly or not, they were blamed for male unemployment or viewed as a drain on family resources.

There were any number of caricatures, from harmless moral guardians of a previous generation, like Miss Fairfield in Clemence Dane's first play, *Bill of Divorcement* (1921) and Margaret Kennedy's spinsters in *Escape Me Never* (1933), through to the grotesques of Rodney Ackland's adaptation of Hugh Walpole's novel, *The Old Ladies* (1935) and Richard Llewellyn's *Poison Pen* (1939): the inference in these latter plays is that being older and unmarried leads to fantasy, neurosis, and psychosis. Female dramatists are more sympathetic, particularly in taking up the connection between spinsterhood and penury, as in *Busman's Honeymoon*, written for the stage by Dorothy L. Sayers in 1936, before being adapted the following year into the eleventh and last novel featuring her detective, Lord Peter Wimsey. In this, Miss Agnes Twitterton's hopes of climbing out of poverty through inheritance and marriage are both dashed when her uncle, murdered by her avaricious fiancé, is discovered to be bankrupt. The subject is also considered in more detail in McCracken's play, *Living Room* (1944), in which the fortunes of two unmarried sisters, Vicky and Deborah Benton, have drastically declined as they have aged, and they struggle with the contradictions of their middle-class upbringing. Untrained for any profession, and having no one to marry, they are unable to cope financially once the family funds have dried up. Society wants to ignore the problem, Deborah explains, but 'Because our poverty isn't picturesque, because it doesn't hit you in the eye, and we don't shout about it from the house-tops, it's ignored.'[28]

Dodie Smith too hints at the way in which women were caught between pre-1914 sexual customs and post-1918 freedoms. Better known as the author of *I Capture the Castle* (1949) and *The One Hundred and One Dalmatians* (1956), her first play, *Autumn Crocus* (1931), centres on Fanny, a spinster teacher, who is drawn towards an affair with a married Austrian inn-keeper when on holiday. Reminded of British conventions of morality, which run in opposition to the less repressive Tyrol, she resists what is represented as her only chance of passion. The play ends with Fanny realizing that there is apparently nothing left for her but to grow old. This was a plight with which many female members of the audience felt empathy, as shown by the scores of letters received by Smith.[29] In the play, Miss Mayne, who leads an equally inhibited life as a vicar's sister, also starts to feel more alive in these new surroundings, and finds herself drawn to the lifestyle of a couple in the hotel, who have left Britain behind, in order to travel abroad together as 'a serious experiment' into their sexual reactions.[30] They cite the influence of Richard von Krafft-Ebing, whose works were amongst the first to study female sexual pleasure, and it is no coincidence that Smith repeats the word 'modern' throughout the play, representing a break between the old and the new, even if this was not entirely clear-cut.[31]

Agatha Christie never allowed her most famous subversion of the spinster type, Miss Marple, to appear on stage, but refers to spinsters stereotypically in most of her plays, including *And Then There Were None* (originally titled *Ten Little Niggers*, 1942), *Appointment with Death* (1945), and *The Mousetrap* (1952). Juxtapositions are also made between older unmarried women and those of the younger generation, who use their single status to revel in their sexual freedom. In her first play, *Black Coffee* (1931), for example, one of these 'modern' women, Barbara Amory, bewilders her elderly spinster aunt by flippantly remarking, 'a girl simply can't have too much red on her lips. She never knows how much she's going to lose in the taxi coming home.'[32] Amory represents the 'flapper', who recurred as a literary and theatrical type throughout the 1920s. She was, Billie Melman tells us, a mass of contradictions: 'sexless but libidinous; infantile but precocious; self-sufficient but demographically, economically and socially superfluous; an emblem of modern times yet, at the same time, an incarnation of the eternal Eve'.[33] The heroine of Kennedy's massively successful bestseller, *The Constant Nymph* (1924) epitomizes this figure. Filmed several times and adapted by Kennedy and Basil Dean as a play two years after publication, it centres on the sexual awakening of the adolescent Tessa who runs away with a much older man, to tragic effect. Although the relationship is never consummated, as is the case in *Autumn Crocus*, its interest in free love and the expression of female sexuality articulated a more generalized feeling that the First World War had led to a fracturing of social mores.

We can see this also in Dane's *A Bill of Divorcement*, although here it is the woman of the older generation, Margaret, who is freed rather than her daughter, Sydney: when Margaret divorces her shell-shocked husband, who has been in an asylum for fifteen years, it is left to Sydney to give up her fiancé to look after the father she barely knows, and this loss of a future for herself leaves her '*flattened against the back of her chair, quivering a little, like a crucified moth*'.[34] The contrast between generations also comes out in Smith's *Touch Wood* (1934). The married Vera, described as a 'nymphomaniac', the first known reference to this on the British stage, is desperate for 'change and excitement', as her long suffering husband puts it, but can only find this through continuous affairs with other men.[35] Elizabeth, an unmarried woman of thirty-eight, admits to having lost her virginity during the war because of life's uncertainty, but now sees 'sex is just a rotten swindle and the only really happy people are those who keep it in a separate compartment of their lives, or get over it altogether'.[36] Those who have borne the brunt of the war – Vera, Elizabeth, and the married but barren Sylvia and

Robin Herriot – feel disengaged from life, a distinct contrast with the energy and idealism of the younger generation.

Significantly, though many young women in interwar plays may seem precocious and forthright, there is still confusion over how this new type of woman should be presented, with opportunity often presented in terms of relationships with the other sex: Tessa in *The Constant Nymph* throws everything up for a married composer, while Mab in *Touch Wood* falls for the married architect, Robin. In another of Smith's plays, *Bonnet over the Windmill* (1937), Janet is happy to give herself to the playwright Kit Carson as a way of inspiring his writing. These young women are shown as trembling on the edge of their future, open to adventure, and full of dreams, and yet all three are ready to see themselves only as muse to the male artist.

If many female characters still looked to men to provide a sense of self-worth, or flailed around trying to make sense of their sexuality, others are shown turning to male-dominated spheres of activity for fulfilment. The nineteenth-century idea of separate spheres was already in contention; the large numbers of men lost during the First World War and the many men left with terrible injuries led to a crisis in masculinity that was further exacerbated by the growing political presence of women.[37] Nicola Gullace argues that in the First World War the argument for female enfranchisement became more persuasive, stating that 'Women's war work, the sacrifices of mothers and wives, and the patriotic performance of well-known suffragists all validated feminists' long-standing arguments about the national and imperial value of female citizenship.'[38] Thus, even given the tragedy of the war, for some women it also came to represent their chance for adventure and escape from marriage and other social conventions that had held them in place for so long. In *Angels at War*, Box intuitively stages this moment of gender transition by feminizing the male trench experience. Several of Sherriff's key war myths are repeated: the naive newcomer, the cynical old-timer, and the tragic and pointless death. Most of the all-female cast, who swear, drink and smoke, have nicknames that sound male (Jo, Vic, Nobby) or genderless (Cocky, Moaner, Skinny). Claire Buck describes how the single room set of *Angels at War* acts as a 'quasi-domestic setting', which 'intensifies the play's thematic preoccupation both with women's new wartime opportunities and freedoms, and with the idea of all-female communities'.[39] Although war is never portrayed as any less than horrific, and the characters are often hostile towards one another, we see how women from disparate backgrounds have been thrown together to encounter a kind of lifestyle far from those encountered – or acceptable – in peacetime.[40] If Sherriff's play focuses on the 'journey's end', though, Box deliberately sets her play in the last days of the war, so as to raise questions about the difficulties for women in fitting back into society after their wartime experiences. As Jo says, 'They sent us out to do men's work ... I'm hanged if I'll be fobbed off with a nursery maid's job.'[41]

A Bill of Divorcement reframes this in relation to political changes that would have great effects on women's lives. Written in 1921 but set at the beginning of the 1930s, it comments on the new British Divorce Laws, very recently brought into being, but not yet enacted. Dane uses time slippage to expose how the social and political changes already occurring for women were also part of a continuum that would revolutionize women's lives in the future.[42] However, it is symptomatic of this complicated period that, although Dane could project the play forward to the next decade, she could not envisage a more optimistic ending to her story, and so, as we have seen, whilst the wife could be set free by the new divorce laws, another woman (her daughter) has to take her place in the household.

This confusion about a woman's role, and indeed where she should situate herself, continues in G.B. Stern's *The Man who Pays the Piper* (1931). Here again there is a concern with the dramatic possibilities of time slips. In the play's 1913 prologue, Daryll exemplifies the *fin de siècle* New Woman and early suffragettes by demanding her right to a latchkey and a paid job. Acts one and two are set in 1926, after the first women have been enfranchised, when the death of Daryll's father and eldest brother forces her to become breadwinner, at which she proves herself highly successful. Act three, set in 1930, a year before the play was written, shows her caught between having a successful career and eventually getting married. As the title would indicate, Daryll is weighed down by duty and responsibility, rather than enjoying the freedom that should have come with a successful career, and bitterly blames the war for forcing a conventional male role on her at an early age: 'we *fathers* of nineteen fourteen ... we're all freaks my generation of girls'.[43] The play ends with her swapping roles with her husband, who is himself worn down by the war and competitive activity; he stays at home ready to welcome back his wife from her 'bachelor rooms' in town when she returns at weekends. While there are some undoubtedly contradictory areas in Stern's play, it not only points to the war being the significant watershed in changing male and female roles, a theme most writers tackled, but also manages to posit a tantalizing view of newly fashioned gender roles.

Maggie Gale asserts that 'Stern's sense that the First World War created a "freak" generation of women connects with the notion of both a "lost generation" and at the same time a new generation. The image of a generation of men lost through war is combined with the image of a new generation of women for whom work and career became either a necessity or simply a burning desire.'[44] It is therefore not surprising to find the interwar dramatists picking up on a favourite theme of suffrage drama, which showed 'recognition ... of the importance of the role of work in establishing women's independence and self-determination'.[45] Teachers, shop workers, and secretaries are amongst the common jobs to be portrayed, though these jobs are not always satisfying because of the drudgery involved and poor economic recompense. Other plays present more unusual fields of endeavour. If Enid Bagnold portrays the dangers of overweening ambition in *Lottie Dundass* (1944), in which a budding actress kills in order to play the leading role, a more inspirational response is provided in the stage adaptation of her novel *National Velvet* (1946), where Velvet Brown, *'a girl with a Chance'*, follows her mother's swimming achievements to become the first female to win the Grand National. Gordon Daviot gives an interesting glimpse of a female philosopher in her play, *The Laughing Woman* (1934), based on the relationship between Sophie Brzeska and Henri Gaudier-Brzeska; in Daphne du Maurier's *The Years Between* (1944), Diana Wentworth takes over her husband's political career when she believes he has died; and Henrietta Angkatell's career as a sculptor is given due seriousness in Agatha Christie's *The Hollow* (adapted from her 1946 novel in 1951).

There is also a connection to be made here between the achievements of women in suffrage plays, such as Hamilton's *The Pageant of Great Women* (1909) and Christopher St John's *The First Actress* (1911), and historical drama during the interwar period. The popularity of the historical or 'bio' play in the 1920s and 1930s shows what Gale calls 'the search for national heroines', a way of inserting, either consciously or unconsciously, the idea of women as political or public beings into social consciousness.[46] Gale goes on to argue that 'as a whole, women had not taken real advantage of their new voting power', and we can certainly see a conflicted relationship with this in many of the plays discussed so far.[47] Katherine Parr, Mary Queen of Scots, Elizabeth I, Nell Gwyn, Sarah Siddons, and the Brontë sisters were amongst the many historical figures deliberately chosen because of their political command, or creativity, and, as feminist critics have frequently observed, putting women's experiences centre stage is part of the process of redefining male-focused history to make a new form of history: literally 'her story'. Even when ostensibly writing plays about men, female playwrights still managed to portray strong women, as with Anne Hathaway in Dane's *Will Shakespeare* (1921) and Queen Anne of Bohemia in Gordon Daviot's *Richard of Bordeaux* (1933). Beyond this, the historical play was used as a means to assert national identity at a time of growing political instability, and to reinforce the notion of the family and home at the centre of the nation's life.

With the approach of the Second World War, a trio of highly popular plays by women engage with this idea. In Smith's *Dear Octopus*, which originally swept to success on a wave of relief over the Munich crisis in 1938, the longevity and solidity of the family is symbolized by the celebrations for Dora and Charles Randolph's silver wedding anniversary, and by the presence of Dora as matriarch. The eldest son gives a toast at the end and reminds the audience of the family's place at the heart of British life: 'it bends, it stretches – but it never breaks'.[48] What could, in another context, have been a picture of suffocating family life, is depicted at this time of imminent war, as part of the nation's armoury against the enemy, where traditional standards are upheld, and the English home is seen as invincible. Again,

Daphne du Maurier's stage adaptation of *Rebecca* (1940) uses the aristocratic symbol of the country house as, in Malcolm Kelsall's phrase, 'a visible sign of "the ancient social order"'.[49] Crucially, and unlike the novel or the film, no dramatic fire destroys the house, and instead evil (Mrs Danvers) is ousted from the nation (Manderley); critics were pleased with the ending of the play 'which they felt was in tune with the turbulent times, so that as husband and wife stand together in perfect accord, the aristocratic Manderley unravaged, the audience are faced with a potent symbol of Englishness at a time of renewed nationalistic pride'.[50] This idea continues in McCracken's *Quiet Weekend* (1941), one of the smash hits of the 1940s. Set at some unspecified time before the start of the Second World War, McCracken fuses the domestic comedy with the pastoral idyll, thus feminizing 'the country-house motif in a way that spoke directly to the increased wartime female audiences through its focus upon the commonplace lives of humdrum people'.[51]

This valuation of a 'domestic femininity' can also be seen in Lesley Storm's *Great Day* (1945). Also set in a village, McCracken's pastoral is replaced by one that is more realistic, dealing as it does with the legacy of the Great War, female mobilization in the present war, and marital discord. The play depicts members of the Women's Institute who put aside their differences to prepare for a visit by Eleanor Roosevelt.[52] Here Storm can be seen to elevate the importance of domestic work, as the women's use of their housewifery skills turns the village into a 'powerful production unit'.[53] Their industrious efforts in providing vast amounts of food and clothing for the troops not only makes an important contribution to the body politic, where 'we all have something to do with each other', but the women gain immeasurably from working, and from acting together as a female collective; as one woman states, they are 'the beginning of something new, make no mistake'.[54]

Whilst commercially timid theatre managements exploited the larger female audiences who had often been released from their usual routines and environment, by producing a steady fare of domestic dramas and comedy, several of these depicted the contradictions between the mobile woman, required by the state to leave her home for the war effort, and the housewife. Others even questioned the stability of the home itself, while looking to the reconstruction of a postwar Britain, which would bring about a greater equality between the sexes.

McCracken's *No Medals* (1944) seems, on the surface, to relate to the wider issue of war and nation, where the family and home are represented as a symbol of national pride and strength. Martha Dacre struggles to look after her fluctuating household, whilst also carrying out her war work. She is 'a martyr to the cause', as indicated by her name, and yet the play consistently dwells on the unpalatable truths about war: bombing raids, family dislocation, and constant fear of death. As a comedy, the play ends happily, but not before Martha finally breaks down, worn out by the constant strain of wartime conditions, and fracturing of the family home. In fact, even given the best endeavours of the time, this idea of the mother figure securing 'the identity of nation as "home"' is a highly unstable one: the 'mobile woman' 'sapped the idea of nation from within; mass mobilisation undermined traditional notions of civil stability', and so 'the idea of home could hardly function as a synecdoche for national unity'.[55]

This breakdown of family life is shown still more starkly in du Maurier's *The Years Between*. Pre-dating the end of the war as well as Labour's landslide election by a few months, it foreshadows the problems of reconstructing Britain in peacetime. Taking over her absent husband Michael's position as MP, Diana competently negotiates a successful career and life as a single mother. When Michael returns unexpectedly from the war (he was thought to be dead), he is unable to recognize the timid, submissive wife he left behind, seeing her now as 'one of those managing, restless women'.[56] Given that women were supposed to slot into male roles 'only for the duration', and that he was a war hero, audiences at the time tended to side with Michael, but du Maurier presents him as being the one out of step in seeking a return to a past that no longer exists. In contrast, Diana sees her work as part of a continuum of change; in a speech she prepares at the end of the play for the Girls' Training Corp, she argues that, in the rebuilding of postwar Britain, equality should become the key, rather than blind service to duty. This awareness of the need of a break with the past would gradually take place at all levels of society, and for women led to the seismic transformations of society brought about by second wave feminism.

In conclusion, most of the plays discussed in this chapter can be described as middlebrow, and as endorsing what were perceived to be 'classic' middle-class values of patriotism, loyalty, duty, and responsibility. They work through a process of what Simon Frith calls 'the pleasure of familiarity'.[57] This perceived conservatism was much derided at the time and subsequently by critics who saw pleasure in the familiar as a sign of political and moral worthlessness. But it is also true to say that whilst these plays often sought to preserve social and political structures, they also brought to the surface tensions between change and stasis. Men may have suffered a crisis in masculinity after the First World War, but we can also point to a similar such crisis in femininity. Women found themselves caught between social and sexual conventions that lingered from the Edwardian period and their new place as enfranchised citizens. In the theatre this was rendered through women's struggle to find a personal and political identity at home, at work, and sexually. It also brought out wider issues of nationhood, with Britain's awareness that the First World War had left it 'lacking the strength of a unified identity'.[58] The demands of the Second World War reinforced the family and home as the nucleus of society, whilst further locating women in the public sphere. Between 1920 and 1945, then, we can see how fissures opened up within society to expose the instability at its heart, along with a vista of opportunity for the future. Ultimately, all of these plays take as their role the task of representing, and even helping to create, the beginnings of a new society in the postwar period.

Notes

1. Several of these women wrote initially, or throughout their career, under pseudonyms; for example, C.L. Anthony (Dodie Smith), Gordon Daviot (Elizabeth Mackintosh, also writing novels as Josephine Tey), Clemence Dane (Winifred Ashton), and Lesley Storm (Margaret McCowie). Maggie B. Gale believes 'the average percentage of plays by women or male/female teams between 1918 and 1962 to be 16.7 per cent', much higher than in current times. Maggie B. Gale, *West End Women: Women and the London Stage 1918–1962* (London: Routledge, 1996), p. 11.
2. He goes on to wonder, 'do I malign her by saying that playwrighting [sic] was for her a hobby rather than a vocation?' W.A. Darlington, 'Esther McCracken: Obituary', *Daily Telegraph* (12 August 1971). In a similar vein, Agatha Christie raised eyebrows by telling interviewers that she could write her novels and plays anywhere, even at the dining table between meals.
3. Sir John Ervine cited in Maggie B. Gale, 'From Fame to Obscurity: In Search of Clemence Dane', in *Women, Theatre and Performance: New Histories, New Historiographies*, ed. Maggie B. Gale and Viv Gardner (Manchester: Manchester University Press, 2000), pp. 121–41, p. 126; Ernest Short, *Sixty Years of Theatre* (London: Eyre and Spottiswoode, 1951), p. 204; Louis MacNeice, cited in Gale, 'Women Playwrights of the 1920s and 1930s', in *The Cambridge Companion to Modern British Women Playwrights*, ed. Elaine Aston and Janelle Reinelt (Cambridge: Cambridge University Press, 2000), pp. 23–37, p. 25.
4. Lady Effie Bancroft's maiden name was Marie Wilton.
5. Scott McCracken, *Pulp: Reading Popular Fiction* (Manchester: Manchester University Press, 1998), p. 20.
6. Clive Bloom, *Bestsellers: Popular Fiction since 1900* (Basingstoke: Palgrave Macmillan, 2002), p. 12.
7. Anthea Trodd, *Women's Writing in English: Britain 1900–1945* (London: Longman, 1998), p. 48.
8. See, for example, Catherine Belsey, *Critical Practice* (London: Methuen, 1980), and Toril Moi, *Sexual/Textual Politics* (London: Routledge, 1985).
9. Tania Modleski, ed., *Studies in Entertainment: Critical Approaches to Mass Culture* (Bloomington: Indiana University Press, 1986), p. 191. It is also interesting to note the title of Andreas Huyssen's chapter in Modleski's book, 'Mass Culture as Woman: Modernism's "Other"', pp. 188–207.
10. Lynton Hudson, *The Twentieth Century Drama* (London: Harrap, 1946), p. 59. This mirrors the comments made by Nicola Beauman on interwar middlebrow novels, although the sentiment is entirely different: 'They generally have little action and less histrionics – they are about the "drama of the undramatic", the steadfast dailiness of a life that brings its own rewards, the intensity of the emotions and, above all, the importance of human relationships' (Nicola Beauman, *A Very Great Profession: The Woman's Novel 1914–1939* (London: Virago, 1983), p. 5).
11. These critics include James Agate, Harold Hobson, Ivor Brown, W.A. Darlington, and J.C. Trewin.
12. Susan Bennett, 'Theatre History, Historiography and Women's Dramatic Writing', in *Women, Theatre and Performance*, ed. Gale and Gardner, pp. 46–59, p. 50.

13. Elaine Aston and Janelle Reinelt, 'Restrospectives', in *The Cambridge Companion to Modern British Women Playwrights*, ed. Aston and Reinelt, pp. 21–37, p. 21.
14. Gale, 'From Fame to Obscurity', p. 121.
15. Gale, 'Women Playwrights of the 1920s and 1930s', pp. 23–37, p. 24.
16. Alison Light, *Forever England: Femininity, Literature and Conservatism between the Wars* (London: Routledge, 1991), p. 13.
17. Claire Tylee, *The Great War and Women's Consciousness: Images of Militarism and Womanhood in Women's Writing, 1914–64* (Basingstoke: Macmillan, 1990), p. 255.
18. Nevertheless, Clive Barker concludes that there was a refusal, particularly on the part of theatre management, to deal with the literal horror of war, and he sees the rise during the interwar period of Grand Guignol, crime dramas, thrillers, and 'illusory portrayals of Death', as a way to deal with 'the pains of absence created by the mass slaughter of war'. See 'The Ghosts of War: Stage Ghosts and Time Slips as a Response to War', in *British Theatre between the Wars 1918–1939*, ed. Clive Barker and Maggie B. Gale (Cambridge: Cambridge University Press, 2000), pp. 215–43, p. 229.
19. Liz Whitelaw, *The Life and Rebellious Times of Cicely Hamilton: Actress, Writer, Suffragist* (London: Women's Press, 1990), p. 154.
20. Muriel Box, *Angels of War*, in *Five New Full-Length Plays for All-Women Casts*, ed. John Bourne (London: Lovat Dickson and Thompson, 1935), p. 25. Box was also a successful screenwriter and film director, working in a male-dominated industry.
21. Bridget Boland sets her later play, *The Cockpit* (1949), in a German provincial theatre, utilizing similar dramatic techniques to those in the ABCA (Army Bureau of Current Affairs) Play Unit's *What's Wrong with the Germans?* (1944), including staging part of the play in the auditorium. Again the message is that people of either sex will find a way to fight.
22. Clemence Dane, *Shivering Shocks, or, The Hiding Place: A Play for Boys*, in *One-Act Comedies*, ed. Philip Wayne (London: Longmans, 1935), p. 124.
23. Heinz Kosok, *The Theatre of War: The First World War in British and Irish Drama* (Basingstoke: Palgrave Macmillan, 2007), p. 93; Vernon Lee [Violet Page], *Satan the Waster: A Philosophic War Trilogy with Notes and Introduction* (New York: John Lane, 1920), p. 41.
24. Gill Plain discusses the innovativeness of Lee's play in 'The Shape of Things to Come: The Remarkable Modernity of Vernon Lee's *Satan the Waster* (1915–1920)', in *Women, the First World War and the Dramatic Imagination. International Essays (1914–1999)*, ed. Claire Tylee (New York: Edwin Mellen Press, 2000), pp. 5–21.
25. All of this had a basis in reality; in 1915, publication of the Women's Political and Social Union's (WSPU) journal *The Suffragette* ceased and a new one brought out called *Britannia* in an effort to show they were fighting 'for king, for country, for freedom'; others, however, became committed pacifists, joining a No-Conscription Fellowship in December 1914. See Diana Condell and Jean Liddiard, eds, *Working for Victory? Images of Women in the First World War, 1914–18* (London: Routledge and Kegan Paul, 1987), p. 56.
26. Elizabeth Rye, *The Three-Fold Path: A Play in 7 Scenes*, in *Five New Full-Length Plays for All-Women Casts* (London: Lovat Dickson & Thompson, 1935), p. 241.
27. Billie Melman, *Women and the Popular Imagination in the Twenties: Flappers and Nymphs* (Basingstoke: Macmillan, 1988), p. 20.
28. Esther McCracken, *Living Room* (London: Charles H. Fox, 1944), p. 38. This play was previously written as *White Elephants* in 1940, and a couple of scenes also started out in an unpublished one-act play, *The Willing Spirit* (1936).

29. Dodie Smith went on to identify this 'contemporary phenomenon' in her article, 'Legion of Loveless Women', *Pearson's Weekly* (6 May 1931).
30. Dodie Smith, *Autumn Crocus*, in *Three Plays by Dodie Smith* (London: Samuel French, 1939), p. 59.
31. Smith herself had a number of affairs with married men, and moved to America at the outset of war with her lover, who was a conscientious objector.
32. Agatha Christie, *Black Coffee* (London: Samuel French, 1934), p. 7.
33. Melman, *Women and the Popular Imagination*, p. 1.
34. Clemence Dane, *A Bill of Divorcement* (London: Heinemann, 1921), p. 68.
35. Dodie Smith, *Touch Wood*, in *Autumn Crocus, Service, Touch Wood: Three Plays by Dodie Smith* (London: William Heinemann, 1939), p. 334.
36. Ibid., p. 345.
37. See, for example, Jessica Meyer, *Men of War: Masculinity and the First World War in Britain* (Basingstoke: Palgrave Macmillan, 2009).
38. Nicoletta F. Gullace, *'The Blood of Our Sons': Men, Women, and the Renegotiation of British Citizenship during the Great War* (Basingstoke: Palgrave Macmillan, 2002), p. 6. Dan Todman takes a different view, arguing that the vote was initially given to older women in the belief that it would act as a bulwark against the extreme left politics coming out of Russia. However, he does agree that the war gave women an increased confidence, and awareness of different forms of lifestyle. See Dan Todman, *The Great War: Myth and Memory* (London: Hambledon and London, 2005), p. 180.
39. Claire Buck, 'Women's Literature of the Great War', in *The Cambridge Companion to the Literature of the Great War*, ed. Vincent Sherry (Cambridge: Cambridge University Press, 2005), pp. 85–112, p. 99.
40. Ironically, this was taken up by British propaganda films of the Second World War, such as *The Gentle Sex* (1943), to persuade women to sign up to the war effort.
41. Muriel Box, *Angels of War*, p. 73.
42. See Clive Barker's 'The Ghosts of War' for more examples of time slips in interwar plays and their metaphorical meaning.
43. G.B. Stern, *The Man who Pays the Piper* (London: William Heinemann, nd. [1931]), p. 96.
44. Gale, 'Women Playwrights of the 1920s and 1930s', p. 28.
45. Linda Fitzsimmons, 'Typewriters Enchained: The Work of Elizabeth Baker', in *The New Woman and Her Sisters: Feminism and the Theatre 1850–1914*, ed. Viv Gardner and Susan Rutherford (London: Harvester Wheatsheaf, 1992), pp. 189–201, p. 191.
46. See Gale, *West End Women*, Chapter 6.
47. Ibid., p. 142.
48. Dodie Smith, *Dear Octopus* (London: Samuel French, 1939), p. 88.
49. Malcolm Kelsall, 'Manderley Revisited: *Rebecca* and the English Country House', *Proceedings of the Bristol Academy*, 82 (1993): 303–15, p. 303.
50. Rebecca D'Monté, 'Origin and Ownership: Stage, Film, and TV Adaptations of *Rebecca*', in *Adaptation in Contemporary Culture: Textual Infidelities*, ed. Rachel Carroll (London: Continuum, 2009), pp. 163–73, p. 166.
51. Rebecca D'Monté, 'Feminizing the Nation and the Country House: Women Dramatists 1938–1940', in *New Versions of Pastoral: Post-Romantic, Modern, and Contemporary Responses to the Tradition*, ed. David James and Philip Tew (Madison, NJ: Fairleigh Dickinson University Press, 2009), pp. 139–55, p. 150.

52. This had to be taken off when Roosevelt suddenly died.
53. Lesley Storm, *Great Day*, in The British Library, *The Lord Chamberlain's Papers*, 1.14.
54. Ibid.
55. Christine Gledhill and Gillian Swanson, 'Introduction', in *Nationalising Femininity: Culture, Sexuality and the British Cinema in the Second World War*, ed. Christine Gledhill and Gillian Swanson (Manchester: Manchester University Press, 1996), pp. 1–12, p. 5; Antonia Lant, 'Prologue: Mobile Femininity', ibid., pp. 13–32, p. 15.
56. Daphne du Maurier, *The Years Between*, in *The Years Between: Plays by Women on the London Stage 1900–1950*, ed. Fidelis Morgan (London: Virago, 1994), p. 373.
57. Simon Frith, 'The Pleasures of the Hearth: The Making of BBC Light Entertainment', in *Formations of Pleasure*, ed. Hazel Carby et al. (London: Routledge & Kegan Paul, 1983), pp. 101–23, p. 122.
58. Gale, *West End Women*, p. 139.

11
The Woman Journalist, 1920–1945
Catherine Clay

Introduction

On 18 July 1931 the feminist weekly *Time and Tide* printed a verse in its correspondence columns sent in by one of its readers. Under the title 'THE SUCCESSFUL JOURNALIST' it begins:

> Oh! I can write on Rural Deans,
> On sunsets or the loves of queens,
> On patent foods, on beauty's spell,
> Or whether instinct's helped by smell.
> On C.O.S., and S.P.G.,
> The use of coloured mats at tea.
> On autumn tints, on toilet soap,
> The dear deceitfulness of hope.

The list of topics to which 'the successful journalist' can turn her versatile pen is endless. The verse continues in a similar vein for a further twenty-four lines, and eventually concludes with an observation which is apparently broken off by an editorial intervention:

> The public simply loves my 'stuff,'
> And never really has enough;
> But editors whose brows are high
> Unwisely limit the supply,
> And so – – STELLA TOWER
> [Our brow *is* high. – ED.][1]

Time and Tide's editorial assertion in this female-run periodical that its 'brow *is* high' intimates much about the position of the woman journalist. As Patrick Collier has observed, 'the prestige of journalism as a profession was at a historic low' during the interwar years and 'this crisis was, for many observers, consequent with the arrival of women as a force in journalism'. Specifically, as Collier puts it, the decline was perceived to have begun 'when women emerged as consumers, subjects, and writers of news'; staple features of the popular press, from attention-grabbing headlines to gossip columns and advertising, were all markers of journalism's shift 'from its imagined artistic or public service mission into the (feminine) realm of the commodity'.[2] In this context *Time and Tide*'s editorial response to the verse sent in by 'Stella Tower' deliberately distances this journal from the 'stuff' of feminized mass-market newspaper and magazine journalism, and aligns it with the 'high' seriousness of the weekly reviews. At the same time, the title 'THE SUCCESSFUL JOURNALIST' celebrates achievement and, with its headline capitals, uses the very techniques of mass-market journalism to draw attention to the gains that may be made in the profession. Opportunities for women in journalism increased as the newspaper and periodical market expanded during the interwar years and *Time and Tide* frequently carried advertisements for professional courses in journalism carrying such tag-lines as 'Write Your Way To Success!'[3] Appearing in a journal devoted to the advancement of women in all professional fields, this verse and its editorial intervention also promotes the status of journalism as a profession. At once challenging the authority of highbrow editors who 'unwisely' limit the successful journalist's 'supply', the speaker's voice, then apparently silenced by the editor of *Time and Tide*, dramatizes the cultural constraints that accompanied the increased market opportunities for the woman journalist in this period.

'THE SUCCESSFUL JOURNALIST' thus raises important questions about how women journalists positioned themselves in relation to 'highbrow' and modernist cultures in an increasingly hierarchical literary and periodical marketplace. Of course, as the recent materialist turn in modernist scholarship has shown, modernist authors themselves operated across the division they constructed between art and commerce, literature and journalism, and their pronounced antipathy to journalism was part of the rhetoric by which they secured literary reputations and achieved cultural dominance. As Aaron Jaffe writes, 'the most "successful" modernists did not so much repudiate so-called "hack work" as they selectively distanced their imprimaturs from it, by adopting the stance of plausible deniability'.[4] This strategy was adopted by some women writers of the period, for example, Storm Jameson and Rebecca West, both of whom reproduced a modernist disavowal of journalism in the construction of their writing identities.[5] Other women writers, however, more actively resisted the devaluation of journalism in modernist discourse. Winifred Holtby, for example, used her position on *Time and Tide* to rehabilitate journalism as a genre and a profession.[6]

This chapter provides an overview of British women's journalistic activity in the period 1920 to 1945, and considers what this signifies in terms of women writers' literary careers and professional identities. My principal focus, therefore, is the journalism of published women novelists, poets, and dramatists, and not that of women who worked only as professional journalists which, though of vital interest and importance, is beyond the scope of the chapter. My survey is divided into three areas: (1) 'women's journalism', including the feminist press, women's pages, and popular women's magazines; (2) 'literary journalism', including book reviewing in newspapers, periodicals, and mass-market magazines as well as modernist cultural criticism in literary magazines;[7] and (3) 'political journalism', including 'serious' news reporting and political opinion. Many writers worked in some or all of these markets and this journalism must necessarily broaden our more general understanding of women's writing in this period.

Women's journalism

Women's journalism from 1920 to 1945 can be divided into two broad areas: (1) feminist periodical publishing, and (2) the more commercially-oriented journalism of 'women's pages' and popular women's magazines. The origins of a feminist periodical press in Britain can be traced back to the mid-nineteenth-century women's movement and in particular the founding of the *English Woman's Journal* by Barbara Leigh Smith and Bessie Rayner Parkes, leading figures in the Langham Place Circle. Commercial women's magazines have been traced back to at least the end of the seventeenth century.[8] This genre expanded, with the rise of consumer culture, in the closing decades of the nineteenth century, years which also saw the development of the 'woman's page' in regular newspapers to attract female readers. These two areas of women's journalism may at first appear to represent the 'radical' and 'conservative' end of the spectrum respectively. Yet women writers who contributed to feminist periodicals also worked in the expanding women's magazine market. The ways in which women writers' journalistic activity crossed over these spheres deserves more critical attention.

Feminist periodical publishing

In a useful survey of this field, Barbara Green states that: 'In the early years of the twentieth century the feminist periodical press experienced a rapid expansion, fuelled in part by the proliferation of movement papers which served as organs of various women's suffrage organizations.'[9] Leading suffrage journals, including *The Woman's Leader* and *The Vote*, continued well into the interwar years and, according to David Doughan and Denise Sanchez, in the years between 1920 and 1945 fifty-two new feminist periodicals were founded in Britain.[10] As Green explains, these new titles encompassed more than 'the movement papers of large national organizations, but also branch papers, papers affiliated with women's religious organizations, temperance papers, feminist literary reviews, and more'.[11] They also included what Alice Staveley identifies as a distinct genre of women's interwar publishing, the 'women's professional magazine', which flourished following the Sex Disqualification (Removal) Act of 1919.[12] These print organs of professional women's organizations, such as *The Woman Journalist* of the Society of Women Journalists founded in 1894, did not necessarily advertise themselves or their organizations as 'feminist', but they were a significant part of the material culture on which an interwar feminist discourse of women's professionalism was based. In a fascinating discussion of Virginia Woolf and the marketing of *Three Guineas*, Alice Staveley finds the print culture of these organizations to be a vast untapped resource for researching the promotion and reception of women's writing. For example, *The Woman Engineer* (print organ of the Women's Engineering Society) was one of several women's professional magazines which carried reviews and advertisements for *Three Guineas* at the behest of the Woolfs' employee Norah Nicholls who used her contacts for 'drumming up sales for *Three Guineas* among women's groups'.[13]

The most significant feminist periodical for British women writers in 1920–1945 was *Time and Tide*. Not only did it provide a new outlet for women writers of the suffrage generation (for example, Cicely Hamilton and Christopher St John) who continued to rely on journalism for a living, it was also hugely important for a new generation similarly reliant upon journalism and establishing their literary reputations. Magazines like *The Woman Journalist* (re-launched in a new format in 1923) functioned primarily as members' newsletters and it is unlikely that their contributors were paid. Unfortunately very few financial records for *Time and Tide* survive, but it is evident that the journal employed regular staff writers (among them were E.M. Delafield and Winifred Holtby) and paid outside contributors competitive rates. The September 1923 issue of *The Woman Journalist* contained the following notice: '*Time and Tide* ... accepts serious and light articles. Short stories, from 400 to 1,000 words, are given special consideration. Payment is from One to Two Guineas a thousand words.'[14] In 1924 *Time and Tide* published a crop of short stories by new fiction writers: Richmal Crompton, E.M. Delafield, Susan Ertz, Eleanor Farjeon, Ethel Mannin, Viola Meynell, Hilda Reid, Sylvia Thompson, and E.H. Young. Others who had stories in *Time and Tide* between the wars include Rose Allatini, Iris Barry, Stella Benson, Elizabeth Bowen, Winifred Holtby, Pamela Hansford Johnson, Marghanita Laski, Naomi Mitchison, Kate O'Brien, Jean Rhys, Helen Simpson, Doreen Wallace, Sylvia Townsend Warner, and Dorothy Whipple. *Time and Tide* also published women poets who struggled to place their work in male-edited magazines.[15] Its book reviews too were important for the critical reception of women's writing. More inclusive than the literary magazines associated with modernist publishing, such as *The Criterion* and *The Calendar of Modern Letters*, *Time and Tide* thus played an instrumental role in nurturing the creative talent of many British women writers.

The 'woman's page' and popular women's magazines

By the 1920s just about every newspaper featured a woman's page. For commercial women's magazines the interwar years mark a period of expansion. Cynthia White identifies as many as fifty-nine new women's magazines in Britain between 1920 and 1945, including middle-class monthlies and the 'new weekly' of the 1930s which targeted a wider readership. The discourses of domesticity in such titles as *Good Housekeeping, Woman and Home*, and *Home Journal*, have made them appear irretrievable for a progressive feminist politics. *Time and Tide*, for example, self-consciously adopted an oppositional relationship to this genre of women's journalism, and carried features overtly satirizing the world of the woman's page and women's magazines. Throughout January 1924 it printed a spoof 'men's page', and in May 1927 feminist activist Crystal Eastman stated categorically 'I suppose there is nothing more irritating to a feminist than the average "Woman's Page" of a newspaper' in an article pointing out that 'women's interests to-day are as wide as the world', far exceeding the genre's regular supply of recipes and romance.[16] In September 1927 and August 1928 *Time and Tide*'s regular 'In the Tideway' column used satire to ridicule the narrow interests of the 'women's weeklies'.[17] In the 1930s the continuing popularity of the woman's page was taken up satirically in the hands of the journal's most famous humorous author, E.M. Delafield.[18]

Time and Tide was highly critical of the failure of this type of women's journalism to engage women readers on wider political and cultural subjects. However, recent scholarship has begun to challenge this view, with Fiona Hackney stating that commercial women's magazines 'weren't the retrograde organs of conservatism that others have assumed them to be'.[19] Indeed, women readers at the time challenged this feminist demonizing of popular women's journalism. Following the publication of Crystal Eastman's article on the woman's page, two readers, including the editor of the woman's page at the *Sheffield Daily Telegraph* wrote in to *Time and Tide* to point out that the woman's page of the provincial papers had already moved with the times and provided more substantial material for women, representing a wide range of interests.[20] Furthermore, the fact that many British women writers wrote for this women's journalism market, including feminist women associated with *Time and Tide*, requires us to pay this material closer scrutiny.

One particularly significant women's magazine was *Good Housekeeping*. Launched in 1922 it was the most successful of the new women's monthlies marketed at middle-class readers after the First World War and, according to Brian Braithwaite, 'concerned itself from the start with the burning issues of the day, particularly as they affected women'.[21] In 1928 (the year that all women over the age of twenty-one received the vote) the magazine carried several articles on 'new professions for women', including one contributed by Storm Jameson on 'Advertising as a Career for Women', thus seeking to engage women readers beyond the narrow confines of the home. Another significant title launched in 1925 was *Modern Woman* which, according to Hackney, 'presented some of the most clearly progressive models of modern womanhood available in commercial women's magazines'. In particular, she discusses the use novelist Leonora Eyles made of her column in *Modern Woman* 'to increase what she termed "sex knowledge"'. 'At a time when *The Daily Express* operated a policy banning discussion of the subject, [Eyles] bravely promoted scientific methods, recommending Stopes's publications and the Society for Constructive Birth Control.'[22] Another writer for *Modern Woman* was Stevie Smith who contributed regular book reviews to the magazine for ten years from 1941. According to Laura Severin, 'Smith attempted to disrupt the influence of domestic ideology on her women readers by recommending not only romances but a wide variety of reading.'[23] British women writers thus contributed to what Hackney describes as 'the multiplicity of varied, and sometimes contradictory versions of modern womanhood that appeared in women's magazines' and also viewed these publications as an opportunity to educate women, to 'change and improve their readers' lives'.[24] Indeed, while Lady Margaret Rhondda once referred to 'our best known and most respected authors' writing for women's magazines 'on their off days', evidence suggests that women writers in fact approached their work in this field with far more seriousness, and political intent.[25]

Another reason for British women to value their journalistic work in the women's magazines was the publicity this brought them for their literary work as novelists, playwrights or poets. *Good Housekeeping* in particular had a 'reputation for superior fiction and topical feature articles' by leading women writers of the period including Rose Macaulay, Rebecca West, and Virginia Woolf.[26] For its book reviews it drew upon such figures as Clemence Dane and Winifred Holtby. As well as providing a lucrative income, magazines like *Good Housekeeping* had very large national readerships, and by distributing women writers' names throughout middle-class households they undoubtedly served to bolster literary reputations and book sales. The role of women's magazines in publicizing women writers' literary careers is further illustrated in a feature article published in *Good Housekeeping* in November 1936. The article, 'Sharing a Flat with an Author – who happens to be E.M. DELAFIELD', was written by Lorna Lewis, an author of children's books and regular book reviewer for *Time and Tide*. Illustrated with photographs of both authors, and the stylish Bloomsbury flat they occupied, the article recounts with affectionate amusement the 'whirlwind' itinerary of Delafield's public and private engagements and:

> a great deal of talk against a roaring background of wireless; a great deal of going out and eating strange little meals at strange little teashops in the neighbourhood; and a great deal of filling of hot-water bottles to keep our knees warm as we sit at our respective desks.[27]

'Many authors live like this', writes Lewis, in the confidential tone characteristic of the new celebrity culture that played an important role in turning writers like E.M. Delafield into household names.[28] Lewis's article also represents a more popular form of 'literary journalism', to which I turn next.

Literary journalism

Given the increased demarcation between literature and journalism in this period, 'literary journalism' may appear a contradiction in terms. In fact, this speaks powerfully to a concerted attempt by certain critics to exercise their authority in a rapidly expanding print marketplace. According to Patrick Collier, in order to maintain artistic integrity, modernist writers and critics 'needed to define a sphere of literary journalism that fell on the proper side of the art/commerce and high/low lines so they could explain and disseminate the principles of modernism'.[29] In a modernist context, 'literary journalism' thus emerges as a rarefied species of journalism, a sphere of cultural rather than commercial activity in which modernists positioned themselves as 'upholder[s] of standards in a degraded journalistic world'.[30] One particular source of anxiety was what Collier describes as 'a broader sense of crisis and failure in book reviewing' as newspapers responded to the expansion of the book market by publishing an increasing number of relatively short reviews for millions of readers.[31] This situation generated anxieties about literature in an age of mass communication, producing further distinctions between 'book reviewing' (devalued, and associated with journalism) and 'literary criticism' (valued, and associated with literature).[32] Such divisions are extremely limiting, however, for a discussion of British women writers for whom book reviewing in newspapers and magazines was frequently an important source of income, as well as a means of contributing to contemporary critical debates.

Literary magazines and modernist cultural criticism

Modernist cultural criticism is identified primarily with the literary magazine. As the editors of *The Oxford Critical and Cultural History of Modernist Magazines* explain, 'magazines ... belonged to the institutions that sustained and promoted modernism', and, as the excellent scholarship in this volume shows, 'participated in the *making* of a "modernist" cultural aesthetic and the institution of modernism'.[33] Particularly influential was T.S. Eliot's *The Criterion*, founded in 1922, which, as Jason Harding argues, was 'crucial to the dissemination and consolidation of modernist writing' and to the development of 'critical standards'.[34] Also highly influential were Edgell Rickword's *The Calendar of Modern Letters* (1925–1927) and F.R. Leavis's *Scrutiny* (1932–1953), co-edited with his wife, Q.D. Leavis. On the whole, literary magazines were not the most hospitable outlets for women's literary journalism. Between 1920 and 1945 as many as forty-three new literary magazines were founded in Britain, the vast majority controlled by male literary editors.[35] While women sometimes gained entry as contributors of creative work, and in some (for example, *The Adelphi* and *The [Monthly] Chapbook*) were encouraged to participate in critical debate, rarely did women writers achieve the status of critics.[36] Two major critical voices did emerge, namely Virginia Woolf and Rebecca West.

Interestingly, both Woolf and West disparaged journalism, thus reiterating the modernist construction of the literature/journalism divide. As Leila Brosnan has argued, Woolf frequently figured journalists and journalism as 'abject', while West privately declared, in a letter dated in 1922, 'I hate, hate, HATE journalism.'[37] However, both were engaged in journalistic activity of some kind throughout their professional writing careers, and their articles and reviews were instrumental in building their reputations as literary critics. As Brosnan points out, Woolf was able to use her family and friendship networks to secure a position as 'an "insider" in the literary world at large'.[38] She enjoyed relative freedom, for example, in the literary pages of the *Nation and Athenaeum* edited by her husband. Moreover, her friendships with other editors holding key positions in the world of journalism facilitated her access to *The Criterion*, the *New Statesman*, *Life and Letters*, and the *Sunday Times*.[39] *The Common Reader* in 1925 consolidated Woolf's status as a critic and essayist, but it was her connection with *Vogue* in the same year that Brosnan identifies as particularly important to Woolf's own appreciation of her 'value as a commodity within the world of journalism' and her ability to manipulate this to material advantage.[40] West was not graced with the same familial and friendship connections that eased Woolf's entry into journalism. She first made her name as a journalist in articles for radical feminist and socialist periodicals including the *Freewoman*, the *Daily Herald*, and the *Clarion* during the years immediately before and after the First World War.[41] During the 1920s she developed her reputation as a literary critic in reviews of contemporary novels for the *New Statesman* and in theatre criticism for *Time and Tide*. West consolidated her reputation as a critic with the publication of *The Strange Necessity* in 1928 and her name, like Woolf's, was by now much sought after by magazine editors.

As Pykett says of West, journalism needs to be recognized as 'a distinctive form of literary work' by which women writers constructed themselves as modern women of letters.[42] More dispersed, however, than the weekly or monthly commentaries written by literary editors such as Eliot, women's journalism had a more fugitive existence and risked getting lost in the modernist ferment. The practice of publishing selections of literary journalism in book form (repeated by Woolf in the second series of *The Common Reader* published in 1932, and by West in the publication of *Ending in Earnest* in 1931) can be read as a tactic for survival. Replicating a distinction between the low-status work of book reviewing and the high-status work of literary criticism, this move raises the status of the published work from ephemeral 'review' to permanent 'essay'. Woolf and West both found ways, therefore, to work literary and journalistic markets to their advantage, despite the obstacles placed in the way of women by male literary gatekeepers. Indeed, one might argue that their greatest contribution to modernist cultural criticism was directly occasioned by the hostile and exclusionary practices of their male contemporaries. In the case of Woolf, Hermione Lee observes that such seminal essays as 'Modern Fiction' and 'Character in Fiction' 'came out of Woolf's arguments with [Arnold] Bennett, [Desmond] MacCarthy and [John Middleton] Murry' and that while we often read them as 'self-ignited, free-standing meditations on what she felt the novel should do and be ... they were, in their inception, angry reactions to reviews of her work'.[43] Similarly, West's most incisive literary criticism may be seen as a rejection of the kind of modernist stance embodied in such figures as Eliot and Leavis.[44] In particular, Patrick Collier credits West for her effort in the late 1920s and 1930s to 'mainstream modernism, to construct a more democratic, inclusive, and politically-engaged version of experimental literature than one would later inherit from Eliot and Pound through their mid-century critics'.[45]

Book reviewing in newspapers, periodicals and mass-market magazines

Opportunities for book reviewing were far more available to women writers in newspapers, periodicals, and mass-market magazines than literary magazines associated with modernist cultural criticism. In particular, the reviewing of fiction was regarded as amenable to women, and several best-selling authors, for example, Phyllis Bentley, Rosamond Lehmann, and Dorothy L. Sayers, became well-known 'novelist–critics'.[46] It was even possible for women to make a career in literary journalism. For example, Naomi Royde-Smith, who became the first female literary editor of a London newspaper, the *Westminster Gazette* (1912–1922), worked for several years between the wars as a freelance book reviewer and drama critic.[47] The evidence suggests that many British women writers resisted Modernism's distinction between 'high' and 'low' reviewing. Clemence Dane, Winifred Holtby, and Stevie Smith regularly reviewed novels for mass-market women's magazines *Good Housekeeping* (Dane and Holtby) and *Modern Woman* (Smith), publications aimed at middle-class women readers, the very audience that modernist cultural critics perceived as a threat to public taste. Book reviews in newspapers and popular magazines were a vital component of what Rosa Maria Bracco describes as the 'virtual industry [that] had grown around middlebrow fiction' by the 1930s.[48] As members also of selection committees for literary prizes and book clubs, such as the *Femina–Vie Heureuse* prize and the British Book Society, women writers were actively involved in the critical reception of 'middlebrow' novels in these years.[49] Book reviewing, and its associated apparatus of literary prizes and clubs, thus played an important role in promoting the work of women writers excluded by modernist institutions and networks.

Book reviewing brought financial remuneration. It was also part of the 'literary work' through which women writers promoted themselves and their friends. Of Stevie Smith, Laura Severin argues that she self-consciously used her book reviews both 'to assert herself into the literary hierarchy' and 'to bring women writers from the margins into the fold' and other women too used their positions as reviewers to bring their friends and fellow writers to the attention of a wider public.[50] This can be seen, for example, in the early review columns of *Time and Tide*, which was particularly supportive of women's writing. From 1920 to 1926 'New Novels' were reviewed by Rose Macaulay, Sylvia Lynd, and Naomi Royde-Smith, all close friends and part of an alternative network to Bloomsbury, which came to represent Modernism for an English audience. Located in west rather than central London, the Thursday evening literary soirées hosted by Macaulay and Royde-Smith in South Kensington in the 1920s, and the Friday evening parties hosted by Robert and Sylvia Lynd in Hampstead in the 1930s, brought together writers and critics whose influence in literary London has been overshadowed by their more famous modernist contemporaries.[51] In 1928 *Time and Tide*'s 'literary turn' marked a new orientation towards modernist cultures as it harnessed Bloomsbury in its own bid for cultural authority. However, throughout the 1930s the journal continued to review the work of writers who have been left out of modernist accounts, and its larger number of reviewers (necessitated by the expansion of its books section) included Margery Allingham, Vera Brittain, Mary Butts, Lettice Cooper, Olive Heseltine, and Naomi Mitchison. *Time and Tide*'s first literary editor was in fact male: R. Ellis Roberts, former literary editor on the *New Statesman*, was appointed to the journal's staff in 1933. However, within two years the position was taken up by Theodora Bosanquet, and the literary editorship remained in female hands until 1950.[52]

Political journalism

Of the types of journalism considered so far, political journalism was the most difficult field for women to enter. From the late nineteenth century until the Second World War women were far more often the subjects than the reporters of news in the mainstream newspaper press.[53] A key challenge for the woman journalist venturing into the sphere of political journalism was to overcome her status as an often trivialized subject of mainstream press reporting in order to become a respected reporter of 'serious' news herself. In the years between 1920 and 1945 women did begin to make incremental advances in the male-dominated world of political journalism, and the Second World War in particular is widely regarded as a breakthrough moment in women's 'serious' news reporting.[54] Writers who have been remembered primarily for their literary work also played a part in these developments.

Women reporters and 'serious' news

One significant barrier faced by women reporters was their exclusion from the very institutions and networks where 'serious' news was made. In 1928 Vera Brittain recorded that 'several thousand women are employed ... in regular journalism', but 'for the most part as reporters and as writers of social notes and fashion articles'.[55] Crucially, while a few exceptional female journalists from the nineteenth century onwards had demonstrated women's capabilities for 'serious' news reporting, as a rule women were still not given journalistic assignments in such fields as politics, economics, and international affairs. Yet this limitation was not simply a matter of prejudicial attitudes among male newspaper editors. Other institutions played a part by denying women access to the sources of information upon which all news reporters were reliant. One small victory was noted by *The Woman Journalist* in January 1925: 'Miss Rebecca West in being admitted to the House of Lords as representative of the *Daily News*, with the usual Press privileges, has established a journalistic record. No lady journalist has hitherto been so admitted.'[56] But women's entry into political journalism remained exceedingly difficult. Almost a decade later *Time and Tide* reported angrily on the exclusion of women from a dinner given by the Royal Institute of International Affairs at which General Smuts (former Prime Minister of South Africa) 'made a speech of world importance'.[57]

From the mid-1930s onwards, events in Europe drew many British writers into politics, including women writer-activists who reported on what was happening on the international stage. Spain became the focal point for much anti-fascist writing and resistance of the period, and among the writers involved in this struggle was Communist Party member Sylvia Townsend Warner who joined an ambulance unit in the Spanish Civil War and reported on the Spanish situation in the *Left Review*, the *New Statesman*, and *Time and Tide*.[58] Another writer-activist was Storm Jameson. Jameson travelled to Vienna, Budapest, and Prague during the 1930s where she witnessed first-hand the effects of the growth of Nazism. Jameson headed a campaign to provide asylum for refugee writers from Europe, became the president of PEN in 1938, and in a prominent article published in the *Times Literary Supplement* in 1940 called upon writers to take up their pens as defenders of European civilization.[59] Similarly, Rebecca West used her position and contacts as a public intellectual to report on the worsening situation in Europe. Accounts of her journeys through Yugoslavia in 1936, 1937, and 1938 were published in the American monthly magazine, *Atlantic*, anticipating her monumental work *Black Lamb and Grey Falcon*. Thus, despite the barriers politically-engaged women found ways to circumvent official rulings and report on the most important political developments of the decade.

Women and political opinion journalism

In shaping political opinion, as in the reporting of 'serious' news, women journalists faced significant barriers on account of their sex. Leader columns in the newspapers and weekly reviews, or 'journals of opinion', were heavily male-dominated; for example, Adrian Smith, describing the *New Statesman* in these years, explains that while women were involved in the production of this journal 'their influence over editorial content and policy was non-existent'.[60] In this context the success of *Time and Tide*, the first and only paper of its kind to be directed and staffed by women, is highly significant. From its inception its coverage extended beyond traditional 'women's interests' and in the 1930s *Time and Tide* completed its transition from a woman-focused to an internationally-oriented journal for an intelligent liberal-left public made up of men and women. Crucially, even as the journal admitted more male contributors women continued to occupy key editorial and staff positions. Several British women writers contributed signed leading articles during the interwar years, among them, Vera Brittain, Lettice Cooper, Richmal Crompton, Clemence Dane, Mary Agnes Hamilton, Cicely Hamilton, Winifred Holtby, and Ellen Wilkinson. An important feature was the paper's 'Notes on the Way' column which from 1932 attracted leading male writers of the period, including T.S. Eliot, E.M. Forster, Aldous Huxley, and Wyndham Lewis. It also carried contributions from Stella Benson, Winifred Holtby, Rose Macaulay, Rebecca West, Ellen Wilkinson, and the critically neglected Jewish liberal-left writer Marghanita Laski.

All these women were encouraged by Lady Margaret Rhondda, who throughout her publishing and editing career was actively committed to the promotion of women in professional life, including journalism. A council member of the Society of Women Journalists in the early 1920s, Rhondda was a founding member of the Six Point Group (1921) and the Open Door Council (1926), both of which campaigned for equal opportunities in the workplace. She was also the first president of the Women's Press Club of London, founded in 1943. Arguably her most important protégée was Winifred Holtby who served as a director of *Time and Tide* from 1926, and until her tragic death in 1935 contributed signed and unsigned material virtually every week. Holtby's position on *Time and Tide* was instrumental in her development as a political journalist; responsible for home news she also used the journal to comment upon the causes she was most passionate about: racial equality in South Africa, feminism, disarmament, and peace.[61] Having acquired a reputation as one of the most brilliant journalists in London, Holtby was invited in 1933 by the new editor of the *News Chronicle* 'to join his panel of political writers for the Leader page – the first woman to do so on that and, I believe, on any London daily'.[62] This promotion to the leader page of a mainstream London newspaper was a remarkable achievement, making Holtby a pioneer in political journalism of the time.

Vera Brittain, Holtby's lifelong friend, also established herself as a freelance journalist and 'achieved a reputation as one of England's most effective writers on topics concerned with feminism and pacifism' during the interwar years.[63] Like Holtby, Brittain resisted the modernist subordination of journalistic work to literary activity, explaining in 1925 to her future husband, George Catlin, that: 'There is less division than you perhaps think between my literary and political work. The first ... is simply a popular interpretation of the second; a means of presenting my theories before people who would not understand or be interested in them if they were explained seriously.'[64] Rose Macaulay also used journalism to shape political opinion. In the 1930s she contributed a large number of political opinion pieces and commentary to the leading weekly reviews, including a regular column 'Marginal Comments' in the *Spectator* where she wrote against Fascism and, according to Jane Emery, resisted the pressure of the Establishment, challenged the decisions of leaders, and 'protested against domestic and international policies which offended her sense of justice'.[65] An active member of the National Council for Civil Liberties, and a sponsor of the Peace Pledge Union, Macaulay also put her political findings and opinions into fiction, notably her 1940 novel set during the Spanish Civil War, *And No Man's Wit*. For many British women writers of this period, literary work, journalistic activity, and politics were intertwined.

Conclusion

Journalism represents a neglected but vital part of British women's writing in the years 1920 to 1945. As the print marketplace expanded, and opportunities for women to work as journalists increased, many women writers of fiction, poetry, and drama also worked in a variety of journalistic markets and challenged the literature/journalism divide constructed by their modernist contemporaries. At one level journalism was a job, providing a source of income necessary for independent existence. But it was not reducible to this, nor was it ever merely a 'supplement' to women writers' literary work. Rather, women writers' journalism was motivated by their desire to build literary reputations, publicize causes, challenge dominant discourses, and make a difference to readers' lives. The range of women's journalistic activity in this period is striking. Straddling both 'high' and 'low' spheres women writers responded enthusiastically to the demands of the market, and engaged with multiple readerships with political as well as literary intent. To become a 'successful journalist' was not to abandon literary ambition, but to embrace professional and political as well as artistic ideals.

Notes

1. *Time and Tide* (18 July 1931): 861.
2. Patrick Collier, 'Journalism Meets Modernism', in *Gender in Modernism*, ed. Bonnie Kime Scott (Urbana: University of Illinois Press, 2007), pp. 188–9.
3. This advertisement for the London Editorial College was on the cover of the 22 February 1929 issue and addressed women readers with its strapline 'Read What Women Say'.

4. Aaron Jaffe, *Modernism and the Culture of Celebrity* (Cambridge: Cambridge University Press, 2005), p. 177.
5. Catherine Clay, 'Storm Jameson's Journalism 1913–33: The Construction of a Writer', in *Margaret Storm Jameson: Writing in Dialogue*, ed. Jennifer Birkett and Chiara Briganti (Cambridge: Cambridge Scholars Press, 2007), pp. 37–52.
6. Catherine Clay, 'Winifred Holtby, Journalist: Rehabilitating Journalism in the Modernist Ferment', in *Winifred Holtby, 'A Woman in Her Time': Critical Essays*, ed. Lisa Regan (Cambridge: Cambridge Scholars Press, 2010), pp. 65–88.
7. I use Stefan Collini's definition of literary journalism as 'a wide range of contributions to those cultural and intellectual discussions that are carried on in the "literary" pages of newspapers and periodicals' and consider women working 'within' and 'outside' modernist institutions and networks. Stefan Collini, 'The Critic as Journalist: Leavis after *Scrutiny*', in *Grub Street and the Ivory Tower: Literary Journalism and Literary Scholarship from Fielding to the Internet*, ed. Jeremy Treglown and Bridget Bennett (Oxford: Oxford University Press, 1998), p. 153.
8. Cynthia White, *Women's Magazines 1693–1968* (London: Michael Johnson, 1970).
9. Barbara Green, 'The Feminist Periodical Press: Women, Periodical Studies and Modernity', *Literature Compass*, 6:1 (2009): 194.
10. David Doughan and Denise Sanchez, *Feminist Periodicals 1855–1984* (Brighton: Harvester, 1987).
11. Green, 'The Feminist Periodical Press', p. 195.
12. Alison Staveley, 'Teacups and Turbines: Negotiating Modernity in the Inter-war Women's Professional Magazine', paper given at the 10th annual conference of the Modernist Studies Association, Nashville, Tennessee, November 2008.
13. Alison Staveley, 'Marketing Virginia Woolf: Women, War and Public Relations in *Three Guineas*', *Book History*, 12 (2009): 299.
14. Anon., 'Home Market', *The Woman Journalist* (September 1923).
15. Jane Dowson, *Women's Poetry of the 1930s: A Critical Anthology* (London: Routledge, 1996).
16. Crystal Eastman, 'What Shall We Do with the Woman's Page?', *Time and Tide* (20 May 1927): 470.
17. 'In the Tideway', *Time and Tide* (2 September 1927 and 17 August 1928).
18. E.M. Delafield, 'All about Us Girls', *Time and Tide* (10 November 1934): 1417–18, and 'The New Rosamond', *Time and Tide* (30 May 1936): 785–6.
19. Fiona Hackney, '"Women are News": British Women's Magazines 1919–1939', in *Transatlantic Print Culture, 1880–1940*, ed. Ann Ardis and Patrick Collier (Basingstoke: Palgrave Macmillan, 2008), p. 129.
20. 'Correspondence', *Time and Tide* (27 May 1927): 502.
21. Brian Braithwaite, *Women's Magazines: The First 300 Years* (London: Peter Owens, 1995), p. 32.
22. Hackney, '"Women are News"', p. 123. A feminist and socialist, Eyles also wrote for *Time and Tide* and for the women's pages of *The Miner* and the *Daily Herald*. See Fiona Hackney's entry on Eyles, in *Encyclopedia of British Women's Writing, 1900–1950*, ed. Faye Hammill et al. (Basingstoke: Palgrave Macmillan, 2006), pp. 85–6.
23. Laura Severin, *Stevie Smith's Resistant Antics* (Wisconsin: University of Wisconsin Press, 1997), p. 17.
24. Hackney, '"Women are News"', pp. 116, 117.
25. Viscountess Rhondda, 'Woman's Place', *Time and Tide* (9 December 1927): 1111.
26. Hackney, '"Women are News"', p. 118.

27. Lorna Lewis, 'Sharing a Flat with an Author – Who Happens to be E.M. Delafield', *Good Housekeeping* (November 1936): 42–3, 124–7.
28. See Faye Hammill, *Women, Celebrity and Literary Culture between the Wars* (Austin: University of Texas Press, 2007).
29. Patrick Collier, 'T.S. Eliot and the "Journalistic Struggle"', in *Challenging Modernism: New Readings in Literature and Culture, 1914–45*, ed. Stella Deen (Aldershot: Ashgate, 2002), p. 194.
30. Patrick Collier, *Modernism on Fleet Street* (Aldershot: Ashgate, 2006), p. 48.
31. Ibid., pp. 72–3.
32. Ibid., p. 26.
33. Peter Brooker and Andrew Thacker, eds, *The Oxford Critical and Cultural History of Modernist Magazines* (Oxford: Oxford University Press, 2009), pp. 2, 11.
34. Jason Harding, 'The Idea of a Literary Review: T.S. Eliot and The Criterion', in *The Oxford Critical and Cultural History of Modernist Magazines*, ed. Brooker and Thacker, p. 349.
35. Alvin Sullivan, ed., *British Literary Magazines: The Modern Age, 1914–1984* (Westport, CT: Greenwood Press, 1986). Only one of the literary magazines listed by Sullivan was edited by a woman, Ethel Gutman's *Bermondsey Book* (1923–1930). Edith Sitwell's edited *Wheels*, founded 1916, ended in 1921, and Laura Riding, overlooked by Sullivan but discussed in *The Oxford Critical and Cultural History of Modernist Magazines*, was the editor of two short-lived but important magazines, *Epilogue* (1935–1937) and *Focus* (1935). This relatively small number of women literary editors contrasts with 'a striking number of women editors active during the rise and flowering of modernism', E. Marek, *Women Editing Modernism* (Kentucky: University Press of Kentucky, 1995), p. 4.
36. Georgina Taylor, *H.D. and the Public Sphere of Modernist Women Writers 1913–1946* (Oxford: Oxford University Press, 2001), p. 73. Eliot's appointment of Janet Adam Smith as chief reviewer of contemporary poetry in *The New Criterion* in 1936 was unusual. See Jason Harding, *The Criterion: Cultural Politics and Periodical Networks in Inter-war Britain* (Oxford: Oxford University Press, 2002), pp. 164–6.
37. Leila Brosnan, *Reading Virginia Woolf's Essays and Journalism* (Edinburgh: Edinburgh University Press, 1999), pp. 70–91; Collier, 'Journalism Meets Modernism', p. 192.
38. Brosnan, *Reading Virginia Woolf's Essays and Journalism*, p. 47.
39. Ibid. Leonard Woolf was literary editor of the *Nation and Athenaeum* from 1923 to 1930.
40. Ibid., pp. 49–58.
41. Lyn Pykett, 'The Making of a Modern Woman Writer: Rebecca West's Journalism, 1911–1930', in *Journalism, Literature and Modernity from Hazlitt to Modernism*, ed. Kate Campbell (Edinburgh: Edinburgh University Press, 2000), p. 177.
42. Ibid., p. 172.
43. Hermione Lee, '"Crimes of Criticism": Virginia Woolf and Literary Journalism', in *Grub Street and the Ivory Tower*, ed. Treglown and Bennett, p. 123.
44. See Collier, *Modernism on Fleet Street*, pp. 181–2, for a discussion of West's battle with Eliot and the New Humanists.
45. Ibid., p. 173.
46. Bentley reviewed novels in the *Yorkshire Post*, Lehmann in the *Spectator*, and Sayers in the *Sunday Times*.
47. George M. Johnson, ed., *Dictionary of Literary Biography, Vol. 191: British Novelists between the Wars* (Detroit: Gale Research, 1998), p. 278.

48. Rosa Maria Bracco, *Betwixt and Between: Middlebrow Fiction and English Society in the Twenties and Thirties* (Parkville, Victoria: University of Melbourne, History Department, 1990), p. 48.
49. Committee members of the *Femina–Vie Heureuse* prize included Rebecca West, May Sinclair, Margaret Kennedy, and Violet Hunt. See Hammill et al., *Encyclopedia of British Women's Writing*, p. 191. The British Book Society selection committee included Clemence Dane and Sylvia Lynd.
50. Severin, *Stevie Smith's Resistant Antics*, p. 80.
51. Sarah Lefanu, *Rose Macaulay* (London: Virago, 2003), pp. 152, 185–6.
52. Bosanquet was succeeded by the historian Cicely Veronica Wedgwood in 1943; the literary editorship passed to John Betjeman in 1950.
53. At end of the nineteenth century the 'New Woman' became 'a symbol of modernity in the press' (Margaret Beetham, 'Periodicals and the New Media: Women and Imagined Communities', *Women's Studies International Forum*, 29:3 (2006): 235); 'in the inter-war years "modern" women made headlines' (Hackney, '"Women Are News"', p. 114).
54. Anne Sebba, *Battling for News: The Rise of the Woman Reporter* (London: Hodder and Stoughton, 1994).
55. Vera Brittain, *Women's Work in Modern England* (London: Noel Douglas, 1928), p. 90.
56. *The Woman Journalist* (January 1925).
57. 'Review of the Week', *Time and Tide* (17 November 1934): 1463.
58. Wendy Mulford, Introduction to Sylvia Townsend Warner, *After the Death of Don Juan* (London: Virago, 1989), pp. xv–xvi. This 1938 novel, and also *Summer Will Show* (1936), express Warner's anti-fascist politics in fictional form.
59. 'Fighting the Foes of Civilizaton: The Writer's Place in the Defence Line', *Times Literary Supplement* (7 October 1939). Cited in Jennifer Birkett, *Margaret Storm Jameson: A Life* (Oxford: Oxford University Press, 2009), p. 186.
60. Adrian Smith, *The New Statesman: Portrait of a Political Weekly 1913–31* (London: Frank Cass, 1996), p. 59.
61. Clay, 'Winifred Holtby, Journalist', pp. 73–8.
62. Winifred Holtby, *Letters to a Friend*, ed. Alice Holtby and Jean McWilliam (London: Collins, 1937), p. 458. The editor would have been Vernon Bartlett, one of the best-known names in diplomatic journalism at the time.
63. Paul Berry and Mark Bostridge, *Testament of a Generation: The Journalism of Vera Brittain and Winifred Holtby* (London: Virago, 1985), p. 30.
64. Ibid.
65. Jane Emery, *Rose Macaulay: A Writer's Life* (London: John Murray, 1991), p. 245. Macaulay also wrote frequently for the *New Statesman*, and occasionally *Time and Tide*.

Part IV
The Mobile Woman

Part IV
The Mobile Woman

12
Caught in the Triple Net? Welsh, Scottish, and Irish Women Writers

Katie Gramich

Joyce's Stephen Dedalus in *Portrait of the Artist as a Young Man* famously declares: 'When the soul of a man is born in this country there are nets flung at it to hold it back from flight. You talk to me of nationality, language, religion. I shall try to fly by those nets.'[1] Like Joyce himself, a number of the metropolitan, modernist women discussed elsewhere in this volume appeared to do just that; indeed, their flouting of rooted national identities was often at the heart of their self-conscious literary experimentation. Juxtaposed with such escapees are those others who chose to embrace nationality, language, and religion, not as nets to restrict but as ties to bind them to their countries, physically or imaginatively. Irish, Scottish, and Welsh women writers of this period are, arguably, particularly susceptible to making this choice, though their concern with nation and language, if not always with religion, does not necessarily entail the resistance to change which Joyce and his fictional creation were clearly seeking to avoid.

As Simone de Beauvoir rather peevishly put it in her introduction to *The Second Sex* in 1949, 'For a long time I have hesitated to write a book on woman. The subject is irritating, especially to women; and it is not new.'[2] Indeed, in 1949, it was not new. For women writers of the previous three decades had been exploring in their fiction exactly the question de Beauvoir confronts squarely in her ground-breaking book: 'What is a woman?'[3] Female writers from Scotland, Wales, and Ireland were among the foremost of those exercised by the question which, for them, was inflected by other pressing questions related to national identity and allegiance, politics, religion, and tradition. Clearly, the grouping of Irish, Scottish, and Welsh women writers together in this chapter is a controversial approach and, of course, some of the writers who appear here could just as easily be discussed in other contexts and in other comparative groups; nevertheless, as I hope to demonstrate, there are marked areas of commonality among these women writers which do set them slightly apart from English female authors of the time.

One of the first things the Welsh novelist and short story writer, Kate Roberts (1891–1985), who began publishing in the mid-1920s, notes in her extensive correspondence with the Welsh poet and dramatist, Saunders Lewis, is her debt to the Irish short story writer, Jane Barlow, whose volume *By Beach and Bogland* (1905), she says, showed her that something could be done with the short story form in Wales.[4] Roberts was also an admirer of Joyce but declared, explicitly, that unlike Joyce's Stephen Dedalus and Joyce himself, she did not feel the need to 'fly by the nets' of nationality, language, and religion.[5] Instead, she devoted herself to chronicling the world that she knew in her native tongue, Welsh, and, although she knew the work of Virginia Woolf and Simone de Beauvoir, she felt her primary allegiance must be not to an international feminist ideal but to her own language and people. Roberts thus had a more problematic relation to feminism than either Woolf or de Beauvoir, partly, at least, as a consequence of belonging to a minority language grouping and an embattled culture rather than having emerged – as did Woolf and de Beauvoir – from imperial cultures of international prestige. Roberts asks 'what does it mean to be a Welsh woman?' and she gives the answers in her extraordinary oeuvre, written over a period of some sixty years.

Roberts's first collection of short stories, *O Gors y Bryniau* (*From the Marsh in the Hills*, 1925) draws strongly on her own background in the village of Rhosgadfan in Snowdonia, a mixed area of slate-quarrying and small farming. These stories deal with the lives of the quarrymen of the Caernarfonshire slate mines, referring to the frequent deaths and accidents in the quarries. Roberts renders with palpable authenticity the lives of hardship and poverty struggled through by people in this north-west corner of Wales. She places women at the centre of her fictional world. If the dark hole of the quarry yawns threateningly in the background, the foreground is the domestic hearth ruled over by her formidably capable womenfolk.

'Y wraig weddw' ('The Widow', written in April 1924) provides an example of this central focus on women's feelings and experiences; the widow of the title is Dora Lloyd, who has lost her husband five years previously. At the start of the story we see her in a typical self-searching mode of women's fiction, standing in front of the mirror, contemplating herself. Her clothing is coded, recording precisely the number of years which have passed since her widowhood: the year before, her silk blouse had black stripes and was done up to the top; this year the blouse is white and she leaves the top buttons undone. This detail is indicative of the care and precision with which Roberts always describes women's clothing; it invariably constitutes a sartorial code, indicative of the woman's personality, status, or desires. Like so many of the male characters in these stories, Ned, her husband, was killed in the quarry; the pain of his loss is now beginning to diminish and grow more distant.

Dora is reluctantly preparing to go and visit her sister-in-law on a holiday (Whitsun) when they traditionally reminisce about Ned, but she is now thinking of Bob Ifans, himself a widower, who has made her fall half in love with him on account of his kindness to her. She decides to wear a blue skirt, rather than the black, in order to prepare her sister-in-law for the news of her developing relationship with Ifans. However, on her way out Dora learns from a neighbour that Bob has not even placed a gravestone on his first wife's grave and suddenly knows that she can have nothing more to do with him. She immediately returns to her house and changes from her blue skirt into the black one before going on to visit her sister-in-law. In the end we see her milking her cows and singing 'Mae gennyf cwpwr cornel, / A'i lond o lestri te ...' ('I've got a corner cupboard / With a china tea set inside...') as if she has resigned herself to what she already has, rather than searching for another being upon whom to lavish her affection.

Roberts's best-known work is the 1936 novel, *Feet in Chains*, which focuses on the microcosm of the Gruffydd family through three generations, charting the changes in Welsh society between 1880 and the end of the First World War. Despite the impressive span of this novel, Roberts was arguably a better short story writer than a novelist, and she excels particularly at the representation of female epiphanies, such as is found in the 1937 story 'Protest March', which bears comparison with the Scottish novelist, Dot Allan's 1934 novel, *Hunger March*. Roberts's succinct style is well displayed here; in the space of just seven pages she manages to suggest the whole history of the Rhondda Valley. She sketches an extensive historical hinterland by focusing intensely on one married couple, Bronwen and Idris. Through this couple, Roberts indicates much, not just about gender relations, but about the relationship between the individual and society, between duty and desire, hope and despair. This is one of Roberts's most political stories, for Bronwen goes on a protest march against the introduction of the means test that will exacerbate further the misery of the unemployed in the Rhondda during the Depression. Bronwen still believes, albeit vestigially, that there is a point to political action such as this, whereas her husband, Idris, has lost hope entirely, literally turning his face to the wall in despair. But Bronwen's hopes are dashed and she returns home after the march with mixed feelings of humiliation and sadness. And yet there is an epiphanic moment in the end; as so often in Roberts's work, this hope is expressed in a domestic gesture of kindness. Idris makes tea for Bronwen, and this simple act – suggesting his desire to nourish, sustain, and console her – gives her some hope again at the end of the story, after the dispiriting experience of the march itself.

Roberts's characters are often hampered by ignorance: Bronwen, for example, is perplexed by the political orator at the protest march because he refers to the 'proletariat' and she does not know the meaning of the word. These characters are suffering individuals whose pain is the more poignant because they themselves do not understand why they find themselves living in poverty and misery. Like the North Welsh characters of her other works, they are able to survive through their heroic stoicism. But Kate Roberts suggests that stoicism is not enough. There is always a hint that education (a coming to consciousness and an analysis of their own situation in the world) is needed for the Welsh people to effect a change in their circumstances.

Kate Roberts's recurring focus on the development of a woman's self-consciousness may be fruitfully compared with that found in the work of her close Scottish contemporary, Nan Shepherd (1893–1981). Shepherd published three novels in rapid succession between 1928 and 1933, to 'immediate critical acclaim'.[6] *The Quarry Wood* (1928) was the first of these novels, followed by *The Weatherhouse* (1930) and *A Pass in the Grampians* (1933). Just as Roberts is a writer committed to her language and Welsh culture as well as to a working-class identity, so Nan Shepherd writes in a distinctive Scots idiom which requires a glossary and which is redolent of a particular way of life and a particular place in north-east Scotland in the early twentieth century. Shepherd's protagonist in *The Quarry Wood* is Martha Ironside and the novel's plot may be seen as a *Bildungsroman* charting Martha's difficult journey towards getting an education and establishing an independent life. Four years before the publication of Lewis Grassic Gibbon's novel of female development written in a flexible Scots idiom, *Sunset Song*, Shepherd was writing in a similarly inward, lyrical, and dialectal vein, and interrogating analogous tensions relating to gender and national identity.

However, *The Quarry Wood* differs markedly from Kate Roberts's habitual representation of the 'Welsh Mam' as a redoubtable and admirably stoical figure; Shepherd boldly presents a particularly unflattering portrait of the mother, Emmeline, who is slovenly, snobbish, and actually opposed to her own daughter's educational aspirations: 'Not an exercise book was purchased but it was audibly grudged.'[7] Nevertheless, there is here, as in Kate Roberts's writing, much emphasis on domestic work, as well as something largely absent in Roberts – long, lyrical descriptions of landscape and weather. There is an analogous preoccupation with the economic realities of life for a poor family, so that Martha's winning of a bursary is as significant an event in the family's life as the son, Owen's, winning of a scholarship in Roberts's *Feet in Chains*.[8]

Martha has to struggle hard to obtain the university education that she has set her mind to at an early age; the struggle is against patriarchal prejudices which are often, paradoxically, upheld by conservative womenfolk. *The Quarry Wood* satirizes effectively notions of middle-class respectability which leave no room for female self-fulfilment (a theme that recurs in Willa Muir's *Imagined Corners*): Martha's Leggatt aunts, for instance, are the embodiment of staid respectability, requiring a stiff dose of syrup of figs before bed every night. Martha succeeds in getting an education at Aberdeen University and becomes a teacher, but she is less fortunate in her affairs of the heart. She is in love with a fellow student, Luke, who marries her friend, Dussie. Unlike her lecturer, Lucy Warrender, 'an ardent feminist',[9] Martha is often irritatingly passive and has what is for a twenty-first-century feminist reader a worrying penchant for self-renunciation. Occasionally, though, her sexual desire does assert itself, particularly in an epiphanic scene in the 'quarry wood' of the title, where she shares an illicit midnight kiss with the married Luke, and Shepherd launches into an embarrassingly Lawrentian passage, in which Martha's 'whole being cried "Take me, take me!"'[10] Fortunately, perhaps, Luke is deaf to Martha's mute corporeal cries, and an impending affair is averted.

Martha's next suitor, Roy Foubister, who is a colonial farmer in the Transvaal, entrances her with his travel tales. She is held rapt, Desdemona-like, by his dashing stories; unfortunately, he is an unreconstructed patriarch with rather crude ideas of sexual conquest: 'A riderless girl! All he need do was to mount.'[11] Martha rejects him, to the reader's relief, since he reveals his true colours when the story of her kissing Luke in the quarry wood comes to light: 'And you thought you'd palm another man's property off on me, did you?'[12] Finally, realizing the inadequacy and selfishness of both Luke and Roy in their relations with her, Martha decides to dedicate herself to educating the infant Robin, the latest in a long line of foster children taken in by her mother. In this way, the novel's main theme of education is seen to be perpetuated in the next generation. The fact that the young child is a boy suggests that Martha's task is specifically to inculcate more enlightened attitudes towards gender.

Martha is also intensely aware of her Scottish identity. In a memorable early scene in the novel she learns about the boundaries of Scotland from her father, Geordie, and repeats it to herself, translating it from her father's Scots into 'proper' English: '*Scotland is bounded on the south by England, on the east by the rising sun, on the north by the Arory-bory-Alice, and on the west by Eternity.*'[13] This poetic vision simultaneously fixes in Martha's mind the distinctiveness of Scotland, setting it apart from elsewhere, specifically from England, and manages to express its relationship to infinity and the way that it fills her entire personal universe.

Shepherd and Roberts were writing in a period often regarded as a 'Renaissance' in the literary culture of their respective countries. In Scotland, the critical history of the period is usually dominated by male writers such as Hugh MacDiarmid and Lewis Grassic Gibbon who, with their different but equally compelling political agendas and their willingness to experiment with language and genre, tend to overshadow the more modest, less declamatory writing of their female peers. In Wales, the 1930s saw a flowering of literature in both Welsh and English, with the bold reinvention of the Welsh nation in the Welsh-language work of Saunders Lewis, the self-consciously new Anglophone Modernism of writers such as Dylan Thomas and Glyn Jones, and the industrial fiction 'from below' by working-class writers such as Lewis Jones. Certainly, Kate Roberts's work can be seen as analogous to the latter, while Lynette Roberts's poetry is increasingly being seen as a cornerstone of Welsh Modernism, but, on the whole, Welsh and Scottish women writers tend to be marginalized by mainstream accounts of these 'Renaissances'. In Ireland, the Celtic 'Renaissance' had occurred even earlier in the form of the Irish Literary Revival from the 1890s onwards. Yet again, though, women writers are often omitted from or marginalized in accounts of the phenomenon.

In each of the three nations under discussion, there were prominent Home Rule movements, already in the case of Ireland partially successful by 1922 in obtaining autonomy from the British state. Wales and Scotland in the 1920s and 1930s were in the process of forming distinct nationalist political parties. Women writers, unsurprisingly, held a range of different political perspectives on nationalism, depending on many variables, such as their class position, linguistic and religious allegiances, and their personal and familial relations with England. Even a passionately committed nationalist like Kate Roberts very rarely uses her fiction to express party political views in the way that male writers such as Hugh MacDiarmid and Lewis Jones openly did.

As John Wilson Foster points out, despite the Home Rule movement, the Celtic Revival, and the establishment of the Irish Free State, there continued to be 'a steady volume of human ... and cultural traffic between Ireland and Britain'.[14] As in Wales and Scotland, Irish women writers did not readily toe any party line; rather, they tended to adopt a notably internationalist outlook. Kate O'Brien and Elizabeth Bowen wrote subtly and sympathetically about both sides of the internal Irish conflict. But Irish women writers were not solely concerned with 'the national question'; like their Welsh and Scottish counterparts, they were concerned with gender, education, religion, class, and economics. Foster argues that in the period 1922–1940 there were in fact three 'Irelands' from which fiction was produced: firstly, the writing of the Irish Free State, secondly, what he calls the 'Ladies' Road', and finally, fiction from Northern Ireland.

Writing by male authors from the Irish Free State tended to critique the narrowness of the new state. Liam O'Flaherty's *The Black Soul* (1924), for instance, is comparable to the blistering attack on the hypocrisy of the Welsh chapel of his Welsh contemporary, Caradoc Evans in his *My People* (1915). Irish women writers, on the other hand, often focus on the Irish country house, using it as a setting to dramatize issues of belonging and identity. Such a trope is clearly indebted to a long history of Irish women's writing, reaching back to Maria Edgeworth's *Castle Rackrent* (1800). Elizabeth Bowen's *The Last September* (1929) and Molly Keane's *Mad Puppetstown* (1931) are examples of the Irish country house novel, concerned with place and property and dramatizing the dilemma of the Anglo-Irish and the question of whether those of Anglo-Protestant descent have any claim to 'belong' to Ireland or if Ireland has claims upon them.

The recurrent motif of the burning of the country house suggests that this generation of writers was very acutely aware of living through the end of an era and a particular way of life which had its peculiarities and its virtues. Although the Irish great house novel can be seen as a distinctive genre, strong parallels can be found in Welsh writing, notably in Eiluned Lewis's *Dew on the Grass* (1934), discussed below. The Irish writer Molly Keane (1905–1996), writing under the pseudonym 'M.J. Farrell', published her great house novel, *Mad Puppetstown*, in 1931. Its first part, whose central consciousness is eight-year-old Easter Chevington, bears remarkable similarities to *Dew on the Grass*, with its nine-year-old heroine, Lucy Gwyn. Both gentry houses are large, sprawling, fascinating worlds for their child protagonists to discover; both girls have formidable 'native' nannies with colourful dialects, encounters with poachers, and dangerously overactive imaginations. However, the chronological span of Molly Keane's novel is greater, bringing Puppetstown into the modern world of the First World War and the Easter Rising, whereas Lewis's *Dew in the Grass* leaves Lucy and her world arrested on the brink of modernity. In the second chapter of *Mad Puppetstown* there is a distinct shift in tone, from the pleasant nostalgia of the earlier period to a modern era of loss and uncertainty, in which Easter's father, as well as many of the dashing young officers glimpsed earlier, are killed in the Great War. In the third chapter of the novel, the war ends and is succeeded by 'strange days for the gentry of Ireland' in which:

> the morning paper ... might tell of the murder of a friend, or the burning of a house that had lately been like Puppetstown, careless in its wide hospitality ... Curiously untouched by it, as by the greater war, life at Puppetstown went on, as though no tide could lick close enough ever to suck Puppetstown to destruction.[15]

The Naylor family in Danielstown, the 'Big House' in Elizabeth Bowen's magisterial novel *The Last September* (1929), adopt a policy of 'not noticing'[16] the unrest that is going on all around them, exactly like the inhabitants of Puppetstown, led by the indomitable Aunt Dicksie, who simply hang on, taking strength from the solidity and presence of the house itself. The ending of the novel has Easter return to a dilapidated, decayed Puppetstown but suggests survival and a renewed sense of belonging in the Ireland she has yearned for during her years of exile in England.

While the great house survives in Molly Keane's nostalgic vision, in Edith Somerville and Martin Ross's *The Big House of Inver* (1925) the house is burnt, and with it the privileged and profligate history of the Anglo-Irish Prendevilles. Like Bowen's novel, this too ends in that 'last September'. Although the novel is set in the past, it is clear that Somerville, in completing the novel she had first conceived with her cousin and fellow writer, Martin Ross, before the latter's death, had in mind the much more recent conflagrations of the Irish Civil War. Again, though, as in the positive conclusion to Molly Keane's novel, *The Big House of Inver* ends, self-consciously, on a note of reconciliation, when Shibby, the illegitimate daughter of the house, and her sworn enemy, Johnny, join forces to try to drag to safety from the burning building old Captain Jason Prendeville. Both this novel and Keane's differ markedly from the novels of female development authored by Scottish women writers of the period, but bear strong resemblances to the chronicles of family and place favoured by many Welsh women writers. It is Irish women writers, perhaps unsurprisingly, given the inescapably violent facts of Irish history, who seem most intent upon chronicling the ways in which the forces of history impinge upon the individual, destabilizing notions of fixed identity or belonging.

Nevertheless, *The Ante-Room* (1934) by the Limerick-born Kate O'Brien (1897–1974) is a novel which bears a close relation to the female *Bildungsromane* of her Scottish contemporaries. O'Brien's vivid portrayal of the warping and destructive nature of an intensely pious Catholic middle-class household has particularly clear parallels with the portraits of restrictive Protestantism in the fiction of Willa Muir. Both writers are similar in their internationalism, their ambivalence towards the homeland, and their attraction to European cultures. O'Brien's recurring theme is the quest for female freedom, both intellectual and sexual; her reward for writing outspoken fiction on these topics was to have several books, including *Mary Lavelle* (1936) and *The Land of Spices* (1942) banned by the Irish Censorship Board in the puritanical atmosphere of the Irish Free State during the 1930s.

Belonging: A Memoir is an autobiographical work by Willa Muir (1890–1970) and one might be forgiven for assuming that it deals with the writer's Scottish birth and identity. On the contrary, however, the work chronicles the author's marriage to the poet, Edwin Muir, and their lifetime partnership and collaboration, notably as translators of European writers such as Franz Kafka. The 'belonging' that the book celebrates is a belonging to each other, not to any place or nation.[17] In fact, when the Muirs returned to live in Scotland in the 1930s after a prolonged period of residence in continental Europe, they were initially unhappy there and failed to respond positively to the newly-awakened Scotland of which Hugh MacDiarmid dreamed. Willa Muir, who has been described as 'one of the finest female intellectuals that Scotland has produced this [the twentieth] century',[18] reveals some of the reasons for her ambivalence about Scottish identity in her early novel, *Imagined Corners* (1931). A brilliant linguist with strongly feminist attitudes, Muir found the patriarchal atmosphere of her native Montrose stifling and promptly satirized it in her first novel. In *Belonging*, she reflects on the partnership with Edwin as a union of two gender dissidents; as she puts it:

> I was no more of a conformist than he [Edwin] was, but the pressures were to reach me from a different angle. He refused to boost himself up the ladder into becoming a dominant male, and I refused to be pushed

down it into female subserviency. Both of us ignored the ladder as if it were not there ....[19]

Imagined Corners (1935) opens in the Scottish town of Calderwick in 1912. It focuses primarily on two women called Elizabeth Shand, one newly married, the other a mature widow returning from the south of France. The novel offers an incisive and satirical view of society in Calderwick: its narrow-minded xenophobia, obsession with propriety, the patriarchal prejudices and pious churchgoing, all of which cover up tensions and breakdowns of the kind evidenced in the madness of young Ned Murray, and in the internecine hatred between sisters Ann and Mary Watson. The book is overtly feminist and shows why the older Elizabeth Shand had to run away from home with the unsuitable married foreigner, Fritz. Her return twenty years later shows that not much has changed in Calderwick but coming back to the town allows her to make peace with her younger, rebellious self and to knit up the two halves of her identity. At the same time, when she leaves Calderwick again for the south of France, she is able to take with her the younger Elizabeth, who has been abandoned by her ne'er-do-well husband, Hector; Elise (the widowed Elizabeth is now known as Elise Mütze) feels that she is helping to clear the way for younger women; 'she felt it might be her Gebiet to clear away stones of prejudice and superstition so that other girls might grow up in a more kindly soil'.[20]

The novel is particularly acid and entertaining in its attack on femininity, as espoused by Mabel Shand, who reads women's magazines and is both obsessed with respectability and ever ready to be flirted with: 'A phrase from one of her [Mabel's] magazines came into her mind as she noted the rustling of her own petticoats: "the delicious frou-frou of femininity". Elizabeth had none of that, not a particle of it.'[21] Nevertheless, the younger Elizabeth does try conscientiously to live up to her role as wife to the boorish Hector:

> The perfect wife was not only selfless and loving – she was sympathetic, understanding, tactful and, above all, charming. ... She must always be pretty – no, not pretty, Elizabeth did not aspire to prettiness – she must always look 'nice'. The frou-frou of femininity was beginning to rustle around Elizabeth.[22]

This satirical portrait recalls Virginia Woolf's description of the feminine role in *A Room of One's Own* (1929) and of the 'Angel in the House' in Woolf's 1942 essay, 'Professions for Women'.[23] But Muir's condemnation of patriarchy has a specifically Scottish accent. She emphasizes, for example, the oppressive influence of religion upon Scottish women's lives. In fact, Muir's unflattering picture of Scottish Nonconformity can be seen to foreshadow Muriel Spark's mockery of Calvinism in *The Prime of Miss Jean Brodie* (1961). In *Imagined Corners*, the bells of Calderwick ring out incessantly every Sunday, from the churches of numerous denominations: 'the United Free, the Congregational, the Wesleyan, the Baptist, the Roman Catholic and the Episcopal – but all were overborne by the peal from the Parish Kirk ...'[24] In this churchgoing society, 'women were the guardians of decorum'.[25] The young Lizzie Shand escapes from the stranglehold of Scottish society where, as she sees it 'man's chief end was to glorify God and woman's to see that he did it'.[26] Fittingly, it is in the family pew at the parish church that the older Elizabeth Shand manages to reconnect with her younger self. The older woman finds her own Bible, with the graffiti from decades before. Thus,

> for a moment or two ... [she] felt not that the long-vanished Lizzie Shand was a ghost, but that she herself was the ghost of that impetuous and resentful small girl. The small girl's emotions touched her again; she was no longer coolly amused at the paltry ugliness of the church, the narrow complacency of the worshippers, she was both furious and miserable at being forced to take part in the service ... God ... was merely an enforcer of taboos, and a male creature at that, one who had no sympathy for little girls and did nothing for them.[27]

It is clear that Muir is no Scottish nationalist; like her character Elise Mütze (née Shand) she will have 'none of your Celtic twilights'.[28] Elise, like her author, is a linguist and European traveller, a cosmopolitan who returns reluctantly after twenty years to her home country for a visit after the death of her German husband, Karl. But then again, she reflects as she travels back from her home in the south of France, 'Karl was a German, but not a typical German; she was a Scot, but not a typical Scot.'[29]

Muir is also astute and acerbic in revealing the xenophobia of small-town Scotland; Calderwick regards the Italian café-owner, Domenico Poggi, with hatred. The representation of the Poggi family also foreshadows later women writers' treatment of the effects of migration and difference on British societies (as in Monica Ali's *Brick Lane* and Andrea Levy's *Small Island*) for the eldest daughter Emilia Poggi, who speaks broad Scots, is chafing against her father's desire for her to marry an unknown Italian, whereas she wishes to marry Charlie, a local boy.

But above all, Muir exposes misogynistic prejudices among her cast of small-town Scottish characters. What is particularly striking is the brilliantly analytical way in which Muir reveals the ways in which patriarchal attitudes infiltrate the lives of even the most well-meaning of men, such as the Reverend William Murray, who

> had not quite escaped the influence of his father, who had ruled his house, as he had ruled his school, on the assumption that the female sex was devised by God for the lower grades of work and knowledge, and that

it was beneath the dignity of man to stoop to female tasks. But although the assumption lay at the back of William's mind it appeared so natural that he had never recognized it ...[30]

Even the obnoxious Hector gains a modicum of sympathy from the reader because of Muir's democratic use of free indirect style, allowing insight into the thoughts and feelings of even the most unsympathetic of characters, though the use of this style sometimes leads to our disliking a character even more. A case in point is Mabel Shand, who appears to fulfil a similar role in the novel to Rosamund in George Eliot's *Middlemarch*: she is a pretty, feminine, empty-headed young woman whom her author clearly despises: 'It was a pity John [her husband] was so old. A woman so well made as she was should have a husband to match her.'[31]

Muir's social satire may be compared with that of Elizabeth Bowen or the Welsh writer Dorothy Edwards. In stylistic terms, she is certainly their equal, particularly in her deft use of free indirect style. Muir, like Kate O'Brien, though, is not one of those writers who willingly embraced the nets of nationality, religion, and language; she escaped those nets and looked back in her fiction to anatomize the society which wove them. Some may regret that she devoted herself in later life to the art of translation; more fiction from this acid and magisterial pen would certainly have been welcome.

Another Scottish writer, Catherine Carswell (1879–1946), who was a neighbour and associate of the Muirs when they lived in Hampstead in the 1920s, can also be seen as writing novels of female development. Her significantly titled autobiographical first novel, *Open the Door!* (1920), concerns Joanna Bannerman's efforts to escape from her repressive religious background to a life of artistic and emotional freedom. There is a strong parallel between the heavy religiosity of the opening, set in Glasgow, and the chapel-dominated world of Welsh women's writing at the time. Carswell writes: 'In 1881 there had swept over Scotland a wave of religious revival ... and in Glasgow alone the registered converts numbered over thirty-two thousand.'[32] Again, as is true of virtually all of the women writers discussed here, Carswell offers an astute satire of men's benighted attitudes towards women, including an interesting portrait of an Italian Futurist, Mario Rasponi, who is obsessed with machines and women's inferiority. Unfortunately, Joanna is impressed by Mario's unwavering certitude and marries him. Both Carswell and Nan Shepherd show the influence of D.H. Lawrence in their work, especially in their rendition of sexual relations, an aspect which sometimes tends to counteract the feminist ideology of their works and to infuse it with a discomfiting masochism.

The repeated focus on the individual in these novels of female development might tend to suggest that women writers ignored the lot of the masses during the Depression but this is far from the case. Alongside the fiction of Kate Roberts, which documents poverty in this period unflinchingly, one can place some of the novels of Dot Allan (1892–1964), a somewhat unexpected champion of the poor, since she herself was born into a wealthy Glaswegian merchant family. Her 1928 novel, *Makeshift*, is a *Bildungsroman* dramatizing the conflict between marriage and the desire to be a writer on the part of Jacqueline, the protagonist. The novel opens with a dramatic account of the suicide of Jacqueline's mother, a seamstress whose unavailing struggle against poverty leaves her in despair. The novel's menfolk tend to be misogynistic and hostile to women's suffrage: 'He [Torrance, Jacqueline's friend] was violently opposed to all forms of women's rights ... The mind of woman was not that of a normal human being, he was wont to declare, but of one warped by reason of her sex.'[33] By the end of the novel, Jacqueline simply escapes, catching the midnight express for London. The journey towards independence is one traced by many of these women writers. Allan's work is somewhat melodramatic and overwritten but it does foreground women's work, while *Hunger March* (1934) is surprisingly innovative formally, in that the action is confined to one day, that of the hunger march in one city (Glasgow). It narrates the interlinking stories of a dozen characters on that momentous day and although Allan is occasionally uncertain in her representation of the voices of working-class characters, her attempt to ventriloquize the downtrodden produces what the *Times Literary Supplement* called at the time 'an honest, inspiring book'.[34]

Very far indeed from the real world of hunger marches is the fictional world of Dorothy Edwards (1903–1934). One of the most untypical and intriguing of Welsh women writers, Dorothy Edwards, published only two volumes of fiction, *Rhapsody* (1927) and *Winter Sonata* (1928) before her tragically early suicide in 1934. Only one of her short stories, 'The Conquered', engages directly with the Welsh landscape and Welsh identity; the other stories being set in recognizably English country houses during the summer. Edwards's work as a whole may be seen as a sophisticated exercise in satire through her skilful and subtle ventriloquism of a male, English voice. Arnold Bennett, who praised her 'subtle and intriguing talent',[35] bracketed her with contemporary English women writers such as Virginia Woolf and Vita Sackville-West, but Edwards's Welshness manifests itself in a far more sardonic representation of an English class structure in relation to which she herself was a dissenting stranger. Frederick Trenier, for example, the male narrator of 'The Conquered' is revealed as an egocentric prig through his own, smug words: 'I have been nearly everywhere.'[36] He spends his summer holiday with his aunt and cousins on the Welsh border and there meets Gwyneth, 'a very charming Welsh lady',[37] possessor of a country house and a voice of equal loveliness. Her house stands in a historicized landscape which bears a Roman road and a hill 'where the ancient Britons made a last stand against the Romans, and were defeated'.[38] The gentrified Gwyneth, though, identifies completely with 'the conquerors'. Inscribed within this story is a subtext relating to Wales's 'conquered' position; implicitly identified with the ancient Britons, the Welsh are a defeated people who have been stripped of their language and their pride. Gwyneth represents the advantages to be had from complicity. The fact that Edwards's title is identical to that of Naomi Mitchison's 1923 historical novel can hardly be coincidental, especially since Mitchison's text also focuses on the conquering of a Celtic people by an imperial power; Mitchison, too, draws implicit parallels between past conquests and the present state of Scotland, just as Edwards does in relation to Wales. In this way, unexpected resonances can be clearly heard among the women writers of the 'Celtic fringe'.

A completely different class perspective is found in the work of Elena Puw Morgan whose fiction is notable for its powerful focus on female servants living in conditions of poverty and deprivation. Her 1939 work, *Y Wisg Sidan* (*The Satin Dress*), is a historical novel set in rural Wales in the late nineteenth century, revolving around the experiences of Mali Meredur, the central female character. She inherits a beautiful, wine-red satin dress from her mother and this object of desire is her only comfort in a life of dire poverty and exploitation. After escaping from her cruel brother, Mali spends most of her life as 'third servant' on the large farm of Plas-yr-Allt, where the 'Master' seduces and then ignores her. Mali has an illegitimate child whom she abandons on the doorstep of the manse. Despite his treatment of her, Mali continues to idolize Tim Huws, the 'Master' of Plas-yr-Allt. In terms of plot, structure, and style, this novel is sophisticated; told largely from Mali's point of view, there are extended passages of free indirect discourse, which sometimes shift to the point of view of Tim Huws. One key episode in the plot – where Mali and Tim first meet at a fair – is, in effect, narrated twice, from each of their contrasting points of view. Both gender and heredity are important concerns in the novel. Mali conforms to gender expectations in her (to the reader) frequently infuriating passivity and self-sacrifice and yet she also exhibits extraordinary resilience and loyalty. Despite the suffering she experiences, ultimately the plot of the novel traces a trajectory of empowerment and vindication for Mali. The final scene of the novel depicts her burning the red dress; the image is suitably ambiguous but it could indicate the end of Mali's 'curse' of bad luck, always associated with the dress and the illicit desires it represents.

Eiluned Lewis's *Dew on the Grass* again takes the reader upwards in the social hierarchy. Like the Irish country house novels of the period, Lewis's description of the homestead of Pengarth emphasizes its ancient, rambling nature – it seems like an untidy, organic outgrowth of the land itself. Lewis is also concerned with the tense relation between Wales and England, Welsh and English identities, in this borderland setting. Lucy Gwyn, the protagonist, is aged eight; she and her siblings live in a Welsh rural environment which seems blessed by the Creator whose generosity and beneficence is rendered in the image of dew upon the grass. Yet there is also the strong suggestion that the Edenic aspects of the rural world which Lucy sporadically experiences come to an end with the passage from childhood to adulthood.

Lucy's family, the Gwyns, are Anglo-Welsh landed gentry; their estate appears to be extensive, and the 'home farm' is run by a large complement of servants. Lucy and her three siblings have a formidable Welsh nursemaid, Louisa, there are two or more housemaids, a parlour-maid, cook, stable-boy, farm labourers, gamekeeper, and coachman. Thus, this novel offers a view of servants' lives from a very different class perspective to that offered in the work of Elena Puw Morgan or, indeed, Kate Roberts. The Gwyn family maintains a close and friendly relationship with the servants but there is a definite sense of social hierarchy. Lucy is largely unaware of class distinctions, although there are indications that poverty and want exist in this society. Interestingly, these occur towards the end of the novel, reflecting Lucy's growing awareness of the adult world around her. Most poignant of all is Lucy's encounter with an unnamed tramp near the end of the novel. It is a tangible irruption of history into the timeless world of Pengarth, for the tramp is a refugee from the industrial unrest and poverty of the South Wales valleys.

Dew on the Grass presents a contradictory representation of Welsh identity. As is the case with Elizabeth Bowen and Molly Keane's representations of the Anglo-Irish, Lewis's markers of the gentry's Welshness are incorporated within a dominant social identity defined by Britishness and class allegiance. There are, moreover, indications that the new sense of working-class identity which was historically crystallizing in the South Wales valleys at the time is viewed as something threatening and alien. While the Welsh servants and tenants of Pengarth are apparently content with their station, the tramp's voice represents the rumbling murmur of social change which will soon threaten and destroy the stable world of Pengarth forever and will, at the same time, lead to a new, and politicized, form of Welsh identity.

Unfettered by Joyce's 'triple net', these Welsh, Irish, and Scottish women writers can be seen to be breaking new fictional ground, be it in the expression of female aspiration and desire, or in the call for political change, emancipation, social justice or the dismantling of class hierarchies. Some writers mark national difference in the use of the Celtic languages or distinctive dialect, while some adopt modernist forms and strategies to express complex psychological states in their often lyrical construction of time and space.

Welsh, Scottish, and Irish women's literary production in this period is characterized by its diversity of style and perspective. There is, though, a shared interest in issues of belonging and identity and in the changing lives and expectations of women in 'Celtic' countries which were experiencing modernity in ways that differed significantly from England or the United States. The effect of the First World War and the Depression and, in Ireland, of the Irish Civil War and Partition, may be seen in the imaginative responses of Welsh, Scottish, and Irish women writers and the ways in which they represent their respective nations to Britain and the wider world.

Notes

1. James Joyce, *Portrait of the Artist as a Young Man* (Ware: Wordsworth Editions, 1992), p. 157.
2. Simone de Beauvoir, Introduction, *The Second Sex*, in *The Feminist Theory Reader*, ed. Carole McCann and Seung-Kyung Kim (London: Routledge, 2003) p. 32.
3. Ibid.
4. Kate Roberts, Letter to Saunders Lewis, 11 October 1923, Kate Roberts and Saunders Lewis correspondence, National Library of Wales, 22723D, ff. 5–12; reproduced in Dafydd Ifans, ed., *Annwyl Kate, Annwyl Saunders: Gohebiaeth 1923– 1983* (Aberystwyth: Llyfrgell Genedlaethol Cymru, 1992), p. 6.
5. 'I never escaped. Never wanted to escape', cited in Emyr Humphreys, *The Triple Net: A Portrait of the Writer Kate Roberts* (London: Channel 4, 1988) p. 3.
6. Roderick Watson, Introduction to Nan Shepherd, *The Quarry Wood* (Edinburgh: Canongate, 1987), p. vii.
7. Nan Shepherd, *The Quarry Wood*, p. 22.
8. Ibid.
9. Ibid., p. 105.
10. Ibid., p. 117.
11. Ibid., p. 145.
12. Ibid., p. 161.
13. Ibid., p. 20. Italics are in the original.
14. John Wilson Foster, 'The Irish Renaissance, 1890–1940: Prose in English', in *The Cambridge History of Irish Literature*, ed. Margaret Kelleher and Philip O'Leary, 2 vols (Cambridge: Cambridge University Press, 2006), II, pp. 113–80, p. 113.
15. M.J. Farrell, *Mad Puppetstown* (London: Virago, 1985), pp. 124–5.
16. Elizabeth Bowen, *The Last September* (London: Vintage, 1998), p. 6.
17. See: Willa Muir, *Belonging: A Memoir* (London: Hogarth Press, 1968), p. 316: 'We belonged together.'
18. Kirsty Allen, Introduction to Willa Muir, *Imagined Selves* (Edinburgh: Canongate, 1996), p. v.
19. Muir, *Belonging: A Memoir*, p. 138.
20. Muir, *Imagined Selves*, p. 281. ('Gebiet' = 'field' or 'territory'.)
21. Ibid., p. 84.
22. Ibid., p. 127.
23. '…I discovered that if I was going to review books I should need to do battle with a certain phantom. And the phantom was a woman, and when I came to know her better I called her after the heroine of a famous poem, "The Angel in the House". It was she who used to come between me and my paper when I was writing reviews. It was she who bothered me and wasted my time and so tormented me that at last I killed her. You who come of a younger and happier generation may not have heard of her – you may not know what I mean by the Angel in the House. I will describe her as shortly as I can. She was intensely sympathetic. She was immensely charming. She was utterly unselfish. She excelled in the difficult arts of family life. If there was chicken, she took the leg; if there was a draught she sat in it – in short she was so constituted that she never had a mind or a wish of her own, but preferred to sympathize always with the minds and wishes of

others. Above all – I need not say it – she was pure...' Virginia Woolf, 'Professions for Women', in *The Death of the Moth and Other Essays* (London: Hogarth Press, 1942) pp. 149–54 (p. 150).
24. Muir, *Imagined Selves*, p. 67.
25. Ibid., p. 77.
26. Ibid., p. 77.
27. Ibid., p. 185.
28. Ibid., p. 147.
29. Ibid., p. 150.
30. Ibid., p. 16.
31. Ibid., p. 38.
32. Catherine Carswell, *Open the Door!* (Edinburgh: Canongate Classics, 1996), p. 13. Compare the opening of Kate Roberts's novel, *Feet in Chains* (1936), which describes a vast open-air prayer meeting in Snowdonia, or, earlier, 'Allen Raine's' representation of the 1904–1905 religious revival in Wales in her 1906 novel, *Queen of the Rushes*.
33. Dot Allan, *Makeshift* and *Hunger March*, ed. Moira Burgess (Glasgow: Association for Scottish Literary Studies, 2010), p. 59.
34. Anonymous review, *Times Literary Supplement* (17 May 1934), quoted in Moira Burgess, Introduction to Allan, *Hunger March*, p. 189.
35. Arnold Bennett, quoted in Roland Mathias, *Anglo-Welsh Literature: An Illustrated History* (Bridgend: Seren, 1986), p. 79.
36. Dorothy Edwards, 'The Conquered', in *Rhapsody* (London: Wishart and Co., 1927), pp. 53–7, p. 53.
37. Ibid., p. 54.
38. Ibid., p. 62.

13
Women's Writing in the Second World War

Gill Plain

The Second World War is seldom regarded as a 'literary' war: its dominant images come from the cinema and newsreels, rather than from poetry or prose, and it is hard to identify a 'canon' of either male or female war writing. As many writers acknowledged at the time, the sheer immensity of the conflict – its geographical extent, political complexity, and human scale – resisted interpretation or summation. While the press called for literary mobilization, repeatedly asking 'where are the war poets?', writers themselves were asking what, after World War One and the Spanish Civil War, could possibly be left for the war writer to say?[1]

One answer to this dilemma involves rethinking the parameters of 'war writing', and is perhaps most clearly articulated by Elizabeth Bowen's preface to *The Demon Lover* (1945). This short essay constitutes one of the most important literary reflections on conflict and creativity to emerge from the war years, capturing both the necessity of writing and the 'hallucinatory' quality of the lived experience from which such writing emerged.[2] In Bowen's analysis, the war permeated literature and culture. Texts bore the imprint of conflict even as they consciously turned from its direct representation. Writing became a mode of resistance and release, the consolatory fantasies of the imagination permitting an assertion of self in the 'stupefying' climate of war (p. 49). In a context in which what 'was happening was out of all proportion to our faculties for knowing, thinking and checking up', individual writers could not hope to be representative. Rather, the fragments of writing produced in the war period come to have complex cumulative meanings. Irrespective of subject matter or style, the stories written by Bowen and her contemporaries were incremental parts of a much larger narrative, and these fragments of 'the particular' (p. 52) constitute a literary response to the Second World War. Describing her own work, Bowen suggests a mode of writing as possession, a communal colonization of the 'private imagination':[3]

> The stories had their own momentum, which I had to control. The acts in them had an authority which I could not question. Odd enough in

their way – and now some seem very odd – they were flying particles of something enormous and inchoate that had been going on. They were sparks from experience – an experience not necessarily my own.

(p. 47)

Bowen's essay makes a persuasive case for reconceptualizing war writing in terms that shift the emphasis away from combat, the dominant discourse of First World War writing, to a more nebulous and inclusive concept of cultural dislocation. However, it is not so easy to argue that Bowen's concept of 'resistance writing' (p. 50) is specifically gendered. Women who documented the quotidian were part of a larger body of civilian writers responding to a conflict that rewrote the rules of engagement. This was, in Annemarie Tröger's phrase, a 'war against civilian populations', and this relocation of the battlefield dissolved the previously clear-cut distinction between combatant and non-combatant.[4] Writers, journalists, and filmmakers consolidated the transition by adopting a rhetoric that merged the identities of soldier and civilian into a democratic national body. Yet this levelling is illusory. While the civilian population en masse had little by way of agency – they remained largely powerless in the face of aerial bombardment and unprecedented government intervention in the business of private life – there remained within the so-called 'People's War' a fundamental, gendered hierarchy of value.

In an influential essay of 1984 Margaret and Patrice L.-R. Higonnet argue that the 'double helix' structure of gender systems ensured that the Second World War initiated only short-term change in gender roles. The nation's demand that women enter the public sphere is understood to be only 'for the duration': their status as subordinate citizens is unchanged, and traditional roles and responsibilities easily resumed with the cessation of hostilities:

> The image of the double helix allows us to see that, although the roles of men and women vary greatly from culture to culture, their relationship is in some sense constant. If men gather and women fish, gathering will be thought more important than fishing; in another society where men fish and women gather, fishing will be more prestigious. The actual nature of social activity is not as critical as the cultural perception of its relative value in a gender-linked structure of subordination.[5]

As women moved into the factories, onto the land, and into the armed forces, industrial labour ceased to signify 'masculine' authority. Instead combat, still exclusively reserved for men, became the benchmark of cultural value in British society. The structural inequality symbolized by the double helix was further complicated by the expectation that women would assume a form of dual subjectivity, taking on traditional males roles while simultaneously exhorted to remember their femininity. 'In a period of national austerity' observes Pat Kirkham, 'the British state called upon its women to make enormous material sacrifices *vis-à-vis* their appearance, but to look as if they had not'.[6] Women were told that beauty was a 'duty', urged by advertisements and magazine articles to maintain their looks for the benefit of national morale. Men, they were warned, would expect nothing less, and the national significance of women's appearance was underscored by the government's decision to protect the limited production of cosmetics (p. 15). Kirkham argues that beauty regimes could be a valuable aid to normalization in the uncertain climate of war, but the coercive effect of articles urging women not to 'get slack' should not be underestimated.[7] A final burden specific to women in wartime was that of domesticity. However seismic and demanding the changes in their public roles, women were still expected to run households, do the shopping (a significant challenge in the face of rationing and queues), and care for children. Women's new wartime occupations were in addition to, not instead of, traditional roles.

Women thus continued to experience war differently to men, not least because of the conventional, often misogynistic, discourses that surrounded them. Jenny Hartley's comprehensive study of British women's fiction in the period details some of the many hostile representations that emerged in the fiction of male writers such as Evelyn Waugh and Henry Green.[8] Hartley might equally have included Graham Greene and W. Somerset Maugham, who together with Waugh perpetuate the powerful binary opposition of head versus heart, mind versus body. Women, we learn from Greene's *The Ministry of Fear* (1943) and Maugham's *The Razor's Edge* (1944) are incapable of understanding the public sphere or the public good. Their horizons are limited to the domestic and the private: they love men, not nations. In the case of good women, this gives rise to commendable loyalty; in the case of bad, to corrupting, destructive sexual desire. Either way, these unthinking creatures cannot be trusted with matters of national importance, nor can they understand the meaning of abstract concepts such as patriotism. These corrosive stereotypes featured in attenuated but nonetheless pervasive form in the cinema, in magazines, and in advertising, and this cultural climate is significant.[9] Just as Bowen's elegant prose illustrates that all wartime writing is at some level resistance writing, so – in a context that determinedly designates women as 'other' – all women's writing encapsulates something distinct and different from that of their male contemporaries.

Women's wartime writing is thus inevitably shaped by their gendered subjectivity, but while women may be homogenized by gender, they are equally rendered separate by discourses of class, region, race, and religion. As the work of the neglected short story writer Elizabeth Berridge suggests, the fault lines of the Second World War were as much geographic and generational as gendered. In 'To Tea With the Colonel' Berridge sets the metropolis against the provinces in her depiction of Miss Morton's alienation from the county town in which she has taken refuge after the bombing of her London room. Conscious of her outsider status, Miss Morton longs for the 'blessed anonymity of a London bus', but as the story progresses, she unexpectedly finds friendship with another woman who bears 'the mark of spinsterdom upon her'.[10] However, the gendered commonalities of the two women cannot breach the gulf of Blitz experience. Miss Morton, experiencing a sudden cathartic urge to speak, describes the horror of waking to find 'what should be outside on the roof' invading the imagined 'invulnerability' of private space (p. 93). As she reaches for words, her friend Miss Lumley recoils from this unwelcome exposure:

> She looked uncomfortable, almost hurt. Weren't Londoners supposed to be like the R.A.F.? Not mentioning things like actual death and mutilation. Of course it was to be expected that a near-miss should make people voluble. The relief, of course. *Another second, and ...*
> 'How dreadful for you,' she said.
>
> (p. 93)

The polite banality of Miss Lumley's response succinctly encapsulates the chasm of incomprehension opened up by bombing, but Berridge's story is equally concerned with the more fundamental division of class. The Colonel of the title is Miss Lumley's father, a relic of a past age, whose deafness symbolizes his insulation from the realities of a changing world. Asked to provide the Colonel with his tea, Miss Morton obliges to please her friend, but left alone to the task she feels 'the ghost of a parlourmaid's panic' (p. 99). Her class resentment and her 'hatred for people who had never known the nightly horror of sirens' (p. 98) coalesce into the story's second cathartic outburst. Miss Morton voices the frustrations of a life of dependency in a bitter attack on the privileges of the gentry, to which the unhearing Colonel responds with a courtesy that at once relieves and crushes Miss Morton: she is freed by her outburst, but reduced to tears. The story ends on this tableaux, and Berridge offers the reader no insight into the complex emotions behind Miss Morton's tears. They are, we conclude, born of trauma, resentment, frustration, and guilt, her moment of rebellion undone by the impenetrable conventions of middle-class politeness.

The complex dynamics of Berridge's stories force a recognition of the plurality of wars fought by British women in the 1940s. In response, women's writing of the period encompassed everything from the modernist experimentation of Virginia Woolf to the genre comforts of Georgette Heyer's Regency romances, and some sense of the diversity of this cultural production can be found in anthologies such as Catherine Reilly's *Chaos of the Night: Poetry and Verse of the Second World War* (1984) and Jenny Hartley's *Hearts Undefeated: Women's Writing of the Second World War* (1994). Many women turned to the short story, a form that experienced a renaissance during the war – being ideally suited to the burgeoning magazine culture of the period, and the fragmented concentration of both writers and readers – but familiar forms such as detective fiction also remained popular. Most of the pre-eminent writers of the interwar period – Margery Allingham, Agatha Christie, Gladys Mitchell – wrote prolifically during the war years. The extent to which their fictions actually engaged with the war, though, varied considerably. Some Christie novels, in the words of Stephen Knight, 'superintend contemporary battles from a distance': the conflict is present only at the level of socio-cultural disturbance, implicit in the anxieties and preoccupations of characters, rather than articulated through specific events.[11] *The Moving Finger* (1943) is typical of this submerged encounter with the conflict. Although its hero is a wounded airman, the novel avoids explicit engagement with the war, preferring instead to refract the conflict through its analysis of community cohesion, shifting gender patterns, and the spectre of psychological disturbance. *N or M?* (1941) by contrast offers a direct address to war, mobilizing the ageing Tommy and Tuppence Beresford as the last line of resistance against a fiendish 'fifth column' conspiracy. The date of publication is significant here, indicating the book's status as a response to national jeopardy; but beyond this, Christie's spy novel works as a traditional clue-puzzle mystery. A seaside boarding house provides the contained community of suspects, and red herrings are constructed through the topical deployment of racial and gender stereotypes. National identity is reassuringly presented as written on the body, but this potential source of comfort is somewhat undermined by the difficulty characters experience in correctly deciphering corporeal language. Nonetheless, in presenting the reader with two profoundly ordinary detective figures, a fantasy of agency is created. While not quite 'Millions Like Us', *N or M?* does present 'detectives like us', in marked contrast to the detached intelligence of a figure such as Hercule Poirot. Margery Allingham undertakes a similar democratization of detective agency in her 1941 thriller, *Traitor's Purse*. Here, the customary controlling intelligence of Albert Campion is significantly undermined by his memory loss, an inadmissible weakness that makes him profoundly dependent on others, in particular his fiancée Amanda and his manservant Lugg. This is golden age detection reconstructed for the people's war, as a fifth column assault on the national economy is defeated by a coalition spanning class and gender divisions. By contrast, Allingham's late war novel, *Coroner's Pidgin* (1945) offers a rather different perspective on coalition politics. The book is significantly less serious in tone. Corpses are moved around with cavalier abandon, and the threat of a Nazi conspiracy seems to generate less anxiety than keeping up appearances. This is a comedy of manners as much as a detective novel, and while Lugg remains central, Amanda is notably absent, engaged in a new form of 'war work': the production of babies.[12]

A more conventional idea of war work formed the basis of much women's documentary writing. Monica Dickens comically recounted her experiences as a nurse in *One Pair of Feet* (1942), while Inez Holden's *Night Shift* (1941) exposed a complex factory subculture, where working men and women survive at the limits of economic security. The workers support the war effort, but refuse the bland comforts of patriotic or national sentiment. Theirs is a personal war for survival fought against a set of personalized enemies, not all of whom are German. Air raids are the work of 'him', 'a personified god of evil', but 'he' is just a part of the problem:

> Besides this great 'He,' this fire-breathing, bomb-throwing, stinking jack-booted son of sweat there were a variety of smaller enemies called 'they,' only 'they' were much closer, always under foot or just around the corner; a set of empowered rats who built bad houses, muddled the insurance schemes, wilfully ignored the cost of living and were maliciously given over to making life more difficult.[13]

The alienation of industrial labour emerges powerfully from Holden's novel, in which the workers exist only in their factory context, hermetically sealed from the wider world. Here, as in Diana Murray Hill's *Ladies May Now Leave Their Machines* (1944), enclosed space and physical and mental exhaustion combine to create a carceral and dehumanizing environment, profoundly counter to the dominant wartime myths of community spirit and cooperation.[14]

For other women, writing was a means of escape. Georgette Heyer's historical novels were consistently successful, taking their readers to a richly imagined world of plenty, where spirited heroines needed only their wits to do battle. As Alison Light has noted of Daphne du Maurier's *Frenchman's Creek* (1941), the past is a space of 'wish-fulfilment' within which desire can be articulated and explored. The space of history enables du Maurier's heroines to trespass 'on the territory of adventure romances' giving them 'a claim to a physical existence of the kind which in realist fiction only the most daring or bohemian of authors might have attempted'.[15] For Naomi Mitchison, by contrast, the past becomes a space for the negotiation of the political as well as the personal. Her epic historical novel *The Bull Calves*, is set in the aftermath of the Jacobite rebellion of 1745, offering an extended meditation on ideas of loyalty, forgiveness, and belonging. As Mitchison's fractured family of Lowlanders struggles to reconcile its factions and forge new relationships with its Highland 'others', the possibility of reconstruction is imagined in the face of the Second World War's remorseless destruction.[16] The 1930s also proved a popular 'historical' setting, providing a temporal space outside the war that nonetheless permitted the discussion of contemporary issues, as is evident from Mary Renault's psychoanalytical experiment *The Friendly Young Ladies* (1943). Renault's acutely observed account of one man's determination to reassert heterosexual authority in the face of two women's happy indifference is simultaneously comic and bleak, and indicates the extent to which desire remained a battlefield within women's writing. Dorothy Whipple's *They Were Sisters* (1943), for example, while not attempting to imagine the transgressive possibilities of Renault's novel, nonetheless exposes the violent and abusive power of patriarchal heterosexuality. Charlotte is utterly destroyed by the psychological cruelty of her husband Geoffrey, a slow process painfully and perceptively mapped out from the point of view of her sister and daughter, both of whom are powerless to help. This is not 'war' writing as it is traditionally understood, but Virginia Woolf would have recognized the potent link between the domestic patriarch and the 'creature, Dictator as we call him when he is Italian or German, who believes he has the right ... to dictate to other human beings how they shall live'.[17]

'One had to laugh': women writers' refusal of seriousness

In Jan Struther's story 'Gas Masks', faced with the almost unthinkable implications of having her children fitted for the monstrous rubber appendages, Mrs Miniver resorts to the comforts of national habit. British middle-class culture insists that terrors and fears are not to be articulated, they must be euphemized, avoided, repressed. 'One had to laugh' thus becomes a stock mode of self-management, a method of normalizing the abnormal and coping with situations far beyond individual control.[18] Yet beyond the sanity-preserving necessity of humour, women writers in the Second World War repeatedly push further into modes of comedy that set them at a distance from the war's uniformity. These women do not necessarily oppose the war, but they do produce fictions that question the dominant cultural ethos and expose the construction of a national mythology.

The impetus to criticize, however, significantly precedes the outbreak of war. Virginia Woolf's *Three Guineas* (1938) is a powerful satirical attack on the patriarchal structures that link domestic tyranny to political dictatorship. In response to a correspondent who wants to know how women can help prevent war, Woolf replies with a comprehensive account of the institutional forces that still deny women political power. Woolf's strategy is one of defamiliarization. By claiming to find the familiar incomprehensible, or by exposing custom to clinical scrutiny, she reveals the prejudice and fear that underpins social norms. The book is decorated with images of men wearing the formal regalia of rank and privilege. Soldiers, judges, churchmen, and academics process in images customarily associated with dignity, but which here signify absurdity and excess. For Woolf's reader, the emperor is not naked, but ridiculously overdressed in a style that for women would be deemed 'unbecoming and immodest': 'A woman who advertised her motherhood by a tuft of horsehair on the left shoulder would scarcely, you will agree, be a venerable object.'[19] Absurdity is a crucial weapon in Woolf's attack, frequently achieved by allowing patriarchal commentators to condemn themselves. Seeming to agree with C.E.M. Joad's insistence that women belong in the home attempting to curb the self-destructive tendencies of 'incurable male mischievousness' (p. 50), Woolf offers a paraphrase of his argument that reduces it to its ridiculous essentials:

> According to Mr Joad you [women attempting to earn their living in the professions] are not only extremely rich; you are also extremely idle; and so given over to the eating of peanuts and ice-cream that you have not learnt how to cook him a dinner before he destroys himself, let alone prevent that fatal act.
>
> (p. 51)

Equally incendiary material is found in the book's extensive footnotes, most of which are written in a voice of pseudo-scientific rationality. For example, noting the findings of a 1936 commission on women's suitability for the ministry which concluded that men would not be able to concentrate on God in the presence of a woman minister, Woolf responds: 'In the opinion of the Commissioners, therefore, Christian women are more spiritually minded than Christian men – a remarkable, but no doubt adequate, reason for excluding them from the priesthood' (p. 181). Woolf's irony is comic, but her purpose in this anxious, liminal space between wars, is corrective. In the words of Lisa Colletta, 'a useful response to the tyranny of those in power is to pelt them with laughter', and Woolf's satire is an attempt to challenge, through the only means available to her, the coercive power of a criminally destructive culture.[20] To prevent war, she believes, women – and like-minded men – must adopt an attitude of indifference (p. 123). They must formulate themselves as 'outsiders' and refuse to participate in the narratives of belonging and exclusion that have for centuries generated fear and hatred. Crucial to the success of Woolf's radical polemic is a refusal to take seriously the sacred cows of patriarchal culture, but this rhetorical strategy has its limits. As Colletta observes, 'living in the shadow of war is much like living in the shadow of the gallows; one can have a variety of responses, but there is very little to be done about the actual circumstances' (p. 56).

This fatalism is another factor underpinning women writers' refusal of seriousness. As the threat of war turned into actuality, there could be little hope of satirical correction. Rather, writers such as Nancy Mitford adopted a bathetic approach to the crisis, turning the sublime terror of aerial warfare into the ridiculous hyperbole of farce:

> Sophia Garfield had a clear mental picture of what the outbreak of war was going to be like. There would be a loud bang, succeeded by inky darkness and a cold wind. Stumbling over heaps of rubble and dead bodies, Sophia would search with industry, but without hope, for her husband, her lover, and her dog.[21]

Mitford's broad comedy simultaneously celebrates and ridicules cherished national characteristics, from the sentimental love of animals to ingrained snobbery (p. 146). She also mocks the widespread desire to be part of war. After the initial shock of seeing her first sandbag, Sophia treats war as an adventure, fantasizing about becoming a glamorous spy, while remaining oblivious to the Nazi conspiracy taking place under her nose. The plot focuses on the disappearance of a national institution, Sir Ivor King, the 'King of Song', on the eve of his inauguration of 'the most formidable campaign of Propaganda through the medium of Song that the world has ever seen' (p. 66). To the dismay of the government, and his god-daughter Sophia, the King of Song reappears on the airwaves as the 'Leider König', broadcasting Song Propaganda from Germany. Mitford's comedy exposes the crude assumptions of wartime propaganda, spoofing the rhetoric of both German and British state broadcasting (pp. 99–100). An absurd climax sees both Sophia's beloved bulldog and the King of Song rescued from captivity by her lover in drag, while the Nazi spies 'scuttle' themselves in the sewers. British victory is achieved not through combat or military intelligence, but through the camp knowingness of pantomime.

Mitford acknowledged that *Pigeon Pie*, written in late 1939, was 'an early and unimportant casualty of the real war which was then beginning', and even allowing for the characters' hyperbolic 'Britishness', their casual racism and xenophobia is jarring. Sophia uncomfortably replicates wider cultural assumptions of women's inability to see beyond the private sphere, and the concluding vision of war as a cricket match with hindsight seems painfully naive (p. 167). But Mitford's fantasy of civilian agency is nonetheless symptomatic of a refusal to take the enemy at his own estimation. Reducing the Nazi threat by making fun of Hitler and the perceived 'professionalism' of his armies was part of a widespread debunking ethos that suggested that proficiency in war was an unforgivable social faux pas. Such an attitude was not confined to a middle class that still fetishized the values of sporting amateurism, it was equally evident in working-class responses. As Holden's factory workers' language suggests, 'that man' is an uninvited guest with far too great a sense of his own importance, just one more problem amongst many.[22]

A different mode of comic resistance is evident in Elizabeth Bowen's *The Heat of the Day* (1948), which works in part through the formal structure of 'Shakespearean' comedy. Although disguised by the temporal shifts of the discourse, the plot presents both the Blitz and the love affair of Robert and Stella as a state of topsy-turveydom. In this paradoxically enchanted space, 'this tideless, hypnotic, futureless day-to-day', the lovers are freed of social constraint and public responsibility.[23] Only the arrival of the counter-spy Harrison disrupts their 'hermetic world' (p. 90) and brings the pressure of historical time to bear upon their charmed habitat. Harrison is hardly an innocent, but he brings with him the force of the law, ensuring that order will be restored. In the case of Stella, and the other central female character

Louie, this means marriage and motherhood: the self-contained and independent Stella will marry a brigadier; the disorderly, promiscuous Louie will become an 'orderly mother' (p. 329). Before this conventional ending, though, comes disruption and dissent, and within London's uncanny Arden, the working-class figures of Connie and Louie take on the shape of rude mechanicals, their absurd dialogues a medium for Bowen's subversive assault on government propaganda and the pervasive war mentality.

The principal target of the novel's comedy is the press. Bowen turns newspapers into government agents seeking to negate private doubts and manipulate subjective desires through an all-embracing rhetoric of public inclusion. The impact on Louie is revelatory, transforming her from a dysfunctional, non-conforming woman into a docile, regimented citizen. '[H]aving begun by impressing Connie', Bowen writes, 'newspapers went on to infatuate Louie out-and-out' (p. 151). Reading the papers, Louie basks in 'warmth and inclusion', repeating their glib comforts in her dialogues with Connie. Her infatuation only ends when the papers report Stella's presence at the death of Robert Kelway. In recognizing as flawed lives that she had, from a distance, reified, Louie finds that there was 'nobody to admire' (p. 307). In a logic entirely appropriate to her character's difficulty in understanding the relationship between the individual and society, she abandons the public morality of the press for the 'vagrant habits' (p. 307) of personal need. It is, thus, the failure of her 'betters' to be better, that leads Louie back to the corporeal consolations of sex – and, in a final twist of Bowen's irony, to the responsible citizenship of maternity.

Connie and Louie, the wartime odd couple, represent one of the few benign examples of domesticity in *The Heat of the Day*. Other houses seem to overwhelm or distort their inhabitants, driving them, in the extreme cases of Cousin Nettie and Robert Kelway, to madness and treachery. These instances are pertinent reminders that the coercive power of the family and domestic space does not evaporate in time of war, as is demonstrated by its traces even within the public narrative of women's documentary fiction.

Double standards: documentary, domesticity, death

'Why be married if you had to clean out the bath every time before you used it?'[24] This reflection by Edward Ledbetter, the 'hero' of *The Fancy*, Monica Dickens's 1943 novel about aircraft factory workers and rabbit breeding, is the more damning for the fact that Edward is, for the most part, a sympathetic character. A charge hand overseeing a bench of women workers, he struggles to do his job fairly while coping with his wife's indifference and the demands of his beloved rabbit club. Yet Edward is also a man of his time, as is demonstrated by his reflections on women:

> As he came off the track into the Inspection Shop, Edward's eyes went at once to his bench of girls. He was beginning to feel quite possessive about

them. They were in his charge, and if the A.I.D. threatened to make trouble for one of their mistakes, Edward would cover up for them and make excuses and even put the blame on himself, if necessary. After all, you had to make allowances for girls. It was not like working with men. Girls had nerves, which were always playing them up. He knew that from Connie.

(p. 78)

The style here is typical of Dickens. The third person narrative slides seamlessly into free indirect discourse, giving an intimate portrait of Edward at a carefully controlled distance. This strategy is replicated for the other characters with significant narrative arcs: Sheila, the well-to-do middle-class girl infatuated with a self-centred, parasitic journalist; Wendy, so withdrawn and vulnerable that Edward comes to think of her as one of his rabbits; Kitty, the wartime bride; and Dinah, a benchmark of sanity in her 'common sense' approach to life and her cheerful companionate marriage.

In this central core of characters the novel can be seen to have a 'group hero' – a formulation typical of documentary writing and film production of the war years. War work, however, is not the focus of the narrative: rather, its unpleasant necessity is humanized by the personal and domestic concerns of the characters. *The Fancy* is self-consciously inclusive, and beyond the focus on the group hero, succinct portraits are painted of less fully developed but significantly representative characters: a mother who will lose her son; a woman who discovers that she and her husband have nothing in common; and Rachel, a comic embodiment of hyperbolic femininity who '[radiates] sex like a gas-stove radiating heat' (p. 297). As the simile suggests, Rachel's vampishness is hardly seen as a threat to national security. Rather, the more threatening figures of the narrative exist beyond the factory in the figures of Connie, Edward's slovenly yet aspirational wife; Mr Holt, Wendy's half-mad tyrannical father; and Dexter Bell, estate agent and black marketeer, a man exploiting the war for his own benefit.

As this summary suggests, the novel depicts a wartime culture that is both reassuringly inclusive and plausibly realistic. Elements of gentle comedy work to defuse potentially disturbing situations, as does the broadly happy ending. Few characters think in terms of national goals, and the 'enemy' is conspicuously absent. For all that the women have become war workers, this is in essence a domestic novel – and it is here that textual tension becomes evident. In the supposedly 'normal' world beyond the war machine, Dickens presents a telling indictment of the double burden placed on women. These impossible pressures are first articulated by a character known only as 'the pot hat' (pp. 52–3), and her comic presentation softens the brutal truth of her complaints about inadequate nursery provision and the logistics of looking after a family while working full time. Thereafter, double standards appear everywhere: David, the journalist, expects Sheila to jump to his every whim (pp. 143–6), and when they need a new flat, he refuses to help with what he calls 'woman's work' (p. 237). Even in the happy marriage of

Dinah and Bill, the domestic burden – the logistical business of surviving on rations – falls entirely on the woman (p. 268). On the rare occasions when male characters enter kitchens, it is for comedy alone: their incompetence in this domestic arena is understood and accepted (pp. 193, 201).

Seemingly, then, *The Fancy* shows us a world of ingrained sexism, evident even to the most obtuse of readers. But Dickens too is a product of her time, and the events of the novel suggest that reimagining women's roles is less straightforward than it might seem, even in the rupture of wartime. In choosing to 'live in sin' with David, Sheila might be seen to represent a challenge to sexual mores, but her romantic adventure brings her only unhappiness, debt, and blackmail. Dexter Bell's attempted seduction implicitly emerges from Sheila's own indeterminate state: neither married, nor a virgin, she must inevitably be a whore. Ultimately, the book treats Sheila's transgression as a growing-up process. Living together outside marriage is not seen as a viable option for an adult middle-class woman, and Sheila must learn to respect her class and gender position.

A similar ambivalence is evident in the central romance of Edward and Wendy. While the father's death frees Wendy and her mother from patriarchal bondage, the women emerge from their ordeal as vulnerable and helpless figures, aligned with traditional values of passivity and domesticity. The moral failings of Connie, by contrast, are symbolized by her lack of housewifely virtues. As Edward's anxiety about the bath indicates, marriage brings with it a duty of care, which Connie singularly fails to fulfil. In comparison, the newly liberated Wendy is revealed to be a domestic goddess: 'Wendy had told him only the other day how she had spent the whole weekend doing what she called "Autumn cleaning". Spring cleaning was such fun, she said, she didn't see why it should only be enjoyed once a year' (p. 310). Arguably, Connie's departure with Dexter Bell is entirely reasonable, but the text affords her no sympathy. She is a superficial, nagging, gossipy, humourless, and soul-destroying presence. With bad teeth and slovenly habits she becomes physically repulsive to Edward, and what began as a reasonably balanced portrait of two people who should never have married ends as an indictment of the woman who rejects her domestic role.

Yet the weight Dickens places on domesticity simultaneously emerges from another, specifically wartime imperative. *The Fancy* is also a novel about making a home – a once straightforward process rendered provisional by war. Her characters struggle to make homes in whatever transient spaces life affords them, including, in the case of the decrepit Urrys, a tube station platform. Space is at a premium, those in need of it are exploited and abused: not for nothing is the novel's chief villain an estate agent. In a world characterized by overcrowding, the 'private imagination' acquires a tangible, territorial dimension.

The relationship between private space and subjective integrity is a major preoccupation of wartime women's writing. In Elizabeth Berridge's short story 'Chance Callers' a young couple, Frank and Beryl, seek a house in which to rebuild their relationship after wartime separation. Both have changed almost beyond recognition: Frank through his experience as a prisoner of war, and Beryl through her enforced independence, evacuation, and the belief that her husband had died. Each seeks in the other traces of the person they once knew, each tries to perform a peacetime identity long-since evaporated. The idea of a house, symbol of stability and normality, provides common ground and common purpose and when Beryl sees the half-empty house of Captain Banks, she eyes it 'hungrily' (p. 120). In a story that typifies Berridge's concern with generational change, loss, and mourning, the young couple's needs are satisfied through an act of profound generosity that stems from the aching power of grief. Mourning the loss of his invalid brother, it is the Captain's suicide that will enable the couple's future.[25]

Private space is equally important within the fragmented form of Frances Partridge's diary, published as *A Pacifist's War*. Partridge, a writer on the fringes of the Bloomsbury group, spent the war at Ham Spray house in Wiltshire with her husband Ralph, a conscientious objector. The diary is a remarkable testament to the difficulty of assimilating the war at both the macro level of strategic engagement, and the micro level of individual disruption and emotional dislocation. Its effect is cumulative: an attempt at self-assertion in the face of the war's crushing totality:

> I have no desire whatever to write anything in this diary, and my only reason for doing so is to show that I am still alive, and not unhappy I might even say. But I have never in my life been less aware of my surroundings, got less pleasure from the visible world, nor felt more completely insulated from thrills of excitement.
> (13 February 1942)[26]

Here, in the private space of words not intended for publication we find the voice of not-coping, a voice which at times finds its greatest consolation in the contemplation of suicide (14 May 1940). For the reader, though, Partridge's words of 13 February 1942 reveal more than the diarist might immediately recognize. In the statement of sensory numbness, Partridge is confessing deep unhappiness. Throughout the book, her frustration with the war is set against the forces of consolation: passages celebrating the value of civilization, the redemptive beauty of nature, music, books, and conversation. Partridge is enriched by nature, enlivened by intellectual and emotional engagement with the world. To confess her detachment and indifference is to acknowledge, implicitly, the war's destructive impact. She has grown 'a cataract ... over the surface of [her] consciousness' (p. 130), she is only half alive.

The diary's impact then emerges from the gradual accretion of irreconcilable emotions and desires, and from this incremental form comes a meditation on the meaning of domestic space. Home for Partridge is a refuge where she restores herself and her faith in human nature. Her books, her gramophone, her violin, and her husband turn the space into a repository of culture. While her rational mind tells her that 'we are sailing along in a boat which has a hole at the bottom', she feels safe within 'our magic Ham Spray circle' (12 April 1941). But when the space evades her control, through the invasion of recalcitrant friends, family, evacuees, and soldiers, it becomes a location that threatens to consume her: 'very quietly but quickly the eiderdown of this rustic, practical life has risen round our necks smothering us' (8 June 1942).

The doubleness that Partridge finds in domestic space is typical of a final pervasive presence in women's wartime writing: the uncanny. In Freud's analysis, the uncanny is a state of ambivalence and indeterminacy in which the familiar becomes frightening, secrets are exposed, the dead return, and the living bear the imprint of death. It is the pressure of the uncanny that links the 'anonymous presence' of 'yesterday's dead' in Bowen's *The Heat of the Day* (p. 91) to the domestic gothic of Dorothy Whipple's *They Were Sisters*, where Charlotte's torment is an open secret rendered untouchable by middle-class mores. It is equally evident in the haunting absences of Partridge's diary, which tries but fails to evade the corrosive force of death. Partridge writes explicitly about the politics of war, the state of the nation, and the opinions of her friends, but there is one thing that her diary scarcely touches upon: the intimate pain of loss. During the period 1939–1945, Partridge loses her sister, her mother, and her friend Rollo, a RAF pilot. This final war-specific death is the only one to be the focus of a diary entry, but even this is brief. In the next paragraph, Partridge turns her attention again to the rational and the abstract, discussing her 'absolute conviction that progress can never be achieved by force or violence, only by reason and persuasion' (20 January 1943). Throughout the text, death is marginalized, placed in footnotes, or given expression through the fears of Partridge's young son Burgo (pp. 155, 193). This might be an act of editorial self-protection – the book is composed of extracts from her diary – but these omissions stand in stark contrast to the imagery of the text, which, as the war progresses, turns increasingly towards disease, decay, and the pathologized body. The war is 'a hole in a tooth' (p. 175), those living through it 'like people in the waiting room of a hospital' (p. 192): ultimately, Partridge's energetic defence of civilization seems haunted by the knowledge of its failure.

The omissions, or constraints, of Partridge's diary return us to Bowen's preface to *The Demon Lover*, in many respects the keynote of this discussion. Bowen constructs wartime writing in terms of emotional displacement, imaginative resistance, communal experience, and uncanny possession. These categories are not discrete, and as the undercurrents of Partridge's diary suggest, the defence mechanisms of writers – be they comedy or community – are haunted by the insistence of death. As Kate McLoughlin has argued, the destructive force of war has always resisted direct articulation, leading writers to adopt a range of rhetorical strategies to displace the depiction of events that present a practical and ethical challenge to realist representation.[27] Central to this process is silence: signifying absences and a refusal to speak are recognized strategies of 'writerly tacitness': 'in the lexical gaps, the spaces separating lines, the structural interstices of fragmented writing' the presence of the unspeakable can be felt, as well as the traumatic silence of grief (p. 17). War's resistance to representation is present in the diverse strategies and preoccupations of women's wartime writing. It is there in Partridge's omissions, in the violent imagery that disturbs the complacent pastoral surface of Woolf's *Between the Acts* (1941), in the gothic framework of Holden's industrial communities, in the horror of Berridge's story 'Lullaby', in which a child will burn to death, comforted by the mechanical recording of its absent mother's voice. The rhetoric of war insistently demands a normalizing process, a belief in 'business as usual', and the national persona of Britishness is complicit in the construction of a self-protective carapace of emotional inarticulacy. But war has to find expression somewhere, and in much women's war writing it finds this in the uncanny reinscription of women's 'traditional' concerns: domesticity, motherhood, love. These components of idealized femininity, symbols for which the nation fights, are equally the spaces most vulnerable to war's contamination. And here perhaps lies the substance behind Bowen's claim that all wartime writing is a mode of resistance. Irrespective of subject matter, to create in the face of destruction is to contribute to a literature of war, and whether women wrote 'safe' domestic novels, complex modernist experiments or fragments of documentary, their legacy bears witness to the urgent necessity of writing in the face of a war that was, and indeed remains, beyond assimilation.

Notes

1. Angus Calder, *The People's War: Britain 1939–1945* (London: Jonathan Cape, 1969), pp. 517–18. Robert Hewison describes the climate of 1939 as one of disorientation and pessimism that led to a 'general loss of confidence among writers'. Hewison, *Under Siege: Literary Life in London 1939–45* (London: Methuen, 1977), pp. 9–12.
2. Elizabeth Bowen, *Collected Impressions* (London, Longmans Green and Co., 1950), p. 49.
3. This phrase comes from Adam Piette, *Imagination at War: British Fiction and Poetry 1939–1945* (London: Macmillan, 1995), p. 1. Piette argues that the drive to transform 'private imagination into public spirit' had a devastating impact on British culture (p. 2), and while Bowen's preface offers a rather more optimistic reading of the war's dissolution of boundaries, it is notable that many of her short stories find little comfort in communality.
4. Annemarie Tröger, 'German Women's Memories of World War II', in *Behind the Lines: Gender and the Two World Wars*, ed. Margaret Randolph Higonnet et al. (New Haven: Yale University Press, 1987), p. 285.

5. Margaret Higonnet and Patrice L.-R. Higonnet, 'The Double Helix', in *Behind the Lines*, ed. Higonnet et al., p. 34.
6. Pat Kirkham, 'Beauty and Duty: Keeping Up the (Home) Front', in *War Culture: Social Change and Changing Experience in World War Two Britain*, ed. Pat Kirkham and David Thoms (London: Lawrence and Wishart, 1995), p. 13. See also Sonya O. Rose, *Which People's War? National Identity and Citizenship in Wartime Britain 1939–1945* (Oxford: Oxford University Press, 2003). Rose notes in addition that at the same time as women were urged to be 'truly feminine' (p. 136) their sexuality was regarded as dangerous, disruptive, and a threat to the nation.
7. Jane Waller and Michael Vaughan-Rees, *Women in Wartime: The Role of Women's Magazines 1939–1945* (London, MacDonald Optima, 1987), p. 81.
8. Significantly, Hartley also notes ambivalence regarding wartime roles in the work of a number of women writers (Jenny Hartley, *Millions Like Us: British Women's Fiction of the Second World War* (London: Virago, 1997), p. 108). Hartley's book achieves a breadth of coverage that this chapter cannot hope to replicate, and should be consulted by readers looking for further information about the preoccupations of women writers in the period.
9. A rich selection of material is provided by Waller and Vaughan-Rees, *Women in Wartime*.
10. Elizabeth Berridge, *Tell It To a Stranger* (London: Persephone Books, 2000), pp. 90, 94.
11. Stephen Knight, 'Murder in Wartime', *War Culture*, ed. Kirkham and Thoms, p. 162.
12. See Gill Plain, *Twentieth-Century Crime Fiction: Gender, Sexuality and the Body* (Edinburgh University Press, 2001); '"A Stiff is Still a Stiff in This Country": The Problem of Murder in Wartime', in *Conflict, Nationhood and Corporeality in Modern Literature: Bodies-at-War*, ed. Petra Rau (Basingstoke: Palgrave, 2010), pp. 104–23; Phyllis Lassner, 'Under Suspicion: The Plotting of Britain in World War II Detective Spy Fiction', in *Intermodernism: Literary Culture in Mid-Twentieth-Century Britain*, ed. Kristin Bluemel (Edinburgh: Edinburgh University Press, 2009), pp. 113–30.
13. Inez Holden, *Night Shift* (London: John Lane, 1941), p. 108.
14. See Sara Wasson, *Urban Gothic of the Second World War: Dark London* (Basingstoke: Palgrave, 2010) for a persuasive reading of these texts as uncanny manifestations of nineteenth-century industrial practice. Haunted by 'Gothic, mechanised ghosts', argues Wasson, these texts represent the wartime factory as 'spaces of marginalisation and dark cravings for death' (p. 104).
15. Alison Light, *Forever England: Femininity, Literature and Conservatism between the Wars* (London: Routledge, 1991), p. 173.
16. See Gill Plain, *Women's Fiction of the Second World War: Gender, Power and Resistance* (Edinburgh: Edinburgh University Press, 1996), pp. 139–65.
17. Virginia Woolf, *Three Guineas* (London: Hogarth, 1986), p. 61.
18. Jan Struther, *Mrs Miniver* (London: Virago, 1989), p. 63.
19. Woolf, *Three Guineas*, p. 25.
20. Lisa Colletta, *Dark Humor and Social Satire in the Modern British Novel* (Basingstoke: Palgrave, 2003), p. 38.
21. Nancy Mitford, *Pigeon Pie* (Harmondsworth: Penguin, 1961), p. 7.
22. The extent of the refusal to dignify Hitler with a name is evident in the title of the popular BBC comedy series ITMA ('It's That Man Again').
23. Elizabeth Bowen, *The Heat of the Day* (Harmondsworth: Penguin, 1962), p. 100.

24. Monica Dickens, *The Fancy* (Harmondsworth: Penguin, 1964), p. 309.
25. The complexity of 'home' is central both to Berridge's stories, and to those of Elizabeth Bowen, whose much-anthologized story 'Mysterious Kôr' provides an intense imagining of war's encroachment on the private – and the mind's defences against such attack.
26. Frances Partridge, *A Pacifist's War* (London: Phoenix, 1978), p. 126.
27. McLoughlin notes the inhibiting factors of censorship, squeamishness, and the risk of depicting something a sadist might enjoy. 'War and Words', in *The Cambridge Companion to War Writing*, ed. Kate McLoughlin (Cambridge: Cambridge University Press, 2009), p. 16.

14
Women Writing Empire
Lisa Regan

In 1924 Virginia Woolf attended the British Empire Exhibition at Wembley: a celebration of colonial unity showcasing commodities and goods from around the empire. Like the ritual of Empire Day and later the Empire Marketing Board, the exhibition was designed to promote a new vision of empire that shifted away from pre-war expansionist, masculine militarism towards the familial dynamic of the Commonwealth (which now included newly-acquired mandates in Africa, the South Pacific, and the Middle East).[1] It did so in the wake of social and political unrest in the colonies and at home following the First World War. The Irish War of Independence broke out in 1919, the same year as the Amritsar massacre in northern India when unarmed Indian protesters were killed by British troops. That year also witnessed riots and racial violence against black workers in several major British cities, which later spread to the Caribbean.[2] Gazing upon the exhibition's spectacle of unity, Woolf, whose grandfather James Stephen (known as 'Mother Country Stephen') had helped to formulate that very imperialist rhetoric of family genealogy, was not convinced: 'How, with all this dignity of their own', she asks looking at the spectators, 'can they bring themselves to believe in that?'[3] For her, '[f]erro-concrete is fallible' to 'violent commotion', a sign that this new narrative of empire is incapable of withstanding the forces of nature rising against it. The storm she witnesses, which sends the crowds dashing for cover as the exhibition is reduced to 'ruins', portends the collapse of an empire already 'perishing', which she noticeably does not lament.[4]

As a recent collection of essays on women's writing on empire in the 1930s demonstrates, 'Many other British women in the interwar period also reflect in their writing English ambivalence about empire in the context of anti-imperialist unrest abroad' and share Woolf's attention to the fallibility of the imperial narrative.[5] Sylvia Townsend Warner, in her revision of *Robinson Crusoe*, *Mr. Fortune's Maggot* (1927), expresses a profound scepticism about Englishness and the imperial mission. Nancy Cunard, as Tory Young argues, 'broke with her mother to break with empire' when she defended her

Women Writing Empire 251

relationship with the African-American musician Henry Crowder in *Black Man and White Ladyship* (1931).[6] And Rebecca West, after travelling around Yugoslavia, resolved 'to put on paper what a typical Englishwoman felt' in *Black Lamb and Grey Falcon* (1942) only to find herself 'newly doubtful about empires'.[7] Alongside these notable modernists, middlebrow writers such as Rumer Godden and Winifred Holtby also undermined what Edward Said identifies as the nineteenth-century novel's 'consolidated vision' of empire.[8]

Challenges to imperial ideology by women writers also led to cross-national literary and political collaborations and the emergence of postcolonial literatures. For example, this period sees the rise of African and pan-African consciousness of the kind represented in Cunard's ground-breaking collection of essays, literature, and art relating to African culture, *Negro: An Anthology* (1934). In a similar turn to Africa in the 1930s, the Jamaican poet Una Marson moves away from her early Romantic influences to the creolized aesthetic of the Harlem Renaissance. Like her compatriot, Louise Bennett, Marson uses dialect and blues patterns to challenge normative white values, illustrated by poems such as 'Kinky Hair Blues' where the speaker protests, 'I hat dat ironed hair / And dat bleaching skin.'[9] This transition towards indigenous cultures and landscapes also takes place amongst dominion writers. Katherine Mansfield and Jane Mander become important to the corpus of New Zealand literature, whilst the Canadian novelist L.M. Montgomery exemplifies what Faye Hammill reads as 'a recognition of the inadequacy of inherited literary forms for capturing colonial experience'.[10]

Women's literary engagement with empire between 1920 and 1945 coincides with their enfranchisement as imperial subjects (many women having won the vote in Britain and the white dominions by 1928) and with the greater social freedom to venture abroad enabled by cruise operators and air travel. Such emancipation, however, often produces complex and contradictory responses to nation and empire. Virginia Woolf's assertion in 1938 – 'as a woman, I have no country. As a woman I want no country' – highlighted that even with the vote, a woman's nationality was still determined by her husband.[11] Moreover, women were still first and foremost constructed as 'symbolic bearers of the nation',[12] which, as Jane Garrity has shown, induced some female modernists, including Woolf, to reconfigure the masculinist national imaginary as feminine.[13] In spite of this, however, for many women, the empire itself presented new opportunities for self-realization through travel, service, and emigration. Emigration to the colonies had been encouraged since the mid-nineteenth century, particularly for young, single women who might otherwise add to escalating fears about the estimated two million 'surplus' women revealed in the 1921 census.[14] Government-run societies assisted women in this enterprise, and a popular literary genre, the empire romance, promoted emigration as a chance to improve career and marriage prospects.[15] As representatives of the 'mother country' these women were expected to support the imperial project: to marry and domesticate the colony though welfare and missionary work, acting as the moral exemplars of white superiority in matters of sexuality, hygiene, and health.[16] In her travel book, *The Little World* (1925), Stella Benson observed: 'Women come to India, I understand, either because they are married to empire builders or because they want to be', and for a woman to 'admit that she has come to India to see India, will make any well-brought-up empire builder blush'.[17] Some women, however, did travel to 'see' the empire, sometimes becoming politically active as reformers or colonial administrators. Margery Perham toured West Africa to report on indirect rule in Nigeria and Gertrude Bell's extensive travels established her as an authority on the Middle East. Her local knowledge, which had enabled T.E. Lawrence's victory over the Turks in 1917–1918, later led to her integral role as Oriental Secretary in establishing the modern state of Iraq in 1921.[18]

Bell and Perham illustrate how women contributed to the continuing imperial project in this period, even as this project came under scrutiny. Vita Sackville-West, visiting Bell in Iraq on her way to meet her diplomat husband, Harold Nicolson, in Persia, would also witness the inauguration of a new modern state at the coronation of Reza Shah in Teheran in 1926. Despite her close connections with colonial authority in the region, Sackville-West nevertheless exercises a self-consciously anti-imperialist mode of vision. 'I was fit only to report of objects, not as I knew them to be, but as they seemed to me', she insists in *Passenger to Teheran* (1926), 'and to read into them, I might add, a great many attributes they could not really possess.'[19] Women's writing of this period is often marked by tensions of this kind, between resistance and complicity with imperial ideology. The financially independent narrator of *A Room of One's Own* (1929), mindful of the 'transnational complicities' of imperial inheritance,[20] owes her autonomy to the colonial legacy left to her by an aunt who 'died by a fall from her horse when she was riding out to take the air in Bombay'.[21] Later, however, that narrator also remarks, 'It is one of the great advantages of being a woman that one can pass even a very fine negress without wishing to make an Englishwoman of her', openly rejecting masculine imperialist appropriation but deploying the objectifying gaze of modernist primitivism nonetheless.[22]

In what follows, I outline some of these tensions between complicity and resistance in women's writing on empire after the First World War, paying attention to what Simon Gikandi calls 'the ambivalence of imperial femininity'.[23] Many of the writers discussed present imperial space ambivalently: both as a site of freedom or childhood nostalgia *and* as a site of oppression and injustice. This ambivalence surfaces through geopolitical perspectives on the relation between colony and metropole, which are often the product of voyages out from the centre as well as, to borrow Said's phrase, 'the voyage in' from the colonies.[24] Also at stake is the distinction between the self and other, whether that other is colonial or metropolitan; at times this generates cross-cultural and cross-gender identification, and at others underscores cultural and racial difference. I begin by examining how women writers reconceptualize the imperial centre in this period, before moving on to consider how their journeys away from the centre question the imperial narrative and anticipate decolonization.

'While Woolf can certainly be accused of overlooking colonial space on its own terms', Anna Snaith and Michael Whitworth suggest, 'she cannot be charged with ignoring the effects of imperialism on Britain, or more specifically the imperial traces found in the architecture and geography of the metropolis.'[25] Certainly, in *Mrs Dalloway* (1925) London is punctuated by monuments such as 'the Indian and his cross' in Regent's Park and re-envisioned through the eyes of the returning colonial administrator, Peter Walsh.[26] Like Leonard Woolf, whose service in Ceylon between 1904 and 1911 inspired his critique of empire in *Empire and Commerce in Africa* (1920), Peter returns from India to the imperial centre in 1923 with a question. Conscious of intensified Indian nationalism, he asks, 'What did the Government mean – Richard Dalloway would know – to do about India?'[27] But the government do not know, and the authority of the imperial centre is ultimately decentred when the arch-imperialist Lady Bruton appeals to Peter to assuage her anxieties about the decline of empire ('he being fresh from the centre').[28] This instability at the heart of empire later figures in *The Waves* (1931) but this time through the failure of a colonial return: as Jane Marcus argues in her ground-breaking essay, 'Britannia Rules *The Waves*', Percival's death in India initiates the collapse of national and imperial identity amongst those waiting in vain for him at the centre.[29] *The Waves*, however, also explores the unstable relation between margin and centre through the Australian Louis's doomed quest for acceptance in the metropole. His sense of precariousness and alienation – 'I, who desire above all things to be taken to the arms with love, am alien, external' – is mirrored in Bernard, whose Englishness he mimics, whilst his sympathy with Rhoda suggests the overlapping experiences of the marginalized feminine and colonial other.[30] *The Waves* therefore illustrates Gikandi's argument 'that the complicitous relationship between colonial centers and margins is indispensible to understanding Englishness'.[31] Moreover, by incorporating the colonial gaze on the metropole, it acknowledges the influence of 'the voyage in' which would lead to 'massive infusions of non-European cultures into the metropolitan heartland'.[32] This period sees a number of women writers 'voyage in', from the Caribbean, the white dominions, and Africa.

Born in Dominica, Jean Rhys travelled to England in 1907, only to feel, like her protagonist Anna Morgan in *Voyage in the Dark* (1934), alienated and marked out as a white Creole by her accent. 'That awful sing-song voice you had! Exactly like a nigger you talked – and still do', Anna's English stepmother complains, justifying an estrangement which becomes a synecdoche for the mother country's rejection of the colonial daughter.[33] Hester imputes Anna's unconventional femininity to her formative relationships with the black servants and to a questionable racial heritage, insinuating that her mother was 'coloured'. Like the heroine of the short story 'Mixing Cocktails' (1927), Anna Morgan is tainted by her colonial origins and seen by the English as an indeterminate racial and class identity. Likened to the supposedly hypersexualized 'Hottentot' by the other chorus girls, she struggles to secure respectability and slides down the social strata towards prostitution.[34] Despite affirming to her London insurance salesman lover, Walter, that 'I am a real West Indian ... I'm the fifth generation on my mother's side', Anna Morgan, like Rhys herself, is caught between two cultures, accepted neither by the white English nor the black Caribbean society with which she more readily identifies.[35] Like other Rhys heroines, who Mary Lou Emery notes, 'fragment most importantly through suppressed histories and eclipsed geo-cultural locations',[36] Anna's alienation is not simply idiosyncratic but the product of colonialism. Alienation in Rhys's fiction can also be read, in Helen Carr's view, as 'endeavouring to resist or complicate conventional essential-izing definitions',[37] so that even the Parisian heroines, Julia Martin in *After Leaving Mr Mackenzie* (1930) and Sasha Jansen in *Good Morning, Midnight* (1939) bring to mind characters as different as the Dominican mixed race newspaper editor, Papa Dom, in 'Again the Antilles' (1927).

Rhys's gendered perspective on racial and colonial identity invites com-parisons with the black Jamaican poet and dramatist Una Marson who had travelled to London in 1932. Like *Voyage in the Dark*, Marson's *At What Price* (1931), which had been the first black colonial production staged in London, and her later plays *London Calling* (1937) and *Pocomania* (1938) present young heroines struggling for self-realization in the contexts of patriarchal, colonial society.[38] Marson, like Rhys, also experienced that feel-ing of the alienated colonial at the metropolitan centre, made more acute by her racial difference. Her poem 'Quashie Comes to London' expresses the wonder of the colonial visitor to the metropole but concludes with disillusionment: 'dere's plenty dat is really nice / But I sick fe see white face.'[39] In 'Little Brown Girl' this sense of alienation is heightened by the performance of a white metropolitan voice questioning the colonial: 'Little brown girl / Don't you feel very strange / To be so often alone / In a crowd of whites?'[40] 'Nigger', a poem that stands out in Marson's oeuvre for its anti-racist ire, is both a protest and an attempt to educate 'You of the white skinned Race' after encountering racist insults from children in London.[41] It appeared in the first issue of *Keys*, the official journal of the League of Coloured Peoples, founded by the Jamaican-born doctor, Harold A. Moody, who had been crucial in integrating Marson into London's West Indian Community, as well as providing her with accommodation and work when she fell victim to the unofficial 'colour bar' operating in London at that time.[42] Marson's experiences of racial abuse and race politics in London were critical to her development as a writer and activist. As Anna

Snaith notes, 'ironically, it was in the heart of the empire that Marson's anti-imperialism, her feminism, and her West Indian identity deepened'.[43] Other colonial women writers, including those from the white dominions, also experienced this intensified commitment to home and national identity.

In 1908 Katherine Mansfield's desire for social freedom beyond the white settler community had taken her from her native New Zealand to the British metropole. The need to transgress domestic confines informs many of her stories, but as 'The Stranger' (1921) reveals such freedom comes at the cost of estrangement. Having travelled alone to Europe, the wife of this story returns to her husband in New Zealand only to reveal that a man had died in her arms on board ship. The implied intimacy of this final embrace with a stranger underscores her emotional distance from both husband and homeland: a liminality which reflects Mansfield's own experience. Although Mansfield was never to travel home to New Zealand, she made an imaginative return in stories written towards the end of her life. By this time, she had become disillusioned with London where she had always been made to feel 'the little colonial ... a stranger – an alien'.[44] But this nostalgia for her childhood home was, as in Rhys's fiction, troubled by an adult consciousness of social constraints and colonial history. On a 1907 tour of the Ureweras (the North Island Maori territories), Mansfield had witnessed 'the savage spirit of the country' which unnerves her settler narrator of 'The Woman at the Store' (1912),[45] and which haunts her later stories as a reminder of historical conflict between Maori and British forces beyond the colonial garden gate.[46] In 'At the Bay' (1922) Beryl is seduced into stepping up to the garden edge by Mr Kember, who suddenly turns into a 'vile' sexual predator 'as the gate pushed open'.[47] In 'The Garden Party' (1922), Laura, having 'shut their garden gates' behind her, leaves the blinkered shelter of the Sheridan household to confront the tragedy of a local working man's sudden accidental death.[48] In such moments, Saikat Majumdar suggests, 'the feminized upper-middle-class domesticity in Mansfield's stories forms a quiet dialectic with possibilities of trauma and violence lurking within her consciousness of colonial and indigenous landscapes'.[49]

Elizabeth Bowen found much to admire in Mansfield's New Zealand stories, recognizing Mansfield's potential as 'a regional writer', an insight which perhaps owes something to her own status as a writer whom, as she puts it, 'the English at their least friendly might call "colonial"'.[50] A member of the Anglo-Protestant ascendancy in Ireland, Bowen shared with Mansfield that childhood nostalgia for the colonial settlement. For her too, the settlers' domestic sphere is an insulated feminized space hemmed in by a public colonial history of violence. In *The Last September* (1929), set amidst the Irish struggle for independence, the Anglo-Irish Lois asks, 'How is it that in this country that ought to be full of such violent realness, there seems nothing for me but clothes and what people say? I might just as well be in some kind of cocoon.'[51] But this sense of protected inertia is shattered when her fiancé, a British soldier, is shot dead, and Irish nationalists burn down Danielstown, along with two other Anglo-Irish country houses. Though Bowen's own family residence escaped the same fate, she reluctantly recognized the necessity for change following Irish independence: '[t]he big house has much to learn – and it must learn if it is to survive at all', she conceded, 'But it also has much to give.'[52]

Elspeth Huxley, who returned to Britain in 1925, having been brought up in Kenya since 1913, is another writer who blends nostalgia for a colonial childhood with a historical consciousness of colonialism. Regarded by postcolonial critics as an apologist for white settlers, Huxley has been accused of appropriating the voices of colonized Africans to the white woman settler's narrative. Phyllis Lassner, however, detects a more self-conscious narrative voice in Huxley's fiction and life-writing which alerts us to the value of her work as a representation of the white colonial woman's interrogation, not vindication, of the colonial project through multiple perspectives: '[b]y the end of her career, both the Kikuyu and the British have been viewed through the lens of each other' so that 'Huxley constructs a balance in perspective that ... is critically unsettling.'[53] So for example, Huxley's detective melodramas centre on white settler society, whilst *Red Strangers* (1939), an ethnographic family saga, focuses on three generations of Kikuyu between the years 1890–1937. This novel encourages readers to witness the arrival of the British through the eyes of the Kikuyu. The so-called 'progress' brought by the 'red strangers' – the building of Nairobi, the railway, and the road, as well as the introduction of new farming technology and missionary schooling – therefore appears nonsensical and damaging to indigenous communities. Different responses to colonialism are captured through two brothers: Muthengi, a warrior, colludes with British authorities, gaining power by taxing his own countrymen and forcing them into labour, whereas Matu, the shaman, struggles to uphold their agricultural traditions amidst the chaos brought by 'Europeans [who] teach their magic to children, so that uncircumcised boys are like elders, and elders like infants in arms'.[54] Alongside men, British settler women emerge as potent domesticating influences eroding Kikuyu culture. The farmer's wife usurps the shaman's role with her medicines, whilst the female missionary, the mouthpiece of British policy, educates young girls to reject the tradition of female circumcision and is consequently murdered in a nationalist backlash presaging the Mau Mau Emergency.

Huxley's determination to defamiliarize the colonial narrative and the white woman's place within it by 'see[ing] through the eyes of the Other' bears comparison with Rumer Godden, for whom this strategy, as Gayathri Prabhu explains, 'involves creating constant resistance against the imperial norms and restrictions of British India'.[55] Godden, the daughter of a shipping agent, spent most of her early childhood in Bengal and after an education in England returned to live in Calcutta, Darjeeling, and Kashmir. Throughout her life Godden moved frequently between India and Britain, and recent scholarship recognizes how 'her preoccupations reflect the liminal position of a transnational and ... transmodern writer'.[56] In *Black Narcissus* (1939) a small group of nuns move to a remote Indian village outside Darjeeling in the Himalayas at the behest of a local general keen to convert a palace, a former harem, into a school and a hospital. Initially the nuns seem to benefit from their encounter with the colonized 'other', but ultimately Sister Clodagh accepts that they can never convert the palace, 'that she was an interloper in it and the Convent life no more than a cobweb that would be brushed away'.[57] Subverting romance and conversion narratives, the novel ends with the nuns' departure, a foretelling of decolonization also explored in *Breakfast with the Nikolides* (1942). Here, an outbreak of rabies in a rural Bengal community sparks tension between Indians and English settlers and serves as a metaphor for the contagious spread of violence during the Second World War. In this charged atmosphere, the modern veterinary surgeon, Narayan Das, balances his desires for European sophistication with orthodox Hindu culture and the nationalist philosophy of 'non-violence', to become what Lassner identifies as 'a self-made decolonized man'.[58]

Freya Stark was another Englishwoman able to 'see through the eyes of the Other' and anticipate problems of the postwar era. The articles in *Baghdad Sketches*, the first collection of her many travel writings, originally appeared in the *Baghdad Times* during 1931. They recount her experiences of living among the ordinary people of Baghdad and present a wide range of public opinion: from the fashionable anti-British attitudes amongst the effendi (the more westernized professionals and intellectuals of Baghdad) to the lower-class hatred of English travellers. Such reports are the product of Stark's transgression into spaces deemed out of bounds for the white woman by colonial and Muslim society. She visits a Bedouin settlement unaccompanied by an American or European man and, disguised in a veil, infiltrates both a harem and the shrine at the holy city of Kadhimain during Ramadan. Such border crossings enable an anti-imperialist perspective that recognizes 'the Old East, incompatible with all we bring and do'[59] and also presciently fears the western technological encroachments on the region's oilfields as well as the wider ramifications of British administration in Palestine.

Stark's ventures brought social censure from her colonial community, and the same was true of Stella Benson. Benson, who travelled widely before her married life as the wife of a Chinese customs official living in colonial China and Hong Kong, always retained her admiration for the Chinese and her criticism of British colonial society. Hong Kong, she observed in 1920, was 'a solid lump of England' where '[t]he average Hongkonger has a tendency to address all Chinese in a throaty tone of authority as "Boy"'.[60] Her writing often exposes the abuses of British imperial influence in both the treaty ports and the international settlement of Shanghai. *Goodbye, Stranger* (1926) achieves this by presenting the Chinese as the rational onlookers to British colonial chaos and mysticism. The novel centres on the sudden disappearance of Clifford Cotton, a printer for the mission and an unstable personality who imagines he is a changeling. His reappearance, naked, and in a trance-like state, is perceived by the British as an experience of revelation or as though he has been returned by the fairies. For the Chinese, however, his apparently intoxicated state warrants arrest. As Mr Liu explains, 'I know British persons say Chinese law has no rights to punish British criminals and drunks. But I am Chinese. I say British law has no rights to work vengeance on innocent Chinese patriots in Chinese territories.'[61] Liu perhaps refers here to the 'Chinese patriots' killed on 30 May 1925 in Shanghai by the British-led Shanghai Municipal Police during a mass demonstration: the deaths increased nationalist and anti-British feeling.[62] Through Mr Liu, Benson critiques British colonials in China, interrogating not only their fitness to conduct their questionable mission but also the force by which they defend it.

A former suffragette, Benson was one of a number of feminists who became politically active within the empire. Others included Eleanor Rathbone, author of *Child Marriage: The Indian Minotaur* (1934) and the American, Katherine Mayo, both of whom opposed the Hindu custom of child marriage. Benson joined a committee investigating the International Traffic in Women on behalf of the League of Nations. Her initial outrage was not directed against prostitution per se but at the practice by which Chinese girls were sold into prostitution by their parents and treated as slaves once they were transported and licensed in the colony. Her report on this for the League contributed to the abolition of brothels in Hong Kong after 1931.[63] Benson and Rathbone were among many feminists who, as Susan Pedersen observes, 'were quick to see women in colonies or mandates as their specific responsibility, but [who] rarely extended that sympathy to colonized men': one exception was Winifred Holtby.[64]

Holtby, who first met Benson in 1925, also became known for her political activism after undertaking a six-month lecture tour of South Africa for the League of Nations Union in 1926. Struck by the urgent issues of racial segregation and interracial violence in the new dominion, she returned home to publish numerous articles uncovering the disenfranchisement of black South Africans under the 1926 Colour Bar Act and to become a tireless campaigner for black trade unionism in South Africa.[65] Such protests against racial inequality also informed her fiction. A short story, 'The Voorloper Group' (1927), for example, presents a poignant tableau of 'two Zulu servants' who 'teach each other to read out of a child's primer'.[66] Yet Holtby was reluctant to set a novel in South Africa, having only spent a short time there, preferring instead to generate geopolitical perspectives against the background of her native Yorkshire landscape. *The Land of Green Ginger* (1927) begun on Holtby's voyage home, presents Joanna, born in South Africa, who dreams of her birthplace amidst the hardship and isolation of married life on a Yorkshire farm, whilst Sarah Burton of *South Riding* (1936) compares rural feudalism in the East Riding to the treatment of black labourers she witnessed in South Africa.

Holtby belonged to numerous organizations committed to promoting interracial understanding, including the League of Coloured Peoples, through which she formed friendships with Una Marson and Norman Leys (a critic of colonial rule in Kenya) and expanded her political interests to include Jamaica and East Africa, the setting of her fifth novel, *Mandoa, Mandoa!* (1933). In this tale of 'empire building', a British travel company transforms a fictional African country into a new holiday destination backed by a British National Government keen to secure waning imperial influence in Kenya and the Sudan. Although a satirical comment on British encroachments on Africa to boost export markets for failing staple industries, the novel ends ambiguously: British cultural and capitalist imperialism is ultimately overthrown by a nationalist uprising that is neither celebrated nor decried but merely depicted as a starting point for reconstruction.

Mandoa, Mandoa! was also a topical response to the 1930 coronation of Emperor Haile Selassie in Abyssinia and a prescient warning about fascist designs on North Africa. The novel acquired a second round of popularity when Mussolini invaded Abyssinia in 1935. Holtby did not live to see this, but other feminists spoke out in support of Selassie and to condemn Fascism. Sylvia Pankhurst founded the paper *New Times and Ethiopia News* which she used to launch swingeing attacks on the British government's refusal to take military action or to continue sanctions against Italy during the Abyssinian occupation. For Nancy Cunard, as for many of her contemporaries such as Marson, the invasion of Abyssinia became inextricable from their opposition to British imperialism and from their support of the agitation for colonial independence in the Caribbean which accelerated in the context of global economic hardship in the 1930s and 1940s.

Cunard's essay, 'Jamaica – The Negro Island', written after a visit to the island in 1932, declares that '[i]t is ridiculous and bound to strike any traveller there overpoweringly that this island should be anything but a black man's territory.'[67] What Cunard presents as self-evident here is, in fact, as Maureen Moynagh points out, 'politically strategic in relation to a bid for decolonization, and ... rhetorically strategic in relation to Cunard's construction of her partisanship'.[68] Certainly, this essay reads as a prelude to Cunard's involvement with pan-Africanism: it offers space to Marcus Garvey's campaign for the black overthrow of white superiority, even if disagreeing with his refusal to cooperate with white anti-racists.

Cunard returned to the Caribbean on her way back from Chile in 1940, visiting Trinidad, which reinforced her dedication to pan-Africanism and the nationalist movements in the West Indies. Her observations at this time echo Una Marson's poetry of the late 1930s with its increasing nationalist commitment amidst the economic depression, labour strikes, and unrest across the Caribbean. Cunard's 'Psalm for Trinidad', related in both Standard English and Caribbean dialect, voices the case of the exploited ('Workin' man can't eat, can't sleep, can't live properly') and asks, 'What about after de war, man you think it come the Democracy?'[69] This was precisely the question she took up in her collaboration with the Trinidadian-born George Padmore, *The White Man's Duty* (1942). In the wake of the Atlantic Charter, where British and American leaders set out the model for postwar international relations, this pamphlet questions the willingness of the western colonial powers to liberate their own colonial subjects after the war, placing anti-colonial movements in the Caribbean in the wider framework of international resistance to the British empire in Africa, India, and Burma. Much of the intellectual thrust comes from Padmore but Cunard's contribution to this essay, as Maroula Joannou has revealed, underlines her importance in working alongside those black people in Britain attempting to shape their own destiny before the arrival of the Empire Windrush in 1948.[70]

In E.M. Forster's *A Passage to India*, Mrs Moore demonstrates cross-cultural awareness and sensitivity in taking off her shoes before entering the mosque. For Godden, 'That act of understanding and respect, unlocked friendship and welcome so that Mrs Moore grew to know an India she would never have glimpsed if she had stayed in the habits of herself, the Englishwoman; but', she asks, 'how many of us know enough to take off our shoes?'[71] The answer was that a good many more women had by 1945 ventured beyond the 'habits' of the 'Englishwoman' and 'knew' enough not only to take off their shoes but to see, as Woolf had done in 1924, that the 'Empire [was] perishing' and anticipate what that 'perishing' might bring[72] – decolonization and the emergence of new nations, and with that the difficult process of reconstructing new identities and international understanding, as well as the prospect of new forms of imperialism.

Notes

1. On this transition in the culture of empire, see Barbara Bush, 'Gender and Empire: The Twentieth Century', in *Gender and Empire*, ed. Philippa Levine (Oxford: Oxford University Press, 2004), pp. 77–111, pp. 78–80.
2. On the riots as a background to the exhibition, see Mary Lou Emery, *Modernism, the Visual and Caribbean Literature* (Cambridge: Cambridge University Press, 2007), pp. 46–52.
3. Virginia Woolf, 'Thunder at Wembley', in *Virginia Woolf: Selected Essays*, ed. David Bradshaw (Oxford: Oxford University Press, 2008), pp. 169–71, p. 170.
4. Ibid., p. 171.
5. Robin Hackett and Gay Wachman, 'Introduction: Making the Private Public: Women Writers, Modernism, Empire, and War', in *At Home and Abroad in the Empire: British Women Write the 1930s*, ed. Robin Hackett, Freda Hauser, and Gay Wachman (Newark: University of Delaware Press, 2009), pp. 13–30, p. 13.
6. Tory Young, 'Nancy Cunard's *Black Man and White Ladyship* as Surrealist Tract', in *At Home and Abroad in the Empire*, ed. Hackett et al., pp. 154–70, p. 168.

7. Rebecca West, *Black Lamb and Grey Falcon* (Edinburgh: Canongate, 2006), pp. 1089–91.
8. See Edward W. Said, *Culture and Imperialism* (London: Chatto & Windus, 1993), p. 90.
9. Una Marson, 'Kinky Hair Blues', in *The Moth and the Star* (Kingston, Jamaica: self-published, 1937), p. 91.
10. Faye Hammill, *Literary Culture and Female Authorship in Canada 1760–2000* (Amsterdam: Rodopi, 2003), p. 107.
11. Virginia Woolf, *Three Guineas* (London: The Hogarth Press, 1977), p. 197.
12. On the gendered formation of nationalism, see Anne McClintock, *Imperial Leather: Race, Gender and Sexuality in the Colonial Contest* (London: Routledge, 1995), pp. 352–60, p. 354.
13. In *Step-Daughters of England: British Women Modernists and the National Imaginary* (Manchester: Manchester University Press, 2003), Jane Garrity outlines how women writers reclaim the nation through the maternal and lesbian body.
14. The figure is quoted as 19,803,022 females to 18,082,220 males in England and Wales in Virginia Nicholson, *Singled Out* (Harmondsworth: Penguin, 2008), p. 22.
15. On the empire romance, see Billie Melman, *Women and the Popular Imagination in the Twenties: Flappers and Nymphs* (Basingstoke: Macmillan, 1988), Chapter 9.
16. Bush, 'Gender and Empire: The Twentieth Century', pp. 86–95.
17. Stella Benson, *The Little World* (Milton Keynes: Dodo Press, 2010), p. 71.
18. See Georgina Howell, *Gertrude Bell: Queen of the Desert, Shaper of Nations* (New York: Farrar, Straus and Giroux, 2008), Chapters 13–15.
19. Vita Sackville-West, *Passenger to Teheran* (London: Tauris Parke Paperbacks, 2007), p. 45.
20. See Susan Stanford Friedman, *Mappings: Feminism and the Cultural Geographies of Encounter* (Princeton, NJ: Princeton University Press, 1998), p. 127.
21. Virginia Woolf, *A Room of One's Own* (London: Hogarth Press, 1929), p. 56.
22. Ibid., p. 76. See Jane Marcus, *Hearts of Darkness: White Women Write Race* (New Brunswick: Rutgers University Press, 2004), Chapter 2.
23. Simon Gikandi, *Maps of Englishness: Writing Identity in the Culture of Colonialism* (New York: Columbia University Press, 1996), p. 47.
24. Said, *Culture and Imperialism*, pp. 260–1.
25. Anna Snaith and Michael H. Whitworth, 'Introduction' to *Locating Woolf: The Politics of Space and Place* (Basingstoke: Palgrave Macmillan, 2007), pp. 1–28, p. 25.
26. Virginia Woolf, *Mrs Dalloway* (Harmondsworth: Penguin, 2000), p. 26.
27. Ibid., p. 176.
28. Ibid., p. 197.
29. Marcus, *Hearts of Darkness*, Chapter 3.
30. Virginia Woolf, *The Waves* (London: Vintage, 2004), pp. 60–1.
31. Gikandi, *Maps of Englishness*, p. 125.
32. Said, *Culture and Imperialism*, p. 292.
33. Jean Rhys, *Voyage in the Dark* (Harmondsworth: Penguin, 2000), p. 56.
34. Ibid., p. 12.
35. Ibid., p. 47.
36. Mary Lou Emery, *Jean Rhys at 'World's End': Novels of Colonial and Sexual Exile* (Austin: University of Texas Press, 1990), p. 16.
37. Helen Carr, 'Jean Rhys: West Indian Intellectual', in *West Indian Intellectuals in Britain*, ed. Bill Schwarz (Manchester: Manchester University Press, 2003), pp. 93–113, p. 106.

38. Emery, *Modernism, the Visual and Caribbean Literature*, pp. 126–7; Delia Jarrett-Macauley, *The Life of Una Marson, 1905–65* (Manchester: Manchester University Press, 1998), pp. 133–4.
39. Una Marson, 'Quashie Comes to London', *The Moth and the Star*, p. 21.
40. Una Marson, 'Little Brown Girl', *The Moth and the Star*, p. 13.
41. Una Marson, 'Nigger', *Keys*, 1.1 (July 1933): 8–9.
42. On the League, see Jarrett-Macauley, *The Life of Una Marson*, p. 50.
43. Anna Snaith, '"Little Brown Girl" in a "White, White City": Una Marson and London', *Tulsa Studies in Women's Literature*, 27: 1 (Spring 2008): 93–114, p. 96.
44. Katherine Mansfield, *The Katherine Mansfield Notebooks*, ed. Margaret Scott, 2 vols (Canterbury, NZ: Lincoln University Press, 1997), II, p. 166.
45. Katherine Mansfield, 'The Woman at the Store', in *Katherine Mansfield: The Collected Stories* (Harmondsworth: Penguin, 2007), pp. 550–62, p. 554.
46. On the gate as 'demarcation line', see Angela Smith, *Katherine Mansfield: A Literary Life* (Basingstoke: Palgrave, 2000), p. 41.
47. Katherine Mansfield, 'At the Bay', in *Katherine Mansfield: The Collected Stories*, pp. 205–45, p. 244.
48. Katherine Mansfield, 'The Garden Party', in *Katherine Mansfield: The Collected Stories*, pp. 245–61, p. 258.
49. Saikat Majumdar, 'Katherine Mansfield and the Fragility of Pákehá Boredom', *Modern Fiction Studies*, 55:1 (Spring 2009): 119–41, p. 123.
50. Elizabeth Bowen, 'A Living Writer: Katherine Mansfield', in *The Mulberry Tree: Writings of Elizabeth Bowen*, ed. Hermione Lee (London: Virago, 1986), pp. 69–85, p. 77 and p. 79.
51. Elizabeth Bowen, *The Last September* (London: Vintage, 1998), p. 49.
52. Elizabeth Bowen, 'The Big House', in *The Mulberry Tree*, pp. 25–30, p. 30.
53. Phyllis Lassner, *Colonial Strangers: Women Writing the End of the British Empire* (New Brunswick, NJ: Rutgers University Press, 2004), p. 122.
54. Elspeth Huxley, *Red Strangers* (Harmondsworth: Penguin, 2006), p. 304.
55. Gayathri Prabhu, 'In Search of Rumer Godden's India', in *Rumer Godden: International and Intermodern Storyteller*, ed. Lucy Le-Guilcher and Phyllis B. Lassner (Farnham: Ashgate, 2010), pp. 51–64, p. 60.
56. Lucy Le-Guilcher and Phyllis B. Lassner, 'Introduction' to *Rumer Godden: International and Intermodern Storyteller*, pp. 1–20, p. 6.
57. Rumer Godden, *Black Narcissus* (London: Pan Books, 1994), p. 105.
58. Lassner, *Colonial Strangers*, p. 95.
59. Freya Stark, *Baghdad Sketches: Journey through Iraq* (London: Tauris Parke Paperbacks, 2011), p. 174.
60. Benson, *The Little World*, p. 28.
61. Stella Benson, *Goodbye, Stranger* (Milton Keynes: Dodo Press, 2010), p. 168.
62. See Robert Bickers, *Britain in China: Community, Culture and Colonialism, 1900–1949* (Manchester: Manchester University Press, 1999), pp. 3–4.
63. On Benson's activism, see Joy Grant, *Stella Benson: A Biography* (London: Macmillan London, 1987), pp. 283–9.
64. Susan Pedersen, 'Metaphors of the Schoolroom: Women Working the Mandates System of the League of Nations', *History Workshop Journal*, 66 (2008): 188–207, p. 204.
65. Marion Shaw, *The Clear Stream: A Life of Winifred Holtby* (London: Virago, 1999), Chapter 6.

66. Winifred Holtby, 'The Voorloper Group', in *Truth is Not Sober* (London: Collins, 1934), pp. 114–18, p. 118.
67. Nancy Cunard, 'Jamaica – The Negro Island', in *Essays on Race and Empire: Nancy Cunard*, ed. Maureen Moynagh (Peterborough: Broadview, 2002), pp. 97–126, p. 117.
68. Maureen Moynagh, 'Introduction' to *Essays on Race and Empire: Nancy Cunard*, pp. 9–63, p. 38.
69. Nancy Cunard, 'Psalm for Trinidad', in *Poems of Nancy Cunard from the Bodleian Library*, ed. John Lucas (Nottingham: Trent Editions, 2005), pp. 69–71, p. 70 and p. 71.
70. Maroula Joannou, 'Nancy Cunard's English Journey', *Feminist Review*, 78 (2004): 141–63, pp. 158–60.
71. Rumer Godden, 'Water Music (Kashmir, 1944)', in *The River* (London: Pan Books, 2004), pp. 115–24, p. 124.
72. Woolf, 'Thunder at Wembley', p. 171.

15
Women Writing the City
Deborah Longworth

The significance of the urban observer within recent cultural and literary criticism owes much to the writings of German cultural theorist Walter Benjamin on the *flâneur*: essays on Baudelaire, and his large, unfinished study of Paris in the nineteenth century, the *Arcades Project*.[1] Through the renewed interest in Benjamin since the 1980s, the *flâneur* has become the iconic personification of the highly developed perceptive skills of the urban observer, a connoisseur of metropolitan life, skilled at folding himself anonymously into the city streets, and priding himself in his ability to delineate the different types that made up the seemingly faceless urban crowd. Yet for many feminist theorists, noting that the experiences of women have largely been excluded from the literature of urban modernity,[2] the *flâneur* has also been a marker of the social and gender dynamics of the urban environment. The existence of a female urban observer, or *flâneuse*, was anathema to the social and gender configurations of the nineteenth- and turn-of-the-century city. To loiter anonymously on the city streets of the nineteenth-century metropolis was an all but exclusively male luxury. The term 'street-walker' when applied to a man may denote the *flâneur*, but when applied to a woman it refers to the prostitute. 'The literature of modernity describes the experience of men', the cultural theorist Janet Wolff writes. Respectable women could not pursue the same private freedom in public space as men enjoyed; they could not visit restaurants or coffeehouses alone, wander the streets day or night, or loiter on street corners catching the glances of passers-by. Any female equivalent of the *flâneur*, she argues, was thus 'rendered impossible by the sexual divisions of the nineteenth century'.[3] Art historian Griselda Pollock agrees that 'there is no female equivalent of the quintessential masculine figure, the flâneur: there is not and could not be a female flâneuse'.[4]

Neither Wolff nor Pollock deny the existence of women on the streets of the metropolis; indeed they note their significant presence amongst the working classes, as prostitutes, and, in London in 1888, as murder victims. What they do emphasize is women's lack of power as observers of the urban scene. Pollock notes, for example, that '[w]omen did not enjoy the freedom of incognito in the crowd', and that 'women do not look. They are positioned as the object of the flâneur's gaze'.[5] Over the past decade, however, critics have challenged the assumption that walking and observing the city was a necessarily male privilege, arguing that the expansion of the public sphere at the end of the nineteenth century enabled both the legitimate presence of women on the city streets – as employees, journalists, shoppers, and tourists, activities that frequently brought them into the position of leisured observation – and a distinct mode of urban perception belonging to a female urban observer or *flâneuse*. Even as early as 1853, Charlotte Brontë's Lucy Snowe, waking in an inn beneath the shadow of St Paul's in *Villette*, declares that 'Elation and pleasure were in my heart: to walk alone in London seemed in itself an adventure.'[6] By the first decades of the twentieth century, however, women's experiences of urban life had become a frequent theme, and female characters as urban observers a common trope in women's writing. Many, although not all, share the elation of Lucy Snowe. Those such as Dorothy Richardson's semi-autobiographical Miriam Henderson, for example, embracing her impoverished yet independent life in London as one of its *'batteurs de pave'*, and Virginia Woolf's Clarissa Dalloway, setting off through Westminster one sunny morning in June 1923 to buy flowers for her evening party, find the city to be a place of freedom, excitement, and possibility.[7] Others, however, such as Jean Rhys's Sasha Jensen in *Good Morning, Midnight* (1939), remain alienated by or within the cityscape. Rhys's protagonists, constantly moving from one boarding-house or temporary lodging to another, haunting the more déclassé bars and cafés, exemplify what Rachel Bowlby has described as a 'negative *flâneuse*', a woman who seeks invisibility and a place to hide within the city, feeling a discomfort born of a sense of unease and transgression. For Sasha the notion that independent urban life is enabling, pleasurable, or exhilarating is a myth about which she has long been disillusioned. Yet she is an urban observer nonetheless, pathologically attuned to the social and psychological nuances of the spaces and places of the city that frame her existence: 'cafés where they like me and cafés where they don't, streets that are friendly, streets that aren't, rooms where I might be happy, rooms where I never shall be'.[8]

I have written about these issues in depth in *Streetwalking the Metropolis* (2000). For the purposes of this chapter I am interested in exploring what might be read as conscious engagements and deliberate rewritings by women writers in the early twentieth century of the tradition of the male *flâneur*, drawing for contrast on the trope of the urban observer as articulated by Poe and Baudelaire.

'The Man of the Crowd'

Edgar Allan Poe's short story, 'The Man of the Crowd' (1840), with its fascinated yet detached urban observer, hypersensitive to the identifiable features of the different groups that make up the urban crowd, offers a prototype of one significant aspect of the conventional male urban observer: an attitude of detached, rationalizing control over the urban landscape. Poe's anonymous narrator has been convalescing in London after a lengthy illness, and begins his tale at the end of an afternoon that he has spent reading and people-watching from the window seat of a coffeehouse near Piccadilly. Peter Cunningham's *Hand-Book of London* for 1850, which included a section on 'COFFEE, &c., IN LONDON', noted that at the best establishments the price of one shilling entitled the customer to 'a cup of coffee and cigar, and the privileges of the room, the newspapers, chess, &c'.[9] The narrator can thus be assumed to be enjoying a comfortable afternoon in a leisured, male environment. His mindset as he surveys the scene both inside and out, is yet not one of simple idle curiosity, but rather of a heightened alertness and keen attention to surrounding life. 'I felt a calm but inquisitive interest in every thing', he comments:

> With a cigar in my mouth and a newspaper in my lap, I had been amusing myself for the greater part of the afternoon, now in poring over advertisements, now in observing the promiscuous company in the room, and now in peering through the smoky panes into the street.[10]

The coffeehouse is located on 'one of the principal thoroughfares of the city', and as it is now dusk, the time of day when the city is at its busiest, the narrator's attention is soon entirely turned towards 'the tumultuous sea of human heads' that hurry past.[11] At first, he admits, his observation 'took an abstract and generalizing turn', but he quickly becomes absorbed in a more detailed study of the passers-by, 'regard[ing] with minute interest the innumerable varieties of figure, dress, air, gait, visage, and expression of countenance'.[12] Through a process of astute observation and popular physiology, he demonstrates a remarkable ability to deduce the differing social groups and class levels of metropolitan life, remarking the 'noblemen', merchants and lawyers, the 'tribe of clerks', gamblers, pick-pockets, street pedlars, beggars, seamstresses, 'women of the town', drunkards and more, in a Boz-like taxonomy of early nineteenth-century London.

Yet despite the narrator's extraordinary powers of observation, the city ultimately refuses his pretension to an encyclopaedic knowledge of the urban crowd, as suggested by the German saying with which the story opens: *'er lasst sich nicht lessen'* [it does not permit itself to be read]. For as the evening continues, there comes an old man whose strange appearance and fiendish expression even the narrator's analytic observational skills fail to place. The man is thin and his clothes 'filthy and ragged', although of good cut and texture. Through a tear in his cloak, the narrator catches sight of a diamond and a dagger. Filled with an obsessive curiosity by this enigmatic figure, the narrator follows the old man as he weaves through the city streets, noting the way in which his movements become hesitant and increasingly frantic and erratic in relatively quiet or deserted areas, but steadier and more purposeful once immersed again within large groups of people. Together they move through the streets, the narrator compulsively stalking his eccentric prey through the fog of the London night, until they come face to face at daybreak outside the coffeeshop where the narrator's increasingly wild chase had begun hours before. It is only now that the narrator is able to apply a category to this man, one defined by his very elusiveness, and the implicit threat of his ability to confound surveillance. 'The old man is the type and the genius of deep crime', the narrator declares: 'He refuses to be alone. He is the man of the crowd.'[13]

The paradox of being at once separate from, and one with, the rhythms of the city, encapsulated in 'The Man of the Crowd', continues as a central principle in the work of the French poet and art critic Charles Baudelaire. Baudelaire was profoundly influenced by Poe, undertaking a comprehensive translation of his writings between 1852 and 1865, and drew upon 'The Man of the Crowd' when writing his influential essay 'The Painter of Modern Life', published in *Le Figaro* in 1863. In this, Baudelaire called for an art of modernity based on the subject matter of contemporary urban life. Central to the essay is a portrait of the ideal modern artist/writer as an observer of urban life, a *flâneur* whose 'genius is curiosity'.[14] Inspired by the relatively unknown illustrator Constantin Guys, Baudelaire compares him to the figure of the narrator in Poe's story. Baudelaire describes his artist–*flâneur* as someone who 'enters into the crowd as though it were an immense reservoir of electrical energy', and a 'kaleidoscope gifted with consciousness, responding to each one of its movements'.[15]

If Baudelaire here associates the modern artist's fascinated perception of urban life with the keen appreciation of Poe's convalescent narrator, he also seems to identify his desire for mingling with the multitude with that of the mysterious 'man of the crowd'. Indeed Baudelaire's apparent collapsing of the principal characters in Poe's story highlights their implicit identity as strange doubles of each other: the old man addicted to being within the crowd, and the narrator, feverishly exhilarated by the stimuli of the world around him and himself soon plunging into the busy streets. For far from seeking to remain separate from the crowd, Baudelaire's modern artist desires to lose himself within it, to plunge into the randomness and variety of urban life. 'The crowd is his element', he writes. Baudelaire's urban artist is not a detached observer, objectively and authoritatively categorizing the scene around him with a dispassionate eye. Rather, 'His passion and his profession are to become one flesh with the crowd. For the perfect *flâneur*, for the passionate spectator, it is an immense joy to set up house in the heart of the multitude, amid the ebb and flow of movement, in the midst of the fugitive and the infinite.'[16] What Baudelaire articulates in his account of the modern artist who at once desires to be surrounded by the crowd and 'rejoices in his 'incognito', his ability 'to see the world, to be at the centre of the world, and yet to remain hidden from the world', is that it is exactly when one is amidst the crowd that one experiences a truly subjective solitude.[17] Baudelaire's artist–*flâneur*, in his fascination with the transience and contingency of modernity adds a new dimension to the urban observer, one predicated on aesthetic impressions rather than social phenomena.

The *flâneuse*

I want to turn now to examine two 'rewritings' of these twin aspects of the urban observer or *flâneur* – his position of detached, rationalizing authority over the urban scene on the one hand, and his concentration on the sensory and impressionistic aspects of the city on the other – by women writers in the twentieth century. The first is an amusing example of such conscious reshaping by Baroness Orczy in her 'Old Man in the Corner' detective stories, which appeared between 1901 and 1904 in *The Royal Magazine*. Here the all-male coffeehouse of Poe's 'The Man of the Crowd' is substituted by an ABC teashop, one of two chains of self-service eating places pioneered by the Aerated Bread Company and Lyons and Co., and in the 1890s a prominent feature of the central London landscape, serving a varied clientele from lower middle-class workers to wealthier shoppers and tourists. Orczy's teashop is located on the Strand and frequented by a young 'Lady Journalist', finally named in the collected edition as 'Miss Polly Burton'. Introduced in the opening tale, 'The Fenchurch Street Mystery', Polly is a financially independent 'New Woman', who likes to take her lunch while reading the daily newspaper and watching the people who pass on the street:

> Now this particular corner, this very same table, that special view of the magnificent marble hall – known as the Norfolk Street branch of the Aërated Bread Company's depôts – were Polly's own corner, table, and view. Here she had partaken of eleven pennyworth of luncheon and one pennyworth of daily information ever since that glorious never-to-be-forgotten day when she was enrolled on the staff of the Evening Observer (we'll call it that, if you please), and became a member of that illustrious and world-famed organization known as the British Press.[18]

Like the narrator of Poe's 'Man of the Crowd', she is interrupted from her reading of the *Daily Telegraph* (where she is engrossed in the latest crime reports) by a thin, strangely dressed, fidgety old man who visits the teashop for milk and cheesecake, and proceeds to regale her with the solution to a famous unsolved crime, before disappearing suddenly into the street, only to return the next day to unravel another mystery. Alternating between arrogant sarcasm at Polly's obtuseness, and fevered excitement at his own supreme powers of deduction, all the time he compulsively knots and unknots a piece of string. At once irritated and fascinated by this mysterious stranger, Polly finds herself drawn back again and again to the restaurant, an eager student of his process of shrewd observation and deductive reasoning. Unlike Poe's hyper-observant narrator, however, for all her fascination with crime stories, Polly has not herself developed her powers of immediate observation – as the old man explains to his protégée when she fails to recall the appearance of a man who had been sitting next to her earlier in the day:

> you are a journalist – call yourself one, at least – and it should be part of your business to notice and describe people ... the average Englishman, say, of the middle classes, who is neither very tall nor very short, who wears a moustache which is neither fair nor dark, but which masks his mouth, and a top hat which hides the shape of his head and brow, a man, in fact, who dresses like hundreds of his fellow-creatures, moves like them, speaks like them, has no peculiarity.[19]

Polly, however, is a quick student, and it does not take her long to realize that the criminal in the final case of the collection, whom he excitedly describes as 'one of the most ingenious men of the age' and whose defining feature is that he leaves behind him a piece of string tied with knots, is in fact the old man himself. Orczy's man in the corner is a knowing recreation of Poe's 'man of the crowd', 'the type and the genius of deep crime'.[20] For Poe's leisured male protagonist and quasi-detective, however, she substitutes a perceptive young female journalist.

By contrast, perhaps one of the most extended articulations of the figure of the *flâneuse* in the tradition of the impressionistic urban observer of Baudelaire is to be found in Dorothy Richardson's thirteen-volume novel *Pilgrimage* (1915–1967), a semi-fictionalized autobiographical account of her own life in London two decades before; first during a brief period in 1892 as a teacher at a small school in the newly built northern suburb of Finsbury Park, and then from 1896 as a dental secretary, living in a boarding-house in Bloomsbury.[21] Walking in London was a necessity for Richardson, both to and from work during the day, but also a more leisured roaming of the city at night. 'Soon after sunset a message would reach even the most stifling attic', she later recalled, 'brought by the evening air stealing in at its open window', and she would swap the solitude of her small room for the companionship of the Bloomsbury squares, where 'giant trees mingled their breath with mine, their being with my own'.[22] The impoverished yet entrancing London years form the landscape of the middle volumes of *Pilgrimage*, odes to the city written in continuous interior monologue, in which the bond between the semi-autobiographical protagonist Miriam Henderson and the city streets persists beyond the otherwise brief acquaintances or transient friendships of her urban life.[23]

I want to explore two lengthy journeys that Miriam makes through the city, the first on the top of an omnibus following her interview for the teaching post in Banbury Park (Richardson's fictionalized version of Finsbury Park), a journey which takes her from north London, down the length of Seven Sisters Road and Camden Road until she eventually reaches Euston Road, Regent Street, and Piccadilly, where the bus then turns along Hyde Park towards her family home in Putney; and the second a circuitous walk that she takes late at night through Bond Street, Piccadilly Circus, and Shaftesbury Avenue to Bloomsbury. Both scenes, the first over ten pages in length, the second near to fifty, present Miriam as a hypersensitive impressionistic observer of the London landscape, extraordinarily attuned to the subjective effects of different streets and areas. While the younger Miriam responds most directly to the social scene surrounding her, however, the later walk demonstrates an aesthetic perspective alive to the magic and poetry of the city.

The omnibus journey takes place in the second book of *Pilgrimage*, *Backwater* (1916), when Miriam is only eighteen. Finsbury Park was a new suburb in the early 1890s, and the terminus of the tram line. 'They would soon be down at the corner of Banbury Park where the tram lines ended and the Favourite omnibuses were standing in the muddy road under the shadow of the railway bridge', Richardson writes, as Miriam and her mother make their way to the bus depot for their journey home, and Miriam climbs eagerly to the front seat on the top, exclaiming: '"This is the only place on the top of a bus".'[24] Her excitement is soon muted by the monotony of the north London landscape:

> They lumbered at last round a corner and out into a wide thoroughfare, drawing up outside a newly-built public-house. Above it rose row upon row of upper windows sunk in masses of ornamental terra-cotta-coloured plaster. Branch roads, laid with tram-lines led off in every direction. Miriam's eyes followed a dull blue tram with a grubby white-painted seatless roof jingling busily off up a roadway where short trees stood all the way along in the small dim gardens of little grey houses.
> ... The little shock sent her mind feeling out along the road they had just left. She considered its unbroken length, its shops, its treelessness. The wide thoroughfare, up which they now began to rumble, repeated it on a larger scale. The pavements were wide causeways reached from the roadway by stone steps, three deep. The people passing along them were unlike any she knew. There were no ladies, no gentleman, no girls or young men such as she knew. They were all alike. They were ... She could find no word for the strange impression they made. It coloured the whole of the district through which they had come.[25]

The teenage Miriam, aware of her family's increasingly precarious financial situation yet still shaped in attitude by her upper-middle-class upbringing, sits in silence, repulsed by the ugliness and uniformity of the scene, but also its implication of domestic entrapment:

> This new secret was shabby, ugly and shabby. The half-perceived something persisted unchanged when the causeways and shops disappeared and long rows of houses streamed by, their close ranks broken only by an occasional cross-road. They were large, high, flat-fronted houses with flights of grey stone steps leading to their porchless doors. They had tiny railed-in front gardens crowded with shrubs. Here and there long narrow strips of garden pushed a row of houses back from the roadway. In these longer plots stood signboards and show-cases. 'Photographic Studio,' 'Commercial College,' 'Eye Treatment,' 'Academy of Dancing.' ... She read the announcements with growing disquietude.[26]

Finally they reach the intersection with Euston Road that Richardson would always identify as the boundary between London proper and the quiet horror of the suburbs, and the atmosphere of dull oppression lifts, the omnibus now moving through wide streets and past balconied houses. Immediately the preoccupation with the social scene subsides, and Miriam's perceptions focus on the impressionistic beauty of the city light: 'The side-streets were feathered with trees and ended mistily ... At the end of the vista the air was like pure saffron-tinted mother-of-pearl. Miriam sat back and drew a deep breath.'[27] Like a true *flâneur* she is invigorated once she is within the bustling, public world of Regent Street and Piccadilly, and excitedly describes the view to her mother in terms that reveal her easy assumption of the role of urban consumer: 'You'll see our A B C soon. You know. The one we come to after the Saturday pops ... It's just round here in Piccadilly. Here it is. Glorious ... We go along the Burlington Arcade too ... It's simply perfect. Glove shops and fans and a smell of the most exquisite scent everywhere.'[28]

By the time of the second scene, from the seventh *Pilgrimage* book, *Revolving Lights* (1923), Miriam has been working and living permanently in London for several years. Leaving a Fabian Society meeting late at night, she welcomes the London pavements that 'offered themselves freely; the unfailing magic that would give its life to the swing of her long walk home'.[29] Absorbed in her own musings she takes a winding route back to Bloomsbury, a *flâneuse* strolling through the relatively silent city streets, enjoying what she describes as a 'plebian dilettantism'.[30] Of course the *flâneur*'s vision is an essentially moving one, and as she walks the streets and buildings around her ebb and flow, her mind, as Baudelaire had described that of the artist–*flâneur* a 'kaleidoscope gifted with consciousness': 'solid lines and arches of pure grey shaping the flow of the pageant, and emerging, then it ebbed away, to stand in their own beauty, conjuring back the vivid tumult to flow in silence, a continuous ghostly garland of moving shapes and colours'.[31] Highly sensitive to the effect of different streets and places on her perceptions and psyche, she instinctively eschews the more populated and brash modern thoroughfare of Oxford Street for the relative quiet of its surrounding streets:

> Oxford Street opened ahead, right and left, a wide empty yellow-lit corridor of large shuttered shop-fronts. It stared indifferently at her outlined fate ... Oxford Street, unless she were sailing through it perched in sunlight on the top of an omnibus lumbering steadily towards the graven stone of the City, always wrought destruction ... Stay here, suggested Bond Street.[32]

Miriam is no 'woman of the crowd', eager to lose herself within its mass, and remains socially detached and fiercely protective of her independence throughout the *Pilgrimage* novels, embracing the solitude that Georg Simmel identified as so characteristic of metropolitan life:

> her untouched self here, free, unseen, and strong, the strong world of London all round her, strong free untouched people, in a dark lit wilderness, happy and miserable in their own way, going about the streets looking at nothing, thinking about no special person or thing, as long as they were there, being in London.[33]

Miriam's kaleidoscopic consciousness may resemble that of the *flâneur*, but Richardson overtly reverses the feminization and objectification of the city that characterized the figure of the leisured male urban observer. For Miriam the *flâneuse*, London becomes a 'mighty lover', but her bond with the city is at once all-consuming and enabling, 'engulfing and leaving her untouched, liberated and expanding to the whole range of her being ... herself one with it, feeling her life flow outwards, north, south, east, west, to all its margins'.[34] As she approaches Piccadilly, however, and becomes aware of prostitutes in the shadows and men loitering, even Miriam loses her sense of security in the streets, feeling 'the need for thoughtless hurrying across its open spaces'. Piccadilly at midnight remained out of bounds to the respectable young unmarried woman throughout the 1890s and 1900s. Yet Richardson challenges the conventional gendered dynamics of the urban landscape. Miriam's path is blocked – 'There was a solitary man's figure standing near the kerb, mid-way on her route across the island to take to the roadway opposite Shaftesbury Avenue; standing arrested; there was no traffic to prevent his crossing; a watchful habitué' – and she realizes in a sudden flash of recognition that the man is a former suitor from her earlier life, shocked at finding her in such a locale at night and already thinking how he will tell of the encounter to his wife, '"Oui, ma chère, little Mirry *Henderson*, strolling, at midnight, across Piccadilly Circus."' *Flâneur* and *flâneuse* meet briefly in the centre of the island and then 'She rushed on, passing him with a swift salute, saw him raise his hat with mechanical promptitude as she stepped from the kerb and forward, pausing an instant for a passing hansom, in the direction home. It was done ... They had met equally at last.'[35]

Notes

I would like to thank Ysanne Holt and the Tate Gallery for kind permission to rework some material from my essay on the urban observer for its 'Camden Town Online Research Project'.

1. Walter Benjamin, *Charles Baudelaire: A Lyric Poet in the Era of High Capitalism*, trans. Harry Zohn (London: Verso, 1983 and 1999).
2. Raymond Williams, for example, writes in his classic study *The Country and the City* (1973) that from the eighteenth century onwards the representation of the modern city has been associated with an archetypal urban observer: 'a man walking, as if alone, in its streets', *The Country and the City* (London: Chatto and Windus, 1973), p. 233.
3. Janet Woolf, 'The Invisible Flâneuse: Women and the Literature of Modernity', *Theory, Culture and Society*, 2.3 (1985): 45. The nineteenth century witnessed the development of a new metropolitan imagination, concerned with observing and reading the city. Writers such as Charles Lamb, William Wordsworth, Charles Dickens, Edgar Allan Poe, and Charles Baudelaire, created a new mode of urban writing, 'a way of seeing men and women that belongs to the street', written from the perspective of a detached observer wandering amidst the urban crowd (Williams, *The Country and The City*, p. 155) With a penchant for abandoning himself to the bustle and variety of the urban crowd, and never happier than with the façades of buildings as his walls and the sky as his ceiling, this idling urban observer, or *flâneur*, found his ideal habitat in the busy thoroughfares, shopping arcades and coffeeshops of the burgeoning metropolis.
4. Griselda Pollock, 'Modernity and the Spaces of Femininity', in *Vision and Difference: Femininity, Feminism and the Histories of Art* (London: Routledge, 1988), p. 71.
5. Ibid.
6. Charlotte Brontë, *Villette* (London: Vintage), p. 59. See on the *flâneuse*, Rachel Bowlby, *Just Looking: Consumer Culture in Dreiser, Gissing and Zola* (London: Methuen, 1985) and 'Walking, Women and Writing', in *Still Crazy After All These Years: Women, Writing and Psychoanalysis* (London: Routledge, 1992); Anne Freidberg, *Window Shopping: Cinema and the Postmodern* (Berkeley: University of California Press, 1993); and Deborah L. Parsons, *Streetwalking the Metropolis* (Oxford: Oxford University Press, 2000).
7. Dorothy Richardson, *Pilgrimage*, ed. Gillian Hanscombe, 4 vols (London: Virago 1979), II, p. 391.
8. Jean Rhys, *Good Morning, Midnight* (London: Deutsch, 1967), p. 40.
9. Peter Cunningham, *Handbook to London* (London: Bradbury and Evans, 1850), p. xxiv.
10. Edgar Allan Poe, 'The Man of the Crowd', in *Tales of Mystery and Imagination*, (Hertfordshire: Wordsworth, 1993), p. 255.
11. Ibid.
12. Ibid., p. 256.
13. Ibid., p. 262.
14. Charles Baudelaire, 'The Painter of Modern Life', reproduced in *Art in Theory, 1815–1900*, ed. Charles Harrison, Paul Wood, and Jason Gaiger (Oxford: Blackwell 1998), p. 495.

15. Ibid., pp. 496–7.
16. Ibid., p. 496.
17. Ibid.
18. Baroness Orczy, *The Old Man in the Corner*, 1908, online edn (2008): http://www.bibliobazaar.com/, p. 11.
19. Ibid., p. 73.
20. Poe, 'The Man of the Crowd', p. 262.
21. The first eleven books of *Pilgrimage* were published separately: *Pointed Roofs* (1915), *Backwater* (1916), *Honeycomb* (1917), *The Tunnel* (February 1919), *Interim* (December 1919; also serialized in the *Little Review*, June 1919–May 1920), *Deadlock* (1921), *Revolving Lights* (1923), *The Trap* (1925), *Oberland* (1927), *Dawn's Left Hand* (1931), *Clear Horizon* (1935). The twelfth, *Dimple Hill*, was added to the four-volume collected edition *Pilgrimage* (London: Dent and New York: Knopf, 1938). A thirteenth, *March Moonlight*, which Richardson had been working on up to her death, appeared in the revised edition published by Dent in 1967.
22. Dorothy Richardson, 'Yeats of Bloomsbury', *Life and Letters Today* (April 1939): 61.
23. See Dorothy Richardson, *Pilgrimage*, ed. Hanscombe, I, *Pointed Roofs, Backwater, Honeycomb*; II, *The Tunnel, Interim*; III, *Deadlock, The Revolving Lights, The Trap*; IV, *Oberland, Dawn's Left Hand, Clear Horizon, Dimple Hill, March Moonlight*. See *The Tunnel, Interim, Deadlock*, and *Revolving Lights* in II and IV.
24. Ibid., I, *Backwater*, p. 192.
25. Ibid., I, *Backwater*, pp. 194–5.
26. Ibid., I, *Backwater*, p. 196.
27. Ibid., I, *Backwater*, pp. 196–7.
28. Ibid., I, *Backwater*, p. 199.
29. Ibid., III, *Revolving Lights*, p. 236.
30. Ibid., III, *Revolving Lights*, p. 245.
31. Ibid., III, *Revolving Lights*, p. 240.
32. Ibid., III, *Revolving Lights*, p. 246.
33. Ibid., II, *The Tunnel*, p. 76.
34. Ibid., III, *Revolving Lights*, pp. 272–3.
35. Ibid., III, *Revolving Lights*, p. 277.

16
Myths of Passage: *Paris* and *Parallax*
Tory Young

Given the kind of thinking, as well as some of the specific themes, that have entered into, if not transformed, the study of Modernism in recent years, it is difficult to understand why Hope Mirrlees's ambitious 450-line modernist poem *Paris* (1920), which Julia Briggs has termed 'modernism's lost masterpiece',[1] and Nancy Cunard's *Parallax* (1925),[2] which remains virtually unknown, have not been at the centre of the discussion. Hope Mirrlees (1887–1978) wrote only occasional poetry after *Paris* but is more widely known as a novelist, especially for her fantasy *Lud-in-the-Mist* (1926), which is felt to have 'influenced genre fantasy since its republication in the late 1960s'.[3] Whilst studying classics at Newnham College, Cambridge, she developed a close relationship with Jane Harrison, whose own fame has resulted in Mirrlees's achievements being somewhat eclipsed in favour of speculation about the nature of their relationship. Mirrlees's friendship with and influence on her sometime lodger T.S. Eliot is also rarely considered although Julia Briggs has now pointed out good reasons for doing so.

Nancy Cunard (1896–1965) also wrote only one long poem, devoting her life after the 1920s to radical politics and campaigns for racial equality. Her early poems were published in Edith Sitwell's anthology *Wheels* (1916) and in two collections, *Outlaws* (1921) and *Sublunary* (1923). In 1928 she established the Hours Press, publishing key modernists such as Samuel Beckett (his first publication) and Laura Riding; she was also, like Mirrlees, a gifted linguist and translated the poems of Pablo Neruda, among others. Born into the Cunard shipping dynasty, she has been regarded as a glamorous dilettante other than in feminist discussion of her work. Although references to her poetry have been made in surveys by, for example, Janet Montefiore and John Lucas, sustained consideration is only beginning.[4] Susan Stanford Friedman's 1990 account of twentieth-century 'long poems' by women lists Gertrude Stein, Mina Loy, and H.D. as 'the first modern writers in English' to write 'big-long-important poems exploring vast, cosmic questions of history, metaphysics, religion, and aesthetics',[5] and whilst *Paris* and *Parallax* might challenge this account, such feminist recognition of poems by women in genres from which they have been excluded has clearly led to further discoveries and excavations. Both texts are concerned with journeys and gender-related consciousness of urban space; but before returning to consideration of these two important poems in more detail, I shall outline some recent developments within modernist scholarship.

As interest in urban experience in general has increased, so a broad notion of the metropolitan has displaced the particularity of Paris within modernist debate. Similarly, interest in *flânerie*, more generally including discussion of the *flâneuse*, has expanded the figure of the *flâneur*, as theories of geography and space have become ascendant in twenty-first-century approaches to the early twentieth century. It was Walter Benjamin who popularized Baudelaire's *flâneur* and expanded its categories, in his unfinished *Arcades Project*,[6] for the description of consumerism and the increasing commodification of city life. The transition from consumed (prostitute) to consumer (in the department store) is one version of the story of female urban experience in the mid-nineteenth- to early twentieth-century city, and commentators have therefore focused on the invention of the modern department store as a feminized space. But attention has also been focused on representations that depict the misery of those women who worked in the department stores, in novels such as Emile Zola's *The Ladies' Paradise* [*Au Bonheur Des Dames*] (1883) and Jean Rhys's *Good Morning, Midnight* (1939).

Whatever emancipatory promise might have been offered by the department store, the literature of the period also shows how easy it is for a woman to be consumed by both man and capitalism; Rhys's wretched wanderers are trapped in a dismal cycle of yearning for the clothes and hairdressing that will enable them to attract the men who will pay for their clothes and hairdressing. For the Rhys protagonist there is no 'progression' in commodification, and no emancipation in the 'freedom' to walk the streets. But recent criticism, and readings of poems such as *Paris* and *Parallax*, offer radical new insights into the sexual politics of the city, and a reciprocal process whereby representations of women in the city expose the sexual politics of existing critical constructions and conceptual resources.

In the first place, then, it is important to outline the general pressure that feminist critics have applied to the *flâneur* as an obviously gendered concept, as well as some of the more nuanced directions that their critique has taken. Baudelaire's *flâneur* was free to survey and define the city; he could walk the streets without drawing attention to himself in a way that a woman could not. He was 'only at home existentially when he [was] not at home physically' but, crucially, he had a home to return to, unlike the dispossessed street dweller, the 'rag-picker'.[7] Deborah Parsons's study, *Streetwalking the Metropolis* (2000), warns that, however appealing we may find the account of a passage from *flâneur* to *flâneuse* as the tale of women escaping from the domestic private space to the public sphere, we cannot simply establish the *flâneuse* as a new, equally reductive and restrictive scheme.[8] Her examination foregrounds the ambiguities of the *flâneur* suggesting that 'it is the Baudelaire-inspired surrealist rag-picker rather than the autocratic Le Corbusian *flâneur* who would seem to share certain aspects of women's experiences of urban space'.[9] Parsons concentrates on the women writers, mainly of fiction, 'who translate the experience of urban space into their narrative form'.[10] There is a sense in which this kind of argument is emblematic of a significant transition away from early constructions of modernist fiction, accounts that emphasized the special demands of new artistic projects aiming to convey the texture of interiority, and which focused critical attention on narratives of ennui and despair. Such accounts, which understood modernist experiment as being all about the mind, without heed to the historical circumstances of fictional settings, were slowly and systematically replaced by cultural materialist accounts in the later decades of the twentieth century, which enable a more gently positive story to be told.

In 'Voyages by Teashop', an account of the spread of the ABC and Lyons tearooms in London, as well as their appearance in literature of the modernist period, Scott McCracken shows how the Lyons company itself participated in the narrative of consumerism as emancipation: '[h]itherto there had been nowhere "respectable" for Mama and the children to have a cup of tea or a midday meal'.[11] McCracken writes of Dorothy Richardson's Miriam, another prominent exponent of modernist female *flânerie*, that for her 'the networks of ABC and Lyons teashops are enabling rather than part of a nightmare, but part of her liberation is the ability to operate in a non-realist mode that the chain facilitates'.[12] Daydreaming of the future, remembering the past: the streets allow a non-linear passage, which, in the literature of *flânerie* undermines the narrative of the journey as progress. Meanwhile, the liberty of women of all classes and ages to take public transport is also explored in the novels of the late nineteenth and early twentieth centuries, and has been discussed in recent modernist studies with a materialist perspective. The growth of modes of transport during the modernist period leads Andrew Thacker to use the term '*voyageur*' rather than *flâneur* in his study of space and place, *Moving through Modernity*, even though these travellers may not exceed the city's limits.[13] It is clear to see, in these new critical tendencies, that a certain reciprocity is at work between the metaphorical resonances of the journey, or passage, and the very material circumstances in which such journeys are made possible and in which they take place.

In the narrative trope of the journey, a geographical or physical voyage is always a metaphor for a character's psychic development or change of some kind. *Flânerie* potently undermines this idea: the *flâneur* is aimless and unmotivated; he goes where he pleases, on a whim. He is questless. Not only is he strolling, wandering, without direction, but the miniaturization of his domain mocks his wealthy predecessor whose satisfaction and entertainment could be met only by a Grand Tour of countries and continents. For the nineteenth-century *flâneur* the empire and its commodities have been brought to the city. By the twentieth century, advertisements for coffee, chocolate, and tobacco pasted throughout the urban landscape are stereopticon views of the unvisited world beyond. The *flâneur* need not endure the discomfort of a voyage, for his own bed is only a short walk away. It is hard to pin a grandiose tale of spiritual development onto the perambulations of a louche sybarite, and the poems of Baudelaire both celebrate hedonism and depravity and mourn its sicknesses, whilst high modernist texts that explicitly engage with the journey trope such as *Pilgrimage* (1915–1935), *Ulysses* (1922), or *Mrs Dalloway* (1925) determinedly undercut it by placing the journey in a circadian framework of the quotidian and of *flânerie*. The mock epic is one of high Modernism's genres: parodying the journey and the telling of it. And this was often undertaken with more humour than is sometimes acknowledged.

Tourism, perhaps itself regarded as an imitation of travel, seems always to have been open to ridicule. In Elizabeth Bowen's *To the North* (1932), a novel that richly employs the lexicon of travel and transport as metaphors to depict the uncertainties of the interwar period and the women living in it, Emmeline Summers runs a travel agency whose slogan 'Move Dangerously' is designed to appeal to clients who feel that all of 'life, even travel, is losing its element of uncertainty' and aims to 'supply that' even at the expense of enjoyment.[14] The irony of this enterprise, as her interlocutor points out, is that the clients are forewarned with so much 'civic intelligence' about where to go and what to avoid that they are 'always only too safe'.[15] Emmeline assures him that the safety is only physical, suggesting a mental dislocation that is the desirable corollary of travel (and what is missing from tourism, leading 'travellers' to disdain it). In the novel, means of transport connote character traits: Emmeline's own agency is indicated not only by the fact that she runs a travel agency but that she drives a car. But the novel ends in tragedy when she is impelled by '[a]n immense idea of departure' to drive herself and her companion, Markie, against his will to a violent death by car crash.[16] She starts the novel as a modern apparently emancipated woman with her own business, accurately reading the zeitgeist, but her impulse to suicide renders her instead as a tragically vulnerable figure (and, with hindsight, a symbol of interwar society). Although the title of Michael Arlen's bestseller *The Green Hat* (1925) metonymically refers to its protagonist, Iris Storm (based on Nancy Cunard), within it, her modernity and erotic power are loudly proclaimed through her casual ownership of a yellow Hispano-Suiza; '[l]ike a huge yellow insect that had dropped to earth from a butterfly civilisation ... gallant and suave'.[17] Iris is punished for her promiscuity and the lack of patriotism that it is seen to signify, again by driving herself to death, crashing her car into a tree at the close of the novel. These irresistible impulses to crash, interpretable through Freud, express a futurist ideal but one with a depressing resilience for the feminist reader; the motif retains

Myths of Passage: Paris and Parallax 279

currency throughout the century when Thelma and Louise, the celebrated heroines of the 1991 eponymous film, make a short-lived, exhilarating bid to escape from sexual violence and subjugation but speed to death of their own volition.

Whilst F.T. Marinetti's crash left him in a symbolic, muddy, '[m]aternal ditch',[18] according to his treatise on the founding of Futurism, for fictional women in the modernist period, motorized vehicles and the speed they make possible appear as metaphors of forbidden emancipation, of threatening sexuality, and financial independence. Bowen and Virginia Woolf gently mock this in their depiction of adolescents who are technically 'voyageurs' but whose voyaging displays characteristics of *flânerie*; with not yet the agency of adulthood, they must travel by 'omnibus'. In *Mrs Dalloway* (1925) Clarissa Dalloway's daughter Elizabeth has been told by her friend and mentor, Miss Kilman, that 'every profession is open to the women of your generation' but '[s]he inclined to be passive'.[19] She mulls over the choices available to her whilst travelling on the 'omnibus', and the atmosphere of the streets down which she voyages, and the speed with which the vehicle enables her to travel, dictate her feelings about her future career: 'thoughts of ships, of business, of law, of administration, and with it all so stately (she was in the Temple), gay (there was the river), pious (there was the Church), made her quite determined, whatever her mother might say, to become either a farmer or a doctor'.[20] But it turns out that the determination for a career is entirely forged by the speed of the bus, 'rushing insolently up Whitehall', and the viewpoint it affords her of the city; off the bus and back on her feet, her passivity returns and she elects not to tell anyone about her ambitions, finding them instead 'silly', the kind of thing you think when alone in a crowd. The crowds are more stimulating 'than any of the books that Miss Kilman had lent her'.[21] Despite the presence of the bus as automated transport, Elizabeth demonstrates classic *flânerie* here: the city is a text that is read by the dilettante whose intentions are fleeting and unfocused; unlike Baudelaire's *flâneur*, the young woman only reads and elects not to write the city; she rejects the agency offered.

In *To the North* (1932) young women are also reliant on the 'civic intelligence' of guardians about London. Orphaned Pauline, bored and lonely in her uncle's flat, persuades his housekeeper to let her go out into the city, but its landscape is to be viewed as an education from the safe distance of the bus whilst its potential dangers are drolly negotiated through careful choice of route:

> The No. 11 is an entirely moral bus. Springing from Shepherd's Bush, against which one has seldom heard anything, it enjoys some innocent bohemianism in Chelsea, picks up shoppers at Peter Jones, swerves down the Pimlico Road – too busy to be lascivious – passes not too far from the royal stables, nods to Victoria Station, Westminster Abbey, the Houses of

Parliament, whirrs reverently up Whitehall, and from its only brush with vice, in the Strand, plunges to Liverpool Street through the noble and serious architecture of the City. Except for the Strand, the No. 11 route, Mrs Patrick considered, had the quality of Sunday afternoon literature; from it Pauline could derive nothing but edification.[22]

Here the bus is seen to reinforce the passivity that Elizabeth found as a pedestrian in *Mrs Dalloway*. Both Elizabeth and Pauline take the bus as entertainment; they don't need to go anywhere but only to pass time. Their youthful status and gender prevents them from experiencing true *flânerie*, from wandering the streets, from succumbing to the allure of the speeding car, and from the personal development offered by an extended journey, but the bus, a guided tour, offers some of its qualities. The idea of a public transport that allows the possibility of oneiric urban pleasures, of 'sensory impressions' and inspiration to wander and to wonder, refutes the notion of public transport as put to the service of work, rather than leisure, envisaged most famously by Le Corbusier, for whom trains above and below ground are only a means of transporting the individual from home on the outskirts to work in the city centre.[23]

In the rest of this chapter, I wish to consider how voyaging in two long modernist poems by women also disrupts simplified, polarized readings of women as flower-buyers and teashop-visitors or as promiscuous and punished speed addicts. So far, through reference to the journey and the *flâneur's* wanderings as theme and metaphor rather than textual structuring device I have thought about 'gender-related city consciousness' as being 'concerned with the comparative experience of the male and female subject *in* the city', but now seek to reiterate Parsons's position that gender-related city consciousness should be concerned instead with 'their relative formulations *of* the city' and even beyond.[24]

Paris and *Parallax* were both published by the Hogarth Press and typeset by Woolf. Both poems, unvalued on publication but recently brought to light by feminist scholars, benefit from the long perspective of being read in the twenty-first century. The title of Cunard's poem, possibly given by Woolf,[25] and its epigram by Sir Thomas Browne alert us from the very start to its performativity; '[m]any things are known as some are seen, that is by Paralaxis, or at some distance from their true and proper being'.[26] Whilst *Parallax* knew and depended upon its relationship to T.S. Eliot's celebrated poetry, *Paris* knew of the Prufrock poems, the typographical experimentation of Jean Cocteau and Guillaume Apollinaire but not *The Waste Land*, which it preceded. But we do.[27] Like parallax itself, perception depends on where the reader stands. It is my intention here to recognize and present the performative address to the canon within the poems' typographical and thematic journeys. These poems review monumental texts as well as monumental cities, and through the freedoms afforded by poetic language present hybrid voices that can transcend the 'experience of the male and female subject *in* the city'.[28]

Each poem offers up an unusual word upon which its meaning is dependent; for *Parallax*, this is the title, an astronomical term denoting the 'change in the apparent position or direction of an object as seen from two different points', which seems suggestively to offer an idea of its own perspective, as I shall discuss, although this seems to have been completely ignored or unseen by its first readers.[29] For *Paris* the word 'holophrase', taken from philology and meaning 'a single word used instead of a phrase, or to express a combination of ideas', which begins the poem, seems to ask how a grouping of words (Eliot's 'objective correlative'?) can portray or define Paris.[30] Both are suggestive of the dialectic that characterizes the ambitions of modernist literature aspiring at once to a new realism and to a non-naturalism, between dream and nightmare, interiority and the empirical object. Parallax and holophrase stand in defiance of the idea of a journey as progress; both words indicate a kind of Saussurean understanding that a word's meaning is not absolute but relative. For parallax a journey from A to B results in a new perspective of A, whilst the holophrase of *Paris* demonstrates that a *flâneur*'s route through the city, a journey, is needed to portray an entity that is conjured and known by one word alone, the city of Paris. The journey is indeed spatial, but the linear progression from innocence to experience, ignorance to knowledge, is circular, endless, inchoate, multiple.

Mirrlees's *Paris*, written in 1919, is historically specific, set at the time of President Wilson's arrival in the city to cement the Treaty of Versailles and create the League of Nations. Celebrated and assiduously annotated by Julia Briggs, *Paris* was refused status as a poem by its first reviewer in the *Times Literary Supplement*; '[t]his little effusion ... does not belong to the art of poetry'.[31] But although this is an uncomprehending dismissal,[32] the reviewer was struck by the qualities of *flânerie* within the text: '[i]t seems meant by a sort of futurist trick to give an ensemble of the sensations offered to a pilgrim through Paris'.[33] What is the 'futurist trick'? The poem is composed of a series of fragments, juxtapositions of upper and lower case, italics, centred and justified phrases, but sequence is suggested by the repeated pronouncements of a first-person voice or narrator whose journey is revealed through expressions of speed, 'I must go slowly'; sight, 'I see the Arc de Triomphe'; and opinion, 'I hate the Etoile / The Bois bores me' that note the changing location in the city.[34]

The text is circadian; time passes from day through night to the next day's dawn. From start to finish the pilgrim is a devotee of Paris, honouring and saluting the metropolis, its art, writers, history, migrants, and nightlife. (Not then futurist in theme; a resurrection of the paintings from the Louvre rather than the destruction of museums urged by Marinetti.) The pilgrim who worships the city is like a *flâneur*: s/he may be purposeful but travelling on foot allows time for reflection. Towards the poem's end, '[t]he Seven

Stages of the Cross' suggests that the meditations may be slow admiration of the city ('cut in box' referring to topiary? The poem's metaphors so often represent the materiality of Paris) as well as the meditations on suffering in the fourteen Stations of the Cross, cut short. The poem begins and ends with a salutation to the city; this devotion remains in the bowdlerized version Mirrlees presented in 1973 in the *Virginia Woolf Quarterly*, after her conversion to Catholicism. The scabrous lines about the 'Grand Guignol of Catholicism', baby Jesus urinating, and girls taking first communion as 'Charming pigmy brides' were removed 'to correspond with her philosophy and beliefs today'.[35] Mirrlees seemed to find the original poem's offence to lie in such sacrilegious images rather than in the presentation of a pilgrim's dedication to a city.

Briggs notes that the opening address to 'NOTRE DAME DE PARIS' not only conflates Paris with the Virgin Mary but significantly genders the city as female (a common and customary designation as the familiar phrase and book and film title *Paris Was a Woman* and when Edith Piaf sings 'Paris c'est une blonde' indicate). The gender of the first-person voice or narrator also appears to be female, if we read line fourteen's address '*Vous descendez Madame?*' as a question to the speaker who has declared 'I want a holophrase' and whose desire for it – to which I shall return – inspires and structures the poem. The question is asked of a woman on the Metro; is she alighting at this station? But, of course, in a modernist poem composed of fragments, the discovery of such causation intimates the reader's critical approach rather than incontrovertible facts about the text. Suzanne Henig does locate a female overview and seems to identify this as that of Mirrlees herself:

> the poet is not part of the poem or even the actor, though she is the speaker, omniscient, like Prufrock who observes London and through London all cities. Miss Mirrlees observes Paris, humanity and the intricacy and barbarity of human relationships but, like Prufrock, she never involves herself in these struggles and is content to be perpetually the objective recorder and observer.[36]

Henig's account, which is admittedly contained within a short introduction to Mirrlees's entire oeuvre, has a tendency towards generalizations such as these. This is all the more evident in comparison to Briggs's historical and textual research into the poem's references and allusions, which alerts us to the coded (possible allusions to lesbianism suggested by a street name 'close to Natalie Barney's house' and 'referred to in Djuna Barnes's *The Ladies' Almanack*') and the particular (for example, '*Tierre de Sienne*' is the reddish brown colour of soldiers' backpacks).[37] Henig rather oddly compares Mirrlees (not named in *Paris*) with the fictional Prufrock (also unnamed within the body of 'The Love Song of J. Alfred Prufrock'), rather than with

Eliot. The 'Love Song' is more obviously narrated and from one point of view, and the 'narrator' does seem more involved in relationships than Henig suggests. It's not necessary for a poem to have a narrator, figured or otherwise, but the question of voice or narrator is important to my discussion of both *Paris* and *Parallax*. Henig's assertion fails to articulate that it is a feature of modernist collage to juxtapose, for example, the overseeing poetic voice with the individual experience in distinctly drawn, often typographically different, expressions. She fails, therefore, to see the multiplicity indicated in the 'holophrase'. The word 'Paris' is a holophrase and a holophrase is needed to describe the city of Paris.

This chapter is concerned with 'gender-related city consciousness', but unlike most prose fiction, poetry has the facility for an absence of particularity of referents asserting gender. When the woman in the Metro is asked 'Vous descendez?', the question's verb, coming after the advert for Dubonnet depicting a 'Scarlet Woman', has a strongly sexual connotation. For this speaker, the Metro, going underground, has a thrilling *frisson* that is the opposite of Sasha's nightmare of being trapped in the London Underground, unable to find the way out, in *Good Morning, Midnight* (1939). Nor is this the refuge of Londoners seeking asylum from aerial bombardment or the uncomfortably crowded transport of weary shoppers.[38] This speaker, in this line, whilst clearly marked as female, may be fearless because she is a poetic voice, disembodied. Sasha's nightmare is to belong to the city depicted by Benjamin as a kaleidoscope of mirrored surfaces, throwing back one's reflection at every turn. The speaker of *Paris* participates in the city but not in this scopic hell; poetry allows an absence of body not afforded to Rhys's protagonists. The claustrophobic mode of transport, with its tunnel and its crowd (space needs to be made to allow the woman off the train), does not offer the safe perspective and distance given by the London bus to Elizabeth and Pauline but is instead thrillingly immersive. She sees the city and she writes it. The war is over, the peace treaty is being negotiated, the speaker alights at Concorde and 'I can't / I must go slowly' eschews speed in order to absorb and celebrate the city.

The Metro may have been designed for directness, but instead, in denial of Le Corbusier's functionality, the colourful posters and advertisements arouse sensual impressions of foreign tastes and places:

          ZIG-ZAG
          LION NOIR
          CACAO BLOOKER

This speaker shares qualities with the *flâneur*: a sensuousness perhaps even lasciviousness, with no interest in depicting home or family, and an appreciation of art and history alongside contemporary nightlife. Even Mirrlees's revised version of *Paris* is sexually open: the city at night is alive with prostitutes and lesbians. At the close of the poem, at the break of day, an American, apparently short-sighted ('astigmatism') voices *'"I don't like the gurls of the night-club – they love women."'* It is perhaps this reference that the biographers of Jane Harrison, until Briggs the main readers of the poem, have been keen to judge as evidence of a one-sided crush from Mirrlees rather than a sexual relationship between the two. Annabel Robinson claims that Mirrlees wanted fame by association with Harrison and encouraged gossip that they were lovers.[39] Mary Beard reads Woolf's reference to *Paris* as 'very obscure, indecent, and brilliant' as a recognition of lesbianism within it, but like Robinson she goes to some lengths to denigrate this as unreliable and self-serving: '*She would*, of course.'[40] The poem may be a coded love letter to Harrison. Both Beard and Briggs point out that 'holophrase' is a word and concept that Harrison had analysed whilst the 'constellation of Ursa Major' that closes the poem is 'part of the private code between HM and JH'.[41] *Paris* is a resolutely sensual poem from the start: the statues of nymphs may be 'harmless' but the injunction not to fear them still rests upon their 'soft mouths'; Gambetta has a tumescent 'red stud in the button-hole of his frock coat' and is being whispered to while he utters the 'obscene conjugal *tutoiement*'. Here mouths may represent female genitalia and the button-hole the anus. The poem presents the city through the eyes of *Eros* not *amour*.

But *Thanatos* is present too. The poem's playful presentation belies its gravity (although it is at times playful in meaning too). This playfulness takes the form of taxis queueing up on the page, striking marchers proceeding as letters vertically down the page instead of as words across it, and puns that are often dependent on the sound of a French pronunciation suggesting an English word, or some variant on this interplay between the two languages.

> The ghost of Père Lachaise
> Is walking the streets,
> He is draped in a black curtain embroidered with the
> letter H,

Briggs points out that 'H' in French sounds like 'ash' in English with connotations of death and burial, which, as well as anticipating Eliot's wasted land, are a characteristic reminder of the long-dead who have shaped Paris and the more recently dead soldiers whose deaths dominate the poem. The reference is a subtle reminder of the way that death remains as the (unspoken?) subtext of all postwar minds: '[t]he silence of *la grève*', here the French word for strike, referring to the quiet of absent workers but of course calling to mind 'the English expression'.[42] The art works can be resurrected from their wartime tombs but colour is drained from the clothes of widows whose lives could be changed and clothes dyed black 'DEUIL EN 24 HEURES', *'deuil'* the French word for 'dyed' appearing, on the page, sinisterly like the devil, whilst the dying of clothes of course is related in homonym to the dying of people; 'The stage is thick with corpses ...' Ellipses feature throughout the poem depicting absence and a perpetuity; things that cannot be said, and things that will continue: '[l]ittle funny things ceaselessly happening'. Indeed the phrase 'And on and on ...' appears more than once. Briggs asks if 'I want a holophrase' means not that the speaker desires one but instead lacks one? The ellipses are a method of presenting the lack, and again denying the possibility of a complete and total presentation of a city, but also a deceleration of the poem's text time, which along with the pictorial layout ensures that the reader and speaker travel slowly, at the same pace.

Deborah Parsons suggests that '[t]he surrealist would seem a natural *flâneur*, wandering a city in which the past uncannily and repeatedly surfaces in the present'.[43] This definition, for example, is an accurate synopsis of André Breton's wretched 'romance' *Nadja*, in which Breton and his heroine's perambulations through Paris pause at sites of violent historical uprisings, and the text contains photos of empty backstreets. Nadja, narrated, ends up incarcerated; the text, the streets and their significance, the musings on psychiatry are Breton's (it's a particularly unappealing text if we believe Mark Polizzotti's assertion in his introduction that it is based on real events)[44] but Mirrlees laughs at Freud, who has 'dredged the river and, grinning horribly, / waves his garbage in a glare of electricity'. *Paris* is a poem of great optimism. The past 'repeatedly surfaces' in it, but it is the paintings that have been stored during the war that are being lifted from the ground: 'They arise, serene and unetiolated, one by one from / their subterranean sleep of five long years'; flowers bloom and President Wilson is welcomed with his peace treaty. The voice of the poem slows down to appreciate the city and its past, and these moments are shared by the reader through ekphrasis; the depicted real and imagined paintings and sculptures introduce moments of stasis in which to admire the city. Again, the poetic voice's lack of referents produces a shared experience. In an ironic inversion of myth and common perception, underground, the Metro, offers futurist modernity, crush, and speed, whilst history is above ground, confronting the surrealist *flâneur*. Although Henig celebrates the poem's 'timelessness' about a 'universal city', *Paris*'s appealing joyfulness is related to its historical moment: the celebration of the Treaty of Versailles and the establishment of the League of Nations. Its mythic method, Christian iconography, resurrection, bulbous flowers, intertextuality, all antedate *The Waste Land*'s but its own resurrection, nursed so carefully by Briggs, may well occur in the classroom where students respond enthusiastically to this challenge to Eliot's fragmented, apocalyptic pessimism.

When Nancy Cunard's poem *Parallax* was first published by the Hogarth Press in 1925 it was derided as a poor imitation of *The Waste Land*. The *Times*

Literary Supplement's complaint about its lack of 'free inspiration' seems particularly ironic given Eliot's indebtedness to Mirrlees:

> The conclusion is unavoidable that Miss Cunard's poem would never have been conceived in its present shape without the example of Mr. Eliot; and the parallelism even extends to verbal reminiscences in certain passages. But, even when this is recognized, Miss Cunard's poem shows the individuality of its author; she transcribes the emotions of aftermath with remarkable subtlety. It seems to be the creation of a resilient mind, it has a complexity and grasp of reality which is so frequently lacking from women's poetry. 'Parallax,' though not itself truly original, may well be the prelude to a poem of free inspiration.[45]

So, whilst the poem's engagement with Eliot's work (*The Waste Land*, 'Prufrock', 'Preludes') is striking and explicit, this is never considered to be anything other than a sort of involuntary imitation or theft, until David Ayers, attending to a section of the poem devoid of reference to Eliot's poetry and starting with 'Well, instead', proposes that it is a deliberate strategy.[46] Ayers 'suggest[s] that Cunard has created a new rhetorical form, over which she has suspended the name "parallax", in which a systematic reworking and re-presentation of the existing material of a contemporary is used to create a new work'.[47] We have seen that Cunard herself had been reworked frequently in fictions of the day: *The Green Hat*, Aldous Huxley's *Antic Hay* (1923).[48] The cruellest version, however, came to light in Valerie Eliot's facsimile edition of the manuscript of *The Waste Land*. When Ezra Pound undertook his brutal and brilliant editing of the poem, he excised a long and vicious satire of Cunard. In the manuscript Cunard, appearing as Fresca, 'scribbles' miserable, incoherent poetry as a means of alleviating the boredom of insomnia; her verse is only favourably misjudged by indebted fawning acquaintances.[49] Of course, Eliot refers here to Cunard's earlier poems, and, unless Ezra Pound had informed her about them, there is no reason to think that she knew of these excised sections of *The Waste Land* or that *Parallax* might be a response to them, but until recently the verse has fuelled biographical interest and speculation about their personal rather than textual relationship.

Parallax begins with a male narrator, redolent of Eliot in inhabiting a 'rented casement' in London; looking from his window at dawn he makes a plea for transport in time and place to achieve the perspective that the title implies; '[h]e would have every milestone back of him.' However, the male narrator of *Parallax*, 'he', is a hybrid persona made up of a voice that is speaking/reading Eliot and another parallel voice bearing characteristics of Cunard herself, switching between third, first, and occasionally second person (who asks 'does your embitteredness endure forever?'). Here it is not that poetic language allows an absence of certain referents but that it affords a multiplicity of them to create this hybridity. There are many phrases and passages that recall Eliot, mentioning, for example, death in life, London, water. The Eliot voice, with its desire for milestones to be marked and passed (a request for memorialization, a place in the canon?), wants things settled, true perspective, whilst the hybrid voice, who leaves London and travels to 'Provence, the solstice' finds that, away from the city, there are no plaques memorializing artists, no canon: 'In Aix, what's remembered of Cézanne?' Instead, the 'Master's' 'dull' person is remembered by a curmudgeonly waiter whilst 'Beauty' remains 'Unpraised, unhindered, / Defiant, of single mind, / And took no rest, and has no epitaph.' The poem continues with what could be casually misread as a conventional meditation on where beauty lies, in mimesis or its origin, but is as much concerned with the arbitrator – 'What hand shall hold the absolute?' – or more concerned with perspective, of course, when the poem's title is recalled. As Jane Goldman explains, in the poem, Cézanne's 'modern technique ... transcends his geographical, rural, location and speaks directly to the "unreal", and international, cultural dimension of metropolitan centres'.[50] She argues that *Parallax* describes the process of how places – Provence, Paris, London – 'become properly visible' through Cézanne's paintings, Baudelaire's poems. And I would extend this to claim that the poem's hybridity performs the questioning of artistic 'timelessness', of the canon. There are constant references to endurance and lasting, some using the type of poetic, arcane phrasing ('sempiternal') that Pound's dictats for imagism[51] warned against, and that perhaps formed a barrier to recognition of what the poem was doing. For the arcane is set against meditations of evaluation of the new and the rewritten. This section is a recalled conversation between three unidentified speakers:

> And one of us questions, and smiles –
> And one of us, smiling, answers with a gesture only –
> And one: – 'Ah no –
>   The new cannot put out the old –
> ...
> Wrapped, folded together
> The new burns, ripens in the known,
> Folded, growing together –
> Yes – (even to paradox)
> Have I not loved you better, loving again?'

This final line, I argue, is a performative plea; its status as a question within quotation marks indicating uncertainty.

Ayers's recognition of the hybridity of voice tends towards a biographical reading; he finds Cunard in the many references to drinking. In the poem, alcohol is not a way to annihilation, as with Rhys's Sasha, but a means of liberating thought and philosophical investigation, which admittedly has its drawbacks:

> With wine alone one is allowed to think
> Less cumbrously, and if one may recall
> Little, there's always tomorrow –

There's no shame in drunken forgetfulness, instead a recognition of life's transience. The poem questions what is fleeting and what shall endure, and uses metaphors of distillation, along with drinking, to do so. Night-time drinking defers the future – 'defiant tomorrows / pushed back' – prolonging the present, but '[t]his poet-fool must halt in every tavern' to find what the 'alembic [has] burned away' to make 'rare' and 'perpetual'.

The poem travels to constantly question perspective. It exemplifies 'modernism's restlessness and refusal to settle'.[52] It travels from London's Commercial Street (notoriously the haunt of Jack the Ripper), where prostitutes are 'aged by stale demand', to Aix, through Mirrlees's Paris ('From the Seine, up the Quarter, homeward at last / to sleep'), meeting Baudelaire's rag pickers, through France to Italy, and ends

> Along a question –
> Nor of passing and re-passing
> By the twin affirmations of never and for-ever,
> In doubt, in shame, in silence.

Goldman finds the poem to exemplify modernist restlessness but suggests that its textual relationship might be to *Mrs Dalloway* through the idea of parallax (just as Briggs suggests that typesetting *Paris* influenced Woolf's use of white page space in *Jacob's Room*). *Paris* pauses to stop and admire the city, through ekphrasis and typesetting that mimics the city's structures and inhabitants, in a confident and joyful appreciation of the city after war. In contrast, *Parallax* does not stop to describe in detail, nor thrill to the speed of the underground train or a fast car, but begs instead parallax, motion, no settling upon a fixed idea, a fixed canon, a fixed interpretation. We need to keep moving to ascertain, from more than one point of view, true perspective. To return to the question with which the chapter opened, in view of their significance it is indeed surprising that neither *Paris* nor *Parallax* have been allowed to participate as primary sources in the cultural materialist revision of Modernism. The recognition of their performativity as exerting a critique of constructions of Modernism is long overdue.

Notes

1. Julia Briggs, 'Hope Mirrlees and Continental Modernism', in *Gender in Modernism: New Geographies, Complex Intersections*, ed. Bonnie Kime Scott (Urbana and Chicago: University of Illinois Press, 2007), pp. 261–9, p. 261.

Myths of Passage: Paris *and* Parallax 289

2. 'Paris: A Poem by Hope Mirrlees', *Times Literary Supplement* (6 May 1920), p. 285 and Nancy Cunard, *Parallax* (London: Hogarth Press, 1925). All quotations used in the main body of my essay are from Hope Mirrlees, *Paris*, in *Gender in Modernism*, ed. Scott, pp. 261–303. Quotations from *Parallax* are from *Parallax* (Cambridge: Parataxis Editions, 2001).
3. 'Mirrlees, Hope', in *The Cambridge Guide to Women's Writing in English*, ed. Lorna Sage (Cambridge: Cambridge University Press, 1999), p. 435.
4. See John Lucas, *The Radical Twenties: Writing, Politics, and Culture* (Nottingham: Five Leaves Press, 1997) and Janet Montefiore, *Men and Women Writers of the 1930s* (London: Routledge, 1996).
5. Susan Stanford Friedman, 'When a "Long" Poem is a "Big" Poem', in *Feminisms: An Anthology of Literary Theory and Criticism*, ed. Robyn R. Warhol and Diane Price Herndl (New Brunswick: Rutgers University Press, 1997), p. 724.
6. Walter Benjamin, *The Arcades Project*, trans. Howard Eiland and Kevin McLaughlin (Cambridge, MA and London: Belknap Press, 1999).
7. Keith Tester, ed., *The Flâneur* (London: Routledge, 1994), p. 2.
8. Deborah Parsons, *Streetwalking the Metropolis: Women, the City and Modernity* (Oxford: Oxford University Press, 2000), p. 149.
9. Parsons, *Streetwalking*, p. 10.
10. Ibid., p. 7.
11. Lyons & Co. in Scott McCracken, 'Voyages by Teashop: An Urban Geography of Modernism', in *Geographies of Modernism: Literatures, Cultures, Spaces*, ed. Peter Brooker and Andrew Thacker (London: Routledge, 2005), pp. 86–98, p. 93.
12. McCracken, 'Voyages', p. 91.
13. Andrew Thacker, *Moving Through Modernity: Space and Geography in Modernism* (Manchester: Manchester University Press, 2003, 2009), p. 7.
14. Elizabeth Bowen, *To The North* (London: Victor Gollancz, 1932), p. 29.
15. Bowen, *To The North*.
16. Ibid., p. 304.
17. Michael Arlen, *The Green Hat* (London: Capuchin Classics, 2008), p. 14.
18. F.T. Marinetti, 'The Founding and Manifesto of Futurism 1909', in *Futurist Manifestos*, ed. Umbro Apollonio (London: Tate Publishing, 2009), p. 21.
19. Virginia Woolf, *Mrs Dalloway* (London: Grafton, 1992), pp. 146, 145.
20. Woolf, *Mrs Dalloway*, p. 147.
21. Ibid., pp. 146, 147.
22. Bowen, *To the North*, pp. 46–7.
23. Parsons, *Streetwalking*, p. 22.
24. Ibid., p. 7.
25. See David Ayers, *Modernism: A Short Introduction* (Oxford: Blackwell, 2004), p. 31.
26. Cunard, *Parallax*, p. 3.
27. For a discussion of fictional knowledge see Michael Wood, *Literature and the Taste of Knowledge* (Cambridge: Cambridge University Press, 2005).
28. Parsons, *Streetwalking*, p. 7.
29. See *Oxford English Dictionary*, online edition: http://www.oed.com. The word had some currency during the modernist period: most famously, in the Lestrygonians section of *Ulysses*, Leopold Bloom is concerned with the concept but a scan of the *Times Literary Supplement* in the 1920s shows that even then the term was used as a metaphor for re-reading canonical texts (see review of *Horace: A New Interpretation* (7 August 1924)). More recently the term has been used in this way by Slavoj Žižek in *The Parallax View* (Cambridge, MA: MIT, 2006) and the Johns Hopkins University Press who have a series called 'Parallax' in which re-visions of culture and society are presented.

30. See *Oxford English Dictionary*.
31. 'PARIS: A Poem by Hope Mirrlees', *Times Literary Supplement* (6 May 1920), p. 285.
32. See Julia Briggs, '"Modernism's Lost Hope": Virginia Woolf, Hope Mirrlees and the Printing of *Paris*', in Julia Briggs, *Reading Virginia Woolf* (Edinburgh: Edinburgh University Press, 2006), pp. 80–95, 91.
33. Anon, '*PARIS*: A Poem by Hope Mirrlees', *Times Literary Supplement* (6 May 1920), p. 285.
34. Mirrlees, *Paris*, pp. 272, 273.
35. Suzanne Henig, 'Queen of Lud: Hope Mirrlees', in *Virginia Woolf Quarterly*, 1.2 (1973): 1–27, p. 3.
36. Henig, 'Queen of Lud', p. 13.
37. Julia Briggs, 'Hope Mirrlees and Continental Modernism', in *Gender in Modernism*, ed. Scott, pp. 261–303, pp. 299, 296.
38. See Dave Ashford, 'Blueprints for Babylon: Modernist Mapping of the London Underground 1913–1939', in *Modernism/Modernity*, 17.4 (2010): 735–64, for his rich contextual discussion of the Underground in modernist literature. Ashford and other critics note Eliot's use of the Tube as 'a metaphor for descent to the Underworld in *Four Quartets*' (758) but not that there was a precedent in Mirrlees's poem.
39. Annabel Robinson, *The Life and Works of Jane Ellen Harrison* (Oxford: Oxford University Press, 2002), p. 295.
40. Mary Beard, *The Invention of Jane Harrison* (Cambridge, MA: Harvard University Press, 2000), pp. 140, 154.
41. Briggs, 'Hope Mirrlees', p. 303.
42. Ibid., p. 296.
43. Parsons, *Streetwalking*, p. 10.
44. See Mark Polizzotti's introduction to André Breton, *Nadja*, trans. Richard Howard (Harmondsworth: Penguin, 1999).
45. See Edgell Rickword, 'Two Poets', *Times Literary Supplement* (28 May 1925), p. 364. This is a bigger review than was afforded to *Paris* by the relatively unknown Mirrlees.
46. Ayers, *Modernism*, p. 32.
47. Ibid.
48. See Anne Chisholm, *Nancy Cunard* (London: Sidgwick and Jackson, 1979); my own articles 'Nancy Cunard's *Black Man White Ladyship* as Surrealist Tract', in *At Home and Abroad in the Empire: British Women Write the 1930s*, ed. Robin Hackett, Freda S. Hauser, and Gay Wachman (Newark: University of Delaware Press, 2009), pp. 96–118; and 'The Reception of Nancy Cunard's *Negro Anthology*', in *Women Writers of the 1930s: Gender, Politics, History*, ed. Maroula Joannou (Edinburgh: Edinburgh University Press, 1999), pp. 113–22.
49. See T.S. Eliot, *The Waste Land: A Facsimile and Transcript of the Original Drafts Including the Annotations of Ezra Pound*, ed. Valerie Eliot (Orlando, Fla: Harcourt Books, 1971), pp. 38–41.
50. Jane Goldman, '1925, London, New York, Paris: Metropolitan Modernisms – Parallax and Palimpsest', in *The Edinburgh Companion to Twentieth-Century Literatures in English*, ed. Brian McHale and Randall Stevenson (Edinburgh: Edinburgh University Press, 2006), pp. 61–72, p. 67.
51. Ezra Pound, 'Imagisme' (1912), in *Modernism: An Anthology*, ed. Lawrence Rainey (Oxford: Blackwell, 2005), pp. 94–5.
52. Ibid., p. 67.

Electronic Resources

Bloomsbury-related collections: *http://specialcollections.lib.sussex.ac.uk* Materials related to the Bloomsbury Group.
Genesis: *http:www.genesis.ac.uk* Genesis is a women's history resource produced collaboratively by the Women's Library, the Archive Hub and over 200 heritage institutions.
Katherine Mansfield Society: *http://www.katherinemansfieldsociety.org/* Online resources for Katherine Mansfield.
LION: Literature online: *http://lion.chadwyck.co.uk* Enables a wide variety of searches e.g. by authors within literary movements.
Literary Encyclopedia: *www.litencyc.com/* A reliable online encyclopedia written by scholars.
Middlebrow Network: *http://www.middlebrow-network.com/* AHRC-funded network of scholars working on middlebrow writing plus resource bank.
Modernist Journals Project: *http://www.modjourn.org/journals.html*
Modernist Magazines Project: *http://modmags.cts.dmu.ac.uk/* These two websites contain invaluable resource for the study of modernism in e-magazines and journals including digital editions of magazines up to the year 1922.
Orlando Project: *http://www.arts.ualberta.ca/orlando/* Integrated online resource for British women's writing in the British Isles.
Space Between Society: *http://www.spacebetweensociety.org* Inter-disciplinary society dedicated to the literature and culture of the interwar period with annual journal produced at Monmouth University.
Sylvia Townsend Warner Society: *http://www.townsendwarner.com* Online resources for Sylvia Townsend Warner.
Virginia Woolf Society: *http://www.virginiawoolfsociety.co.uk/* Online resources for Virginia Woolf.
Women's Library: *http://www.londonmet.ac.uk/thewomenslibrary/* Britain's most extensive library and resources centre of women's history and literature with online catalogue.
University of Bristol Theatre Collection: *http://www.bris.ac.uk/theatrecollection/* The University of Bristol Theatre Collection is an accredited museum and research centre dedicated to the study of British Theatre History.

Select Bibliography

Primary sources

Allan, Dot and Moira Burgess (eds), *Makeshift* [1928] and *Hunger March* [1934] (Glasgow: Association for Scottish Literary Studies, 2010).
Arlen, Michael, *The Green Hat* (London: Collins, 1924).
Benson, Stella, *The Little World* [1925] (Milton Keynes: Dodo Press, 2010).
Bentley, Phyllis, *Freedom Farewell!* [1936] (London: Gollancz, 1937).
——, *O Dreams, O Destinations: An Autobiography* (London: Victor Gollancz, 1962).
Box, Muriel, *Angels of War*, in *Five New Full-Length Plays for All-Women Casts* (London: Lovat Dickson and Thompson, 1935).
Bowen, Elizabeth, *The Collected Stories of Elizabeth Bowen* [1980] (London: Vintage Classics, 1999).
——, *The Death of the Heart* [1938] (Harmondsworth: Penguin, 1962).
——, *The Heat of the Day* [1949] (London: Vintage Classics, 1998).
——, *The Last September* [1929] (London: Vintage, 1998).
——, *The Mulberry Tree: Writings of Elizabeth Bowen*, ed. Hermione Lee (London: Virago, 1986).
——, *To The North* [1932] (New York: Anchor Books, 2006).
Broster, D.K., *The Gleam in the North* [1927] (Harmondsworth: Peacock, 1968).
——, *The Dark Mile* [1929] (London: Heinemann, 1968).
Butts, Mary, *Scenes From the Life of Cleopatra* (London: William Heinemann, 1933).
Christie, Agatha, *The Murder at the Vicarage* [1930] (New York: Berkeley Books, 1986).
Cunard, Nancy, *Parallax* [1925] (Cambridge: Parataxis Editions, 2001).
——, *Poems of Nancy Cunard from the Bodleian Library*, ed. John Lucas (Nottingham: Trent Editions, 2005).
Delafield, E.M., *The Diary of a Provincial Lady* [1930] (London: Virago Press, 1984).
——, *The Way Things Are* [1927] (London: Virago Press, 1988).
Edwards, Dorothy, *Rhapsody* (London: Wishart and Co, 1927).
Evans, Margiad, *Country Dance* [1932] (London: John Calder, 1978)
Farrell, M.J, *Mad Puppetstown* [1931] (London: Virago, 1985).
Ferguson, Rachel, *The Brontës Went to Woolworths* [1931] (London: Virago, 1988).
Gibbons, Stella, *Cold Comfort Farm* [1932] (Harmondsworth: Penguin, 1983).
Godden, Rumer, *Black Narcissus* [1939] (London: Pan Books, 1994).
——, *Breakfast with the Nikolides* [1942] (London: Pan, 2002).
——, *The River* [1946] (London: Pan Books, 2004).
H.D. (Hilda Doolittle), *Palimpsest* [1926] (Carbondale and Edwardsville: Southern Illinois University Press, 1968).
——, *Collected Poems 1912–1944* (New York: New Directions Publishing Corporation, 1982).
Heyer, Georgette, *The Black Moth* [1921] (London: Pan, 1965).
——, *These Old Shades* [1926] (London: Arrow, 1997).
——, *An Infamous Army* [1937] (London: Arrow, 2001).
Holden, Inez, *Born Old, Died Young* (London: Duckworth, 1932).
——, *Death in High Society* (London: Kegan Paul, 1934).

―, *It Was Different at the Time* (London: John Lane, 1943).
―, *Night Shift* (London: John Lane, 1941).
―, *There's No Story There* (London: John Lane, 1944).
Holtby, Winifred, *Mandoa, Mandoa!: A Comedy of Irrelevance* [1933] (London: Virago, 1982).
―, *The Land of Green Ginger* [1927] (London: Virago, 1983).
―, *South Riding: An English Landscape* [1936] (London: Virago, 2000).
Huxley, Elspeth, *Red Strangers* [1939] (Harmondsworth: Penguin, 2006).
Irwin, Margaret, *Young Bess* [1944] (London: Alison and Busby, 1999).
―, *The Gay Galliard: The Love Story of Mary Queen of Scots* (London: Chatto and Windus, 1941).
King-Hall, Magdalen, *Life and Death of the Wicked Lady Skelton* [1942] (New York: Rinehart, 1946).
Lehmann, Rosamond, *Dusty Answer* [1927] (London: Virago Press, 2000).
Macaulay, Rose, *Crewe Train* (London: Collins, 1926).
―, *Dangerous Ages* (New York: Boni and Liveright, 1921).
―, *Potterism: A Tragi-Farcical Tract* (London and New York: Collins, 1920).
―, *They Were Defeated* [1932] (Oxford: Oxford University Press, 1982).
McCracken, Esther, *Living Room* (London: Charles H. Fox, 1944).
Mansfield, Katherine, *The Katherine Mansfield Notebooks, Volume 2*, ed. Margaret Scott (Canterbury, NZ: Lincoln University Press, 1997).
―, *The Collected Letters of Katherine Mansfield*, ed. Vincent O' Sullivan and Margaret Scott, 5 vols (Oxford: Constable, 1984–2008).
―, *The Stories of Katherine Mansfield*, ed. Anthony Alpers (Auckland: Oxford University Press,1984).
Marson, Una, *The Moth and the Star* (Kingston, Jamaica: published by the author, 1937).
―, 'Nigger', *Keys*, 1: 1 July 1933: 8–9.
―, *Collected Poems and Selected Prose*, ed. Charlotte Mew and Val Warner (Manchester: Carcanet, 1997).
Miller, Betty, *Farewell Leicester Square* [1934] (London: Persephone Books, 2000).
―, *On the Side of the Angels* [1945] (London: Virago, 1985).
―, *Sunday* (London: Gollancz, 1934).
―, *Portrait of the Bride* (London: Gollancz, 1935).
Mirrlees, Hope, 'Paris: A Poem by Hope Mirrlees', *Times Literary Supplement*, 6 May 1920: 285.
Mitchison, Naomi, *Cloud Cuckoo Land* (London: Jonathan Cape, 1925).
―, *The Conquered* (London: Jonathan Cape, 1923).
―, *The Corn King and the Spring Queen* [1931] (London: Virago, 1983).
―, *We Have Been Warned* (London: Constable, 1935).
―, *You May Well Ask: A Memoir 1920–1940* (London: Flamingo, 1986).
Mitford, Nancy, *The Pursuit of Love* [1945] (Harmondsworth: Penguin, 1970).
Muir, Willa, *Belonging: A Memoir* (London: Hogarth Press, 1968).
―, *Imagined Selves* [1931] (Edinburgh: Canongate, 1996).
Reilly, Catherine (ed.), *Women's War Poetry and Verse* (London: Virago, 1997).
Rhys, Jean, *After Leaving Mr MacKenzie* (London: Jonathan Cape, 1930).
―, *Voyage in the Dark* [1934] (Harmondsworth: Penguin, 2000).
―, *Good Morning Midnight* (London: Constable, 1939).
Richardson, Dorothy, *Pilgrimage*, 4 vols [1938] (London: Virago, 1979).
Robertson, E. Arnot, *Cullum* [1928] (London: Virago, 1990).

Ryle, Elizabeth, *The Three-Fold Path: A Play in Seven Scenes*, in *Five New Full-length Plays for All-Women Casts* (London: Lovat Dickson and Thompson, 1935).
Sackville-West, Vita, *Passenger to Teheran* [1926] (London: Tauris Parke Paperbacks, 2007).
Sayers, Dorothy, *Gaudy Night* (London: Gollancz, 1935).
——, *Strong Poison* [1930] (Hodder and Stoughton, 2003).
Shepherd, Nan, *The Quarry Wood* [1928] (Edinburgh: Canongate, 1987).
Sitwell, Edith, *Taken Care of: an Autobiography* (London: Hutchinson, 1965).
Smith, Dodie, *I Capture the Castle* [1949] (London: The Reprint Society, 1950).
——, *Three Plays by Dodie Smith* [1939] London: Samuel French, 1939).
Smith, Stevie, *The Holiday* [1949] (London: Virago, 1980).
——, *Me Again: The Uncollected Writings of Stevie Smith* (London, Virago, 1981).
——, *Novel on Yellow Paper, or, Work it Out for Yourself* [1936] (London: Virago, 1980).
——, *Over the Frontier* [1938] (London: Virago, 1980).
Stark, Freya, *Baghdad Sketches* [1937] (London: Tauris Parke, 2011)
Struther, Jan, *Mrs Miniver* [1939] (London: Virago, 1989).
Vaughan, Hilda, *Harvest Home* (London: Victor Gollancz, 1936).
Warner, Sylvia Townsend, *After the Death of Don Juan* [1938] (London: Virago, 1989).
——, *Collected Poems* (Manchester: Carcanet, 1982).
——, *The Diaries of Sylvia Townsend Warner*, ed. Harman, Claire (London: Chatto and Windus, 1994).
——, *Lolly Willows, or The Loving Huntsman* [1926] (London: Virago, 2000).
——, *Mr. Fortune's Maggot* [1927] (London: Virago, 1978).
——, *Summer Will Show* [1936] (London: Virago, 1987).
Warner, Sylvia Townsend and Valentine Ackland, *Whether a Dove or a Seagull* (New York: Viking, 1933).
West, Rebecca, *Black Lamb and Grey Falcon* (Edinburgh: Canongate, 2006).
Wickham, Anna and R.D. Smith (eds), *Writings of Anna Wickham: Free Woman and Poet* (London: Virago, 1984).
Wingfield, Sheila, *Collected Poems 1938–1983* (London: Enitharmon, 1983).
Woolf, Virginia, *Between the Acts* (London: Hogarth, 1941).
——, *Flush: A Biography* (London: Hogarth, 1933).
——, *Jacob's Room* (London: Hogarth, 1922).
——, *Mrs Dalloway* (London: Hogarth, 1925).
——, *Orlando: A Biography* (London: Hogarth, 1928).
——, *To The Lighthouse* (London: Hogarth, 1927).
——, *The Voyage Out* (London: Duckworth, 1915).
——, *The Waves* (London: Hogarth, 1931).
——, *The Years* (London: Hogarth, 1937).
——, *The Diary of Virginia Woolf (1915–1941)*, 5 vols, ed. Nigel Nicolson and Joanne Trautman (London: Hogarth, 1975–1980).
——, *The Essays of Virginia Woolf*, Vols 1–4, ed. Andrew McNellie (London: Hogarth, 1986–1994).
——, *The Letters of Virginia Woolf (1888–1940)*, ed. Nigel Nicolson and Joanne Trautman (London: Hogarth, 1975–1980).
——, *Virginia Woolf, A Passionate Apprentice: The Early Journals, 1897–1909*, ed. Mitchell A. Leaska (London: Hogarth, 1990).

Secondary sources

Ashford, Dave, 'Blueprints for Babylon: Modernist Mapping of the London Underground 1913–1939', *Modernism/Modernity*, 17.4 (2010): 735–64.

Select Bibliography 295

Aston, Elaine and Janelle Reinelt, 'Restrospectives', in *The Cambridge Companion to Modern British Women Playwrights*, ed. Elaine Aston and Janelle Reinelt (Cambridge: Cambridge University Press, 2000), pp. 21–37.
Ayers, David, *Modernism: A Short Introduction* (Oxford: Blackwell, 2004).
Barbera, Jack and William McBrien, *Stevie: A Biography of Stevie Smith* (London: Macmillan, 1986).
Barker, Clive and Maggie, B. Gale (eds), *British Theatre Between the Wars 1918–1939* (Cambridge: Cambridge University Press, 2000).
Barreca, Regina, *Last Laughs: Perspectives on Women and Comedy* (New York: Gordon and Breach, 1988).
——, *Untamed and Unabashed: Essays on Women and Humor in British Literature* (Detroit: Wayne State University Press, 1992).
Beard, Mary, *The Invention of Jane Harrison* (Cambridge, MA: Harvard University Press, 2000).
Beauman, Nicola, *A Very Great Profession: The Woman's Novel 1914–39* (London: Virago, 1983).
Beer, Gillian, 'Sylvia Townsend Warner: The Centrifugal Kick', in *Women Writers of the 1930s: Gender, Politics and History*, ed. Maroula Joannou (Edinburgh: Edinburgh University Press, 1999), pp. 76–86.
——, *Virginia Woolf: The Common Ground: Essays by Gillian Beer* (Edinburgh: Edinburgh University Press, 1986).
Bennett, Susan, 'Theatre History, Historiography and Women's Dramatic Writing', in *Women, Theatre and Performance: New Histories, New Historiographies*, ed. Maggie, B. Gale and Vivien Gardner (Manchester: Manchester University Press, 2000), pp. 46–59.
Benstock, Shari, *Women of the Left Bank: Paris, 1900–1940* (Austin: University of Texas Press, 1986).
Benton, Jill, *Naomi Mitchison: A Biography* (London: Pandora Press, 1992).
Berry, Paul and Mark Bostridge, *Testament of a Generation: The Journalism of Vera Brittain and Winifred Holtby* (London: Virago, 1985).
Bluemel, Kristin, *George Orwell and the Radical Eccentrics: Intermodernism in Literary London* (Basingstoke: Palgrave Macmillan, 2004)
—— (ed), *Intermodernism: Literary Culture in Twentieth-Century Britain* (Edinburgh: Edinburgh University Press, 2009).
Bowlby, Rachel, *Feminist Destinations and Further Essays on Virginia Woolf* (Edinburgh: Edinburgh University Press, 1997).
Bracco, Rosa Maria, *Betwixt and Between: Middlebrow Fiction and English Society in the Twenties and Thirties* (Victoria: University of Melbourne, 1990).
Briganti, Chiara and Kathy Mezei, *Domestic Modernism: The Interwar Novel and E.H. Young* (Aldershot: Ashgate, 2006).
Briggs, Julia, 'Hope Mirrlees and Continental Modernism', in *Gender in Modernism: New Geographies, Complex Intersections*, ed. Bonnie Kime Scott (Urbana and Chicago: University of Illinois Press, 2007), pp. 261–9.
——, *Reading Virginia Woolf* (Edinburgh: Edinburgh University Press, 2006).
Brittain, Vera, *Testament of Friendship: the Story of Winifred Holtby* (London: Macmillan, 1940).
Broe, Lynn and Angela Ingram (eds), *Women's Writing in Exile* (Chapel Hill: University of Carolina Press, 1989).
Brooker, Peter and Andrew Thacker (eds), *Geographies of Modernism: Literatures, Cultures, Spaces* (London: Routledge, 2005).
——, *The Oxford Critical and Cultural History of Modernist Magazines, vol 1: Britain and Ireland 1880–1945* (Oxford: Oxford University Press, 2009).

Brooker, Peter, Andrzej Gasiorek, Deborah Longworth, and Andrew Thacker (eds), *The Oxford Handbook of Modernisms* (Oxford: Oxford University Press, 2010)

Brosnan, Leila, *Reading Virginia Woolf's Essays and Journalism* (Edinburgh: Edinburgh University Press, 1999).

Brothers, Barbara, 'Writing Against the Grain: Sylvia Townsend Warner and the Spanish Civil War', in *Women Writers in Exile*, ed. Mary Lynn Broe and Angela Ingram (University of Carolina Press, 1989), pp. 350–66.

Bush, Barbara, '"Britain's Conscience on Africa": White Women, Race and Imperial Politics in Interwar Britain', in *Gender and Imperialism*, ed. Claire Midgley (Manchester: Manchester University Press, 1998), pp. 200–23.

——, 'Gender and Empire: The Twentieth Century', in *Gender and Empire*, ed. Philippa Levine (Oxford: Oxford University Press, 2004), pp. 77–111.

Caesar, Adrian, *Dividing Lines: Poetry, Class and Ideology in the 1930s* (Manchester: Manchester University Press, 1991).

Calder, Jenny, *The Nine Lives of Naomi Mitchison* (London: Virago, 1997).

Carlson, Susan, *Women and Comedy: Rewriting the British Theatrical Tradition* (Ann Arbor: University of Michigan Press, 1991).

Carlston, Erin G., *Thinking Fascism: Sapphic Modernism and Fascist Modernity* (Stanford: Stanford University Press, 1998).

Carr, Helen, 'Virginia Woolf, Empire and Race', in *The Cambridge Companion to Virginia Woolf*, ed. Sue Roe and Susan Sellers (Cambridge: Cambridge University Press, 2010), pp. 197–213.

——, 'Jean Rhys: West Indian Intellectual', in Bill Schwartz (ed.), *West Indian Intellectuals in Britain*, ed. Bill Schwartz (Manchester: Manchester University Press, 2003), pp. 93–113.

Cavaliero, Glen, *The Alchemy of Laughter* (Basingstoke: Palgrave, 2000).

Chisholm, Anne, *Nancy Cunard* (London: Sidgwick and Jackson, 1979).

Clark, Suzanne, *Sentimental Modernism: Women Writers and the Revolution of the Word* (Bloomington: Indiana University Press, 1991).

Clay, Catherine, *British Women Writers 1914–1945: Professional Work and Friendship* (Aldershot: Ashgate).

——, 'Winifred Holtby, Journalist: Rehabilitating Journalism in the Modernist Ferment', in *Winifred Holtby, 'A Woman In Her Time': Critical Essays*, ed. Lisa Regan (Cambridge: Cambridge Scholars Press, 2010), pp. 65–88.

——, 'Storm Jameson's Journalism 1913–33: The Construction of a Writer', in *Margaret Storm Jameson: Writing in Dialogue*, ed. Jennifer Birkett and Chiara Briganti (Cambridge: Cambridge Scholars Press, 2007), pp. 37–52.

Colletta, Lisa, *Dark Humor and Social Satire in the Modern British Novel* (London: Palgrave, 2003).

Collier, Patrick, *Modernism on Fleet Street* (Aldershot: Ashgate, 2006),

Collini, Stefan, 'Modernism and the little Magazines', *Times Literary Supplement*, 7 October 2009: 1.

Crangle, Sarah, 'Ivy Compton-Burnett and Risibility', in *British Fiction after Modernism: The Novel at Mid-Century*, ed. Marina MacKay and Lyndsey Stonebridge (Basingstoke: Palgrave, 2007), pp. 99–120.

Cuddy-Keane, Melba, *Virginia Woolf, the Intellectual, and the Public Sphere* (Cambridge: Cambridge University Press, 2003).

Deen, Stella (ed.), *Challenging Modernism: New Readings in Literature and Culture, 1914–45* (Aldershot: Ashgate, 2002).

DiCenzo, Maria, *Feminist Media History: Suffrage, Periodicals and the Public Sphere* (Basingstoke: Palgrave, 2010).

D'Monté, Rebecca, 'Feminizing the Nation and the Country House: Women Dramatists 1938–1940', in *New Versions of Pastoral: Post-Romantic, Modern, and Contemporary Responses to the Tradition*, ed. David James and Philip Tew (Madison, NJ: Fairleigh Dickinson University Press,2009), pp. 139–55.

——, 'Origin and Ownership: Stage, Film, and TV Adaptations of Rebecca', in *Adaptation in Contemporary Culture: Textual Infidelities*, ed. Rachel Carroll (London: Continuum, 2009), pp. 163–73.

Doan, Laura, 'Passing Fashions: Reading Female Masculinities in the 1920s', in *Gender and Modernism: Critical Concepts in Literary and Cultural Studies*, ed. Bonnie Kime Scott, Vol. 4, *Diversity and Identities* (London: Routledge,2008), pp. 297–320.

Doan, Laura and Jane Garrity, 'Modernism Queered', in *Blackwell Companion to Modernist Literature and Culture*, ed. David Bradshaw and Kevin J. Dettmar (Oxford: Blackwell, 2006), pp. 542–50.

Doan, Laura and Jane Garrity (eds), *Sapphic Modernities: Sexuality, Women and National Culture* (Basingstoke: Palgrave Macmillan, 2006).

Donnell, Alison and Sarah Lawson Welsh (eds), *The Routledge Reader in Caribbean Literature* (London: Routledge, 1996).

Dowson, Jane, '*Time and Tide* (1920–76) and *The Bermondsey Book* (1923–30): Interventions in the Public Sphere', in *The Oxford Critical and Cultural History of Modernist Magazines, vol 1: Britain and Ireland 1880–1945*, ed. Peter Brooker and Andrew Thacker (Oxford: Oxford University Press, 2009), pp. 530–51.

—— (ed.), *Women's Poetry of the 1930s: A Critical Anthology* (London: Routledge, 1996).

——, *Women, Poetry and British Modernism 1910–39* (Aldershot: Ashgate, 2002).

—— (ed.), *Women's Writing 1945–60: After the Deluge* (Basingstoke: Palgrave, 2003).

Dowson, Jane and Alice Entwistle, *A Cambridge History of Twentieth-Century Women's Poetry* (Cambridge University Press, 2006).

Doughan, David and Denise Sanchez, *Feminist Periodicals 1855–1984* (Brighton: Harvester, 1987).

Doyle, Laura and Laura Winkiel (eds), *GeoModernisms: Race, Modernism, Modernity* (Bloomington: Indiana University Press, 2005).

Emery, Jane, *Rose Macaulay: A Writer's Life* (London: John Murray, 1991).

Emery, Mary Lou, *Jean Rhys at 'World's End': Novels of Colonial and Sexual Exile* (Austin: University of Texas Press, 1990).

——, *Modernism, the Visual and Caribbean Literature* (Cambridge: Cambridge University Press, 2007).

Esty, Jed, *A Shrinking Island: Modernism and National Culture in England* (Princeton: Princeton University Press, 2004).

Felski, Rita, 'Afterword', in *Women's Experience of Modernity*, ed. Ann. L. Ardis and Leslie W. Lewis (Baltimore: Johns Hopkins University Press, 2003), pp. 290–9.

——, *The Gender of Modernity* (Cambridge, MA: Harvard University Press, 1995).

Finney, Gail (ed.), *Look Who's Laughing: Gender and Comedy* (London: Taylor and Francis, 1994).

Fitzgerald, Penelope, *Charlotte Mew and Her Friends* (London: Collins, 1985).

Ford, Hugh (ed.), *Nancy Cunard: Brave Poet, Indomitable Rebel 1896–1965* (Philadelphia: Chilton Book Company, 1968).

Foster, John Wilson, 'The Irish Renaissance, 1890–1940: Prose in English', in *The Cambridge History of Irish Literature, Vol. 2, 1890–2000*, ed. Margaret Kelleher and Philip O'Leary (Cambridge: Cambridge University Press, 2006), pp. 13–80.

Friedman, Susan Stanford, *Mappings: Feminism and the Cultural Geographies of Encounter* (Princeton: Princeton University Press, 1998).

Gagnier, Regenia, 'Between Women: A Cross-Class Analysis of Status and Anarchic Humor', in *Last Laughs: Perspectives on Women and Comedy*, ed. Regina Barrecca (New York: Gordon and Breach, 1988), pp. 135–48.

Gale, Maggie B., *West End Women: Women and the London Stage 1918–1962* (London: Routledge, 1996).

——, 'Women Playwrights of the 1920s and 1930s', in *The Cambridge Companion to Modern British Women Playwrights*, ed. Elaine Aston and Janelle Reinelt (Cambridge: Cambridge University Press. 2000), pp. 23–37.

Gale, Maggie B. and Viv Gardner, 'From Fame to Obscurity: In Search of Clemence Dane', in *Women, Theatre and Performance: New Histories, New Historiographies*, ed. Maggie B. Gale and Viv Gardner (Manchester: Manchester University Press, 2000), pp. 121–41.

Garrity, Jane, *Step-Daughters of England: British Women Modernists and the National Imaginary* (Manchester: Manchester University Press, 2003).

Gikandi, Simon, *Maps of Englishness: Writing Identity in the Culture of Colonialism* (New York: Columbia University Press, 1996).

Gilbert, Sandra and Susan Gubar, *No Man's Land: The Place of the Woman's Writer in the Twentieth Century*, 3 vols (New Haven: Yale University Press, 1988, 1989, 1994).

Gledhill, Christine and Gillian Swanson, 'Introduction' to *Nationalising Femininity: Culture, Sexuality and the British Cinema in the Second World War*, ed. Christine Gledhill and Gillian Swanson (Manchester: Manchester University Press, 1996), pp. 1–12.

Goldman, Jane, '1925, London, New York, Paris: Metropolitan Modernisms – Parallax and Palimpsest', in *The Edinburgh Companion to Twentieth-Century Literatures in English*, ed. Brian McHale and Randall Stevenson (Edinburgh: Edinburgh University Press, 2006), pp. 61–72.

Grant, Joy, *Stella Benson: A Biography* (London: Macmillan, 1987).

Grover, Mary, *The Ordeal of Warwick Deeping: Middlebrow Authorship and Cultural Embarrassment* (Madison, NJ: Fairleigh Dickinson University Press, 2009).

Habermann, Ina, *Myth, Memory and the Middlebrow: Priestley, Du Maurier and the Symbolic Form of Englishness* (Basingstoke: Palgrave Macmillan, 2010).

Hackett, Robin, *Sapphic Primitivism: Production of Race, Class and Sexuality in Key Works of Modern Fiction* (New Brunswick: Rutgers University Press, 2004).

Hackett, Robyn, Freda Hauser, and Gay Wachman (eds), *At Home and Abroad in the Empire: British Women Write the 1930s* (Newark: University of Delaware Press, 2009).

Hackney, Fiona, '"Women are News": British Women's Magazines 1919–1939', in *Transatlantic Print Culture, 1880–1940*, ed. Ann Ardis and Patrick Collier (Basingstoke: Palgrave Macmillan, 2008), pp. 114–33.

Hall, Lesley A., *Sex, Gender and Social Change in Britain Since 1880* (Basingstoke: Macmillan, 2000).

Hammill, Faye, *Literary Culture and Female Authorship in Canada 1760–2000* (Amsterdam: Rodopi, 2003).

——, *Sophistication: A Literary and Cultural History* (Liverpool: Liverpool University Press, 2010).

——, *Women, Celebrity, and Literary Culture Between the Wars* (Austin: University of Texas Press, 2008).

Hanscombe, Gillian and Virginia, L. Smyers, *Writing for Their Lives: The Modernist Women, 1910–1940* (Boston: Northeastern University Press, 1987).

Hanson, Clare, *Hysterical Fictions: The 'Woman's Novel' in the Twentieth Century* (Basingstoke: Palgrave, 2000).
Harding, Jason, *The Criterion: Cultural Politics and Periodical Networks in Inter-War Britain* (Oxford: Oxford University Press, 2002).
Harris, Alexandra, *Romantic Moderns: English Writers, Artists and the Imagination from Virginia Woolf to John Piper* (London: Thames and Hudson, 2010).
Hartley, Jenny, *Millions Like Us: British Women's Fiction of the Second World War* (London: Virago, 1997).
Suzanne Henig, 'Queen of Lud: Hope Mirrlees', in *Virginia Woolf Quarterly*, 1.2 (1973): 1–27.
Hewison, Robert, *Under Siege: Literary Life in London 1939–45* (London: Methuen, 1977).
Higonnet, Margaret et al. (eds), *Behind the Lines: Gender and the Two World Wars* (New Haven: Yale University Press, 1987).
Hinds, Hilary, 'Ordinary Disappointments: Femininity, Domesticity, and Nation in British Middlebrow Fiction, 1920–1944', *Modern Fiction Studies*, 55.2 (Summer 2009): 293–320.
Holtby, Winifred, *Letters to a Friend*, ed. Alice Alice and Jean McWilliam (London: Collins, 1937).
——, *Women in a Changing Civilization* (London: Bodley Head, 1929).
Hoberman, Ruth, *Gendering Classicism: The Ancient World in Twentieth-Century Women's Historical Fiction* (New York: State University of New York, 1997).
Hopkins, Chris, 'Sylvia Townsend Warner and the Marxist Historical Novel', *Literature and History*, 4.1 (Spring 1995): 50–64.
Howell, Georgina, *Gertude Bell: Queen of the Desert, Shaper of Nations* (New York: Farrar, Straus and Giroux, 2008).
Hughes, Helen, *The Historical Romance* (London and New York: Routledge, 1993).
Humble, Nicola, *The Feminine Middlebrow Novel 1920s to 1950s: Class, Domesticity and Bohemianism* (Oxford University Press, 2001).
Ifans, Dafydd (ed.), *Annwyl Kate, Annwyl Saunders: Gohebiaeth 1923–1983* (Aberystwyth: Llyfrgell Genedlaethol Cymru, 1992).
Jaffe, Aaron, *Modernism and the Culture of Celebrity* (Cambridge: Cambridge University Press, 2005).
Jameson, Storm, *Autobiography of Storm Jameson: Journey from the North*, 2 vols (London: Collins and Harvill Press, 1969).
Jarrett-Macauley, Delia, *The Life of Una Marson, 1905–65* (Manchester: Manchester University Press, 1998).
Joannou, Maroula, *'Ladies, Please Don't Smash These Windows': Women's Writing, Feminism and Social Change 1918–1938* (Oxford: Berg, 1995).
——, 'Nancy Cunard's English Journey', *Feminist Review*, 78 (2004): 141–63.
——, 'The Woman Writer in the 1930s: On Not being Mrs Giles of Durham City', in *Women Writers of the 1930s: Gender, Politics and History*, ed. Maroula Joannou (Edinburgh: Edinburgh University Press, 1998), pp. 1–13.
Kaplan, Cora, *Salt and Bitter and Good: Three Centuries of English and American Women Poets* (New York and London: Paddington Press, 1975).
Kent, Sylvia, *The Woman Writer* (Stroud: History Press, 2009).
Kirkham, Pat and David Thoms (eds), *War Culture: Social Change and Changing Experience in World War Two Britain* (London: Lawrence and Wishart, 1995).
Lassner, Phyllis, *Colonial Strangers: Women Writing the End of the British Empire* (New Brunswick: Rutgers University Press, 2004).

Select Bibliography

——, *British Women Writers of World War II: Battlefields of their Own* (London: Macmillan, 1998).

——, 'Under Suspicion: The Plotting of Britain in World War II Detective Spy Fiction', in *Intermodernism: Literary Culture in Mid-Twentieth-Century Britain*, ed. Kristin Bluemel (Edinburgh: Edinburgh University Press, 2009), pp. 113–30.

Le-Guilcher, Lucy and Phyllis Lassner (eds), *Rumer Godden: International and Intermodern Storyteller* (Farnham: Ashgate, 2010).

Leavis, Q.D., *Fiction and the Reading Public* (London: Chatto and Windus, 1932).

Lee, Hermione, *Virginia Woolf* (London: Chatto and Windus, 1996).

Light, Alison, *Forever England: Femininity, Literature and Conservatism between the Wars* (London: Routledge, 1991).

——, '"Young Bess": Historical Novels and Growing Up', *Feminist Review*, 33 (Autumn 1989): 57–71.

Little, Judy, *Comedy and the Woman Writer: Woolf, Spark and Feminism* (Lincoln: University of Nebraska Press, 1983).

Lucas, John, *The Radical Twenties* (Nottingham: Five Leaves Press, 1997).

Macdonald, Kate (ed.), *The Masculine Middlebrow, 1880–1950: What Mr Miniver Read* (Basingstoke: Palgrave Macmillan, 2011).

MacKay, Marina, *Modernism and World War II* (Cambridge: Cambridge University Press, 2007).

Majumdar, Saikat, 'Katherine Mansfield and the Fragility of Pákehá Boredom', *Modern Fictions Studies*, 55.1 (Spring 2009): 119–41.

Mao, Douglas and Rebecca L. Walkowitz (eds), *Bad Modernisms* (Durham: Duke University Press, 2006).

——, 'The New Modernist Studies', *PMLA*, 123.3 (May 2008): 737–48.

Marcus, Jane, *Hearts of Darkness: White Women Write Race* (New Brunswick: Rutgers University Press, 2004).

Marek, Jane E., *Women Editing Modernism* (Kentucky: University Press of Kentucky, 1995).

Maslen, Elizabeth, 'Naomi Mitchison's Historical Fiction', in *Women Writers of the 1930s: Gender Politics and History*, ed. Maroula Joannou (Edinburgh: Edinburgh University Press, 1999), pp. 138–50.

——, *Political and Social Issues in British Women's Fiction 1928–1968* (London: Palgrave, 2001).

Mathias, Roland, *Anglo-Welsh Literature: An Illustrated History* (Bridgend: Seren, 1986).

McClintock, Anne, *Imperial Leather: Race, Gender and Sexuality in the Colonial Context* (London: Routledge, 1995).

McLoughlin, Kate (ed.), *The Cambridge Companion to War Writing* (Cambridge: Cambridge University Press, 2009).

Melman, Billie, *Women and the Popular Imagination in the Twenties: Flappers and Nymphs* (Basingstoke: Macmillan, 1988).

Mills, Sara, *Discourses of Difference: An Analysis of Women's Travel Writing and Colonialism* (London: Routledge, 1991).

Mitchison, Naomi, 'Writing Historical Novels', *Saturday Review of Literature*, XI. 41 (27 April 1935): pp. 645–6.

——, *You May Well Ask: A Memoir 1920–1940* (London: Gollancz, 1979).

The Modern Girl Around the World Research Group, *The Modern Girl around the World: Consumption, Modernity, and Globalization* (Durham: Duke University Press, 2008).

Select Bibliography 301

Montefiore, Janet, *Feminism and Poetry* (London, Pandora, 1987).
——, *Men and Women Writers of the 1930s: The Dangerous Flood of History* (London: Routledge, 1996).
Moynagh, Maureen (ed.), *Essays on Race and Empire: Nancy Cunard* (Peterborough, Ontario: Broadview Press, 2002).
Nesbitt, Jennifer Poulos, *Narrative Settlements: Geographies of British Women's Fiction between the Wars* (Toronto: University of Toronto Press, 2005).
Nicholson, Virginia, *Singled Out: How Two Million Women Survived Without Men after the First World War* (Harmondsworth: Penguin, 2008).
Orwell, George, 'Bookshop Memories' [1936], in *The Collected Essays, Journalism and Letters, Vol. I: An Age Like This, 1920–1940*, ed. Sonia Orwell and Ian Angus (London: Secker and Warburg, 1968).
Pedersen, Susan, 'Metaphors of the Schoolroom: Women Working the Mandates System of the League of Nations', *History Workshop Journal*, 66 (2008): 188–207.
Pankhurst, Sylvia, 'The Fascist World War', in *The Sylvia Pankhurst Reader*, ed. Kathryn Dodd (Manchester: Manchester University Press, 1993), pp. 213–16.
Parsons, Deborah, *Streetwalking the Metropolis: Women, the City and Modernity* (Oxford: Oxford University Press, 2000).
Piette, Adam, *Imagination at War: British Fiction and Poetry 1939–1945* (London: Macmillan, 1995).
Plain, Gill, *Women's Fiction of the Second World War: Gender, Power and Resistance* (Edinburgh: Edinburgh University Press, 1996).
——, '"A Stiff is Still a Stiff in This Country": The Problem of Murder in Wartime', in *Conflict, Nationhood and Corporeality in Modern Literature: Bodies-at-War*, ed. Petra Rau (Basingstoke: Palgrave, 2010), pp. 104–23.
——, 'The Shape of Things to Come: The Remarkable Modernity of Vernon Lee's *Satan the Waster* (1915–1920)', in *Women, the First World War and the Dramatic Imagination. International Essays (1914–1999)*, ed. Claire Tylee (Lampeter: Edwin Mellen Press, 2000), pp. 5–21.
——, *Twentieth-Century Crime Fiction: Gender, Sexuality and the Body* (Edinburgh: Edinburgh University Press).
Pumphrey, Martin, 'Play, Fantasy and Strange Laughter: Stevie Smith's Uncomfortable Poetry', *Critical Quarterly*, 28.3 (Autumn 1986): 85–96.
Radway, Janice, *A Feeling for Books: the Book-of-the-Month Club, Literary Taste and Middle-Class Desire* (Chapel Hill: University of North Carolina Press, 1997).
Raitt, Suzanne, 'Charlotte Mew and May Sinclair: A Love Song', *Critical Quarterly*, 37.3 (Autumn 1995): 3–17.
Robinson, Annabel, *The Life and Works of Jane Ellen Harrison* (Oxford: Oxford University Press, 2002).
Rose, Sonya, O., *Which People's War? National Identity and Citizenship in Wartime Britain 1939–1945* (Oxford: Oxford University Press, 2003).
Schneider, Karen, *Loving Arms: British Women Writing the Second World* War (Lexington: University Press of Kentucky, 1997).
Scott, Bonnie Kime (ed.), *Gender in Modernism: New Geographies, Complex Intersections* (Urbana and Chicago: University of Illinois Press, 2007).
—— (ed.), *The Gender of Modernism: A Critical Anthology* (Bloomington: Indiana University Press, 1990).
Sebba, Anne, *Battling for News: The Rise of the Woman Reporter* (London: Hodder and Stoughton, 1994).
Shaw, Marion, *The Clear Stream: A Life of Winifred Holtby* (London: Virago, 1999).

Smith, Adrian, *The New Statesman: Portrait of a Political Weekly 1913–31* (London: Frank Cass, 1996).
Smith, Angela, *Katherine Mansfield: A Literary Life* (Basingstoke: Palgrave, 2000).
Snaith, Anna, '"Little Brown Girl" in a "White, White City": Una Marson and London', *Tulsa Studies in Women's Literature*, 27.1 (Spring 2008): 93–114.
Snaith, Anna and Michael H. Whitworth, 'Introduction' to *Locating Woolf: The Politics of Space and Place* (Basingstoke: Palgrave Macmillan, 2007).
Sochen, June (ed.), *Women's Comic Visions* (Detroit: Wayne State University Press, 1991).
Southworth, Helen, *Leonard and Virginia Woolf, the Hogarth Press, and the Networks of Modernism* (New York: Columbia University Press, 2010).
Spalding, Frances, *Stevie Smith: A Critical Biography* (London: Faber, 1988).
Squier, Susan M., 'Rose Macaulay', in *The Gender of Modernism: A Critical Anthology*, ed. Bonnie Kime Scott (Bloomington and Indianapolis: University of Indiana Press, 1990), pp. 252–9.
Stetz, Margaret D., *British Women's Comic Fiction, 1890–1990: Not Drowning, But Laughing* (Aldershot: Ashgate, 2001).
Suh, Judy, *Fascism and Anti-Fascism in Twentieth-Century British Fiction* (New York: Palgrave, 2009).
Taylor, Georgina, *H.D. and the Public Sphere of Modernist Women Writers 1913–1946* (Oxford: Oxford University Press, 2001).
Tester, Keith (ed.), *The Flâneur* (London: Routledge, 1994).
Thacker, Andrew, *Moving through Modernity: Space and Geography in Modernism* (Manchester: Manchester University Press, 2003).
Treglown, Jeremy and Bridget Bennett (eds), *Grub Street and the Ivory Tower: Literary Journalism and Literary Scholarship from Fielding to the Internet* (Oxford: Oxford University Press, 1998).
Trodd, Anthea, *Women's Writing in English: Britain 1900–1945* (London: Longman, 1998).
Tusan, Michelle, *Women Making News: Gender and Journalism in Modern Britain* (Champaign: University of Illinois Press, 2005).
Tylee, Claire, M., *The Great War and Women's Consciousness: Images of Militarism and Womanhood in Women's Writing, 1914–64* (Basingstoke: Macmillan, 1990).
Wachman, Gay, *Lesbian Empire: Radical Crosswriting in the Twenties* (New Brunswick: Rutgers University Press, 2001).
Walkowitz, Rebecca, L., *Cosmopolitan Style: Modernism beyond the Nation* (New York: Columbia University Press, 2006).
Wall, Cheryl A., T*he Harlem Renaissance* (Bloomington: Indiana University Press, 1995).
Waller, Jane and Michael Vaughan-Rees, *Women in Wartime: The Role of Women's Magazines 1939–1945* (London, MacDonald Optima, 1987).
Wasson, Sara, *Urban Gothic of the Second World War: Dark London* (Basingstoke: Palgrave, 2010).
White, Cynthia, *Women's Magazines 1693–1968* (London: Michael Johnson, 1970).
Winning, Joanne, *The Pilgrimage of Dorothy Richardson* (Madison: University of Wisconsin Press, 2000).
Woollacott, Angela, *Gender and Empire* (Basingstoke: Palgrave Macmillan, 2006).
Young, Tory, 'Nancy Cunard's *Black Man White Ladyship* as Surrealist Tract', in *At Home and Abroad in the Empire: British Women Write the 1930s*, ed. Robin Hackett,

Freda S. Hauser, and Gay Wachman (Newark: University of Delaware Press, 2009), pp. 96–118.

——, 'The Reception of Nancy Cunard's *Negro Anthology*', in *Women Writers of the 1930s: Gender, Politics, History*, ed. Maroula Joannou (Edinburgh: Edinburgh University Press, 1999), pp. 113–22.

——, 'Torrents of Trash', *Cambridge Quarterly*, 33 (2004): 187–9.

Zwerdling, Alexander, *Virginia Woolf and the Real World* (Berkeley: University of California Press, 1986).

Index

Abyssinia, 12, 259
Ackland, Valentine, 80, 85–7, 90–1, 163, 173
  For Sylvia: An Honest Account, 87
  Whether a Dove or a Seagull, 35, 82, 172
Actresses' Franchise League, 184
Africa, 6, 36
  see also Kenya; South Africa
Aldington, Richard, 7, 27, 137, 162–3, 167
Ali, Monica, *Brick Lane*, 226
Allan, Dot, 228
  Hunger March, 219, 228
  Makeshift, 228
Allatini, Rose, 8, 202
allegory, 89, 139, 185–7
Allingham, Margery, 101, 108, 144–5, 148, 150, 156, 237
  The Fashion in Shrouds, 108
  Sweet Danger, 108
  Traitor's Purse, 237
Anand, Mulk Raj, 6
Anderson, Margaret, 29
anti-Semitism, 45, 48–9, 147
Apollinaire, Guillaume, 280
Apuleius, *The Golden Ass*, 83
Aragon, Louis, 163
Archdale, Helen, 11
Argentina, 27
Arlen, Michael, *The Green Hat*, 8, 278, 286
Astor, Nancy, Viscountess, 11, 70
Atkinson, M.E., *The Chimney Corner*, 185
Atwood, Clare ('Tony Atwood'), 10
Auden, W.H., 43, 83
Austen, Jane, 5, 14, 60, 103
  Northanger Abbey, 148

Bagnold, Enid, 192
  Lottie Dundass, 192
  National Velvet, 192
Barlow, Jane, 218
  By Beach and Bogland, 218

Barnes, Djuna, 2, 170, 282
  'How It Feels To Be Forcibly Fed', 32
  Ladies' Almanack, 35
  Nightwood, 35
Barney, Natalie, 170, 282
Barry, Iris, 202
Barthes, Roland, 59, 63
Basic English, 46
Baudelaire, Charles, 168, 264, 267, 269, 276–7, 287
  'The Painter of Modern Life', 267
Beach, Sylvia, 163, 168, 170
Beard, Mary Ritter, 112
  Laughing Their Way, 112
Beauman, Nicola, 2–3
Beauvoir, Simone de, 217
  The Second Sex, 217
Beckett, Samuel, 7, 26, 43, 275
Beethoven, Ludwig van, 63
Behn, Aphra, 14, 33
Bell, Gertrude, 252
Bell, Julian, 68
Benjamin, Walter, 264, 276, 283
  The Arcades Project, 264
Bennett, Arnold, 101, 207, 228
Bennett, Louise, 251
Benson, E.F., 101
  Mapp and Lucia, 104
Benson, Stella, 6, 202, 210, 257–8
  Goodbye, Stranger, 257–8
  The Little World, 251
Bentley, E.C., 152
Bentley, Phyllis, 131–3, 207
  Freedom, Farewell!, 132
  Bermondsey Book, The, 163
Bermondsey Bookshop, 163
Berridge, Elizabeth, 235–6
  'Chance Callers', 244–5
  'To Tea with the Colonel', 235–6
Besler, Rudolf, 184
  Kultur at Home, 184
Betjeman, John, 6
Bidder, George, 184
  Patriotic Pence, 184

bi-location, 84, 91
birth control, 204
Blackwood's Magazine, 85
Blake, William, 45
  'Jerusalem', 69–71
  Milton, 70
BLAST, 24, 30, 32
Bloomsbury Group, 57, 69, 102, 208, 245
Bondfield, Margaret, 11
book clubs, 86, 100
Book Guild, 100
Book-of-the-Month Club, 86, 100
book reviewing, 207–8
Book Society, 100
Boots Booklovers' libraries, 99
Bowen, Elizabeth, 11, 13, 90–1, 113, 202, 222, 227, 230, 233–4, 255
  'Daffodils', 124
  The Death of the Heart, 100, 107, 114
  The Demon Lover, 233, 246
  The Heat of the Day, 124, 241, 246
  The Last September, 145, 222–3, 255–6
  To the North, 278–80
Bowes Lyon, Lilian, 163, 177
Box, Muriel, 185–6, 190
  Angels at War, 185, 190
  Peace in Our Time, 185–6
Box, Sydney, 185
Boyle, Kay, 29, 163
Braddon, Mary Elizabeth, 147
breast-feeding, 51–2
Breton, André, 285
  Nadja, 285
Bridges, Robert, 169
Brierley, Walter, 12
  Means Test Men, 12
British Empire, 6–7, 35–6, 221, 250–60
  Exhibition 1924, 250
Brittain, Vera, 2, 9, 11–13, 35, 187, 208–11
Brontë, Charlotte, 33
  The Professor, 149
  Shirley, 154
  Villette, 149, 265
Brontë, Emily, 33, 60
Brontës, 5, 103, 168
Broster, D.K., 131
  The Dark Mile, 135
  The Flight of the Heron, 135
  The Gleam in the North, 135

Browne, Thomas, 71–3, 280
  The Garden of Cyrus, 71–2
  Quincuniall, 173
  Urn Burial, 73
Browning, Elizabeth Barrett, 5, 48
Browning, Robert, 48
Bruere, Martha Bensley, 112
  Laughing Their Way, 112
Bryher, pseud., *see* Ellerman, Winifred
Buchan, John, 101, 147
Buck, Percy, 85–6
Burney, Frances, 14
Butts, Mary, 130, 137, 208
  Scenes from the Life of Cleopatra, 138

Calendar of Modern Letters, The, 202, 205
Cape, Jonathan, publisher, 41, 44–5, 50, 174
Caribbean, 6, 254, 259–60
Carswell, Catherine, 227
  Open the Door!, 227
Catlin, George, 211
cats, 79–83, 90–1
Cézanne, Paul, 287
Chaplin, Charlie, 154
Chapman and Hall, 45
Chatto and Windus, 44
Chaucer, Geoffrey, 89
  Canterbury Tales, 89
Chesterton, G.K., 152
Cheyney, Ralph, 34
  'What is This Modernism?', 34
Chilver, Sally, 45
China, 6, 257–8
Chlumberg, Hans, 186
  Miracle at Verdun, 186
Christianity, 63, 73, 84–5, 90–1, 149, 153–4, 224–6, 282
Christie, Agatha, 3, 144–50, 155, 237
  And Then There Were None, 189
  Appointment with Death, 189
  Black Coffee, 189
  The Hollow, 192
  The Mousetrap, 189
  The Moving Finger, 237
  The Murder at the Vicarage, 148–51, 153
  Nemesis, 151
  N or M?, 237

Cixous, Hélène, 67
Classicism, 24, 131, 137–8
Cleopatra, 138
Close Up (journal), 29
Cocteau, Jean, 280
coffeehouses, 266
Coleridge, Samuel Taylor, 68
  Remorse, 68
Collins, Wilkie, 147, 152
colonialism, *see* British Empire
comedy, 112–29, 148, 155, 183, 193, 237, 239–44
Communist Party, 80, 87, 173
Compton-Burnett, Ivy, 3, 121, 145
Connolly, Cyril, 47
Conrad, Joseph, 14
conservatism, 3, 33, 50–1, 110, 114, 134–5, 145–6, 155, 172, 176–7, 183–4, 194, 203
Cooper, Lettice, 12, 208, 210
Co-operative Working Women's Guild, 15
Cornford, Frances, 161, 163, 177
Coward, Noel, 3, 114
  Private Lives, 152–3
Craig, Edith, 9, 32
crime fiction, 17, 144–56
Crisis (journal), 29
Criterion, The, 202, 205–6
Critic, The, 112
Crocker, Bosworth, 185
  Pawns of War, 185
Crompton, Richmal, 202, 210
Cross, Amanda, pseud., *see* Heilbrun, Carolyn
Cunard, Nancy, 7–8, 12, 26, 57, 89, 163–5, 168, 170, 172–3, 259–60, 275–6, 278
  Black Man and White Ladyship, 250–1
  'Jamaica: The Negro Island', 259
  Negro: An Anthology, 7, 26
  Parallax, 7, 275–6, 280–1, 283, 285–8
  'Psalm for Trinidad', 260
  The White Man's Duty, 260
Cunningham, Peter, 266
  Handbook to London, 1850, 266

Daily Express, The, 44, 204
Dane, Clemence, 8, 204, 207, 210
  Bill of Divorcement, 188–9, 191

Shivering Shocks, 186
Will Shakespeare, 192
Daryush, Elizabeth, 161, 163, 177
Daskam, Josephine, 112
Daviot, Gordon, pseud., *see* Mackintosh, Elizabeth
Deeping, Warwick, 101
Delafield, E.M., 99, 101–2, 119, 202–5
  Diary of a Provincial Lady, 101–2, 114, 118, 125–6
  The Way Things Are, 124–5
Dell, Ethel M., 98
Depression, Great, 11–12, 219, 227
Detection Club, 152
Dial, The, 29, 168
Dick, Kay, 45
Dickens, Charles, 102–3, 152, 154
Dickens, Monica, 237–8
  The Fancy, 242–4
  One Pair of Feet, 237–8
domesticity, 5–6, 11, 49, 66, 104, 109, 113–14, 118, 125–6, 172, 176, 183–7, 190, 193, 203–4, 218–20, 235, 242–7, 255–6, 271
Doolittle, Hilda, *see* H.D.
Doyle, Sir Arthur Conan, 152
  see also Holmes, Sherlock
drama, 182–95
Du Bois, W.E.B., 27, 29, 36
Du Maurier, Daphne, 3
  Frenchman's Creek, 133–4, 238
  Rebecca, 193
  The Years Between, 192, 194

Eastman, Crystal, 203
Eckhardt, Amelia, 108
Edgeworth, Maria, 222
  Castle Rackrent, 222
Edwards, Dorothy, 227
  'The Conquered', 228–9
  Rhapsody, 228
  Winter Sonata, 228
Egoist, The, 28, 169
Einstein, Albert, 1–2, 65
Eliot, George, 5, 33
  Middlemarch, 227
Eliot, T.S., 3, 14, 28–9, 34, 40, 43–4, 163, 167–8, 205–7, 210, 275, 280–1, 286–7
  'The Love Song of J. Alfred Prufrock', 280, 282–3, 286

'Preludes', 286
'Tradition and the Individual Talent', 24, 62
The Waste Land, 1–2, 26, 57, 166, 280, 285–6
Ellerman, Winifred, 29, 137
Empson, William, 16
England, 135–6
English literature, teaching of, 16, 58–60
English Review, The, 27
English Woman's Journal, 201
Epilogue (journal), 163
Equal Franchise Act 1928, 131, 150
Ertz, Susan, 202
escapism, 131, 133–5
Ethiopia, *see* Abyssinia
Evans, Caradoc, 223
  My People, 222
Evans, Cicely Louise, 186
  Antic Disposition, 186
Evans, Margiad, pseud., *see* Whistler, Peggy
Eve (journal), 86
Evening Standard, 46
evolutionary theory, 36
Eyles, Leonora, 204

Faber and Faber, 41, 163
family, 11, 108–10, 117, 120, 123, 145, 183, 192–4, 219–20, 223–4, 242
fantasy, 8, 79, 84, 91, 105, 137, 186, 275
Farjeon, Eleanor, 3, 176, 202
Farrell, M.J., pseud., *see* Keane, Molly
Fascism, 12–13, 88–9, 131, 133, 155, 211, 259
fashion, 8, 218–19
Fauset, Jessie Redmon, 29, 36
femininity, 2, 10, 134, 162–5, 194
feminism, 4, 6–8, 10–18, 25–37, 49–50, 57–73, 131, 138–40, 152–5, 168–74, 184, 187, 192, 201–3
Ferber, Edna, 113
Ferguson, Rachel, 101
  The Brontës Went to Woolworths, 104–6
films, 49, 154
  Brief Encounter, 2
  Thelma and Louise, 279
First World War, *see* World War I
flânerie, 278–81
flâneur, 264–8, 276–8, 281, 285

flâneuse, 268–73, 276–8
Ford, Ford Madox, 27
Forster, E.M., 35, 210
  A Passage to India, 260
Forum, The (magazine), 86
Foucault, Michel, 59, 63
Foyle's bookshop, 100
Frankau, Gilbert, 101
Frazer, James George, Sir, 139
  The Golden Bough, 139
free verse, 167–9
Freewoman, The, 28, 206
French Revolution, 130, 173
Freud, Sigmund, 1, 27, 57, 65, 109, 123, 139, 149, 278, 285
  Why War?, 65–6
Fry, Roger, 59

Galsworthy, John, 101
Gandy, Ida, 186
  In the House of Despair, 186
Garnett, David, 82, 174
Garnett, Edward, 50
Gaskell, Elizabeth, 150, 154
  Cranford, 150, 154
Gawthorpe, Mary, 28
General Strike 1926, 104
Gershon, Karen, 175
Gibbon, Lewis Grassic, 221
  Sunset Song, 220
Gibbons, Stella, 101, 119
  Cold Comfort Farm, 102–3, 114, 118
Gilman, Charlotte Perkins, 28
Gissing, George, 154
  The Odd Women, 154
Gladstone, W.E., 154
globalization, 4, 6, 25–6, 37
Godden, Rumer, 6–7, 251, 256, 260
  Black Narcissus, 257
  Breakfast with the Nikolides, 257
Godwin, William, 153
Gollancz, Victor, publisher, 41, 48–9
Good Housekeeping, 15, 203–4, 207
Gourmont, Remy de, 24–5
  The Natural Philosophy of Love, 24
Grand, Sarah, 154
Graves, Robert, 3, 163, 167
  But It Still Goes On, 184
Great War, *see* World War I
Green, Henry, 43, 235

Greene, Graham, 235
  The Ministry of Fear, 235
Greenwood, Anthony, 12
  Love on the Dole, 12
Griffiths, Hubert, 184
  Tunnel Trench, 184
Grimké, Angela Weld, 33–4
  'Beware Lest He Awakes', 34
  'Your Eyes', 34
Gutman, Ethel, 163
Guys, Constantin, 267

H.D., 2, 9, 24, 27–30, 130, 137, 161, 163, 166–7, 275
  'The Cinema and the Classics', 29
  Palimpsest, 137–8, 141
  Sea Garden, 167
  Trilogy, 176
Hale, Robert, publisher, 48
Hall, Radclyffe, 86
  'Miss Ogilvy Finds Herself', 30–1
  The Well of Loneliness, 9, 35, 50
Hamilton, Cicely, 3, 202, 210
  The Child in Flanders, 185
  How the Vote Was Won, 32
  The Old Adam, 186
  The Pageant of Great Women, 192
Hamilton, Mary Agnes, 210
Hankey, Arthur, Mrs, 184
  A House-Warming in War-Time, 184
Hardy, Thomas, 169, 173
Harlem Renaissance, 6, 34, 251
Harper's Bazaar, 46, 113
Harrison, Jane, 131, 275, 284
Harrow School, 84–5
Hart-Davis, Rupert, 69
Hastings, Beatrice, 29
Hayford, Adelaide Casely, 36
  'Mista Courifer', 36–7
Heap, Jane, 29
Heilbrun, Carolyn, 155
Henderson, Alice Corbin, 29
Heseltine, Olive, 208
Heterodoxy (New York collective), 113
Heyer, Georgette, 129–30, 133–4, 236, 238
  The Black Moth, 133
  An Infamous Army, 134
  These Old Shades, 133–4
Hill, Diana Murray, 238
  Ladies May Now Leave Their Machines, 238
Hirst, Damien, 82
historical fiction, 17, 129–41, 144
Hitler, Adolf, 12, 70, 133, 176
Hogarth Press, 15, 26, 41, 57, 65, 280
Holden, Inez, 6, 40–3, 45–8, 53
  Born Old, Died Young, 47
  'Country House Bridge', 46
  Death in High Society, 46
  diaries, 46–7
  'Fellow Travellers in Factory', 47
  'Fox Hunting – Is It Human?', 46
  It Was Different at the Time, 47
  Night Shift, 46, 238
  There's No Story There, 47
Holmes, Sherlock, 104, 148–9, 151
  see also Doyle, Sir Arthur Conan
Holtby, Winifred, 6, 9–12, 163, 172, 187, 200, 202, 204, 207, 210, 251, 258–9
  The Land of Green Ginger, 258–9
  Mandoa, Mandoa!, 259
  South Riding, 10, 259
  Women and a Changing Civilization, 13, 131
Home Journal, 203
homosexuality, 8–9, 25, 33–7, 80
  see also lesbianism
Horizon, 47
Hours Press, The, 7, 26, 163, 275
Hughes, Langston, 27
Hulme, T.E., 24–5, 33
humour, *see* comedy
Hunt, Violet, 27
Hurston, Zora Neale, 27
Huxley, Aldous, 108, 210
  Antic Hay, 286
Huxley, Elspeth, 6
  Red Strangers, 256
hysteria, 25

imagism, 24–5, 27, 137, 165, 167
imperialism, *see* British Empire
India, 36, 84, 253, 256–7
Intermodernism, 6, 17, 25, 41–53
  see also Modernism; Postmodernism
Ireland, 7–8, 18, 35, 48, 133, 217, 222–31
irony, 5, 31, 81, 83–4, 103, 113, 124–5, 129, 239–40, 242, 285

Irwin, Margaret, 131, 134
  The Gay Galliard, 133
  Young Bess, 133–4

Jackson, Ada, 175–6
  Behold the Jew, 176
  World in Labour, 175
Jackson, Laura, *see* Riding, Laura
James, P.D., 144, 155
  An Unsuitable Job for a Woman, 155
James, William, 27
Jameson, Storm, 2, 11–13, 45, 187, 200, 203, 209
  In the Second Year, 12
  Journey from the North, 11–13
Japan, 29
Jarrow March 1936, 11
Jennings, Gertrude, 184
  Waiting for the Bus, 184
Jewish influences, 12, 44, 48–9, 80, 168, 175–6, 210
Joad, C.E.M., 240
John, Augustus, 46
Johnson, Amy, 108
Johnson, Pamela Hansford, 11, 202
Jones, Glyn, 221
Jones, Lewis, 12, 221–2
  Cwmardy, 12
journalism, 17–18, 25, 29, 32, 40–6, 48, 112–13, 163, 199–211, 201–2, 205–11
Joyce, James, 1–2, 5–6, 14, 27–8, 43, 83, 230
  Finnegan's Wake, 1
  Portrait of the Artist as a Young Man, 217–18
  Ulysses, 1, 15, 40, 278
Jung, Carl Gustav, 27

Kafka, Franz, 14, 224
Keane, Molly, 230
  Mad Puppetstown, 222–3
Kennedy, Margaret, 131
  The Constant Nymph, 189–90
  Escape Me Never, 188
Kenya, 6, 256
Keys (magazine), 254
King-Hall, Magdalen, 133
  Life and Death of the Wicked Lady Skelton, 133–4

Labour Party, 50, 64, 70, 155
Lane, John, publisher, 41, 47
Laski, Marghanita, 11, 202, 210
Lassner, Phyllis, 6
Lawrence, D.H., 27–8, 43, 58–9, 167, 170, 227
  Lady Chatterley's Lover, 102
Lawrence, T.E., 251
Le Corbusier, 6, 279, 283
League of Nations, 65, 185, 281
Leavis, F.R., 16, 43, 205, 207
Leavis, Q.D., 101, 205
Lee, Vernon, 8, 186–7
  The Ballet of the Nations, 8, 186–7
  Satan the Waster, 186
Left Book Club, 48
Left Review, 173, 209
Lehmann, Rosamond, 2, 12, 45, 101, 207
  Dusty Answer, 108–9, 114, 119–23, 126
lesbianism, 2, 8–10, 20–1, 30–1, 34–5, 50, 80, 84–6, 140, 163, 169, 172, 282–4
Levy, Andrea, 226
  Small Island, 226
Lewis, Lorna, 204–5
Lewis, Eiluned, 223, 229–30
  Dew on the Grass, 223, 229–30
Lewis, Saunders, 218, 221
Lewis, Wyndham, 24–7, 33, 210
  Men without Art, 24
Lewisohn, Mary Arnold, *see* Crocker, Bosworth
libraries, 99–100
Little Review, The, 29, 168
Llewellyn, Richard, 188
  Poison Pen, 188
Locke, Alain, 27
Lofts, Norah, 133
London, 6, 27, 35, 41, 68, 116, 208, 236, 255, 264–73, 278–80, 282–3, 286–8
London and National Society for Women's Service, 10
Loos, Anita, 112–13
Lowell, Amy, 24, 28, 34, 167
Loy, Mina, 163, 166–8, 275
  'Anglo-Mongrels and the Rose', 168
  'Modern Poetry', 168
Lukács, Georg, 135, 139, 141
  The Historical Novel, 130
Lynd, Sylvia, 208

MacAlmon, Robert, 170
Macaulay, Rose, 13, 118, 131, 136, 204, 208, 210–11
  And No Man's Wit, 211
  Crewe Train, 102
  Dangerous Ages, 123–4
  Potterism, 114, 118–19, 123, 126
  They Were Defeated, 129–31
MacCarthy, Desmond, 207
MacDiarmid, Hugh, 221–2, 224
Mackintosh, Elizabeth, 144, 155
  The Laughing Woman, 192
  Richard of Bordeaux, 192
MacNeice, Louis, 182
Macpherson, Kenneth, 29
magic realism, 79
Mander, Jane, 251
Mannin, Ethel, 11, 202
Manning, Olivia, 45
Mansfield, Katherine, 6, 14, 28, 30, 40, 57, 251, 255
  'At the Bay', 255
  'Bliss', 9
  'The Garden Party', 255
  'The Prelude', 26
  'The Stranger', 255
  'The Woman at the Store', 255
marriage, 8, 10, 13, 23, 30, 86, 109–10, 113, 133–6, 150, 153, 170, 190, 228, 242–4, 258
Marsden, Dora, 28
Marsh, Ngaio, 144–5, 147, 150, 155–6
  Death at the Bar, 146
Marson, Una, 6, 251, 154–5, 259
  At What Price, 254
  London Calling, 254
  Pocomania, 254
Marxism, 84–5, 89–90, 130, 139, 173
  Communist Manifesto, 81, 140
masculinity, 8, 13, 23–5, 33, 37, 62, 100, 112, 116–17, 147, 149–50, 152, 190, 194, 234, 250–2, 264
Masses, The (journal), 34
Mass Observation, 90
Mata Hari, 154
Matisse, Henri, 6
Maugham, W. Somerset, 235
  For Services Rendered, 184
  The Razor's Edge, 235
  The Sacred Flame, 184

Maxeke, Charlotte Manye, 36
Maxwell, William, 82
Mayo, Kathleen, 258
Mayor, F.M., 15
  The Rector's Daughter, 15
McCracken, Esther, 182
  Living Room, 188
  No Medals, 193
  Quiet Weekend, 193
Mew, Charlotte, 161, 163, 168–9, 171
  The Farmer's Bride, 169
  'On the Road to the Sea', 169
  Saturday Market, 169
Meynell, Viola, 202
middlebrow, 14–18, 97–111, 118, 145, 155, 182–94, 207, 251
Miles, Susan, pseud., *see* Roberts, Ursula Wyllie
Milholland, Inez, 34
Millay, Edna St Vincent, 34, 170
Miller, Alice Duer, 113
Miller, Betty, 6, 40–3, 45, 47–50, 53
  Farewell Leicester Square, 48–9
  The Mere Living, 48–9
  'Next Year in Jerusalem', 48
  On the Side of the Angels, 47–8, 52
  Portrait of the Bride, 48
  Sunday, 48
Miller, Emanuel, 48
Mirrlees, Hope, 2, 26, 275–6, 280–5
  Lud-in-the-Mist, 275
  Paris, 2, 26, 275–6, 280–5
Mitchell, Gladys, 144, 149–50, 237
Mitchison, Naomi, 6, 11–12, 40–4, 49–53, 129, 133, 135–6, 139, 141, 172–5, 202, 208
  Barbarian Stories, 50
  The Bull Calves, 238
  Cloud Cuckoo Land, 51
  The Conquered, 51, 131–3, 229
  The Corn King and the Spring Queen, 51, 139
  An Outline for Boys and Girls and Their Parents, 50
  We Have Been Warned, 12, 50–2
  When the Bough Breaks, 131
Mitford, Mary Russell, 48
Mitford, Nancy, 101
  Noblesse Oblige, 105
  Pigeon Pie, 240–1

The Pursuit of Love, 109
mobility, 7, 17–18, 36, 100, 146, 183, 193–4, 277–81
Modernism, 1–18, 23–37, 40–3, 57–8, 83–92, 98, 137, 145, 148, 165, 167–8, 221, 267, 275, 278, 280–8
  see also Intermodernism; Postmodernism
modernity, 1–18, 23–5, 29, 34–7, 42, 45, 49, 58, 134, 147, 150, 154–5
Modern Woman (magazine), 204, 207
Moir, Phyllis, 64
Molière, 88–9
Monroe, Harriet, 29
Montgomery, L.M., 251
Moore, Marianne, 2, 24, 29, 167–9
Morgan, Elena Paul, 230
Y Wisg Sidan, 229
Mosley, Oswald, 12–13
Mozart, Wolfgang Amadeus, 88–9
Muir, Edwin, 224
Muir, Willa, 224
  Belonging: A Memoir, 224–5
  Imagined Corners, 220, 224–7
Munro, C.K., 186
  The Rumour, 186
Murray, Margaret, 131
Murry, John Middleton, 207
Mussolini, 12, 259

Nation, The (magazine), 86
National Association for the Advancement of Colored People, 29
National Union of Societies for Equal Citizenship, 11
National Union of Women's Suffrage Societies, 11
Nazism, 15, 71, 87, 175, 209, 237, 241
Neruda, Pablo, 275
New Age, The (journal), 29
New Freewoman, The, 28–9
New Republic (magazine), 64, 113
New Statesman, 15, 98, 131, 174, 206, 208–10
New Yorker (magazine), 29, 82, 113
New Zealand, 155
News Chronicle, 210
Nietzsche, Friedrich, 24–5
Nyonin Geijutsu (Japanese journal), 29

O'Brien, Kate, 11, 202, 222, 227
  The Ante-Room, 224
  The Land of Spices, 224
  Mary Lavelle, 224
O'Casey, Sean, 184, 186
  The Silver Tassie, 184, 186
O'Flaherty, Liam, 222
  The Black Soul, 222
Ocampo, Virginia, 27
Ogden, C.K., 46
Open Door Council, 210
Orage, A.R., 29
Orczy, Emma, Baroness, 134–5
  'Old Man in the Corner', 268–9
  The Scarlet Pimpernel, 133
Orwell, George, 6, 49, 98, 101
  Animal Farm, 48
  Down and Out in Paris and London, 48–9
  Keep the Aspidistra Flying, 99
Owen, Wilfred, 173

pacifism, 13, 57, 66, 69, 71, 73, 186–7, 210, 245
Padmore, George, 260
  The White Man's Duty, 260
Paget, Violet, *see* Lee, Vernon
Pankhurst, 259
Paris, 2, 7, 26, 29, 35, 163, 170, 264, 275–6, 280–5, 287–8
Parker, Dorothy, 112–13
Parkes, Bessie Rayner, 201
Parsons, Ian, 44
patriarchy, 5, 51–3, 59–60, 225, 239
Partridge, Frances, 245–7
  A Pacifist's War, 245–7
Peach, Lawrence du Gard, 184
  Shells, 184
Pearl Harbor, 71
Pearson Newnes, publisher, 44
Perham, Margery, 252
Persephone Books, 3
Piaf, Edith, 282
Picasso, Pablo, 6
Pitcher, Velona, 186
  The Searcher, 186
Pitter, Ruth, 163, 177
Plaid Cymru, 136
Poe, Edgar Allan, 265–9
  'The Man of the Crowd', 265–9

poetry, 3, 18, 33–5, 41, 44–5, 81–3, 87–8, 91, 161–77, 221–2, 236, 254, 275–6, 280–8
Poetry (magazine), 29
Poetry Bookshop, London, 163, 169–70
Popplewell, Olive, 187
  The Pacifist, 187
  This Bondage, 187
popular culture, 17, 25, 40, 90, 183
Porter, Horace, Mrs, 184
  Patriotic Pence, 184
postcolonialism, 7, 25, 251, 256
Postmodernism, 17, 42, 145
  see also Intermodernism; Modernism
Potter, Beatrix, 151
Pound, Ezra, 1–2, 7, 14, 24–5, 27, 29, 40, 163, 166–8, 170, 286
  'Hugh Selwyn Mauberley', 1
Power, Eileen, 131
Powys, Theodore, 86
Price, Evadne, 8
Priestley, J.B., 3
  Johnson over Jordan, 186
Proust, Marcel, 14
  Contre Saint-Beuve, 82
psychology, 27–8, 149, 151, 168
publishers, 41, 44
  see also individual names
Pym, Barbara, 118

queering, see homosexuality; lesbianism

racism, 31, 33–4, 36, 254–5
Raine, Kathleen, 173
  'Fata Morgana', 172
Ransom, John Crowe, 34
Rathbone, Eleanor, 6, 11, 258
  Child Marriage: The Indian Minotaur, 258
  The Disinherited Family, 11
Rattigan, Terence, 3
readers, 99–101, 103, 145, 204–5
realism, 13, 27–8, 32, 41, 43, 47, 91, 100, 123, 133–9, 148, 155–6, 165–6, 175, 183, 281
Reid, Hilda, 131, 202
Renault, Mary, 238–9
  The Friendly Young Ladies, 238–8
Rendell, Ruth, 144, 155
Rhys, Jean, 6, 11, 202, 253

  After Leaving Mr Mackenzie, 254
  Good Morning, Midnight, 254, 265, 276, 283, 287
  'Mixing Cocktails', 254
  Smile Please, 36
  Voyage in the Dark, 36, 253–4
Rhondda, Margaret, Viscountess, 11, 204, 210
Richards, I.A., 16
Richardson, Dorothy, 27, 29, 167
  'Continuous Performance', 29
  Dawn's Left Hand, 9
  Pilgrimage, 27, 265, 268–73, 277–8
Ridge, Lola, 34
Riding, Laura, 3, 7, 163–4, 166–7, 275
  'Helen's Faces', 167
  'The Lady of the Apple', 167
  A Pamphlet against Anthologies, 167
  'Postponement of Self', 167
  'The Word "Woman"', 167
Ridler, Anne, 163, 172, 177
Roberts, Kate, 218–22, 227, 230
  Feet in Chains, 219–20
  O Gors y Bryniae, 218
Roberts, Lynette, 3, 221–2
  Gods with Stainless Ears, 175–6
Roberts, Ursula Wyllie, 176
Robertson, E. Arnot, 101
  Cullum, 103, 106
Robins, Elizabeth, 9
Romanticism, 24–5, 42, 62
Rootham, Helen, 164
Rowland, Helen, 112
Rowling, J.K., 144
Royal Society of Literature, 48
Royde-Smith, Naomi, 207–8
Russian Revolution, 30
Rye, Elizabeth, 187
  The Three-Fold Path, 187

Sackville, Margaret, Lady, 162
Sackville-West, Vita, 9, 163, 172, 177, 252
  Passenger to Teheran, 252
Sanborn, Kate, 112
  The Wit of Women, 112
Sappho, 9, 164
Sassoon, Siegfried, 169
Sayers, Dorothy, 108, 144–52, 207
  Busman's Honeymoon, 188

Gaudy Night, 152, 154–5
Strong Poison, 114, 150–4
Schreiner, Olive, 10–11
Scotland, 7–8, 18, 135, 217, 220–31
Scots language, 220
Scott, Walter, 135
  Waverley, 129–30
Scovell, E.J., 161, 177
Scrutiny, 205
Seabury, Florence, 113
Second World War, *see* World War II
Seito (Japanese journal), 29
Seizin Press, 163
sentimentalism, 5, 24, 27, 31, 33–4, 118–19, 161–4, 173
Sex Disqualification (Removal) Act (1919), 202
Shakespeare, William, 60, 63
  Othello, 70
  Two Gentlemen of Verona, 70
Shakespeare and Company, Paris, 163, 168
Sharp, Evelyn, 32
  'The Woman at the Gate', 32
Shaw, George Bernard, 187
shell-shock, 25, 31
Shepherd, Nan, 227
  A Pass in the Grampians, 220
  The Quarry Wood, 220–1
  The Weatherhouse, 220
Sherriff, R.C., 184–5, 190
  Journey's End, 184–5, 190
Simon, Shena, 65
Simpson, Helen, 202
Sinclair, May, 27–8, 40–1, 163, 167–8
  Mary Olivier: A Life, 27–8
  The Tree of Heaven, 31–2
Sitwell, Edith, 3, 41, 43, 161, 163–9, 175, 275
  Bucolic Comedies, 166
  Façade, 114, 165–6
  'Fox Trot', 166
  Gold Coast Customs, 166
  'Hornpipe', 166
  'Modern Poetry', 165
  The Sleeping Beauty, 166
  The Wooden Pegasus, 114
Six Points Group, 11, 210
Sketch, The, 46
slavery, 132

Smith, Barbara Leigh, 201
Smith, Dodie, 103–4, 188–92
  Autumn Crocus, 188–9
  Bonnet over the Windmill, 190
  Dear Octopus, 192
  I Capture the Castle, 103–4
  Touch Wood, 189–90
Smith, Eleanor, 133
Smith, Logan Pearsall, 71–2
  A Treasury of English Prose, 71–2
Smith, Stevie, 6, 40–6, 48, 53, 161, 171–5, 204, 207–8
  A Good Time Was Had by All, 44–5, 174
  The Holiday, 45–6
  letters, 173–4
  Novel on Yellow Paper, 44
  Over the Frontier, 43–5
  poetry, 171–2
  Tender Only to One, 45, 174
Smuts, Jan, 209
social reform, 34
socialism, 11, 28–9, 47, 51, 70, 130, 138–41, 172–6, 206
Society of Women Journalists, 202, 210
Somerville and Ross, 223–4
  The Big House of Inver, 223–4
South Africa, 6
Spanish Civil War, 12, 30–1, 68, 80, 87–9, 173, 209, 211
Spark, Muriel, 113
  The Prime of Miss Jean Brodie, 225
Spender, Stephen, 165
spinsters, 187–9
Spottiswoode, Sybil, 184
  Kultur at Home, 184
Squire, J.C., 162–3
Stalin, Joseph, 83–4
Stark, Freya, 7, 257
  Baghdad Sketches, 257
Stein, Gertrude, 2, 14, 57, 163, 165, 167–8, 275
Stephen, James, 250
Stern, G.B., 27
  The Man Who Pays the Piper, 191
Stevenson, Robert Louis, 135
St John, Christopher, 9, 202
  The First Actress, 192
  How the Vote Was Won, 32
Stone, Reynolds, 81

Stopes, Marie, 204
Storm, Leslie, 193
  Great Day, 193
Strachey, Ray, 131
  The Cause, 131
Stravinsky, Igor, 6
stream of consciousness, 25, 27, 40
Struther, Jan, 3
  'Gas Masks', 239
  Mrs Miniver, 104
Stuart, Muriel, 177
suffragism, 10, 25, 31–2, 162, 184, 187, 190
Sur Press, 27

Taggard, Genevieve, 34
Taylor, Elizabeth, 118
Tey, Josephine, pseud., *see* Mackintosh, Elizabeth
Thomas, Dylan, 221
Thompson, Sylvia, 202
Time and Tide, 11, 86, 163, 169, 172, 199–200, 202–4, 206, 108–10
Tit-Bits, 44
transition (magazine), 29
Tree, Iris, 164–5
Trent, Lucia, 34
  'What is This Modernism', 34
Trevelyan, G.M., 129
Troubridge, Una, 35

United States of America, 24, 26–7, 29, 31–3, 36, 64, 70–1, 112–13, 166–9
universities, 5, 16, 28, 48, 57, 130–1, 135, 154–5, 220

Vaughan, Hilda, 130, 136
  Harvest Home, 136
Virago, publisher, 2–3
Vogue, 15, 206
vorticism, 24–5
Vote, The, 113, 201
Votes for Women (magazine), 113

Wales, 7–8, 18, 135–6, 217–31
Wall, Harry, 184
  Havoc, 184
Wallace, Doreen, 202
Wallace, Edgar, 147
Walpole, Hugh, 68–9

The Old Ladies, 188
war, attitudes to, 2, 65–73, 184–6, 233–47
war work by women, 31, 43, 47, 85, 130, 134, 185, 190, 193, 237–8, 243
Warner, George Townsend, 84–5
Warner, Sylvia Townsend, 5, 8, 11–12, 17, 29, 78–92, 130, 139, 141, 161, 163, 171–3, 202, 209
  After the Death of Don Juan, 12, 83, 88–9, 139
  'Behind the Firing Line', 85
  'Benicasim', 87
  Boxwood, 81–2
  'But at the Stroke at Midnight', 78–81
  The Cat's Cradle-Book, 83, 87, 91
  The Corner that Held Them, 83, 89–90
  diaries, 82, 91–2
  The Espalier, 86, 172
  The Flint Anchor, 80, 83, 87
  'In This Midwinter', 173
  'Journey to Barcelona', 88
  Kingdoms of Elfin, 91
  letters, 82, 92
  Lolly Willowes, 12, 79–82, 84–6, 172
  Mr Fortune's Maggot, 12, 79–81, 83, 86, 250
  Opus 7, 79, 171–2
  parental influences, 84–6
  poetry, 82, 87–8, 91, 171–3, 175
  'The Red Carnation', 88
  'Red Front', 88, 173
  Scenes of Childhood, 87
  Summer Will Show, 12, 80–1, 87, 139–40
  Time Imported, 172
  The True Heart, 8, 12, 83
  Whether a Dove or a Seagull, 35, 82, 172
  'Winter in the Air', 90
  'Women as Writers', 173
Washington Post, 113
Waterloo, battle of, 134
Waters, Sarah, 144
Waugh, Evelyn, 6, 108
Weaver, Harriet Shaw, 28
Webb, Beatrice, 151
Wellesley, Dorothy, 163, 175, 177
Wellington, Duke of, 134

Wells, Carolyn, 112
Wells, H.G., 28
Welsh language, 218–19, 221, 229
West, Rebecca, 27–9, 35, 162, 200, 204, 206–7, 209–10
  Black Lamb and Grey Falcon, 209, 251
  Ending in Earnest, 206
  The Judge, 32
  The Strange Necessity, 206
Wharton, Edith, 187
Wheels anthologies, 164–5, 275
Whipple, Dorothy, 3, 11, 202
  They Were Sisters, 239, 246
Whistler, Peggy, 130, 136
  Country Dance, 135
White, Elizabeth Wade, 87, 89–90
White, T.H., 82
Wickham, Anna, 161–3, 168–71
  'The Angry Woman'
  Fragment of an Autobiography, 170
  The Little Old House, 170
  'Marriage', 170–1
  'Return to Pleasure', 170
  'The Revolt of Wives', 171
  'Suppression', 170
  'The Wife', 171
Wilberforce, Octavia, 9
Wilde, Oscar, 35
Wilkinson, Ellen, 11, 210
Williams, William Carlos, 163
Wingfield, Sheila, 176
  Beat Drum Beat Heart, 176
Wodehouse, P.G., 101, 108, 148–9, 153
Wollstonecraft, Mary, 5, 153
Woman Engineer, The, 202
Woman and Home, 203
Woman Journalist, The, 202, 209
Woman's Leader, The, 201
Women's Auxiliary Army Corps, 185
Women's Library, London, 113
Women's Social and Political Union, 28, 31–2
Wood, Ellen, 147
Woolf, Leonard, 26, 57, 253
  Empire and Commerce in Africa, 253
Woolf, Virginia, 1–2, 5–6, 9–17, 24–8, 35, 40–1, 43–4, 57–73, 91, 102, 108, 113, 115, 136–8, 141, 145, 166–7, 169, 187, 204, 206–7, 236, 250–1, 280, 284

'Anon', 59, 61–4, 67, 71, 73
Between the Acts, 32, 57–9, 61, 114, 117, 130, 247
'Character in Fiction', 66, 207
The Common Reader, 57, 206
The Death of the Moth, 14–15, 98
diary, 68
Flush: A Biography, 57–8
Jacob's Room, 30, 288
Kew Gardens, 26
letters, 68
'The Leaning Tower', 63–4
'Middlebrow', 98
'Modern Fiction', 26–7, 57, 207
'Mr Bennett and Mrs Brown', 57, 66–7
Mrs Dalloway, 1, 9, 30, 114–17, 253, 265, 278–80, 288
Night and Day, 30, 32, 72
Orlando, 35, 114, 117, 130, 137, 140, 145
The Pargiters, 129
'Professions for Women', 225
'The Reader', 59, 63–4
'Reading', 72
'Reading at Random', 58–9
A Room of One's Own, 14, 17, 30, 33, 57–8, 60–1, 65, 80, 108, 117, 129, 225, 252
'Shakespeare's Sister', 60, 62–3, 67, 129
'A Sketch of the Past', 58, 62–4
'A Tap on the Door', 59
'Thoughts on Peace in an Air Raid', 58, 64, 67, 69–72
Three Guineas, 7, 11, 30–1, 57, 59, 69, 117, 202, 239–40
To the Lighthouse, 40, 57, 114, 116–17
'Turning the Page', 59
The Voyage Out, 23
The Waves, 57–8, 253
'Women and Fiction', 147
The Years, 58–9, 67–8
Workers' Educational Association, 15, 63
working-class culture, 11–12, 15, 42–3, 47–9
World War I, 10, 13, 30–1, 35–6, 85, 107–8, 130, 147, 161, 190, 223, 234
  drama, 183–7, 194
  poetry, 173, 175

World War II, 13–15, 25, 30, 41,
    45–6, 67–9, 89–90, 161, 208,
    233–47
  air raids, 67–70, 73, 236, 238
  drama, 193–4
  gender roles, 234–5
  poetry, 175–6, 233
  women's writing, 233–47

Yeats, W.B., 14, 133
Yonge, Charlotte M., 103
Young, E.H., 2, 6, 11, 202
  William, 15
Yugoslavia, 209

Zola, Emile, 276
  Au Bonheur des Dames, 276

CPI Antony Rowe
Chippenham, UK
2016-12-29 15:49